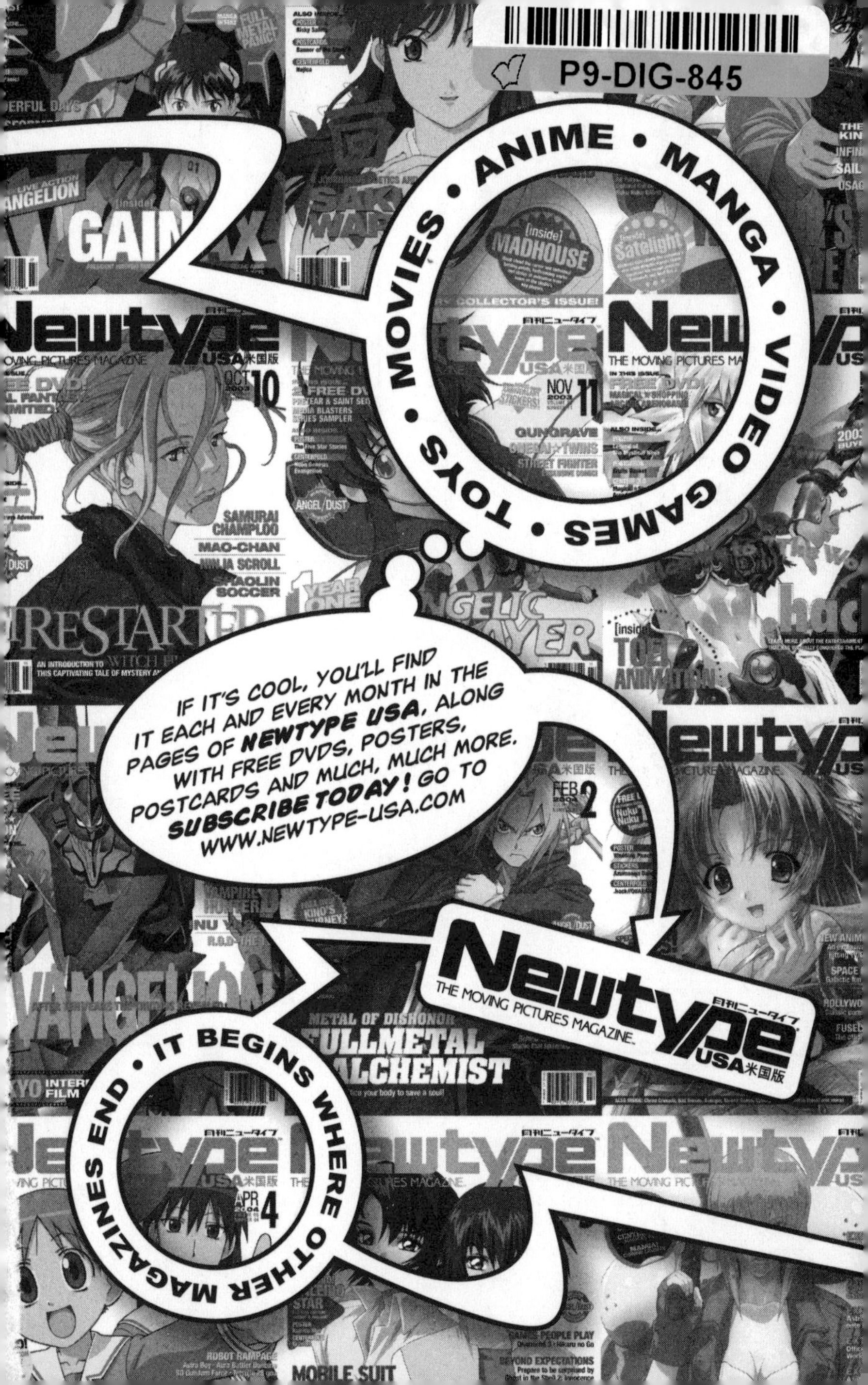
MOVIES • ANIME • MANGA • VIDEO GAMES • TOYS •
IF IT'S COOL, YOU'LL FIND IT EACH AND EVERY MONTH IN THE PAGES OF NEWTYPE USA, ALONG WITH FREE DVDS, POSTERS, POSTCARDS AND MUCH, MUCH MORE. SUBSCRIBE TODAY! GO TO WWW.NEWTYPE-USA.COM
Newtype
THE MOVING PICTURES MAGAZINE.
月刊ニュータイプ
USA米国版
IT BEGINS WHERE OTHER MAGAZINES END •

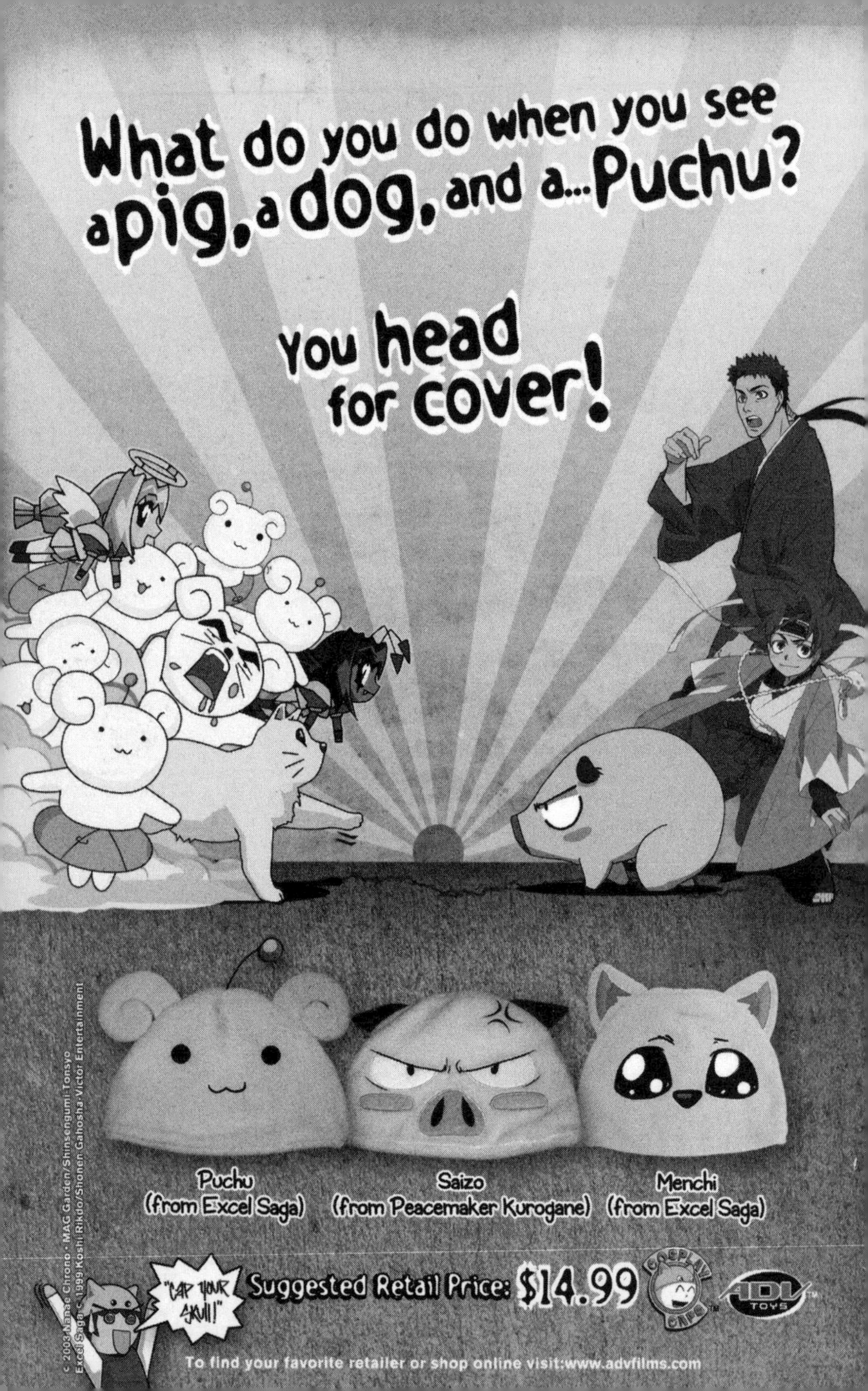
What do you do when you see a pig, a dog, and a...Puchu?
You head for cover!
Puchu (from Excel Saga)
Saizo (from Peacemaker Kurogane)
Menchi (from Excel Saga)
"Cap your skull!"
Suggested Retail Price: $14.99
COSPLAY CAFE
ADV TOYS
To find your favorite retailer or shop online visit:www.advfilms.com
© 2003 Nanae Chrono • MAG Garden/Shinsengumi-Tonsyo
Excel Saga © 1999 Koshi Rikdo/Shonen Gahosha•Victor Entertainment

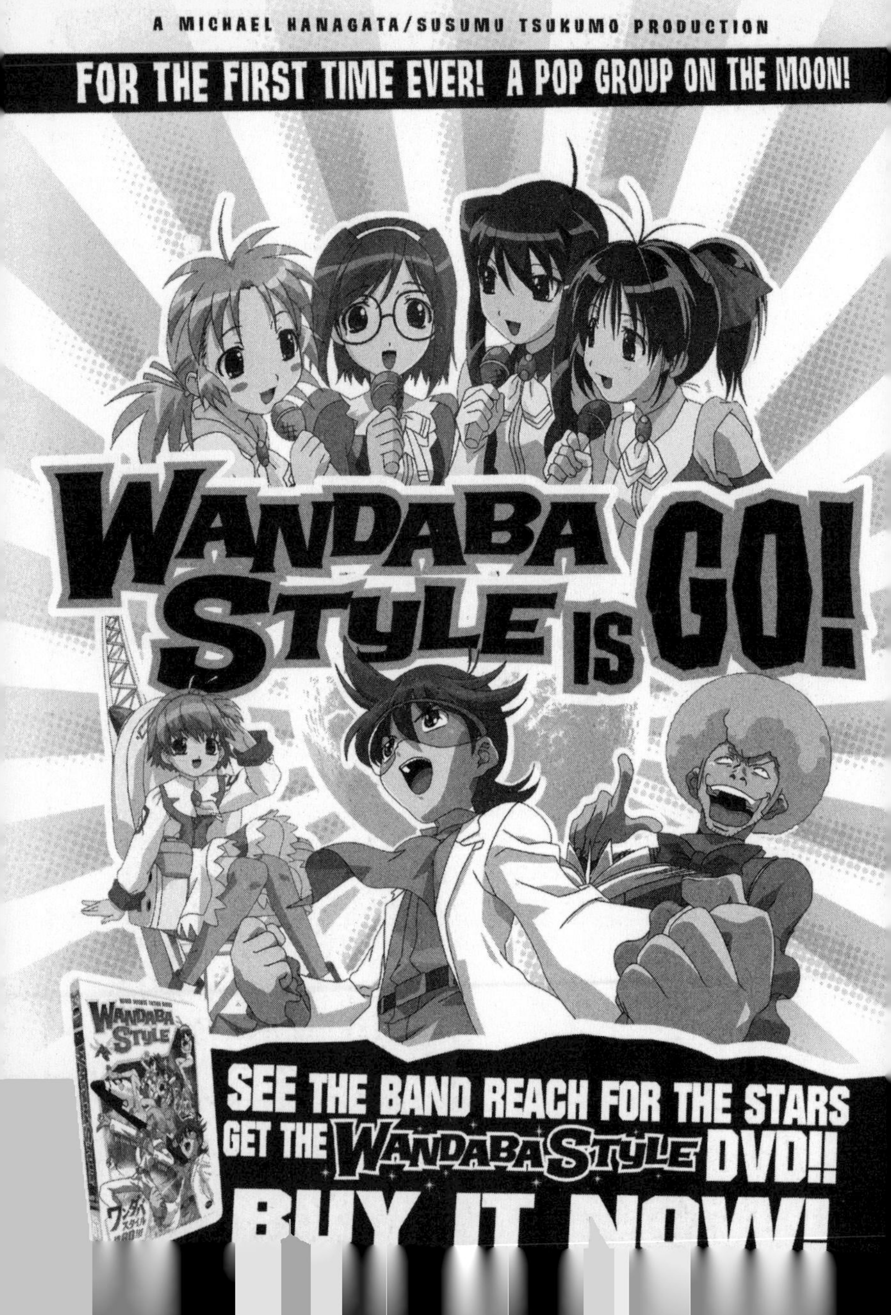
A MICHAEL HANAGATA/SUSUMU TSUKUMO PRODUCTION
FOR THE FIRST TIME EVER! A POP GROUP ON THE MOON!
WANDABA STYLE IS GO!
WANDABA STYLE
SEE THE BAND REACH FOR THE STARS
GET THE WANDABA STYLE DVD!!
BUY IT NOW!

DO YOU HAVE WHAT IT TAKES TO MAKE IT IN CROMARTIE HIGH?

Do you have a tough nickname?

❏ Yes ❏ No

How many fights have you been in?

❏ None ❏ More than 100

❏ 5-10 ❏ None – no one ever had the stones to challenge me

What's in your bookbag?

❏ My homework ❏ Porn ❏ A metal plate

How tough do you look? Check all that apply.

❏ Pompadour ❏ Handlebar mustache ❏ Shaved eyebrows

❏ Carpet of chest hair ❏ Lazy swagger ❏ Menacing glare

Say you checked out eleven adult videos. Three of those were new releases, so you had to return them the next day. How many videos do you have left?

❏ 3 ❏ 8 ❏ 11 – I would never give them back.

How did you rate?

10 points or less	**Errand Boy**
10 – 15	**Wannabe Punk**
30 – 40	**One Badass Dude**
More than 100	**Champ by Default**

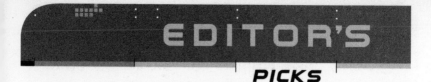

EDITOR'S PICKS

IF YOU LIKED *MORE STARLIGHT TO YOUR HEART* VOLUME 2, THEN YOU'LL LOVE THESE

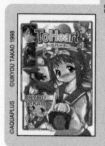

PICK 1

ToHeart
UKYOU
TAKAO

TO HEART

Akari is a shy, sweet teenager, especially when it comes to her childhood chum and crush, Hiroyuki. While this outspoken young man is attempting to break the habits and relationships of his yesteryear, Akari is determined to play the part of girlfriend to her "Hiroyuki-chan." But our naïve sweetheart can't do it alone. She must enlist the help of someone with a great knowledge of household chores, someone who can give her useful instructions, someone who softens the heart of her beloved Hiroyuki—a robot, of course! But as with all matters of the heart, time is of the essence and Akari must put a fast plan in motion to capture the attention of Hiroyuki, in the touching romantic comedy, To Heart.

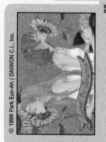

PICK 2

Sweet & Sensitive

SWEET & SENSITIVE

Life is tough for lovesick teenagers! Meet Ee-Ji, a high school freshman suffering from—or is, perhaps, the cause of—an adolescent love triangle. Torn between two men, she is racked with grief over her own indecision. To make matters worse, these two contenders are best friends! This situation has the potential to explode into a sordid mess, but Ee-Ji will have to pick her favorite man first!

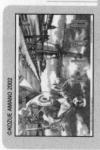

PICK 3

ARIA

ARIA

After moving to the planet Aqua (formerly Mars), Akari Mizunashi has made her home in the charming town of Neo-Venezia. Determined to become an undine, she spends her days training in the labyrinths of canals throughout the city, and finding fascinating adventures within her new planet. She enjoys the primitive lifestyle of her ancestors and has no qualms about doing her own laundry or cooking meals from scratch, and she even enjoys scraping barnacles off of her boat! Pursuing this career and becoming independent are her dreams and, with the help of some curious Martians, underground dwellers and even wild creatures, Akari will one day captain her own gondola through the city of Neo-Venezia.

CHECK 'EM OUT TODAY!

ADV Manga™

www.adv-manga.com

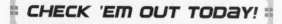

More Starlight To Your Heart
VOLUME 2

© Hiro Matsuba 2003
All rights reserved.
First published in 2003 by MAG Garden Corporation.
English translation rights arranged with MAG Garden Corporation.

Translator **KAY BERTRAND**
ADV Manga Translation Staff **AMY FORSYTH AND BRENDAN FRAYNE**
Editor **JAVIER LOPEZ**
Assistant Editors **MARGARET SCHAROLD AND SHERIDAN JACOBS**

Editorial Director **GARY STEINMAN**
Creative Director **JASON BABLER**
Print Production Manager **BRIDGETT JANOTA**
Pre-press Manager **KLYS REEDYK**
Graphic Artists **NATALIA REYNOLDS AND HEATHER GARY**
Graphic Intern **MARK MEZA**

International Coordinators **TORU IWAKAMI, ATSUSHI KANBAYASHI,**
KYOKO DRUMHELLER & AI TAKAI

President, CEO & Publisher **JOHN LEDFORD**

Email: editor@adv-manga.com
www.adv-manga.com
www.advfilms.com

For sales and distribution inquiries please call 1.800.282.7202

is a division of A.D. Vision, Inc.
10114 W. Sam Houston Parkway, Suite 200, Houston, Texas 77099

English text © 2005 published by A.D. Vision, Inc. under exclusive license.
ADV MANGA is a trademark of A.D. Vision, Inc.

ISBN: 1-4139-0227-8
First printing, April 2005
10 9 8 7 6 5 4 3 2 1
Printed in Canada

PINECONE H.M. NEWS SERVICE (COMIC EDITION) 8

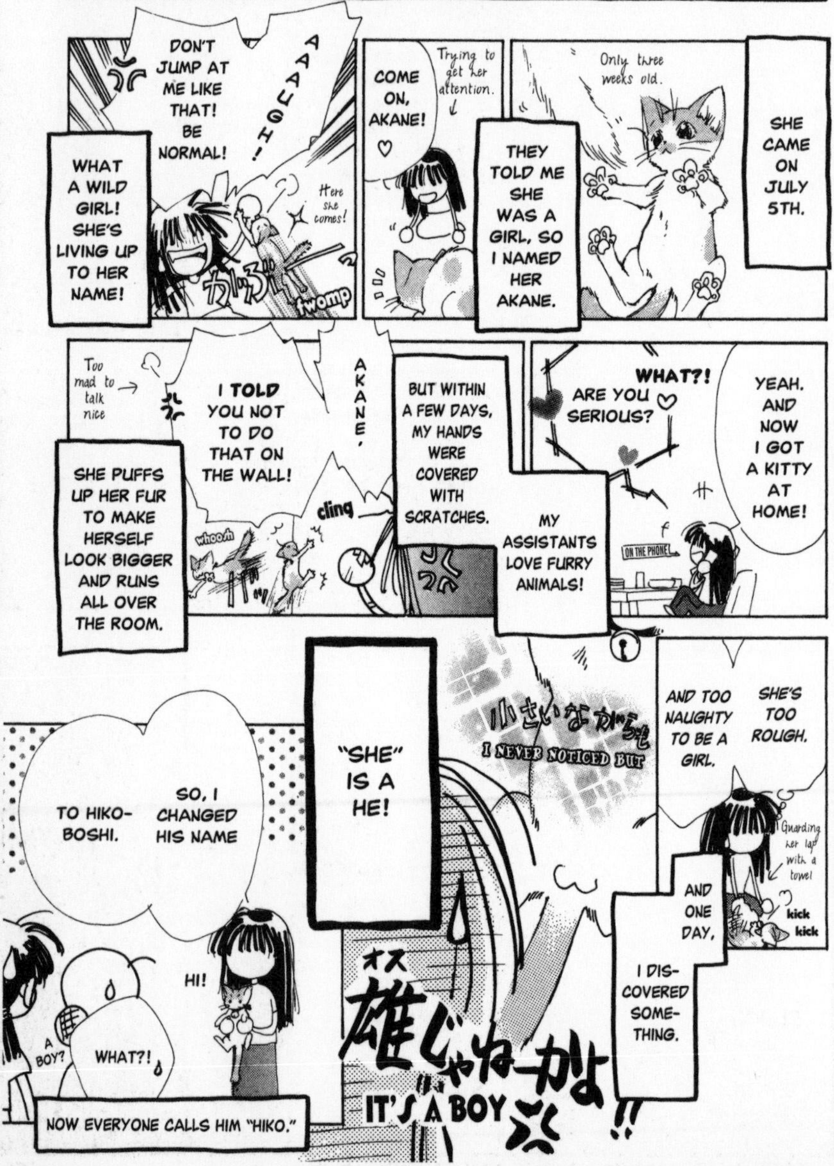
SHE CAME ON JULY 5TH.
Only three weeks old.
THEY TOLD ME SHE WAS A GIRL, SO I NAMED HER AKANE.
Trying to get her attention.
COME ON, AKANE!
Here she comes!
AAAUGH!
DON'T JUMP AT ME LIKE THAT! BE NORMAL!
fwomp
WHAT A WILD GIRL! SHE'S LIVING UP TO HER NAME!
YEAH. AND NOW I GOT A KITTY AT HOME!
ON THE PHONE
WHAT?!
ARE YOU SERIOUS?
MY ASSISTANTS LOVE FURRY ANIMALS!
BUT WITHIN A FEW DAYS, MY HANDS WERE COVERED WITH SCRATCHES.
AKANE,
cling
I TOLD YOU NOT TO DO THAT ON THE WALL!
Too mad to talk nice
whoosh
SHE PUFFS UP HER FUR TO MAKE HERSELF LOOK BIGGER AND RUNS ALL OVER THE ROOM.
SHE'S TOO ROUGH.
AND TOO NAUGHTY TO BE A GIRL.
Guarding her lap with a towel
kick kick
AND ONE DAY,
I DISCOVERED SOMETHING.
I NEVER NOTICED BUT
雄じゃねーかよ!!
IT'S A BOY
"SHE" IS A HE!
SO, I CHANGED HIS NAME
TO HIKO-BOSHI.
HI!
WHAT?!
A BOY?
NOW EVERYONE CALLS HIM "HIKO."

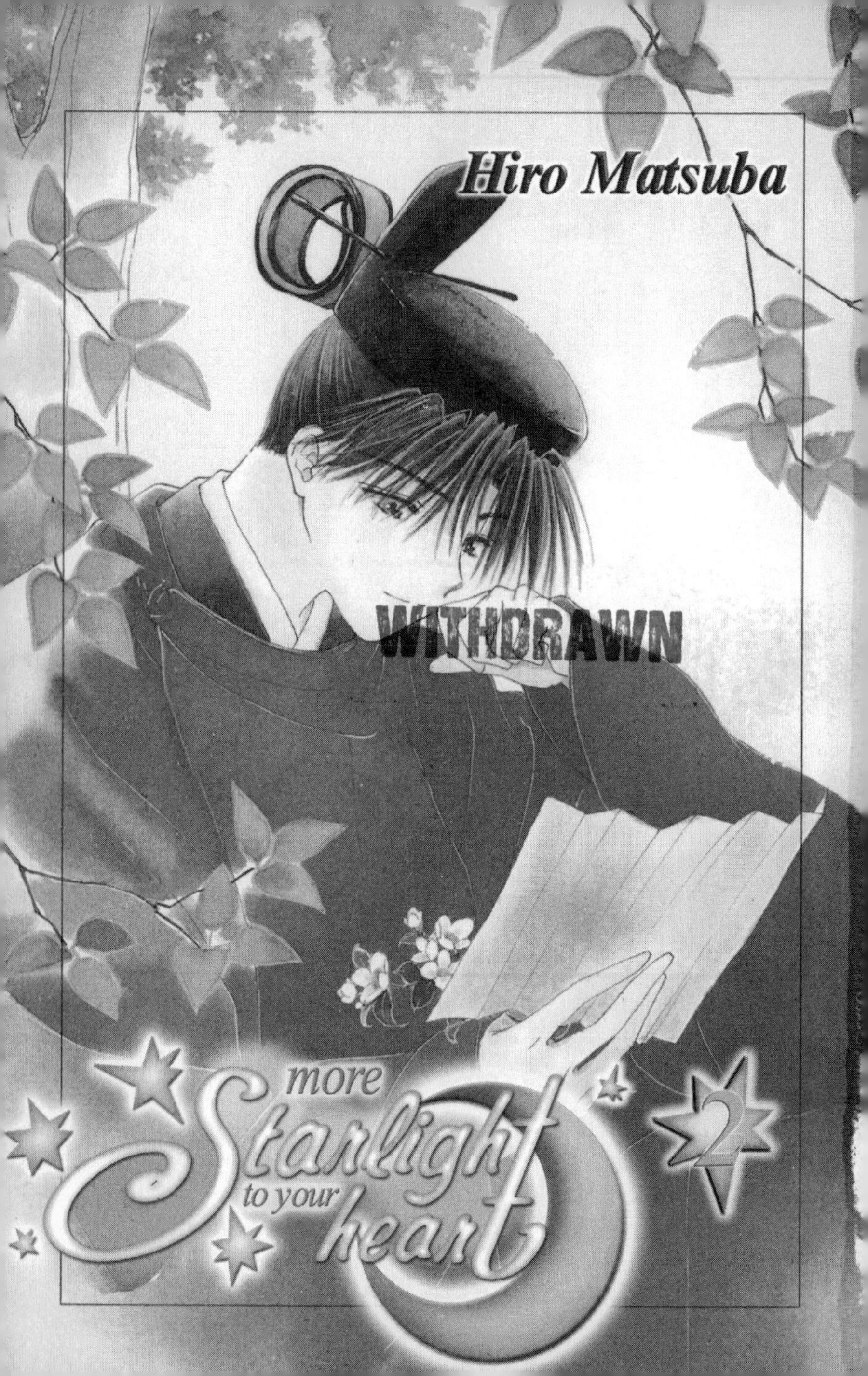
Hiro Matsuba
WITHDRAWN
more
Starlight
to your
heart
2

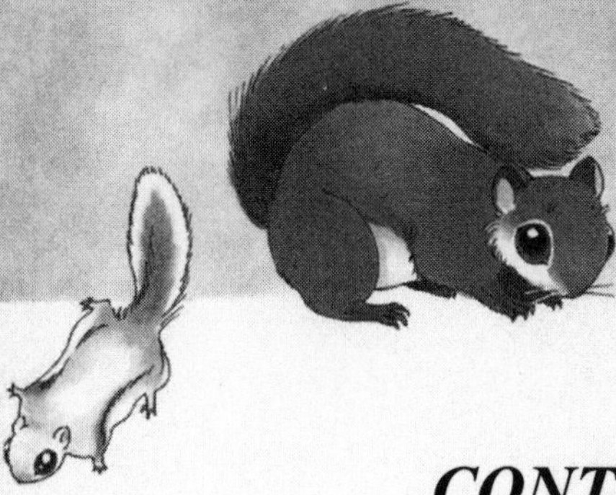

CONTENTS

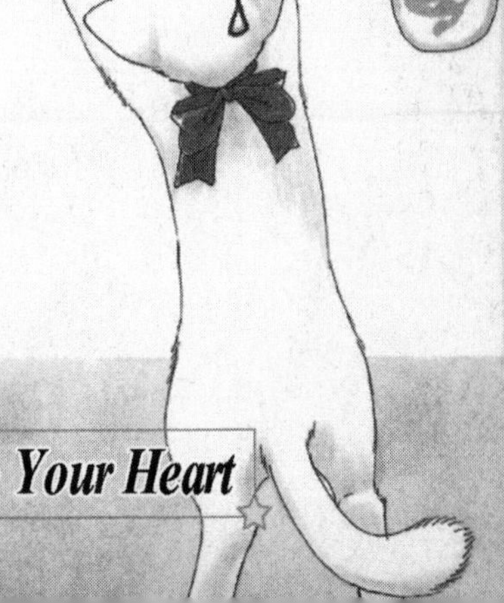

More Starlight to Your Heart

トラブル5 傍にいて…

Trouble 5
Be By My Side

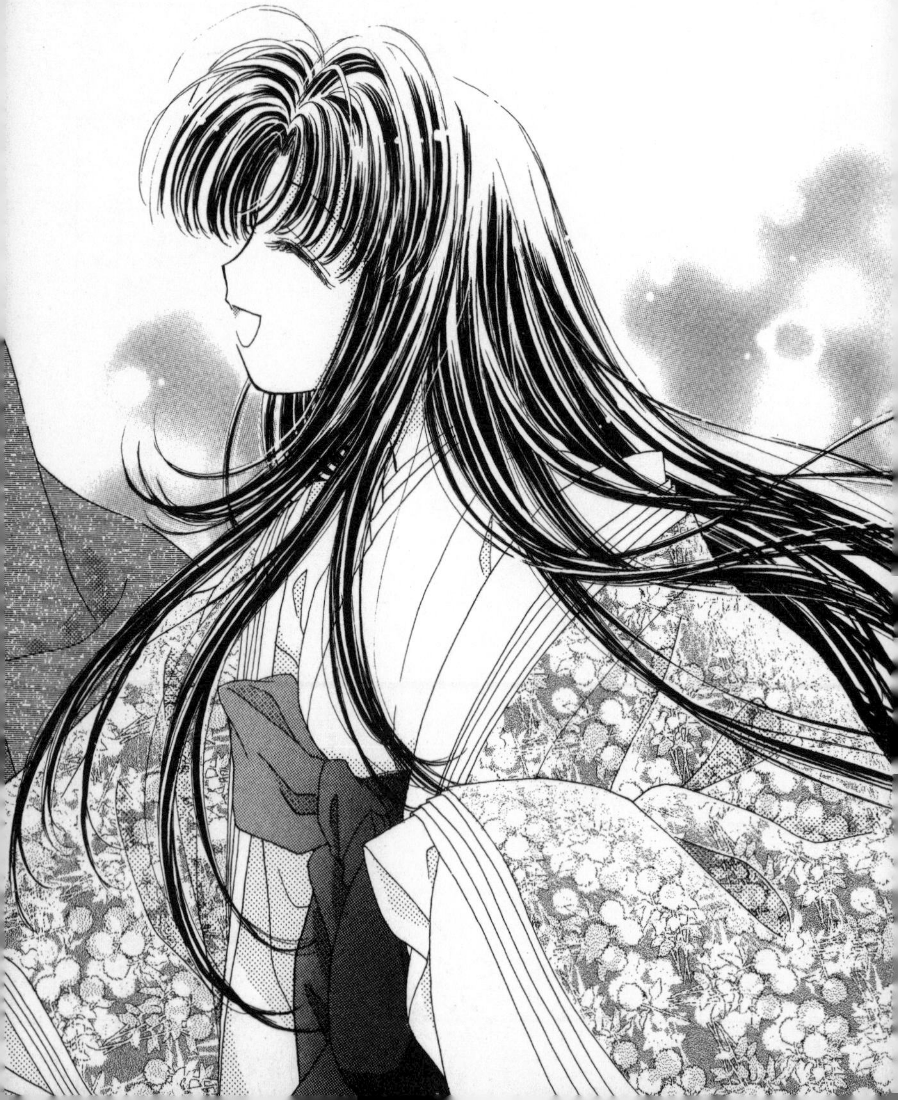

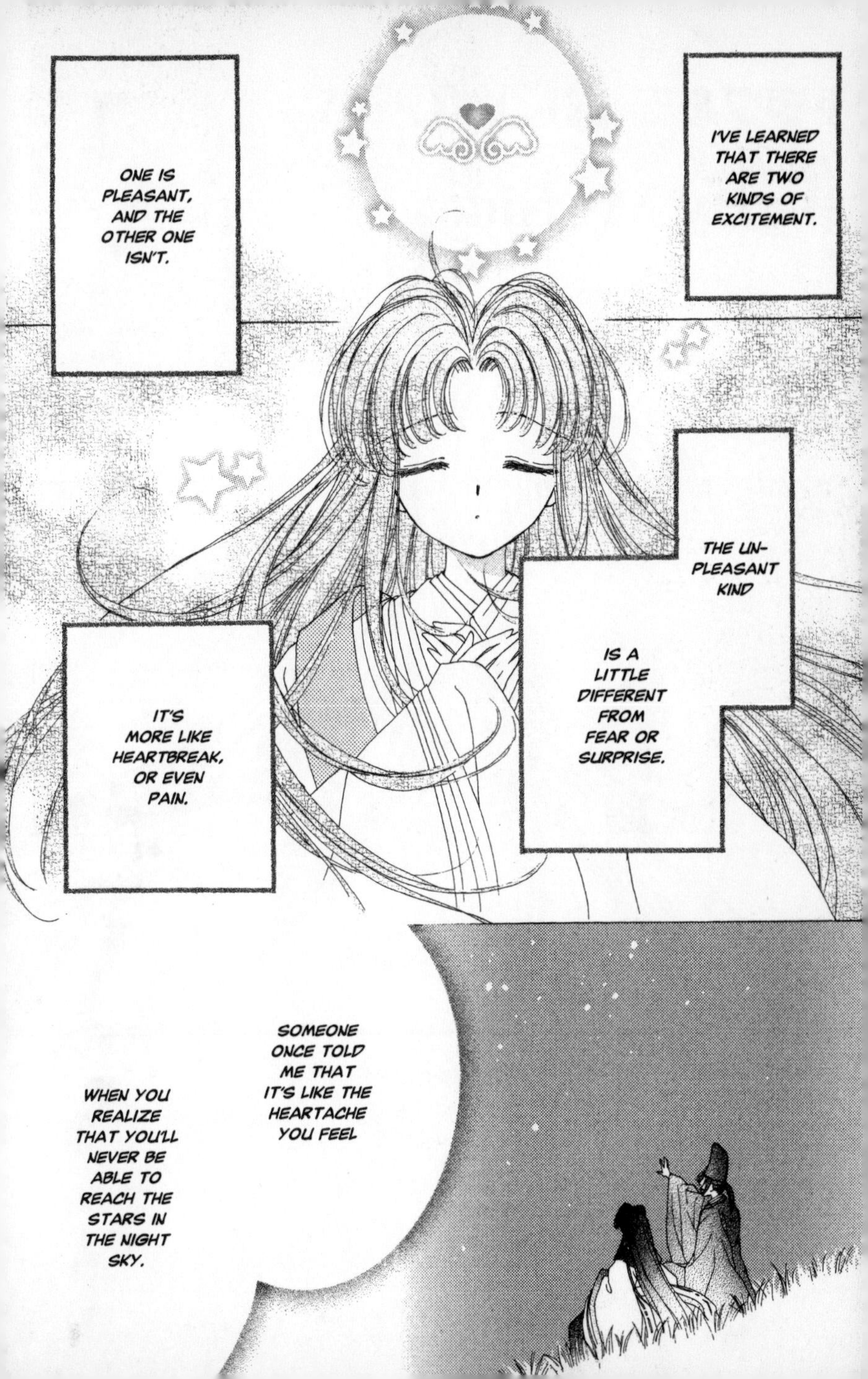
I'VE LEARNED THAT THERE ARE TWO KINDS OF EXCITEMENT.
ONE IS PLEASANT, AND THE OTHER ONE ISN'T.
THE UN-PLEASANT KIND
IS A LITTLE DIFFERENT FROM FEAR OR SURPRISE.
IT'S MORE LIKE HEARTBREAK, OR EVEN PAIN.
SOMEONE ONCE TOLD ME THAT IT'S LIKE THE HEARTACHE YOU FEEL
WHEN YOU REALIZE THAT YOU'LL NEVER BE ABLE TO REACH THE STARS IN THE NIGHT SKY.

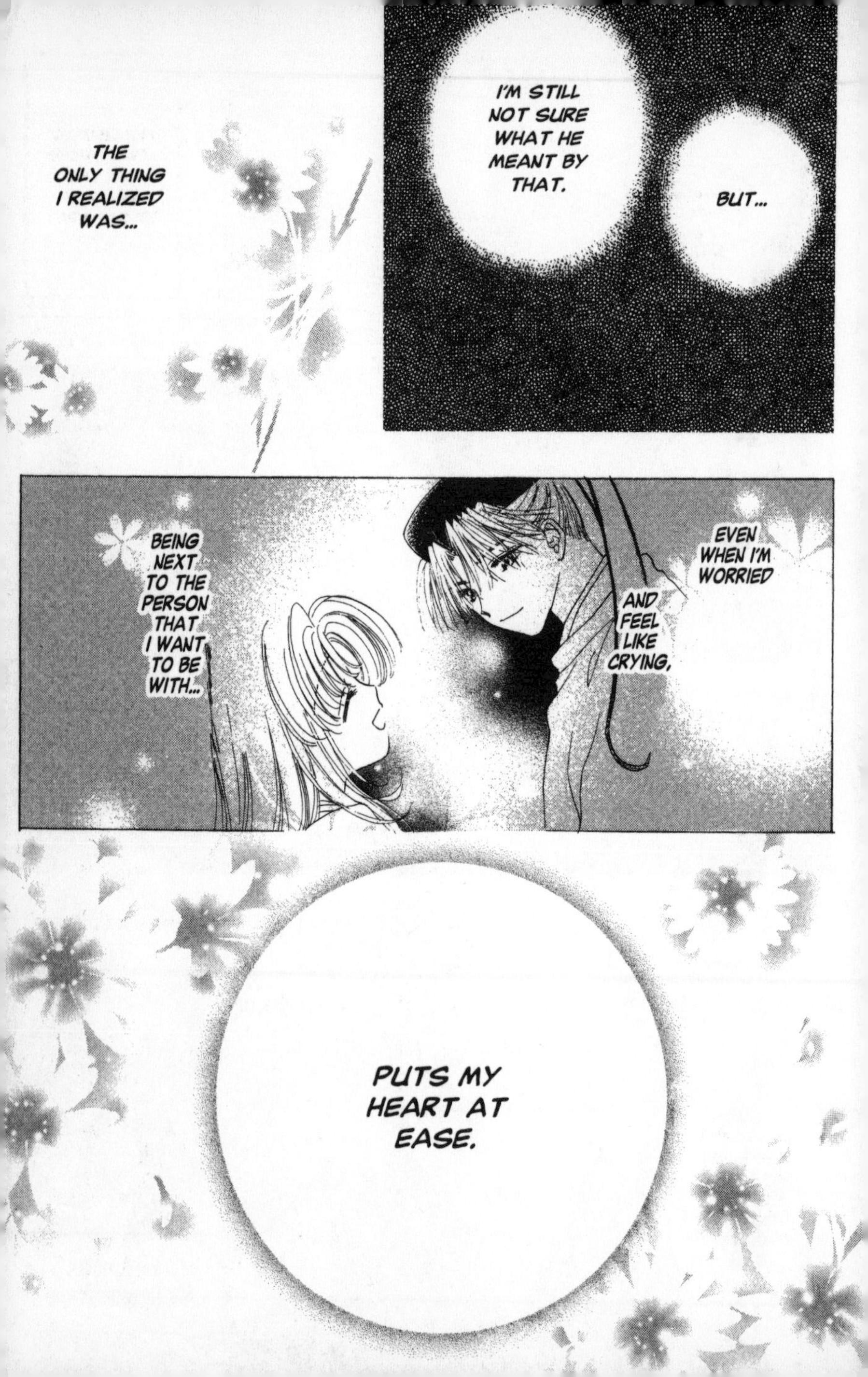
I'M STILL NOT SURE WHAT HE MEANT BY THAT.
BUT...
THE ONLY THING I REALIZED WAS...
EVEN WHEN I'M WORRIED
AND FEEL LIKE CRYING,
BEING NEXT TO THE PERSON THAT I WANT TO BE WITH...
PUTS MY HEART AT EASE.

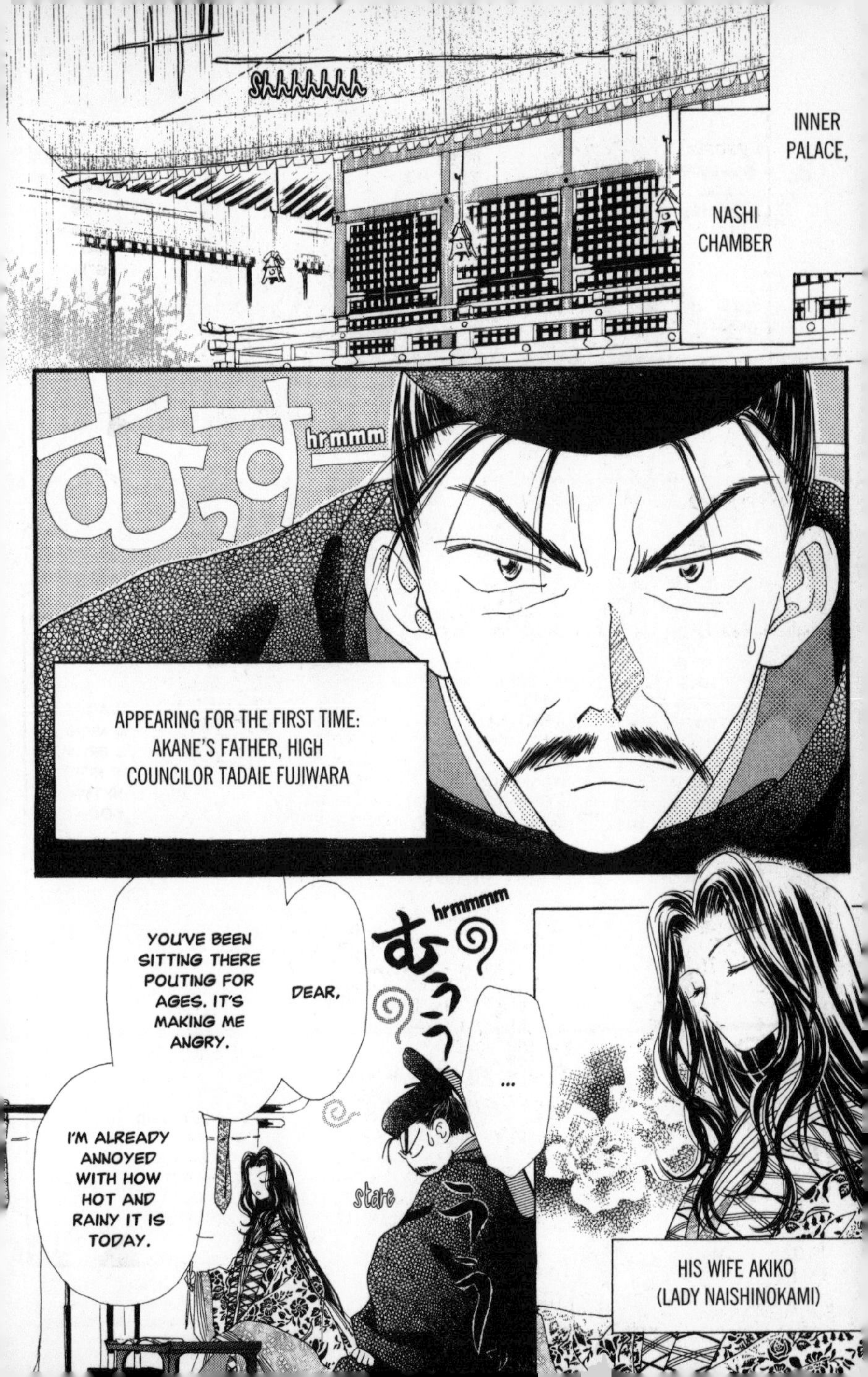
Shhhhhhh
INNER PALACE,
NASHI CHAMBER
むっすー
hrmmm
APPEARING FOR THE FIRST TIME: AKANE'S FATHER, HIGH COUNCILOR TADAIE FUJIWARA
DEAR,
YOU'VE BEEN SITTING THERE POUTING FOR AGES. IT'S MAKING ME ANGRY.
I'M ALREADY ANNOYED WITH HOW HOT AND RAINY IT IS TODAY.
むぅぅ
hrmmmm
...
stare
HIS WIFE AKIKO (LADY NAISHINOKAMI)

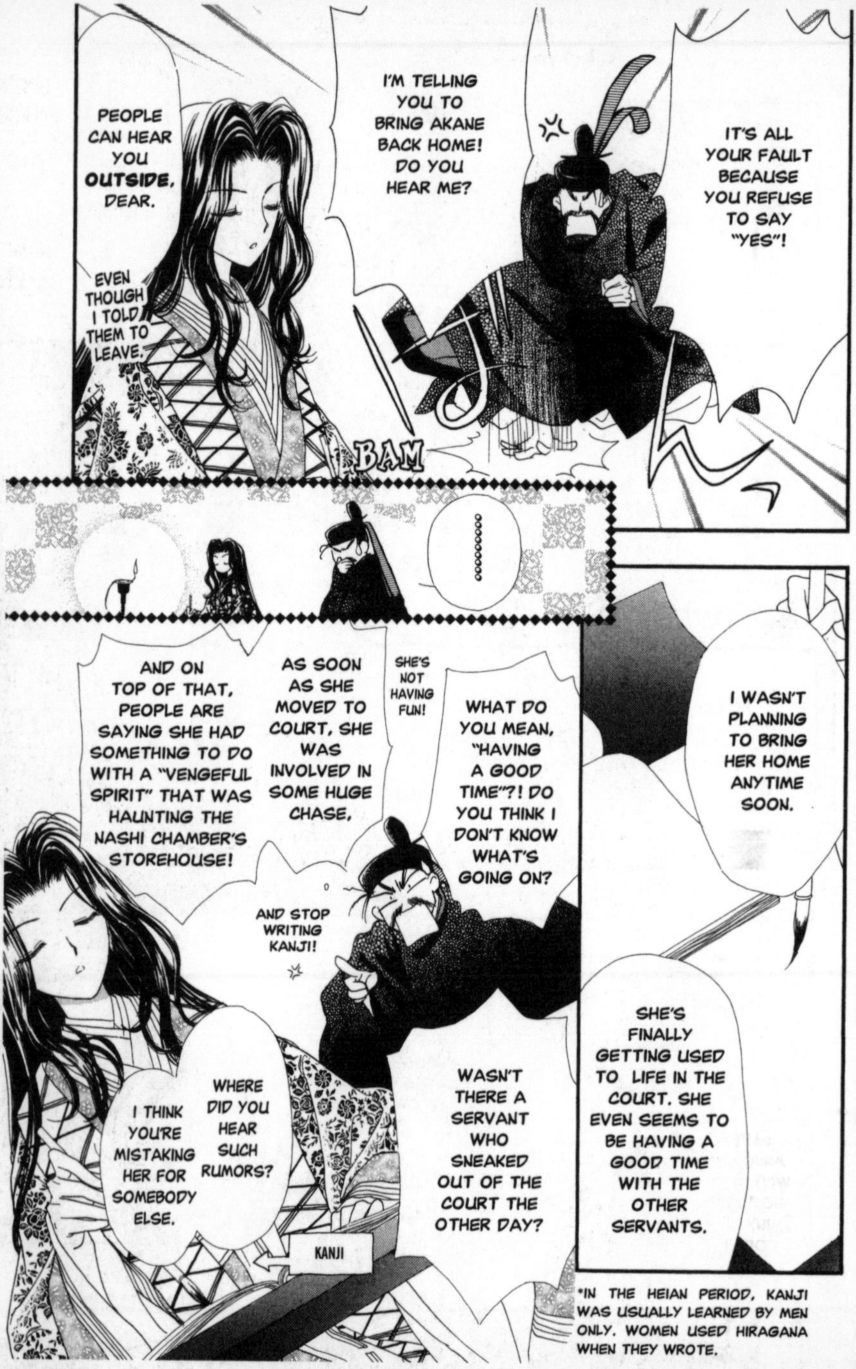
PEOPLE CAN HEAR YOU **OUTSIDE**, DEAR.
EVEN THOUGH I TOLD THEM TO LEAVE.
I'M TELLING YOU TO BRING AKANE BACK HOME! DO YOU HEAR ME?
BAM
IT'S ALL YOUR FAULT BECAUSE YOU REFUSE TO SAY "YES"!
....
AND ON TOP OF THAT, PEOPLE ARE SAYING SHE HAD SOMETHING TO DO WITH A "VENGEFUL SPIRIT" THAT WAS HAUNTING THE NASHI CHAMBER'S STOREHOUSE!
AS SOON AS SHE MOVED TO COURT, SHE WAS INVOLVED IN SOME HUGE CHASE,
SHE'S NOT HAVING FUN!
WHAT DO YOU MEAN, "HAVING A GOOD TIME"?! DO YOU THINK I DON'T KNOW WHAT'S GOING ON?
I WASN'T PLANNING TO BRING HER HOME ANYTIME SOON.
AND STOP WRITING KANJI!
I THINK YOU'RE MISTAKING HER FOR SOMEBODY ELSE.
WHERE DID YOU HEAR SUCH RUMORS?
WASN'T THERE A SERVANT WHO SNEAKED OUT OF THE COURT THE OTHER DAY?
SHE'S FINALLY GETTING USED TO LIFE IN THE COURT. SHE EVEN SEEMS TO BE HAVING A GOOD TIME WITH THE OTHER SERVANTS.
KANJI

*IN THE HEIAN PERIOD, KANJI WAS USUALLY LEARNED BY MEN ONLY. WOMEN USED HIRAGANA WHEN THEY WROTE.

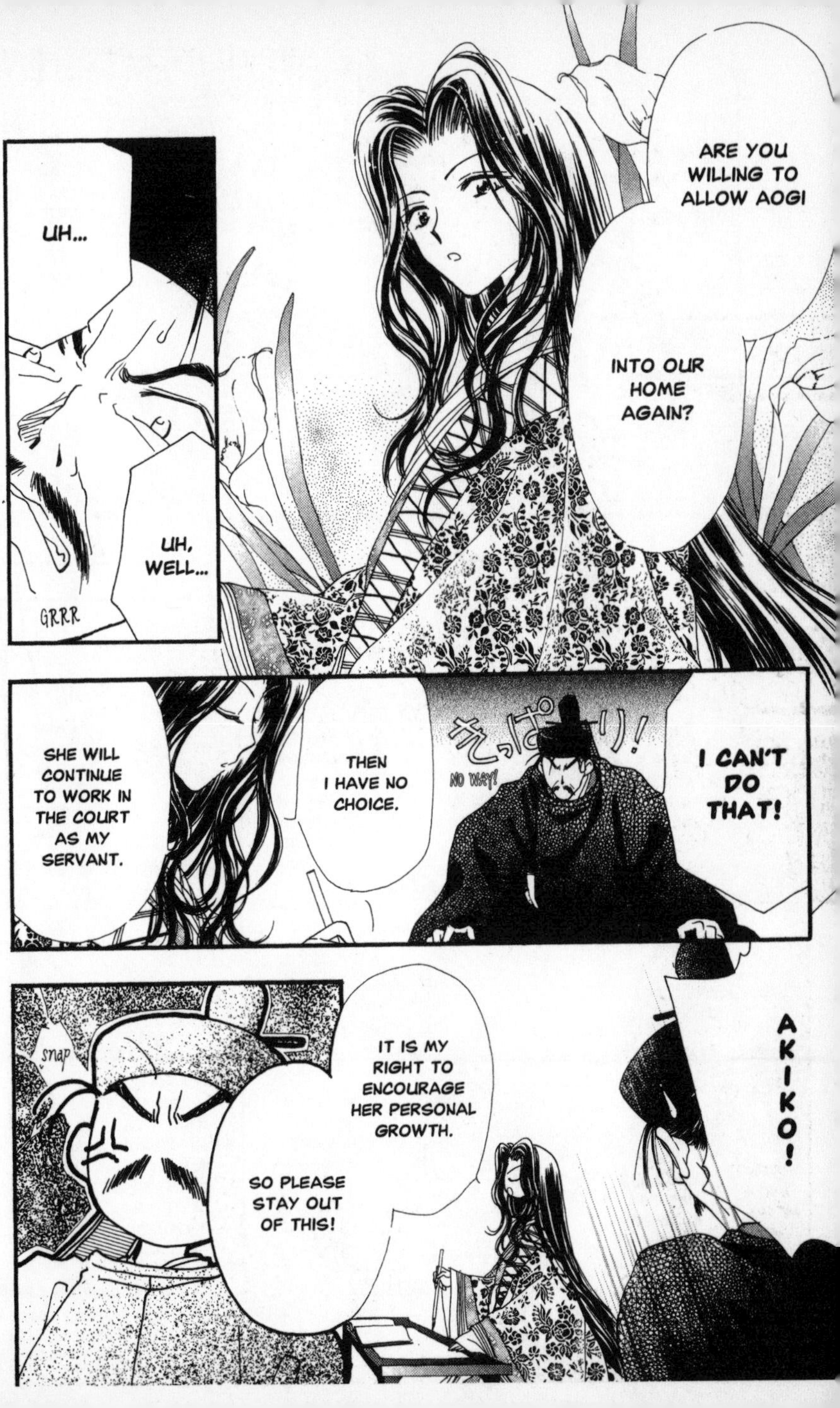
ARE YOU WILLING TO ALLOW AOGI
INTO OUR HOME AGAIN?
UH...
UH, WELL...
GRRR
I CAN'T DO THAT!
NO WAY!
THEN I HAVE NO CHOICE.
SHE WILL CONTINUE TO WORK IN THE COURT AS MY SERVANT.
AKIKO!
IT IS MY RIGHT TO ENCOURAGE HER PERSONAL GROWTH.
SO PLEASE STAY OUT OF THIS!
snap

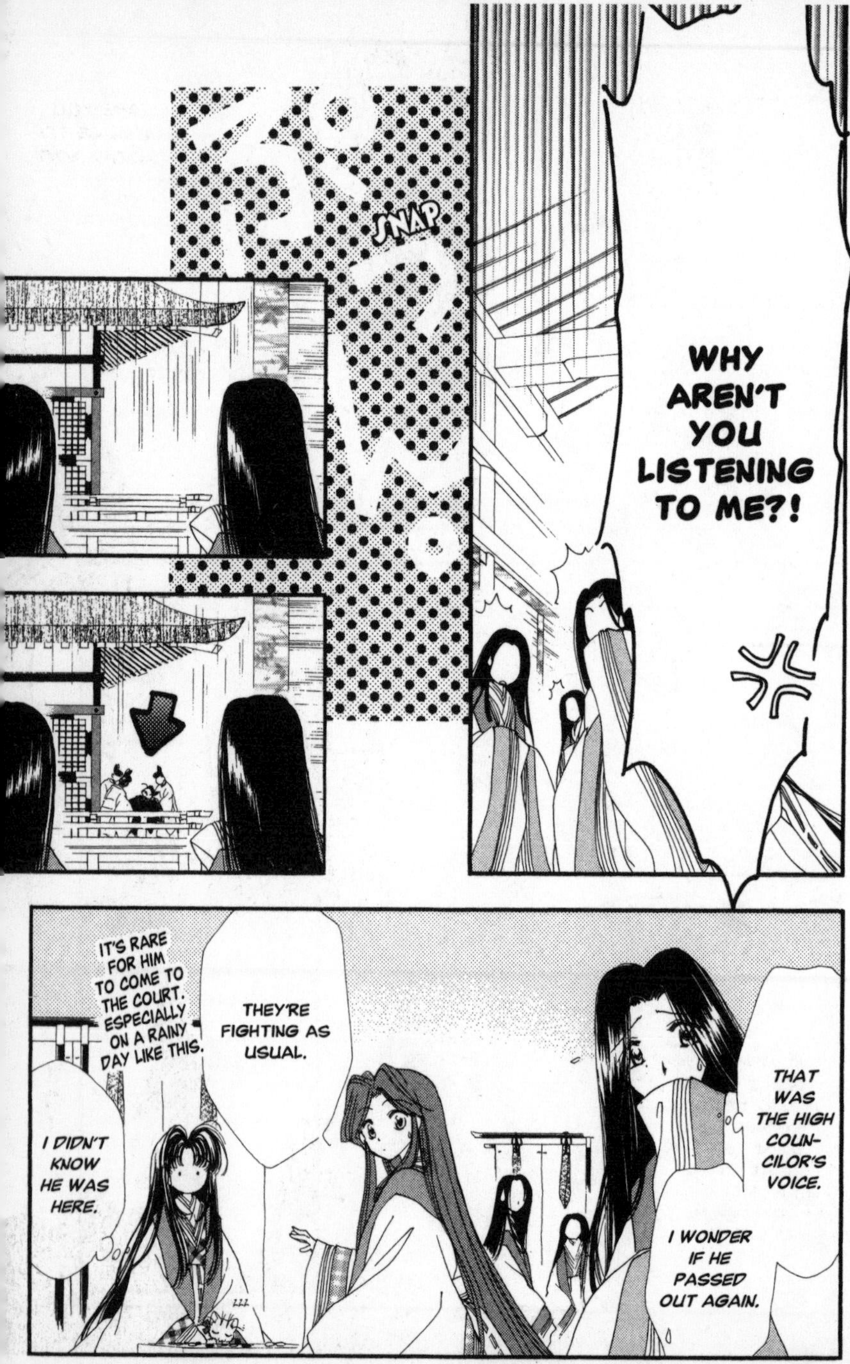
WHY AREN'T YOU LISTENING TO ME?!
SNAP
THAT WAS THE HIGH COUN-CILOR'S VOICE.
I WONDER IF HE PASSED OUT AGAIN.
THEY'RE FIGHTING AS USUAL.
IT'S RARE FOR HIM TO COME TO THE COURT. ESPECIALLY ON A RAINY DAY LIKE THIS.
I DIDN'T KNOW HE WAS HERE.

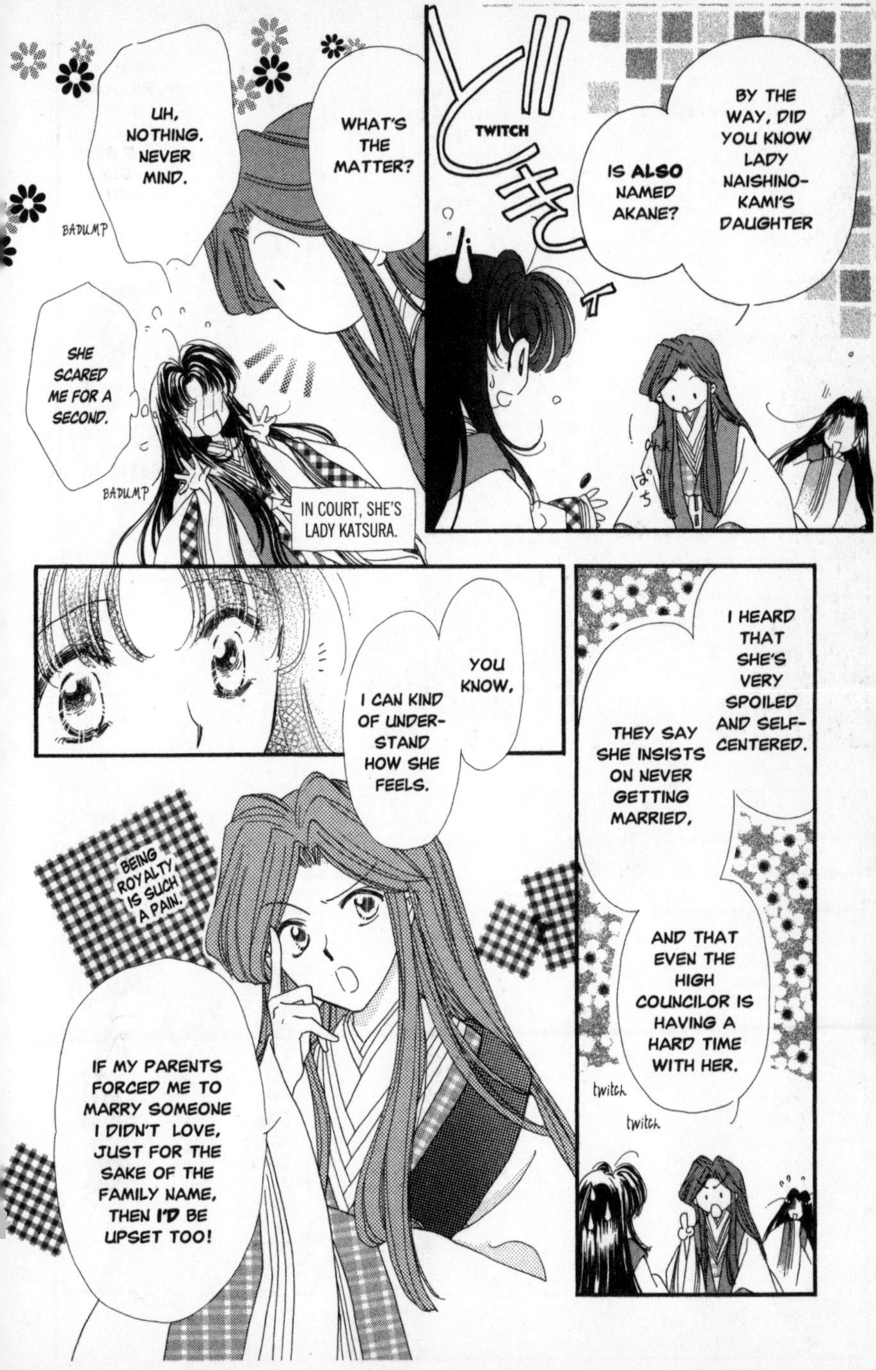
BY THE WAY, DID YOU KNOW LADY NAISHINO-KAMI'S DAUGHTER
IS ALSO NAMED AKANE?
TWITCH
WHAT'S THE MATTER?
UH, NOTHING. NEVER MIND.
BADUMP
SHE SCARED ME FOR A SECOND.
BADUMP
IN COURT, SHE'S LADY KATSURA.
I HEARD THAT SHE'S VERY SPOILED AND SELF-CENTERED.
THEY SAY SHE INSISTS ON NEVER GETTING MARRIED,
AND THAT EVEN THE HIGH COUNCILOR IS HAVING A HARD TIME WITH HER.
twitch
twitch
YOU KNOW,
I CAN KIND OF UNDER-STAND HOW SHE FEELS.
BEING ROYALTY IS SUCH A PAIN.
IF MY PARENTS FORCED ME TO MARRY SOMEONE I DIDN'T LOVE, JUST FOR THE SAKE OF THE FAMILY NAME, THEN I'D BE UPSET TOO!

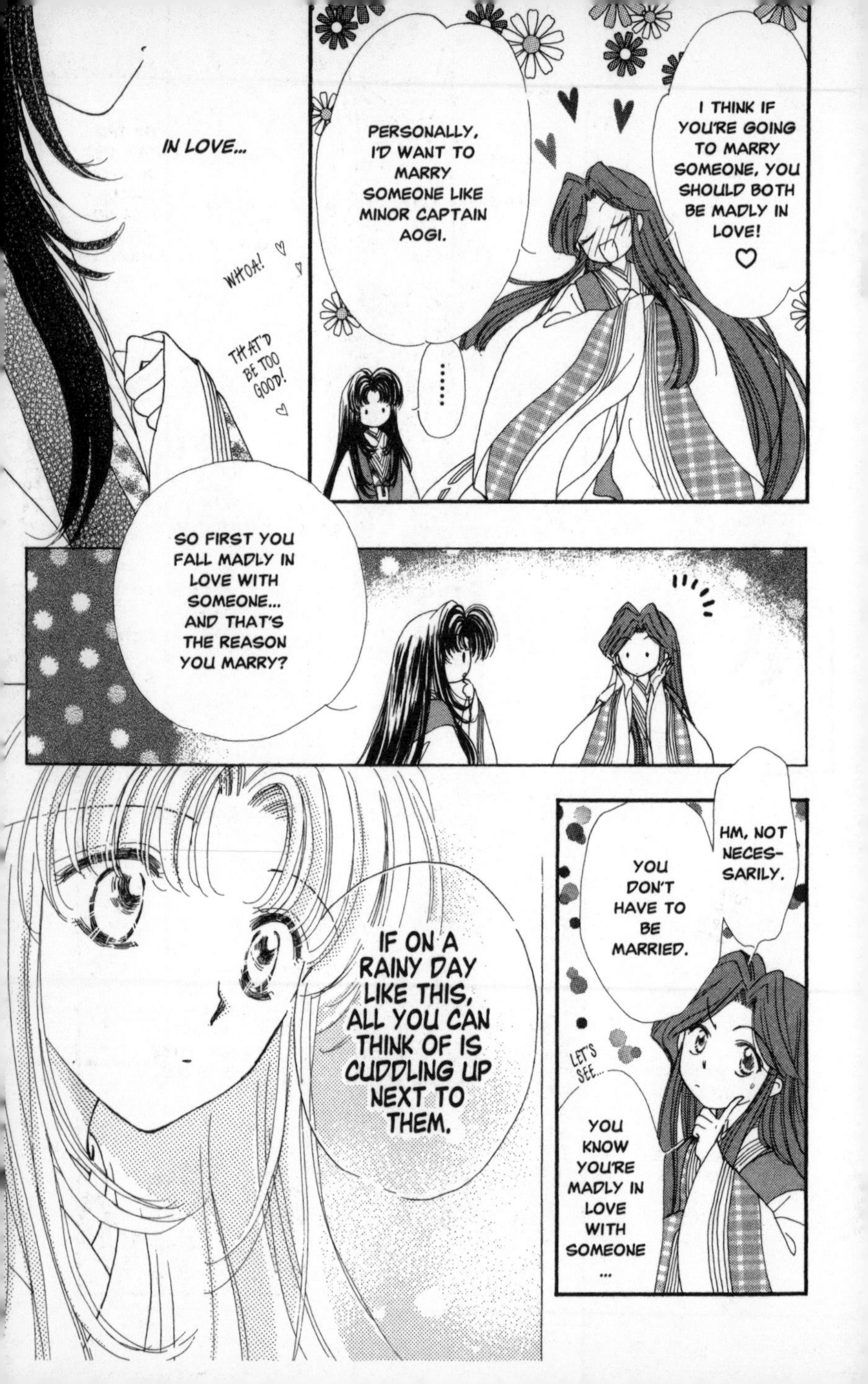

I THINK IF YOU'RE GOING TO MARRY SOMEONE, YOU SHOULD BOTH BE MADLY IN LOVE! ♡
PERSONALLY, I'D WANT TO MARRY SOMEONE LIKE MINOR CAPTAIN AOGI.
......
IN LOVE...
WHOA! ♡
THAT'D BE TOO GOOD! ♡
SO FIRST YOU FALL MADLY IN LOVE WITH SOMEONE... AND THAT'S THE REASON YOU MARRY?
HM, NOT NECES-SARILY.
YOU DON'T HAVE TO BE MARRIED.
LET'S SEE...
YOU KNOW YOU'RE MADLY IN LOVE WITH SOMEONE...
IF ON A RAINY DAY LIKE THIS, ALL YOU CAN THINK OF IS CUDDLING UP NEXT TO THEM.

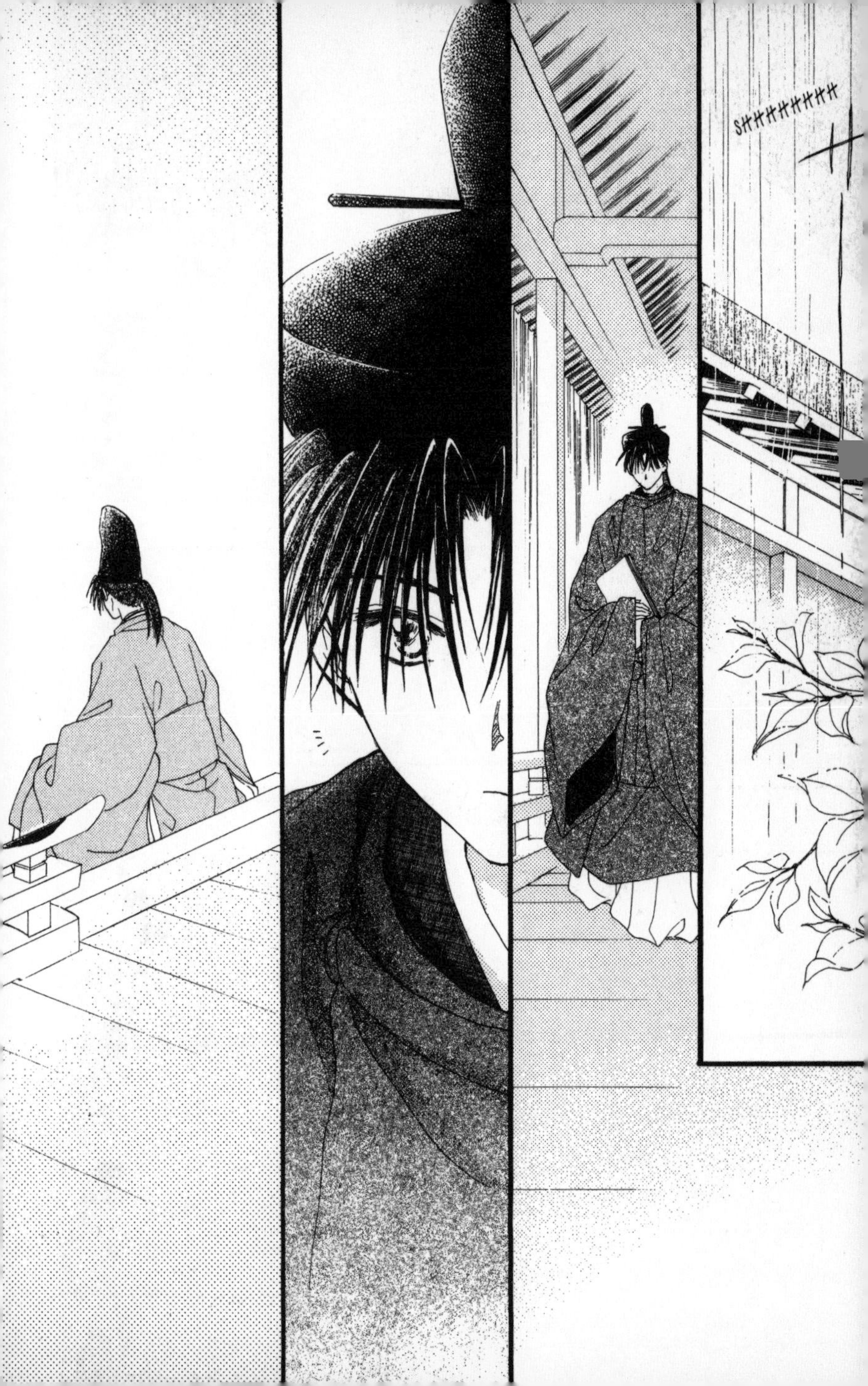
SHHHHHHHH

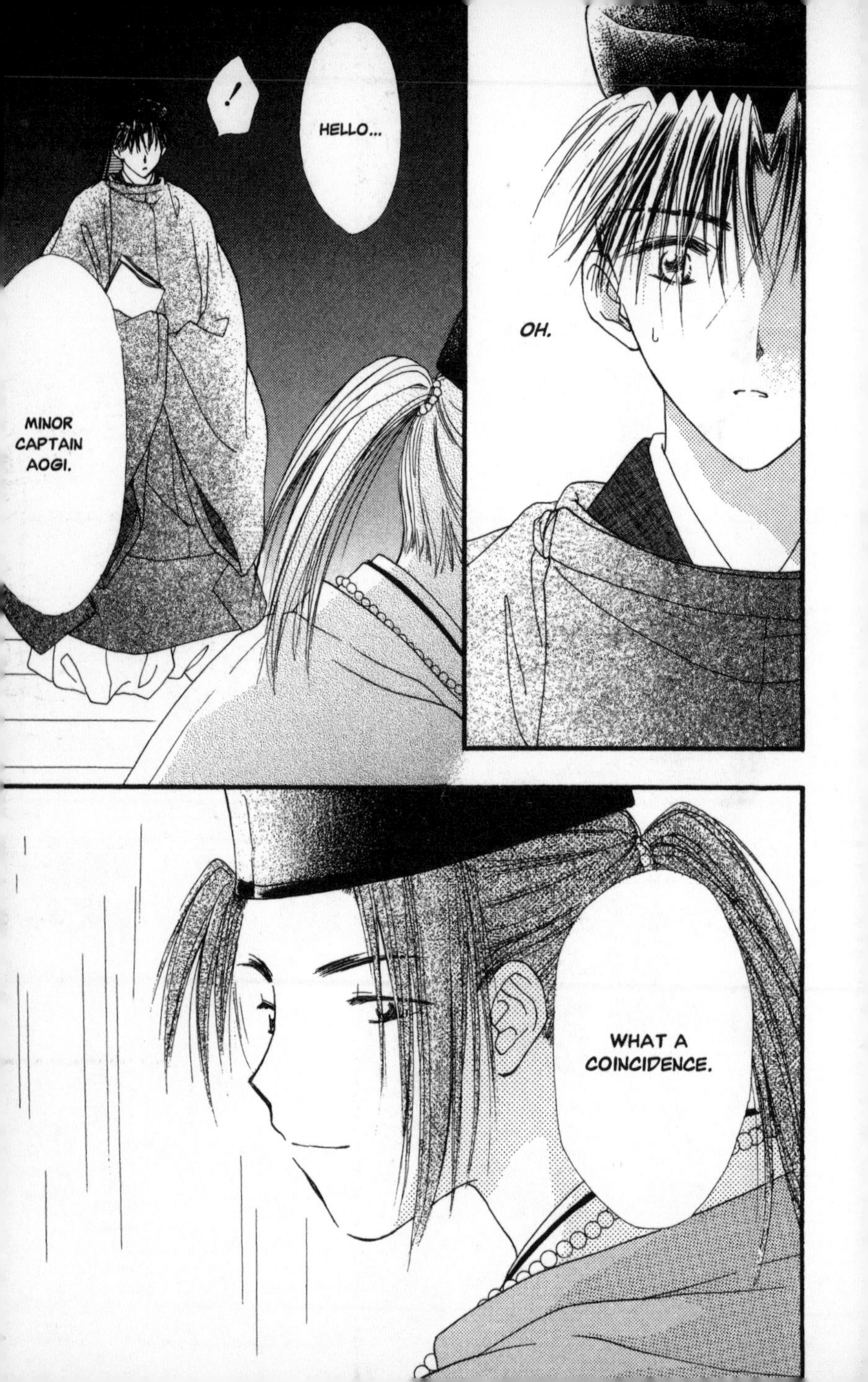
OH.
!
HELLO...
MINOR CAPTAIN AOGI.
WHAT A COINCIDENCE.

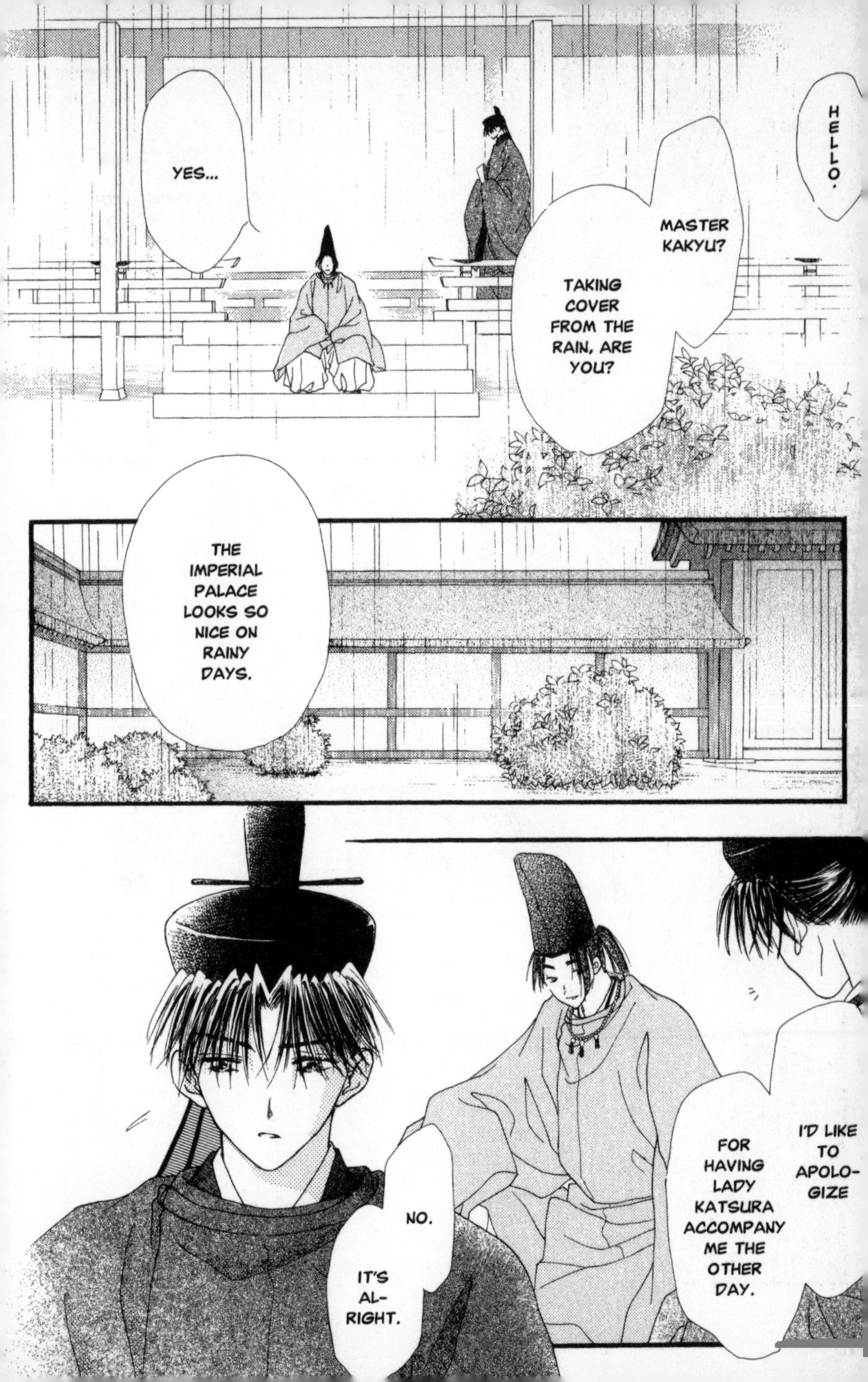
HELLO.
MASTER KAKYU?
TAKING COVER FROM THE RAIN, ARE YOU?
YES...
THE IMPERIAL PALACE LOOKS SO NICE ON RAINY DAYS.
I'D LIKE TO APOLO-GIZE
FOR HAVING LADY KATSURA ACCOMPANY ME THE OTHER DAY.
NO.
IT'S AL-RIGHT.

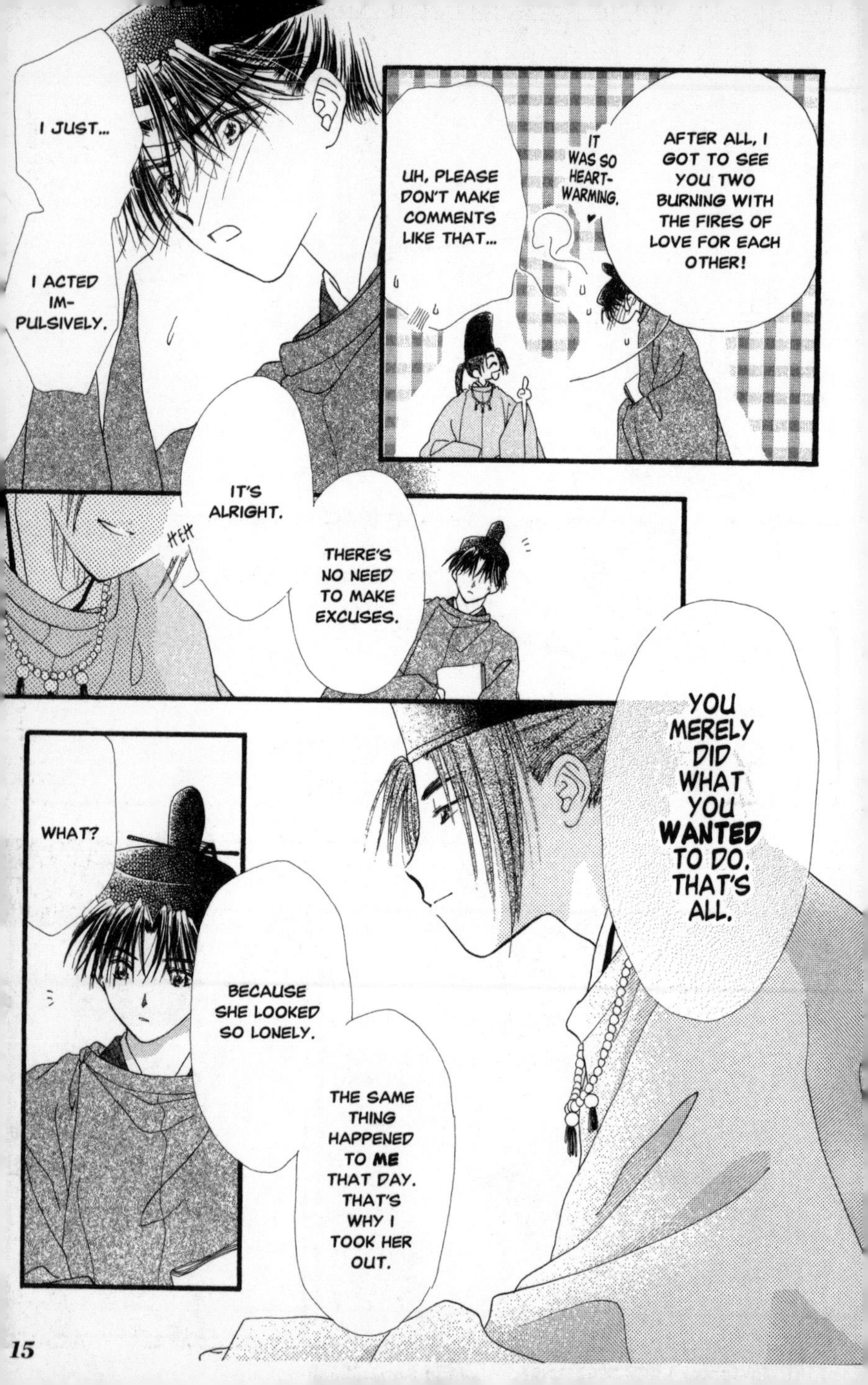

AFTER ALL, I GOT TO SEE YOU TWO BURNING WITH THE FIRES OF LOVE FOR EACH OTHER!
IT WAS SO HEART-WARMING.
UH, PLEASE DON'T MAKE COMMENTS LIKE THAT...
I JUST...
I ACTED IM-PULSIVELY.
HEH
IT'S ALRIGHT.
THERE'S NO NEED TO MAKE EXCUSES.
YOU MERELY DID WHAT YOU **WANTED** TO DO. THAT'S ALL.
WHAT?
BECAUSE SHE LOOKED SO LONELY.
THE SAME THING HAPPENED TO **ME** THAT DAY. THAT'S WHY I TOOK HER OUT.

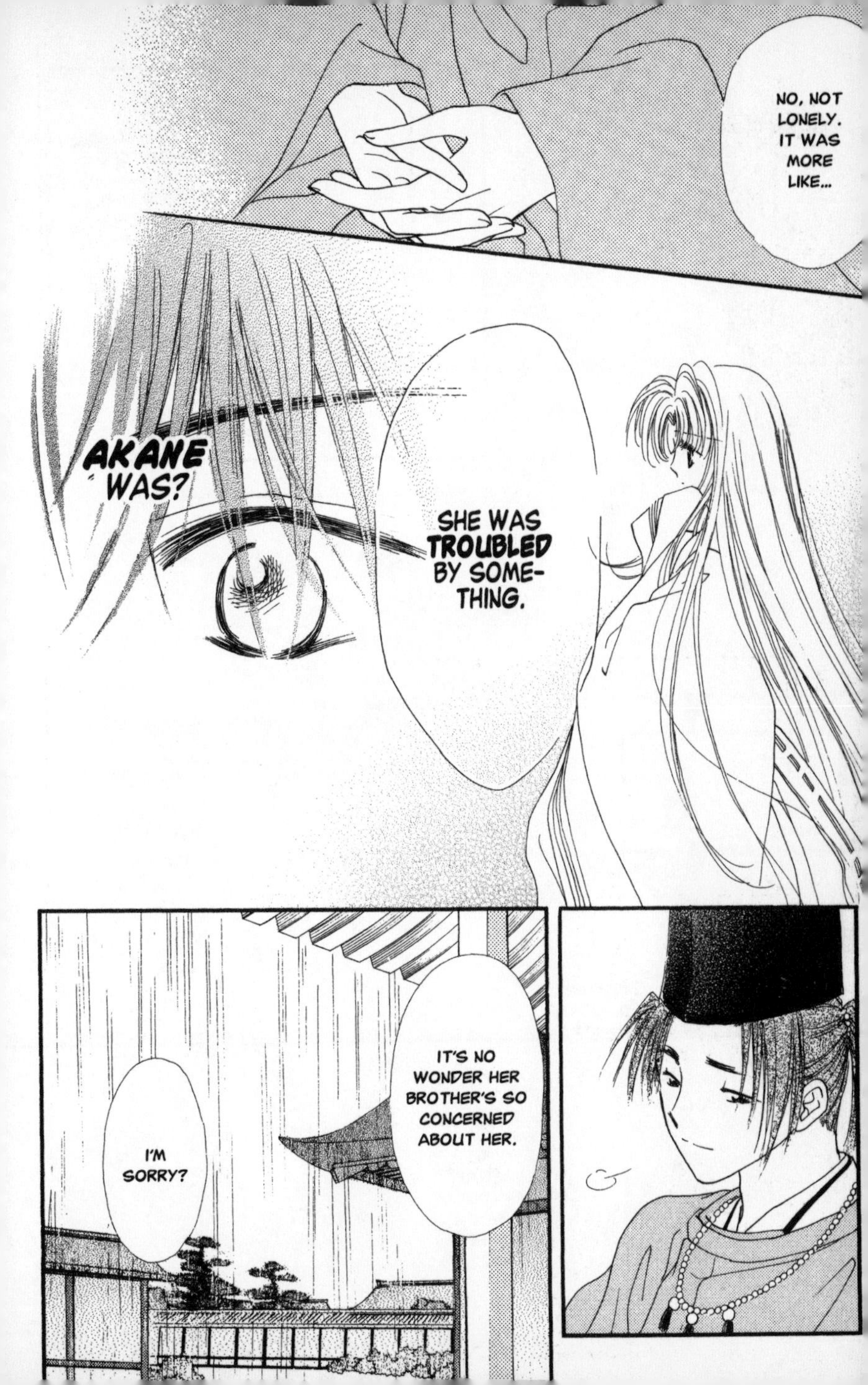
NO, NOT LONELY. IT WAS MORE LIKE...
AKANE WAS?
SHE WAS TROUBLED BY SOME-THING.
IT'S NO WONDER HER BROTHER'S SO CONCERNED ABOUT HER.
I'M SORRY?

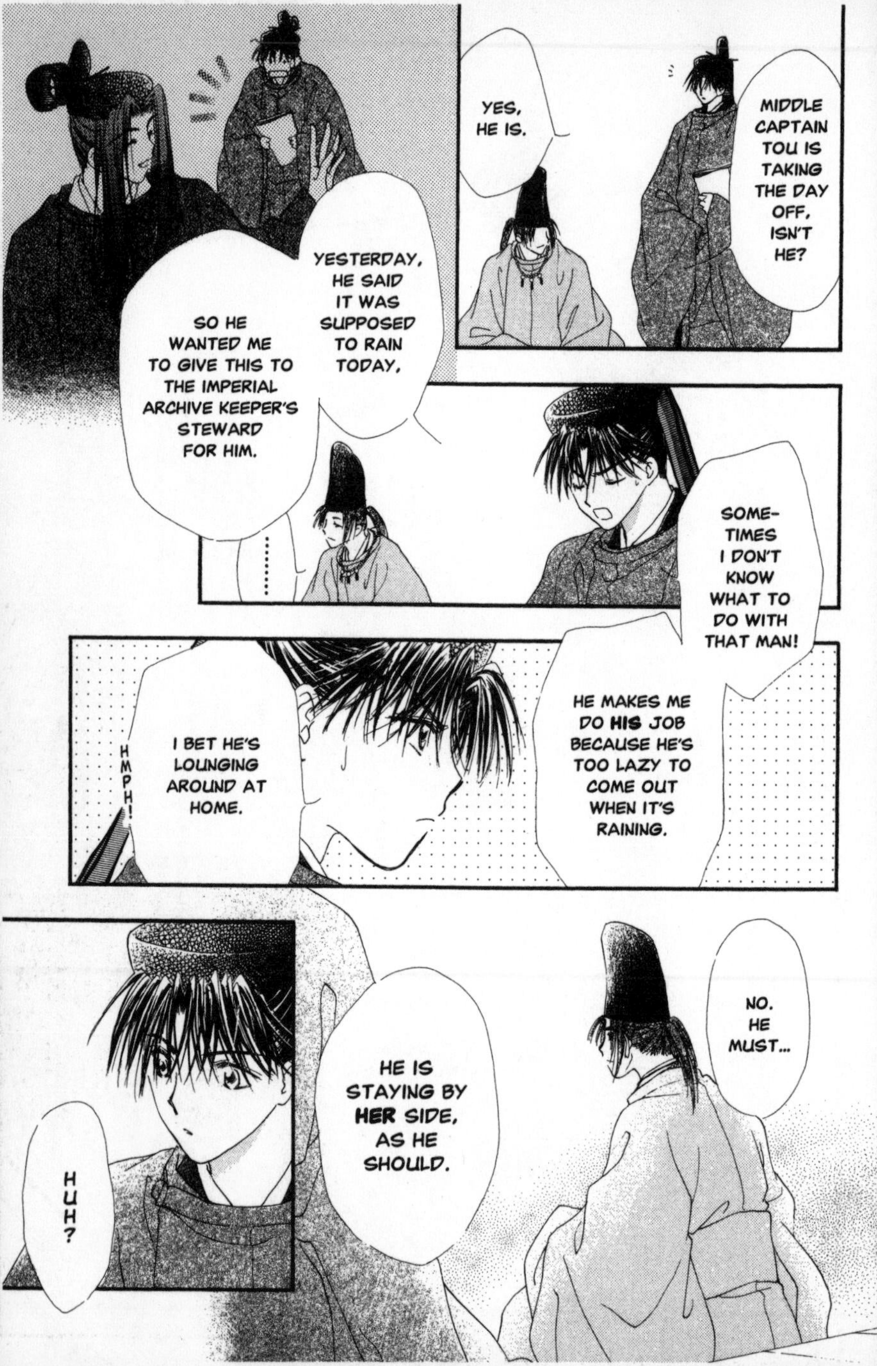
MIDDLE CAPTAIN TOU IS TAKING THE DAY OFF, ISN'T HE?
YES, HE IS.
YESTERDAY, HE SAID IT WAS SUPPOSED TO RAIN TODAY,
SO HE WANTED ME TO GIVE THIS TO THE IMPERIAL ARCHIVE KEEPER'S STEWARD FOR HIM.
SOME-TIMES I DON'T KNOW WHAT TO DO WITH THAT MAN!
......
HE MAKES ME DO **HIS** JOB BECAUSE HE'S TOO LAZY TO COME OUT WHEN IT'S RAINING.
HMPH!
I BET HE'S LOUNGING AROUND AT HOME.
NO. HE MUST...
HE IS STAYING BY **HER** SIDE, AS HE SHOULD.
HUH?

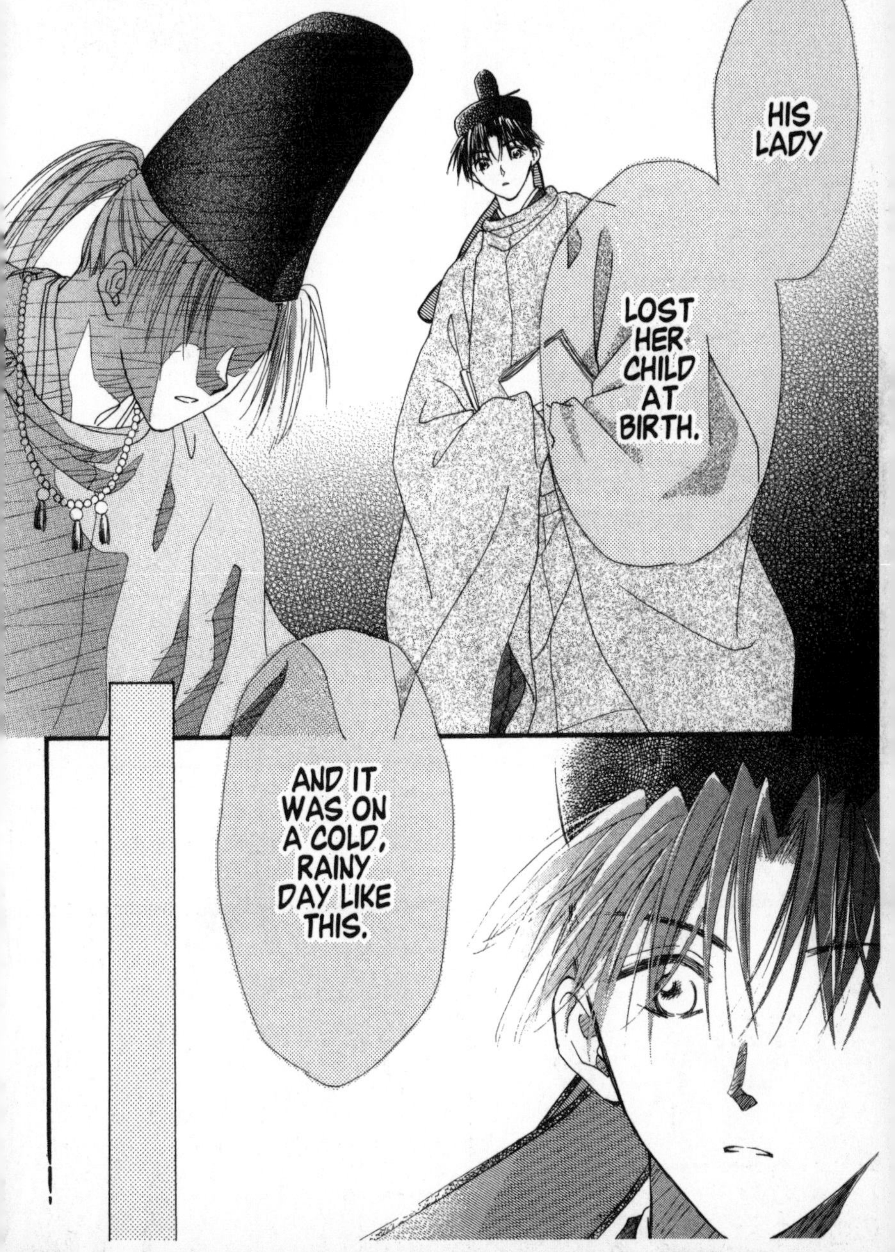
HIS LADY
LOST HER CHILD AT BIRTH.
AND IT WAS ON A COLD, RAINY DAY LIKE THIS.

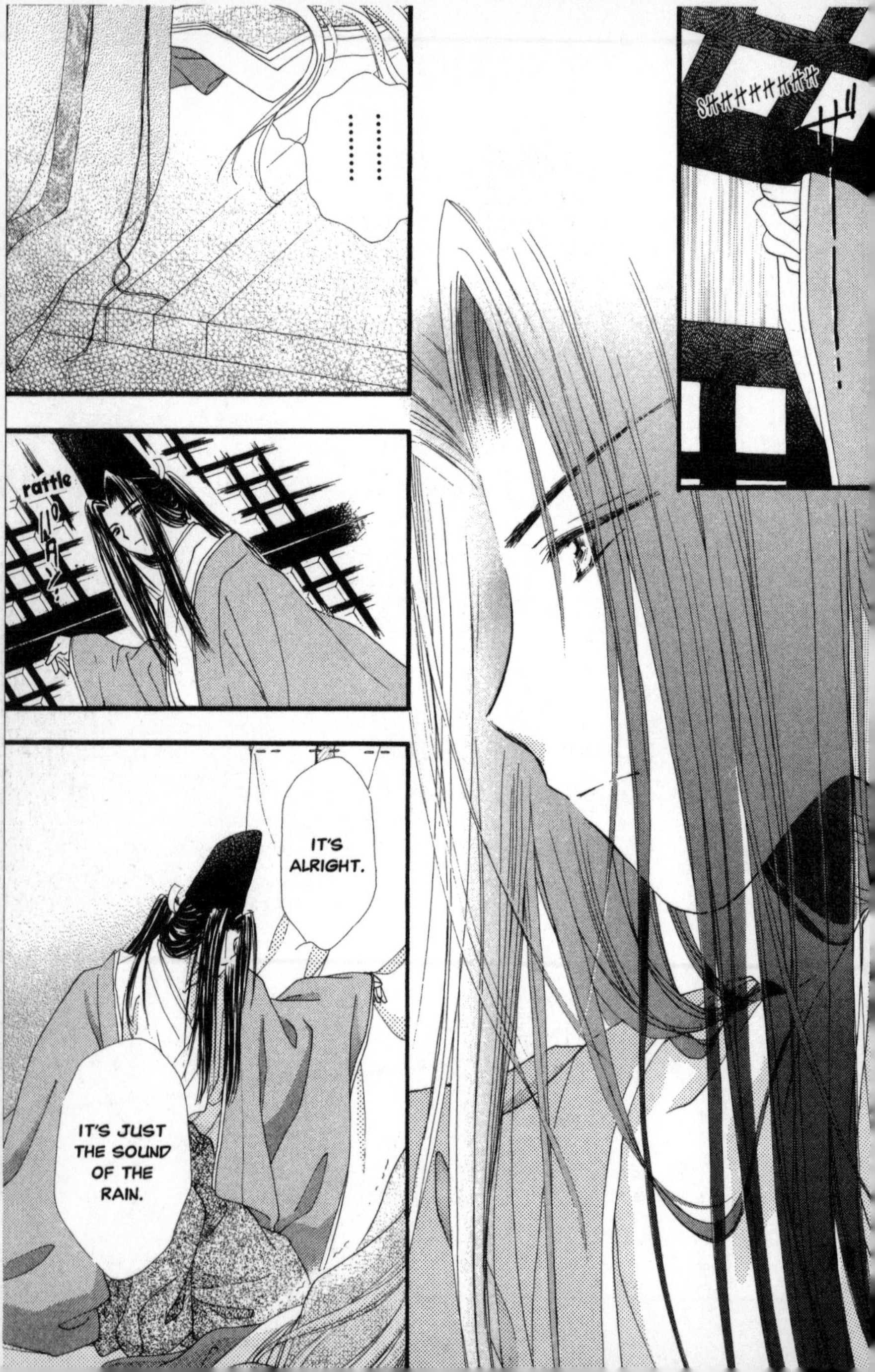
SHHHHHHHHH
......
rattle
IT'S ALRIGHT.
IT'S JUST THE SOUND OF THE RAIN.

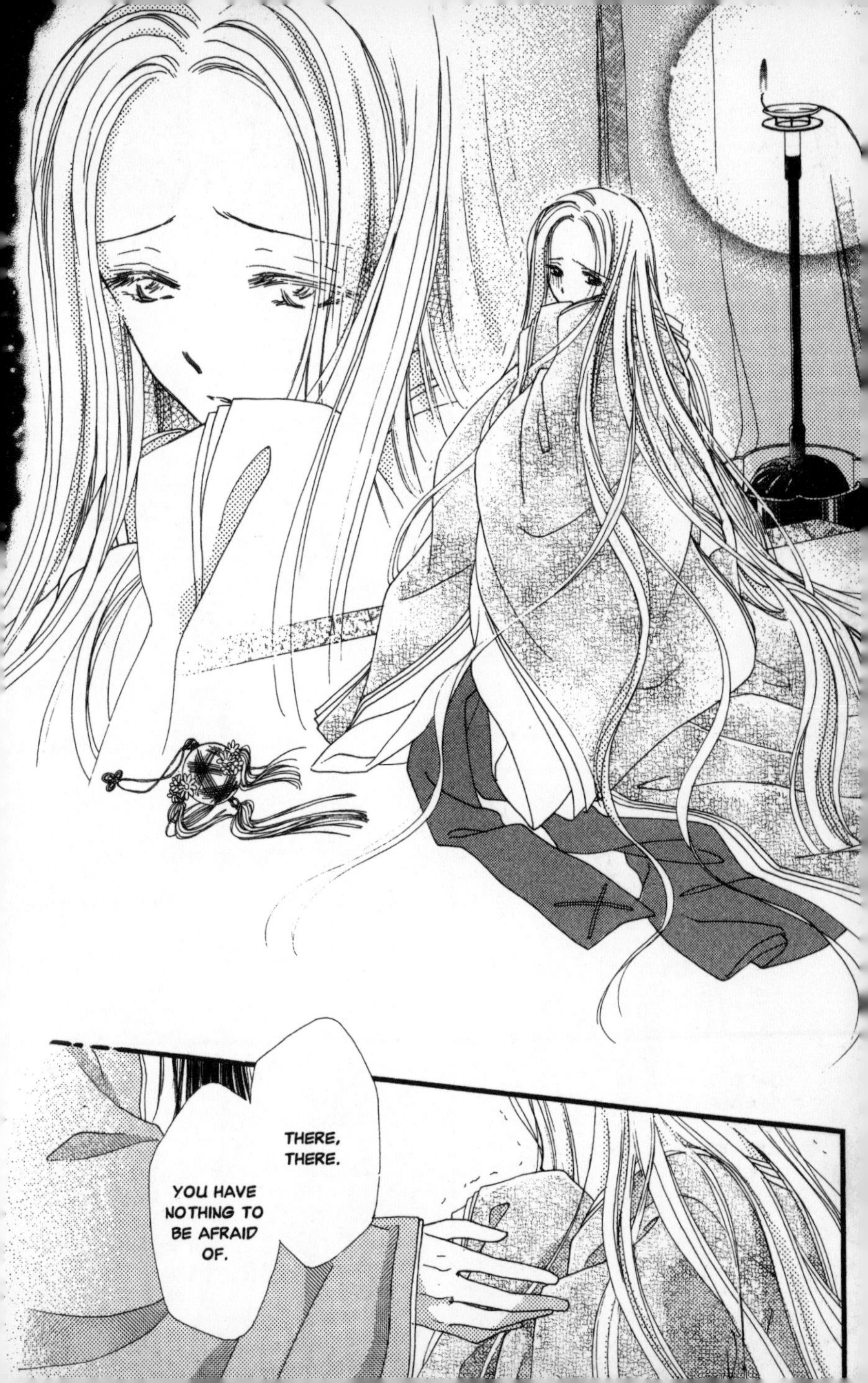
THERE, THERE.
YOU HAVE NOTHING TO BE AFRAID OF.

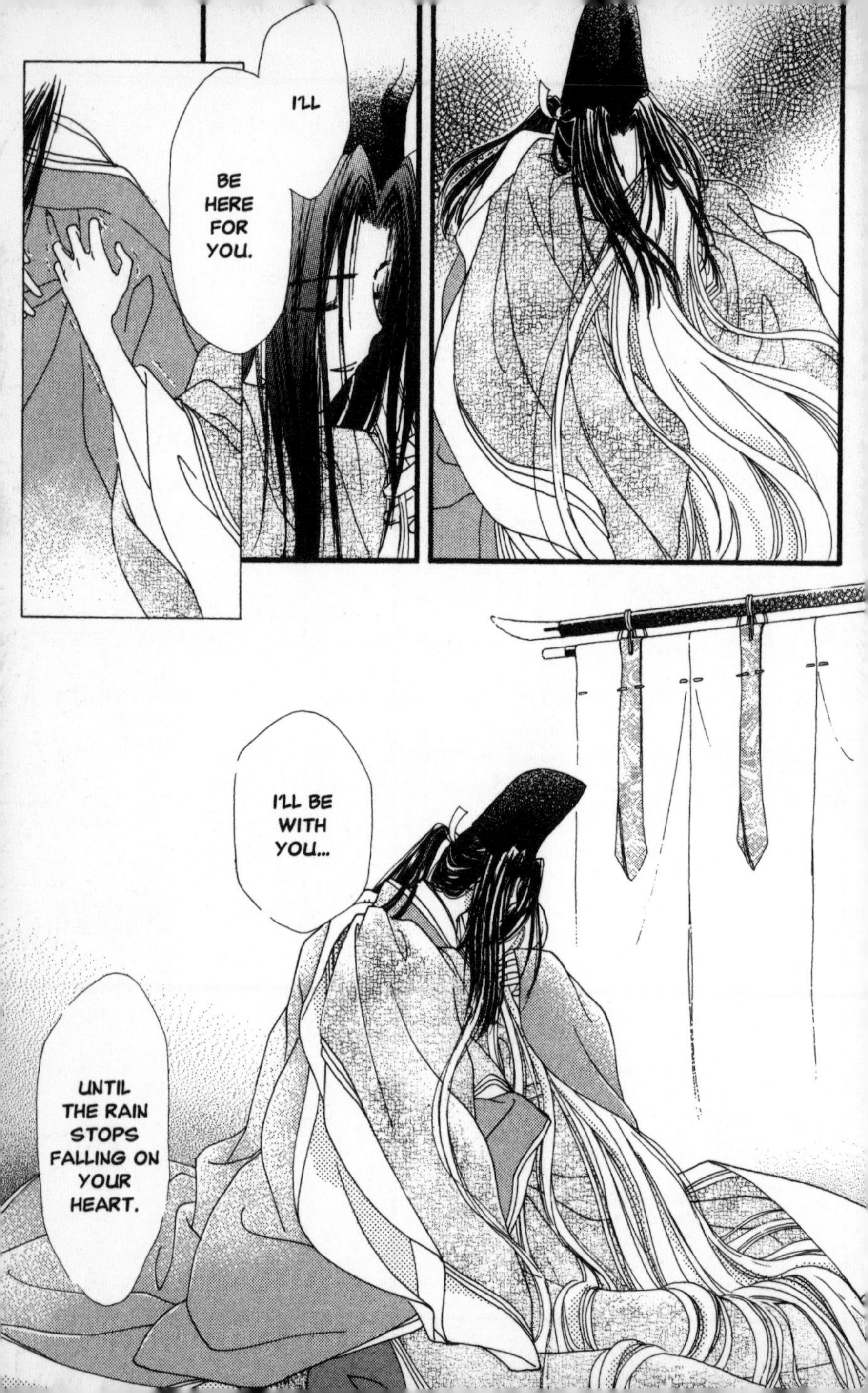
I'LL BE HERE FOR YOU.
I'LL BE WITH YOU...
UNTIL THE RAIN STOPS FALLING ON YOUR HEART.

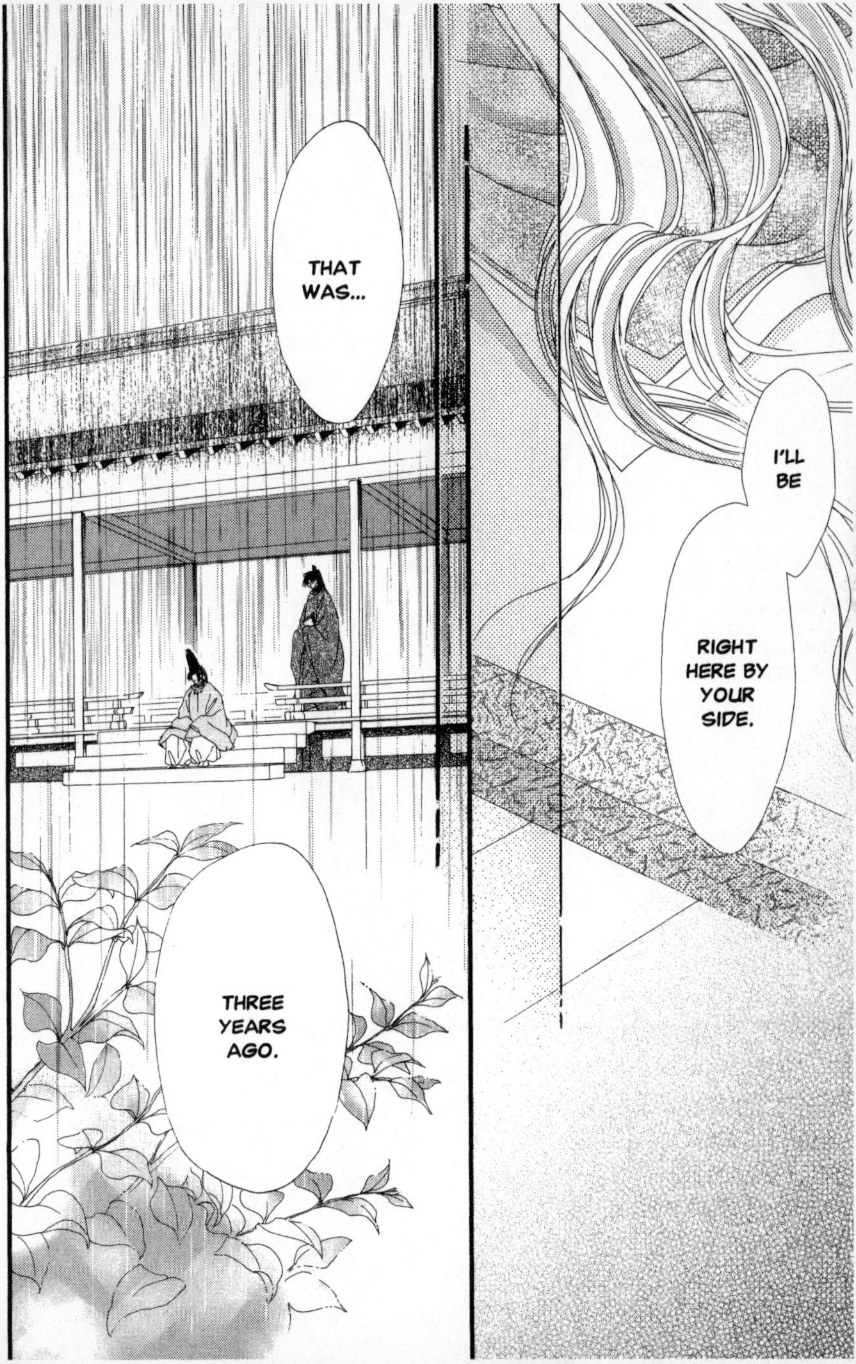
I'LL BE
RIGHT HERE BY YOUR SIDE.
THAT WAS...
THREE YEARS AGO.

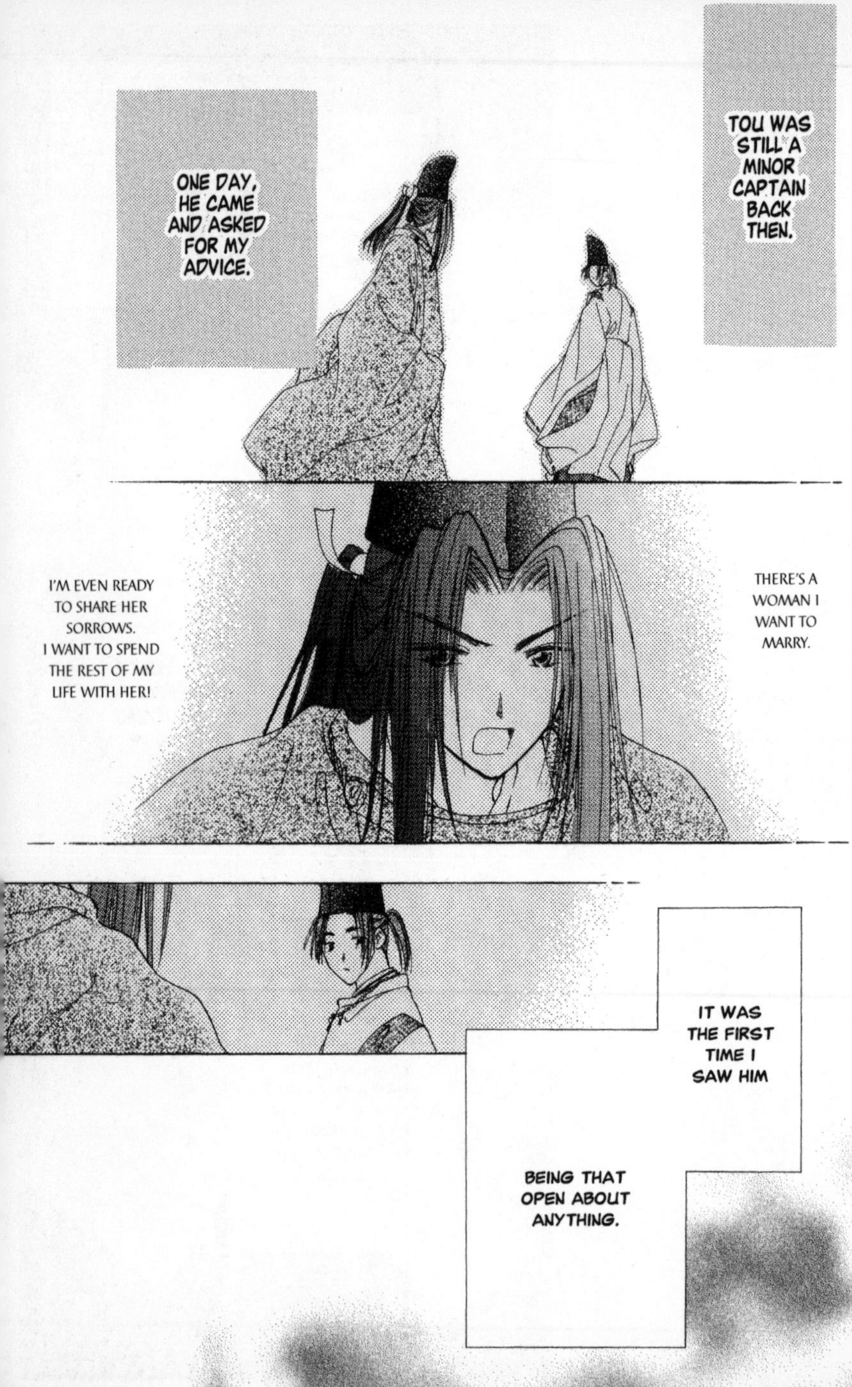
TOU WAS STILL A MINOR CAPTAIN BACK THEN.
ONE DAY, HE CAME AND ASKED FOR MY ADVICE.
THERE'S A WOMAN I WANT TO MARRY.
I'M EVEN READY TO SHARE HER SORROWS. I WANT TO SPEND THE REST OF MY LIFE WITH HER!
IT WAS THE FIRST TIME I SAW HIM
BEING THAT OPEN ABOUT ANYTHING.

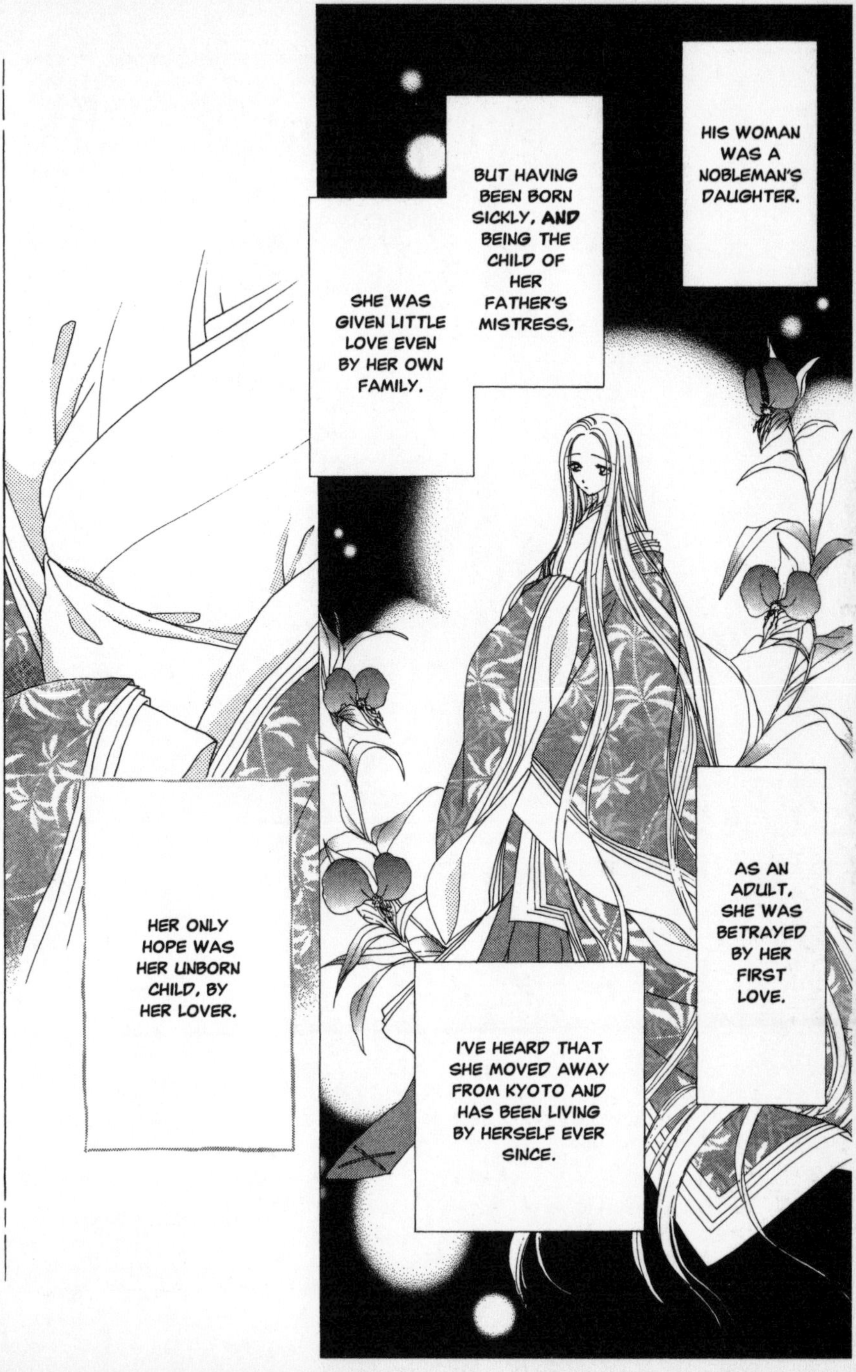
HIS WOMAN WAS A NOBLEMAN'S DAUGHTER.
BUT HAVING BEEN BORN SICKLY, AND BEING THE CHILD OF HER FATHER'S MISTRESS,
SHE WAS GIVEN LITTLE LOVE EVEN BY HER OWN FAMILY.
AS AN ADULT, SHE WAS BETRAYED BY HER FIRST LOVE.
I'VE HEARD THAT SHE MOVED AWAY FROM KYOTO AND HAS BEEN LIVING BY HERSELF EVER SINCE.
HER ONLY HOPE WAS HER UNBORN CHILD, BY HER LOVER.

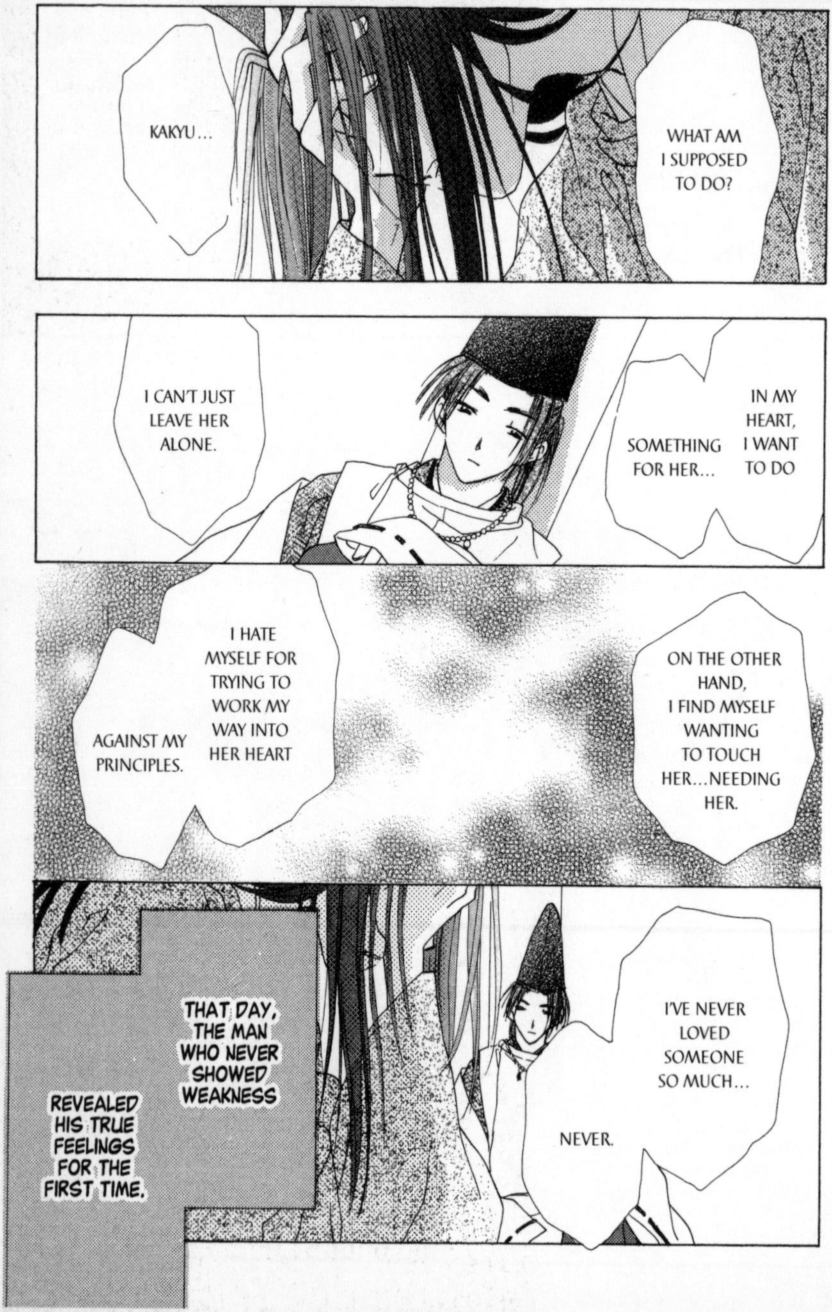
WHAT AM I SUPPOSED TO DO?
KAKYU…
IN MY HEART, I WANT TO DO SOMETHING FOR HER…
I CAN'T JUST LEAVE HER ALONE.
ON THE OTHER HAND, I FIND MYSELF WANTING TO TOUCH HER…NEEDING HER.
I HATE MYSELF FOR TRYING TO WORK MY WAY INTO HER HEART AGAINST MY PRINCIPLES.
I'VE NEVER LOVED SOMEONE SO MUCH… NEVER.
THAT DAY, THE MAN WHO NEVER SHOWED WEAKNESS
REVEALED HIS TRUE FEELINGS FOR THE FIRST TIME.

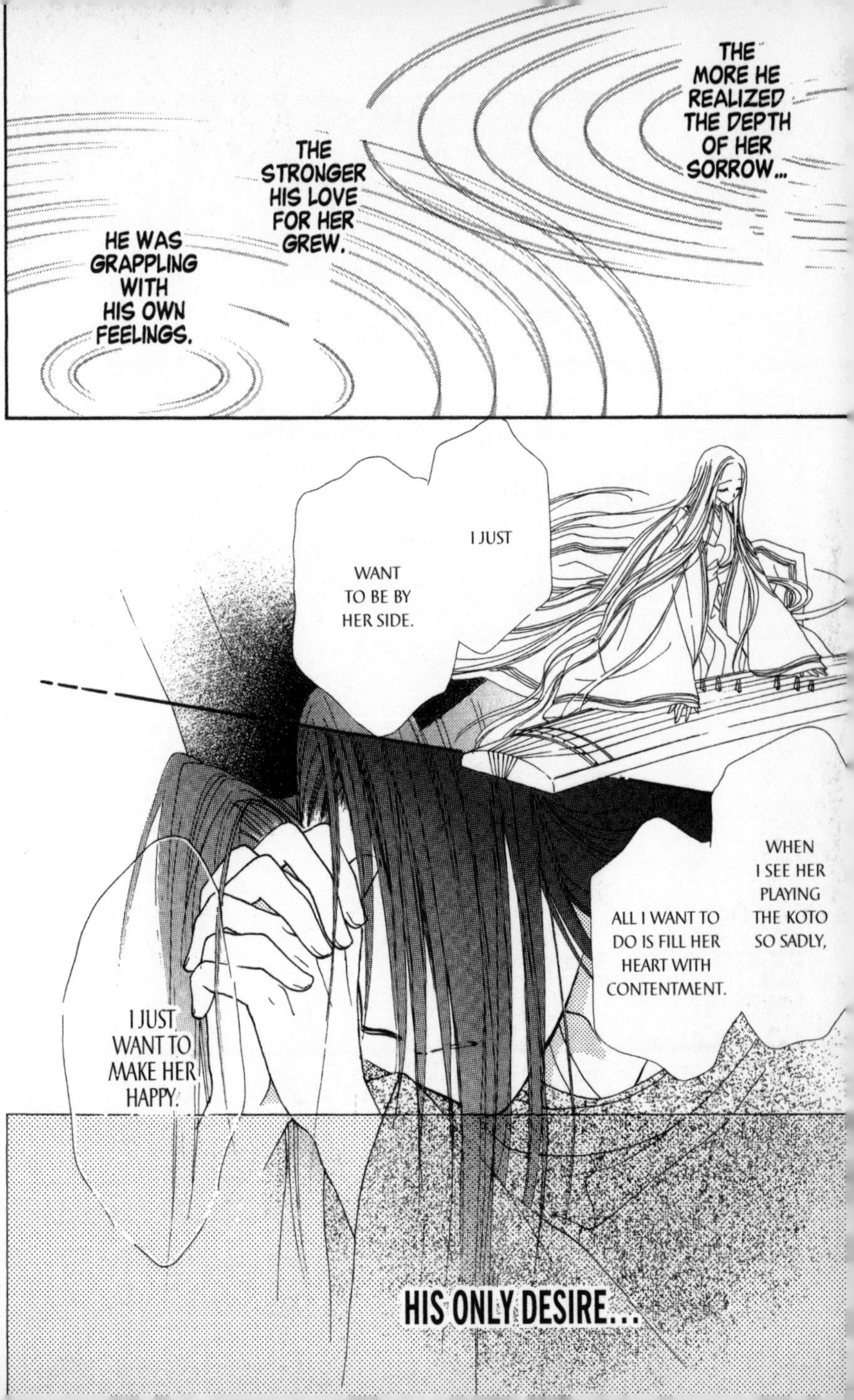
THE MORE HE REALIZED THE DEPTH OF HER SORROW...
THE STRONGER HIS LOVE FOR HER GREW.
HE WAS GRAPPLING WITH HIS OWN FEELINGS.
I JUST WANT TO BE BY HER SIDE.
WHEN I SEE HER PLAYING THE KOTO SO SADLY,
ALL I WANT TO DO IS FILL HER HEART WITH CONTENTMENT.
I JUST WANT TO MAKE HER HAPPY.
HIS ONLY DESIRE...

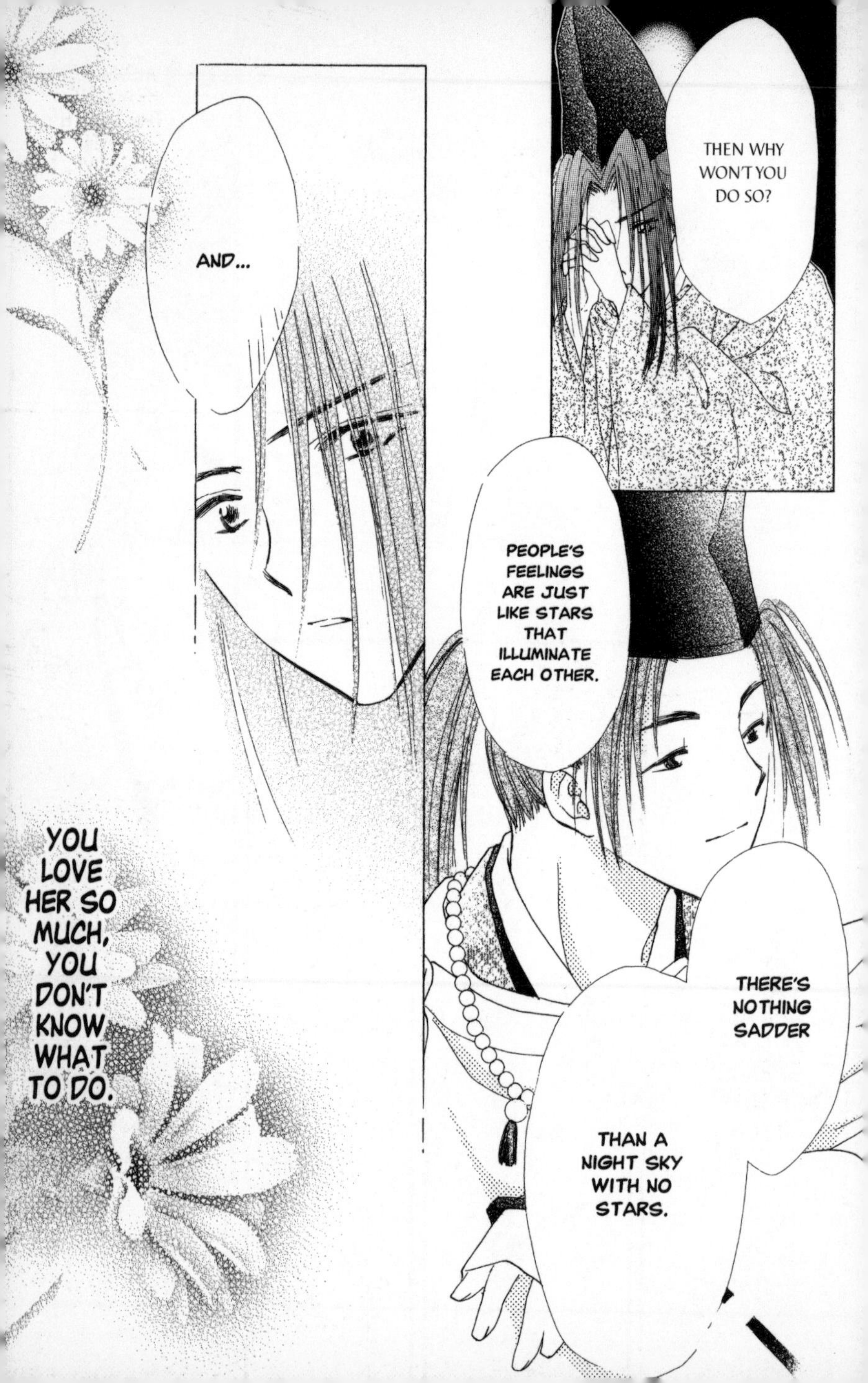
THEN WHY WON'T YOU DO SO?
PEOPLE'S FEELINGS ARE JUST LIKE STARS THAT ILLUMINATE EACH OTHER.
THERE'S NOTHING SADDER
THAN A NIGHT SKY WITH NO STARS.
AND...
YOU LOVE HER SO MUCH, YOU DON'T KNOW WHAT TO DO.

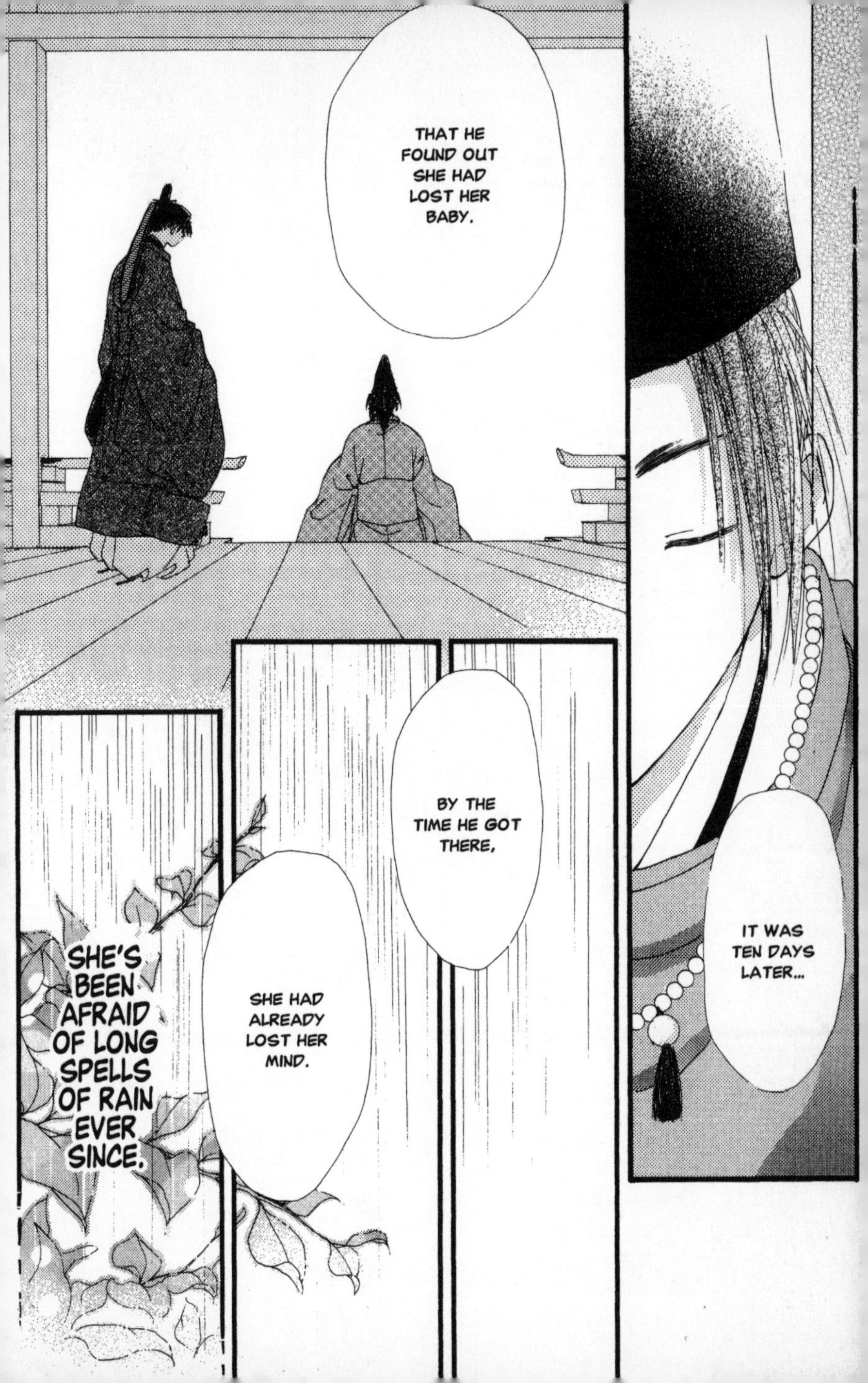
IT WAS TEN DAYS LATER...
THAT HE FOUND OUT SHE HAD LOST HER BABY.
BY THE TIME HE GOT THERE,
SHE HAD ALREADY LOST HER MIND.
SHE'S BEEN AFRAID OF LONG SPELLS OF RAIN EVER SINCE.

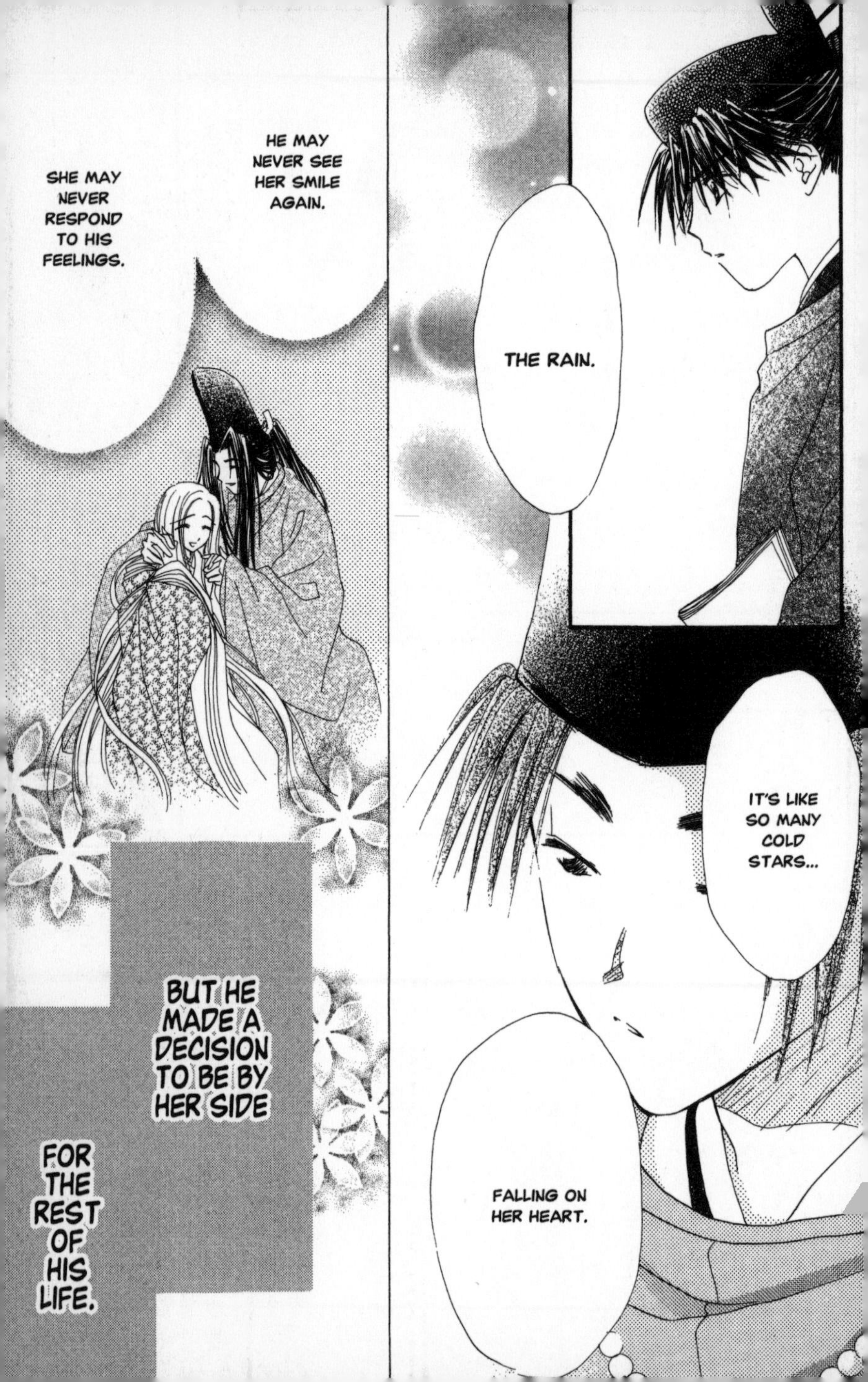
THE RAIN.
IT'S LIKE SO MANY COLD STARS...
FALLING ON HER HEART.
HE MAY NEVER SEE HER SMILE AGAIN.
SHE MAY NEVER RESPOND TO HIS FEELINGS.
BUT HE MADE A DECISION TO BE BY HER SIDE
FOR THE REST OF HIS LIFE.

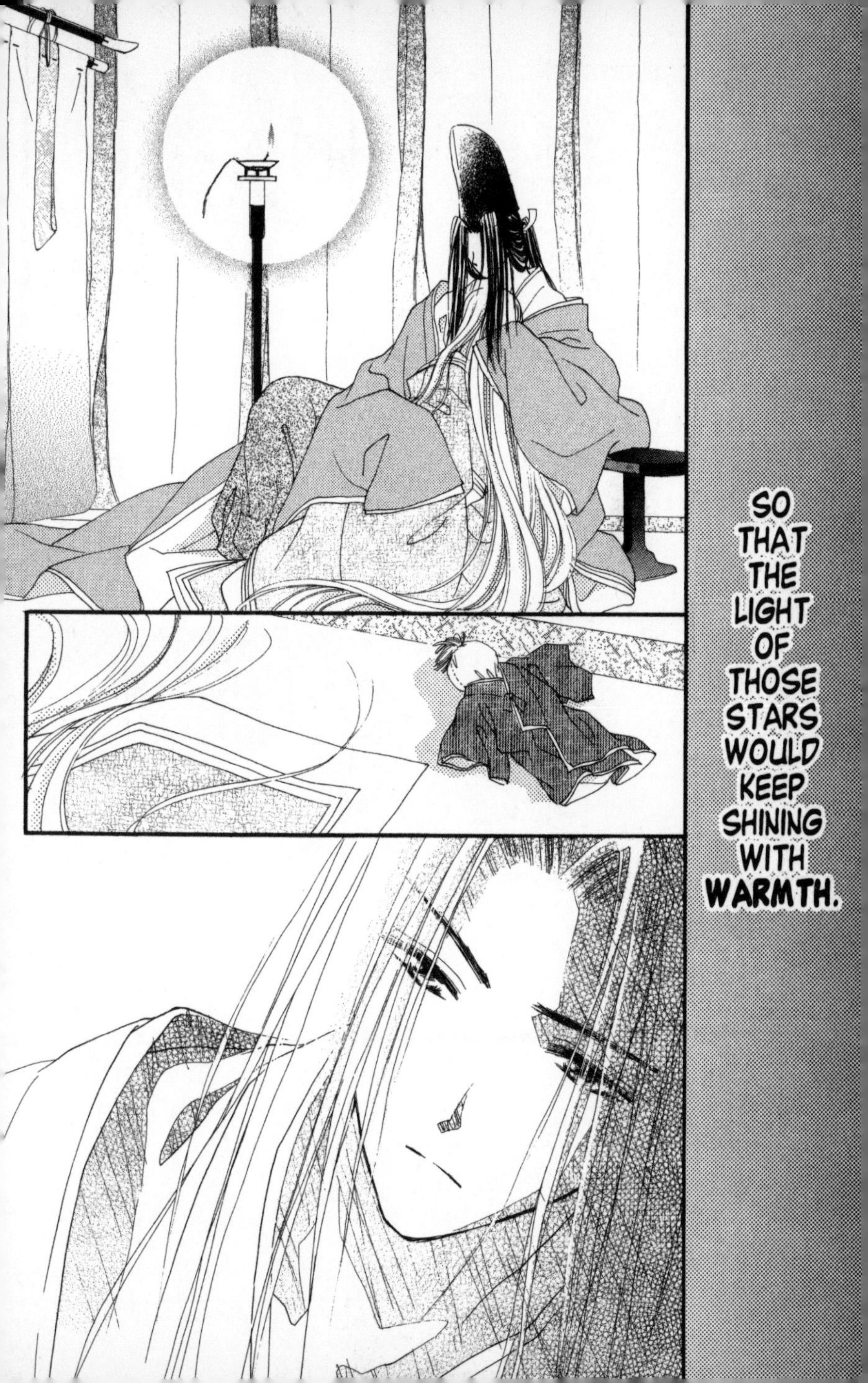
SO THAT THE LIGHT OF THOSE STARS WOULD KEEP SHINING WITH WARMTH.

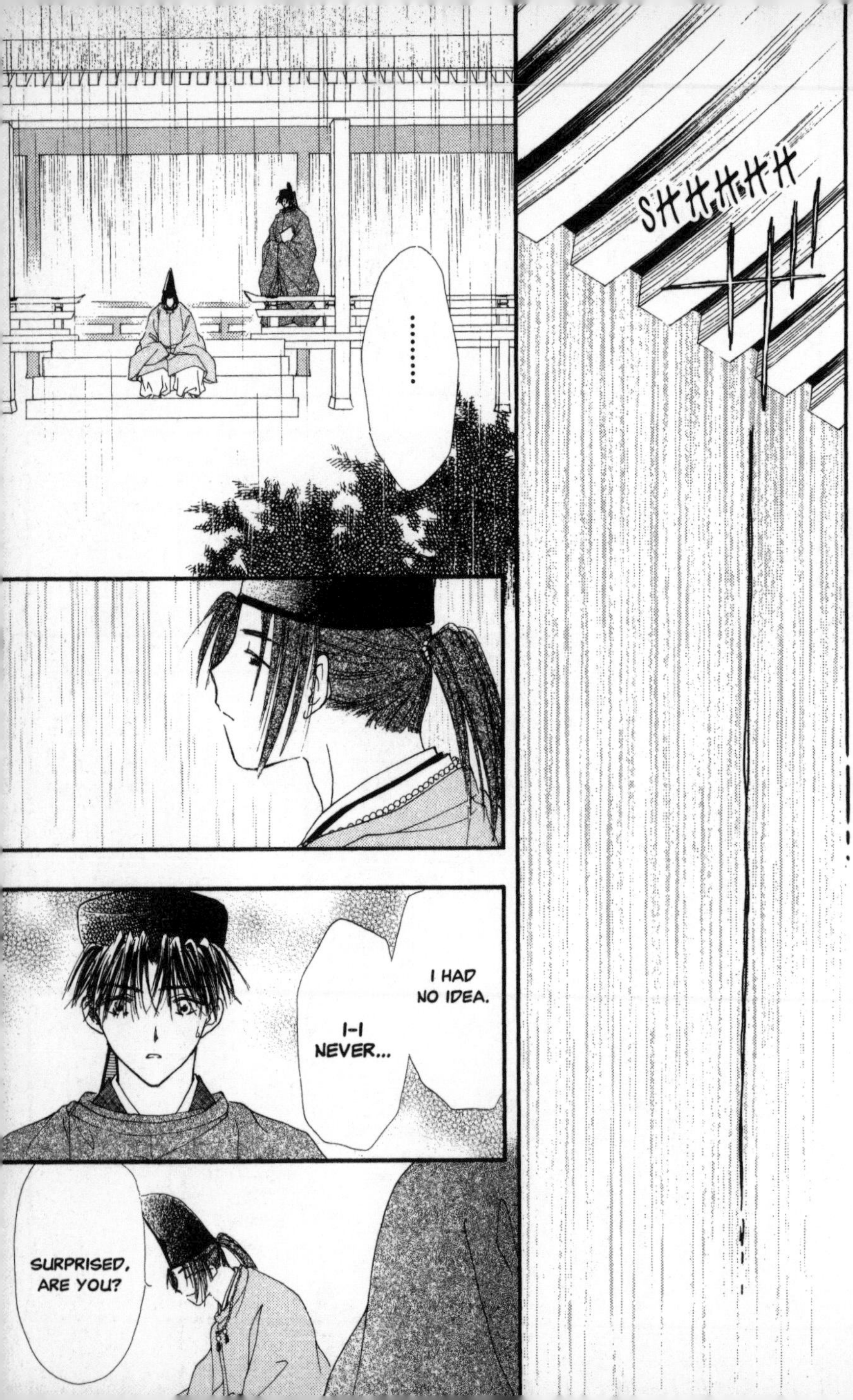
SHHHHH
....
I HAD NO IDEA.
I-I NEVER...
SURPRISED, ARE YOU?

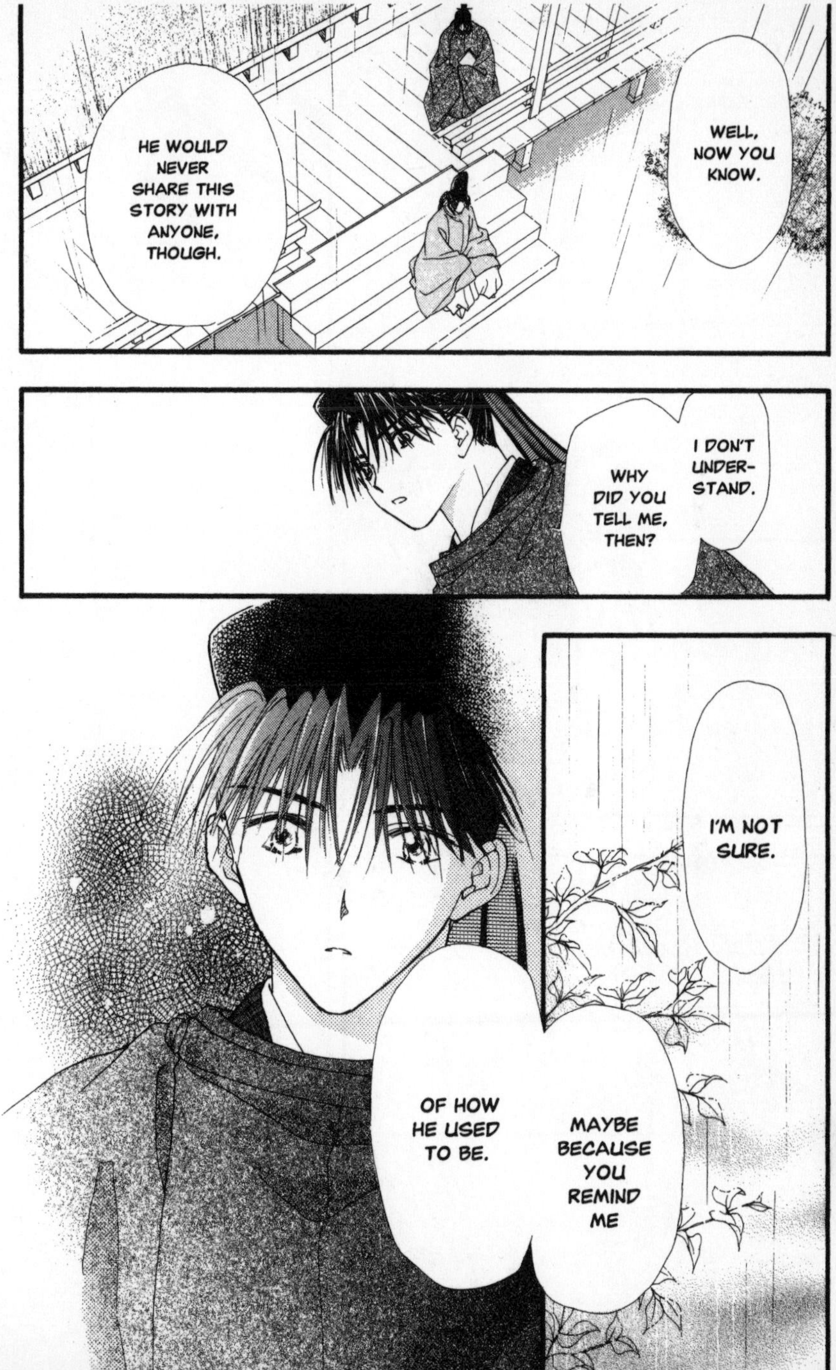
WELL, NOW YOU KNOW.
HE WOULD NEVER SHARE THIS STORY WITH ANYONE, THOUGH.
I DON'T UNDER-STAND.
WHY DID YOU TELL ME, THEN?
I'M NOT SURE.
MAYBE BECAUSE YOU REMIND ME
OF HOW HE USED TO BE.

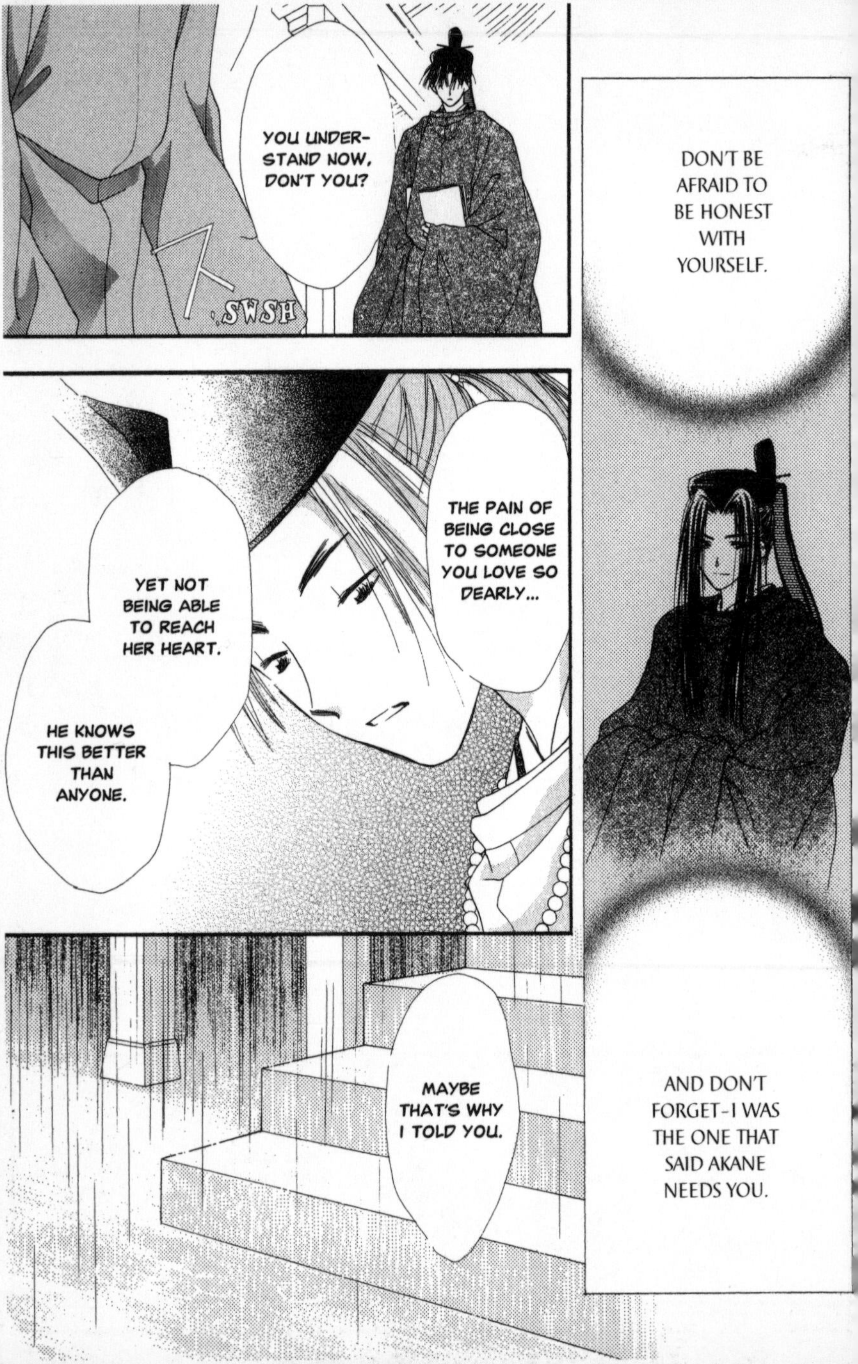
DON'T BE AFRAID TO BE HONEST WITH YOURSELF.
YOU UNDER-STAND NOW, DON'T YOU?
SWSH
THE PAIN OF BEING CLOSE TO SOMEONE YOU LOVE SO DEARLY...
YET NOT BEING ABLE TO REACH HER HEART.
HE KNOWS THIS BETTER THAN ANYONE.
MAYBE THAT'S WHY I TOLD YOU.
AND DON'T FORGET-I WAS THE ONE THAT SAID AKANE NEEDS YOU.

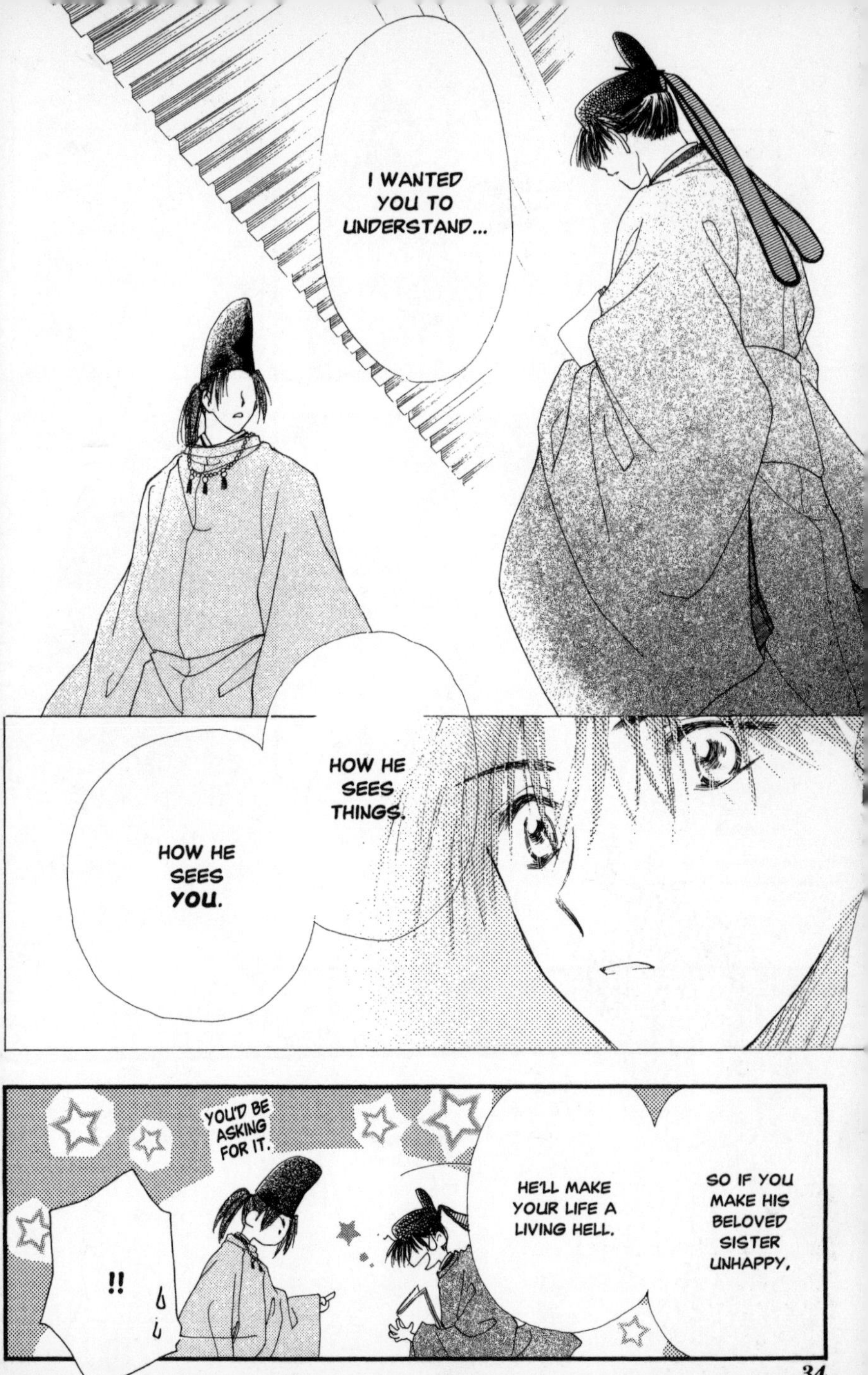
I WANTED YOU TO UNDERSTAND...
HOW HE SEES THINGS.
HOW HE SEES YOU.
SO IF YOU MAKE HIS BELOVED SISTER UNHAPPY,
HE'LL MAKE YOUR LIFE A LIVING HELL.
YOU'D BE ASKING FOR IT.
!!

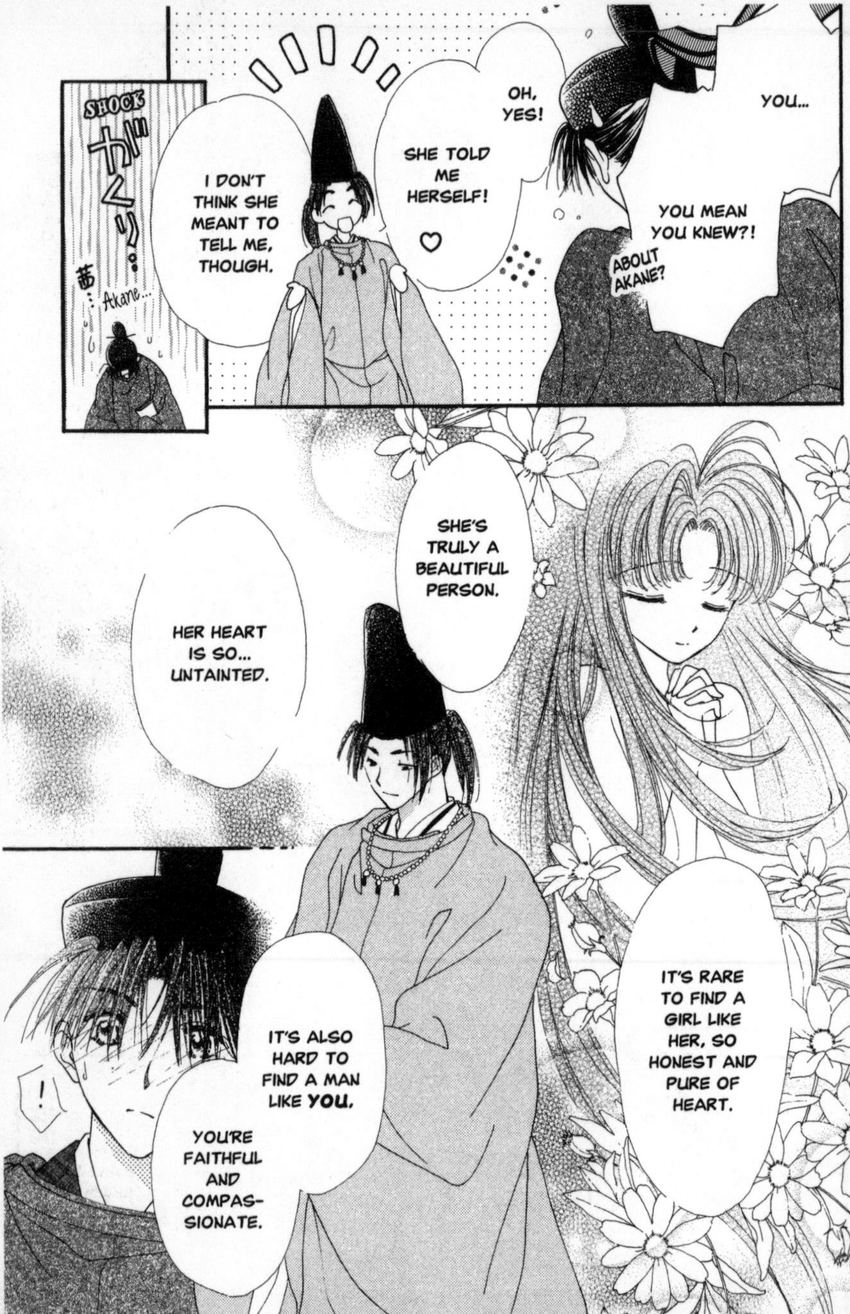
YOU...
YOU MEAN YOU KNEW?!
ABOUT AKANE?
OH, YES!
SHE TOLD ME HERSELF! ♥
I DON'T THINK SHE MEANT TO TELL ME, THOUGH.
SHOCK
がくり。
茜…
Akane...
SHE'S TRULY A BEAUTIFUL PERSON.
HER HEART IS SO... UNTAINTED.
IT'S RARE TO FIND A GIRL LIKE HER, SO HONEST AND PURE OF HEART.
IT'S ALSO HARD TO FIND A MAN LIKE **YOU.**
YOU'RE FAITHFUL AND COMPAS-SIONATE.
!

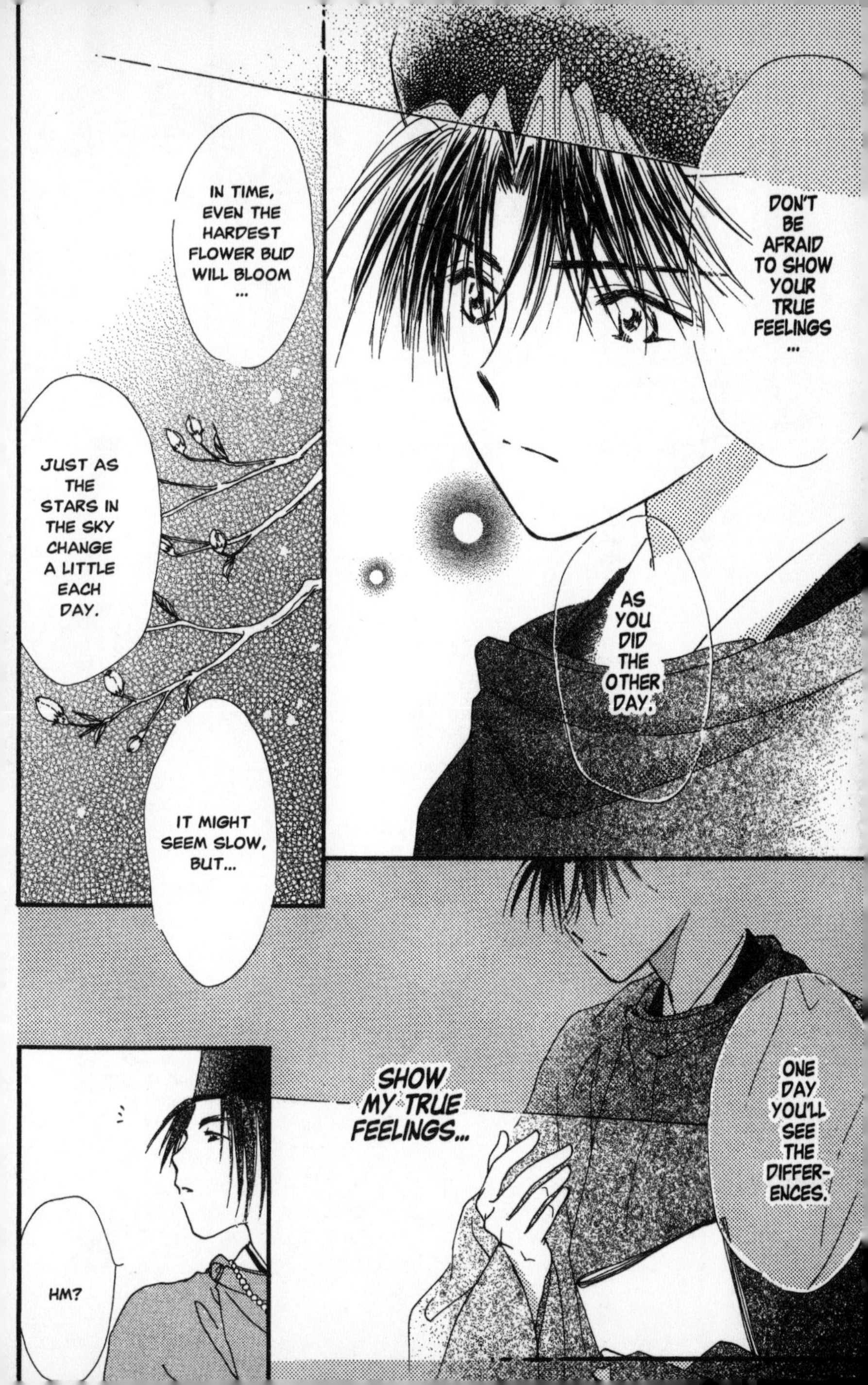
DON'T BE AFRAID TO SHOW YOUR TRUE FEELINGS ...
AS YOU DID THE OTHER DAY.
IN TIME, EVEN THE HARDEST FLOWER BUD WILL BLOOM ...
JUST AS THE STARS IN THE SKY CHANGE A LITTLE EACH DAY.
IT MIGHT SEEM SLOW, BUT...
ONE DAY YOU'LL SEE THE DIFFER-ENCES.
SHOW MY TRUE FEELINGS...
HM?

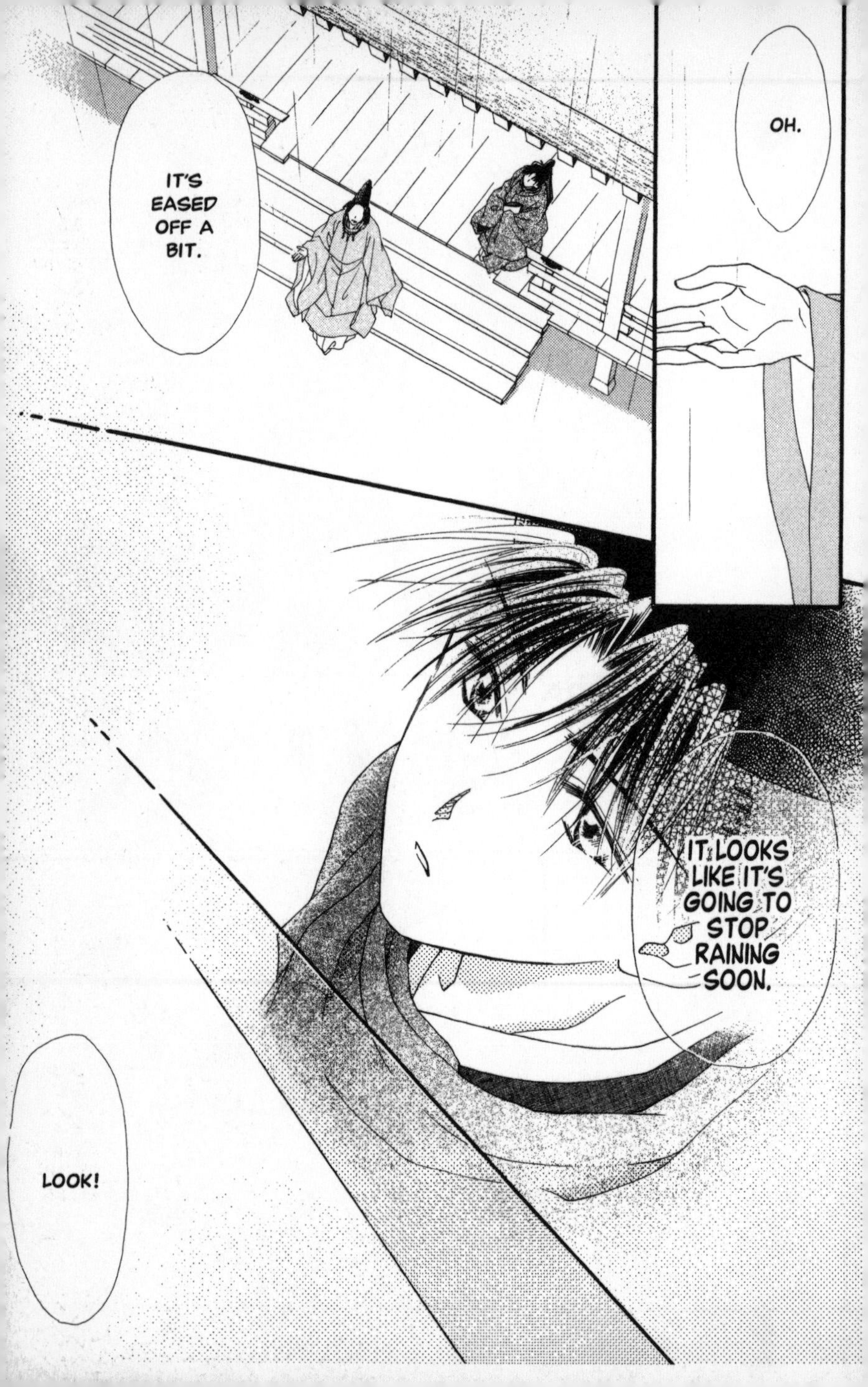
OH.
IT'S EASED OFF A BIT.
IT LOOKS LIKE IT'S GOING TO STOP RAINING SOON.
LOOK!

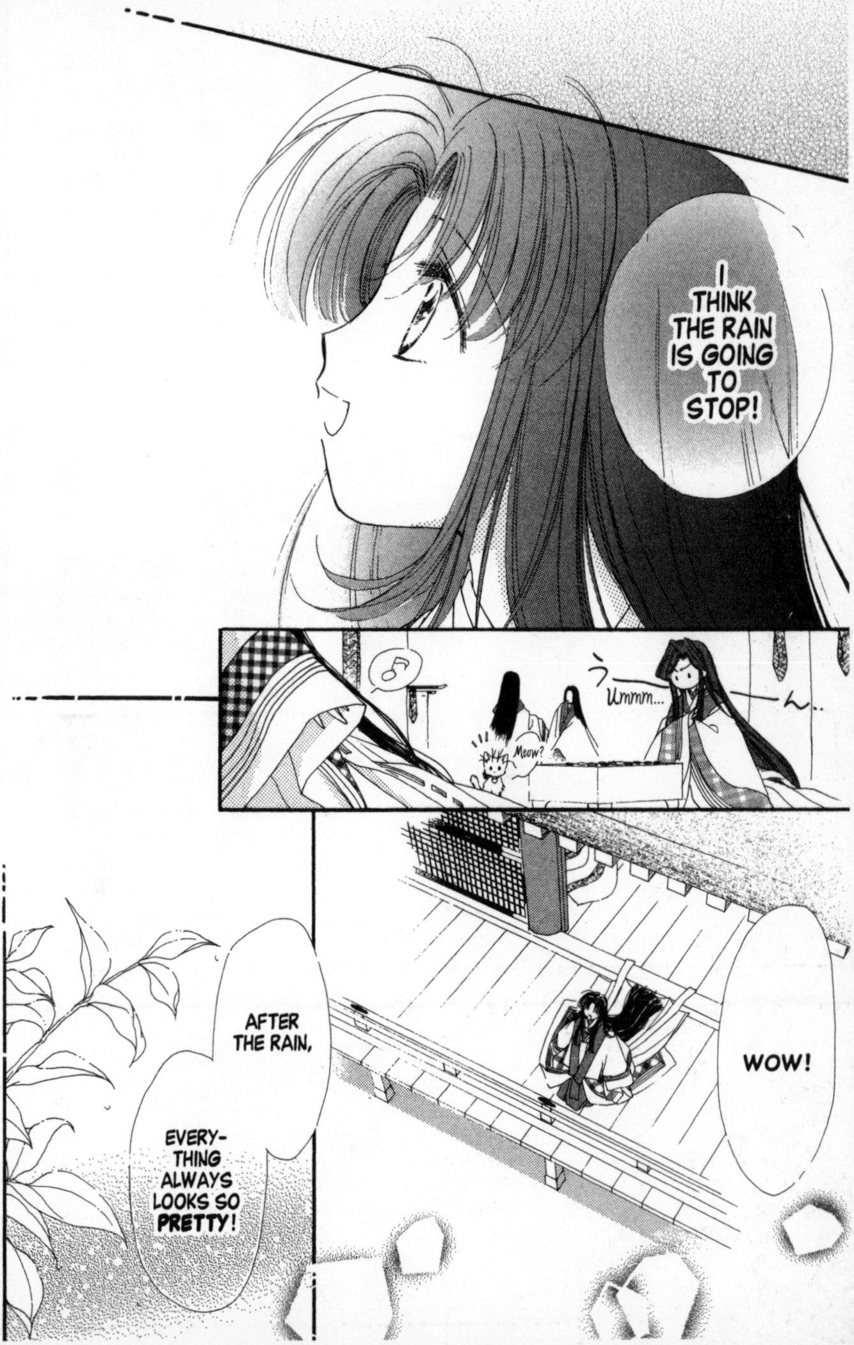

I THINK THE RAIN IS GOING TO STOP!
う——ん..
Ummm...
Meow?
WOW!
AFTER THE RAIN,
EVERY-THING ALWAYS LOOKS SO PRETTY!

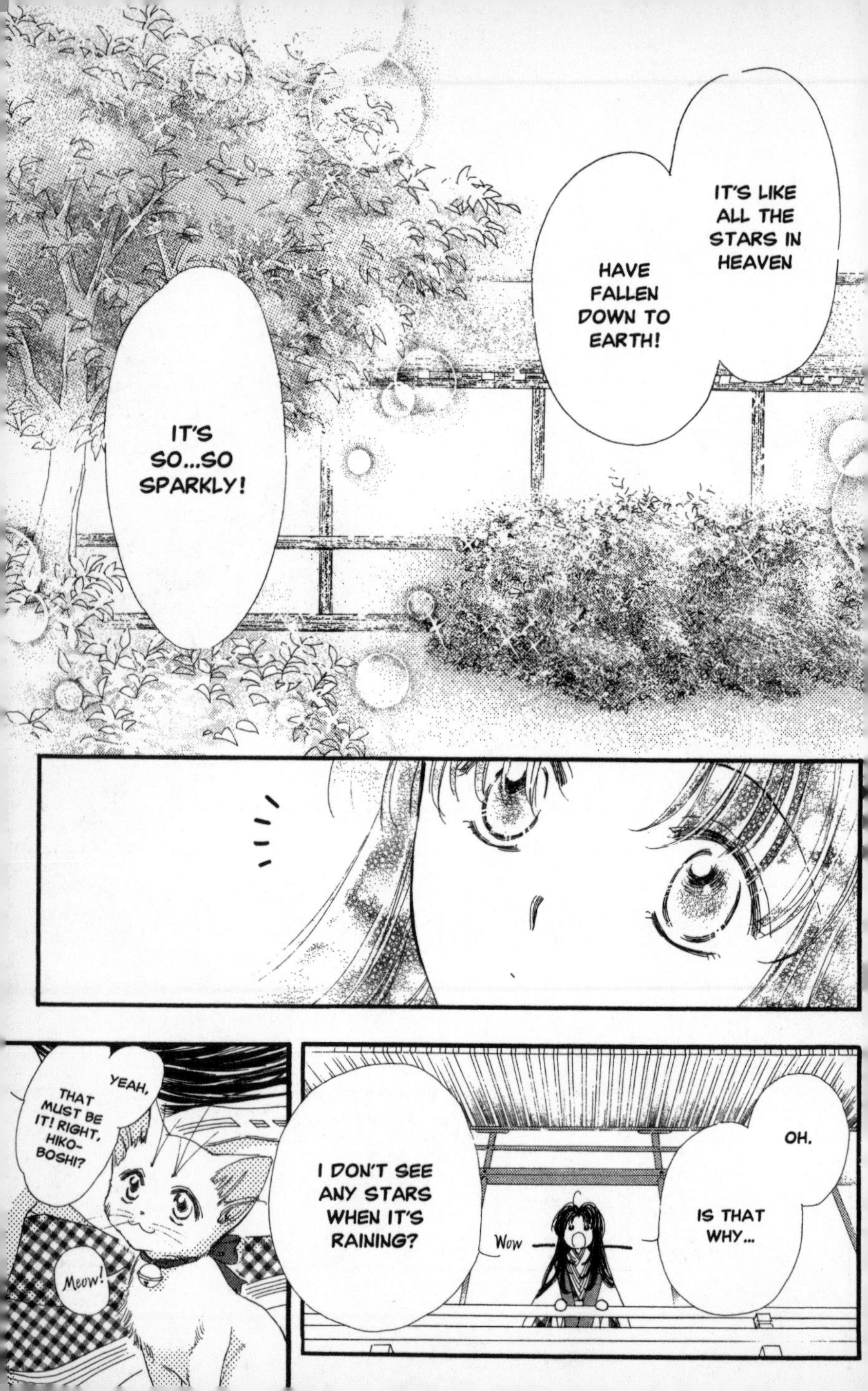
IT'S LIKE ALL THE STARS IN HEAVEN
HAVE FALLEN DOWN TO EARTH!
IT'S SO...SO SPARKLY!
OH.
IS THAT WHY...
Wow
I DON'T SEE ANY STARS WHEN IT'S RAINING?
YEAH, THAT MUST BE IT! RIGHT, HIKO-BOSHI?
Meow!

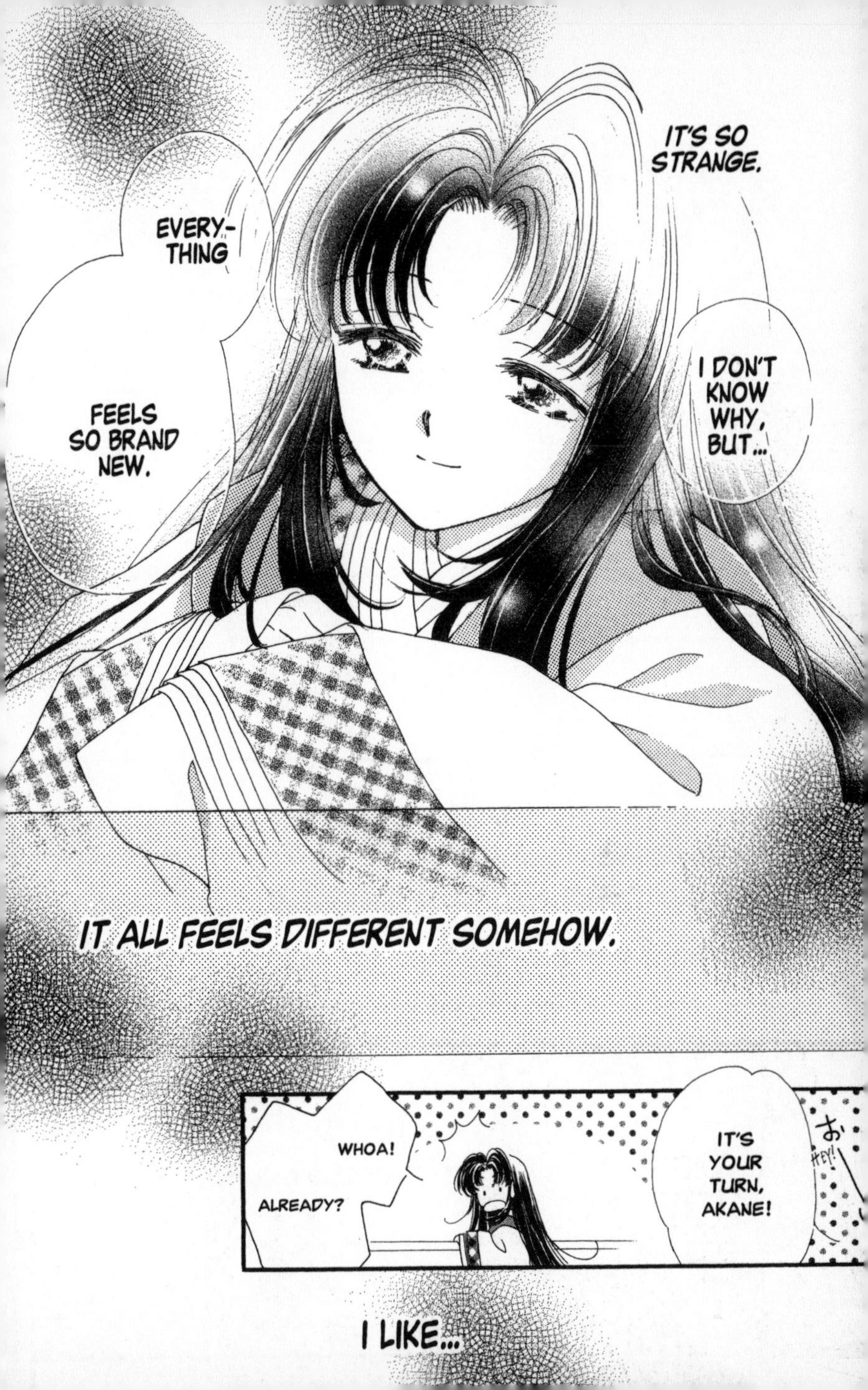
IT'S SO STRANGE.
I DON'T KNOW WHY, BUT...
EVERY-THING
FEELS SO BRAND NEW.
IT ALL FEELS DIFFERENT SOMEHOW.
お
HEY!
IT'S YOUR TURN, AKANE!
WHOA!
ALREADY?
I LIKE...

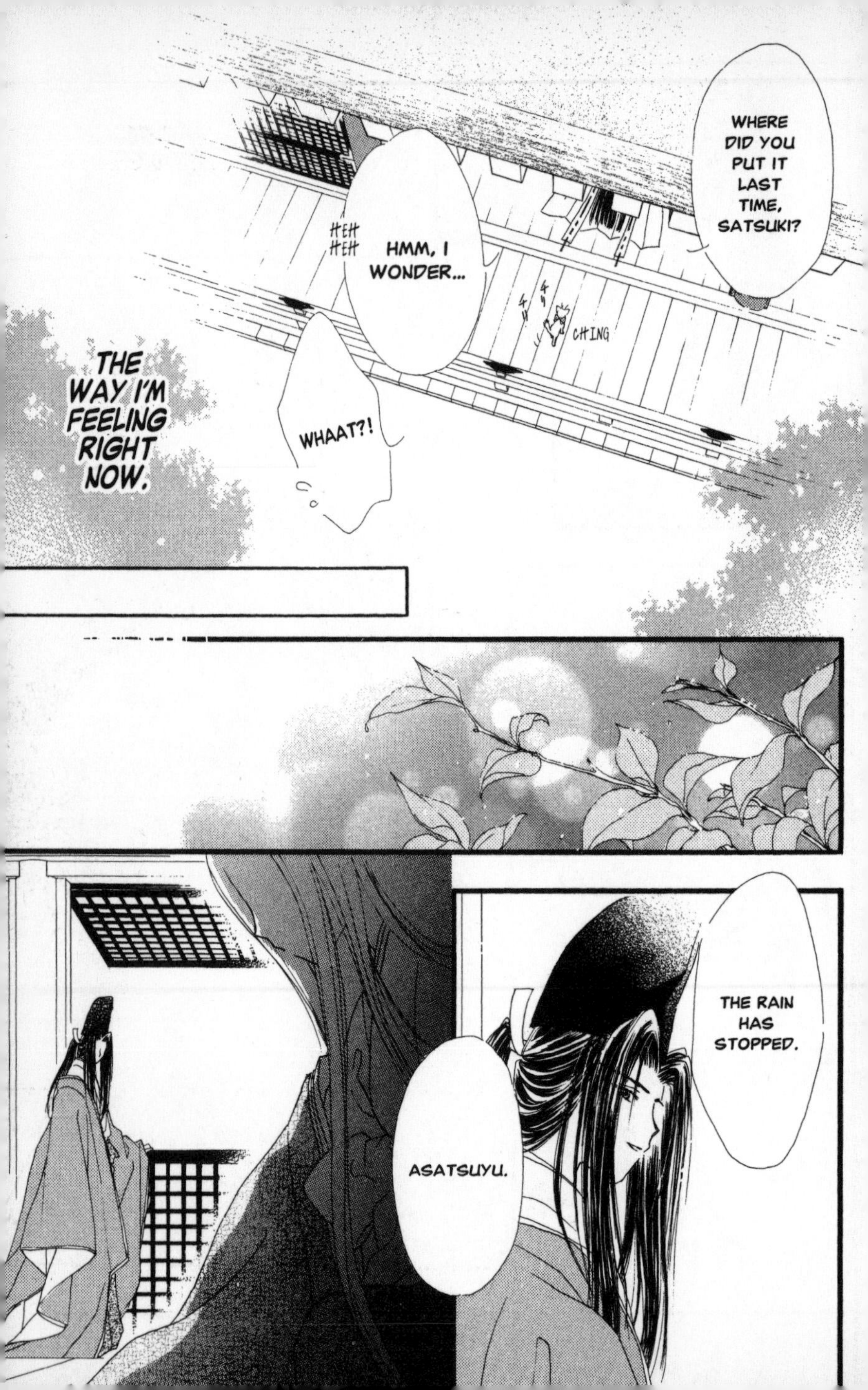
WHERE DID YOU PUT IT LAST TIME, SATSUKI?
HMM, I WONDER...
HEH HEH
CHING
WHAAT?!
THE WAY I'M FEELING RIGHT NOW.
THE RAIN HAS STOPPED.
ASATSUYU.

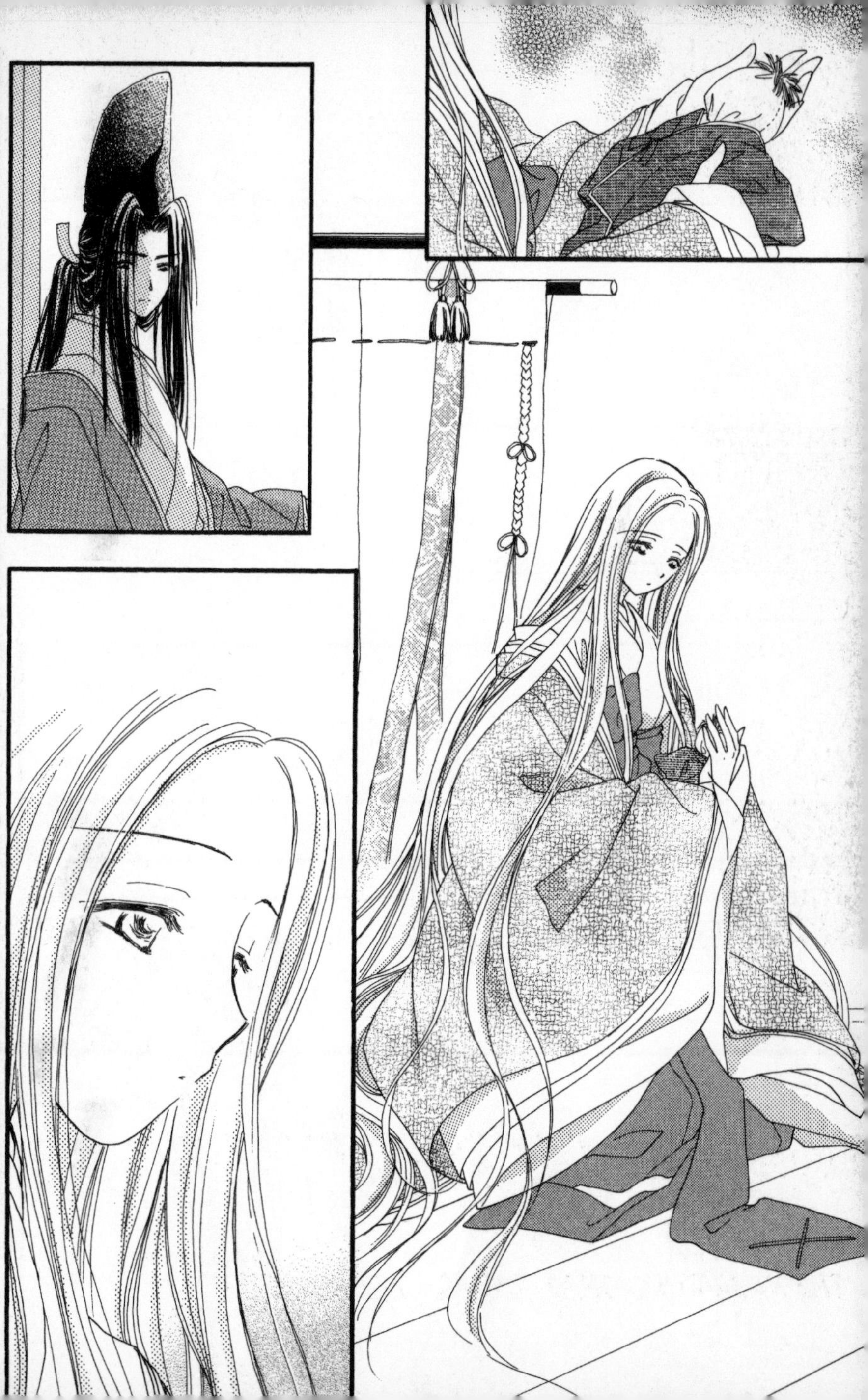

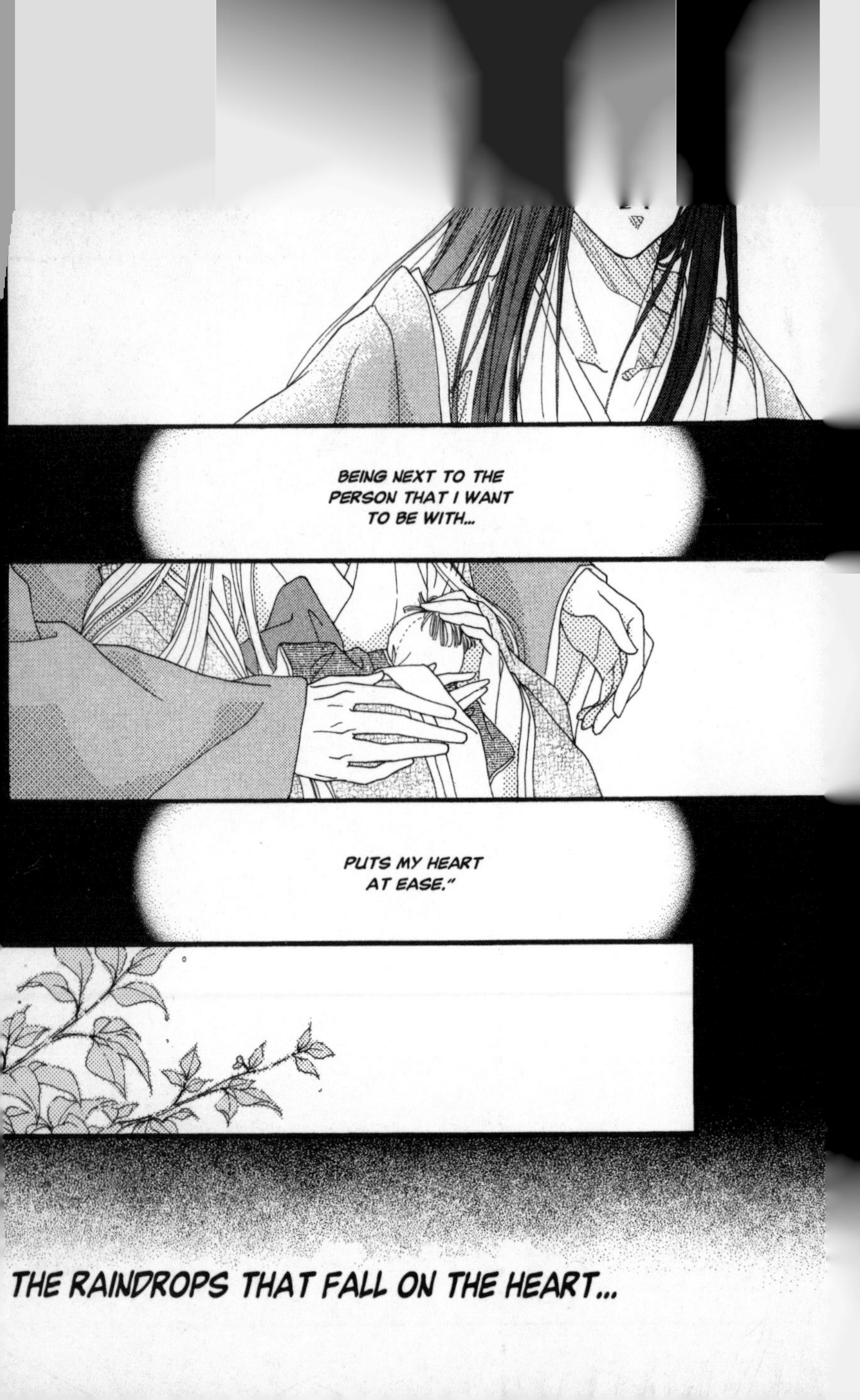
BEING NEXT TO THE PERSON THAT I WANT TO BE WITH...
PUTS MY HEART AT EASE."
THE RAINDROPS THAT FALL ON THE HEART...

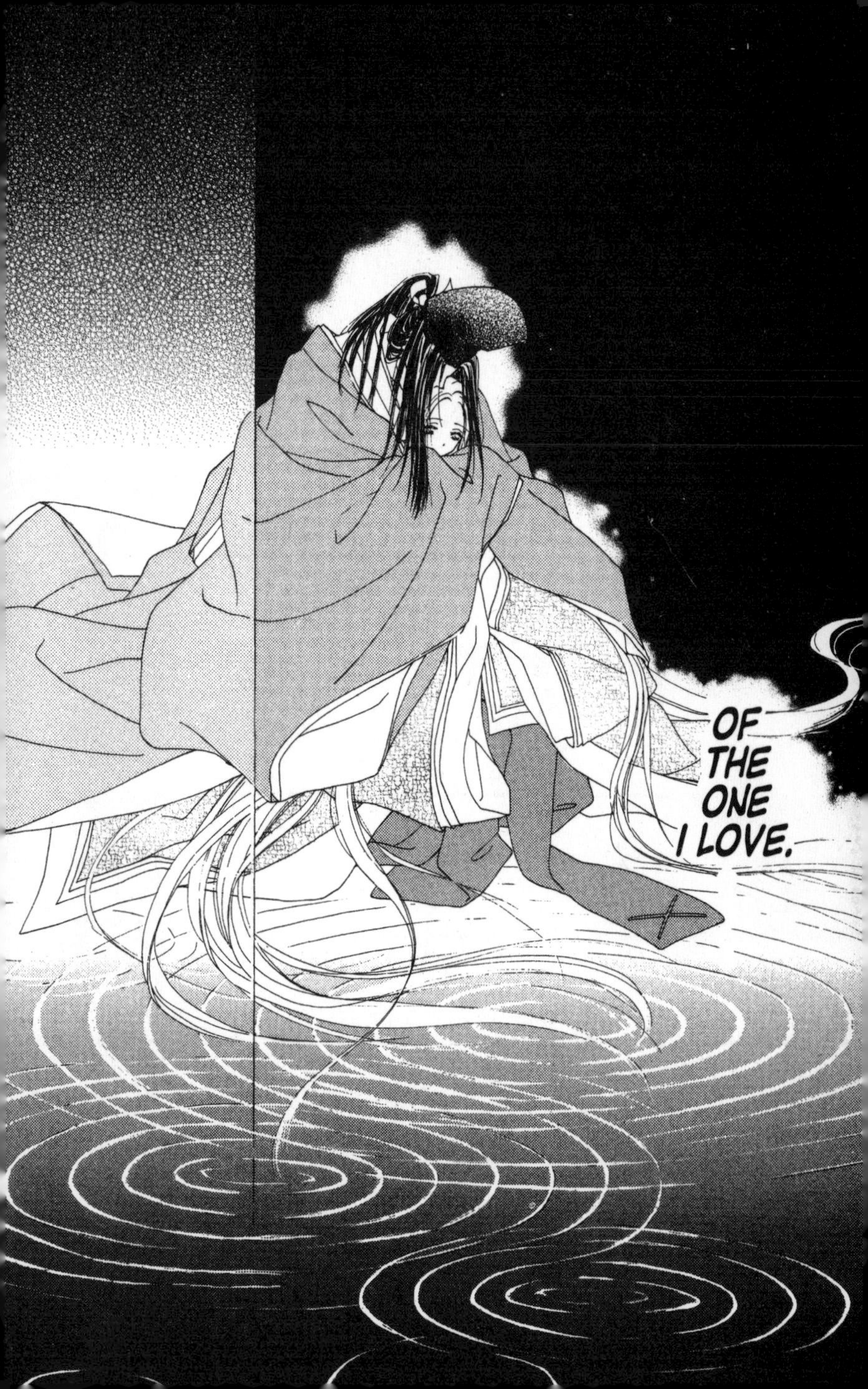
OF THE ONE I LOVE.

トラブル6 星祭り(ほしまつり)

Trouble 6
The Star Festival

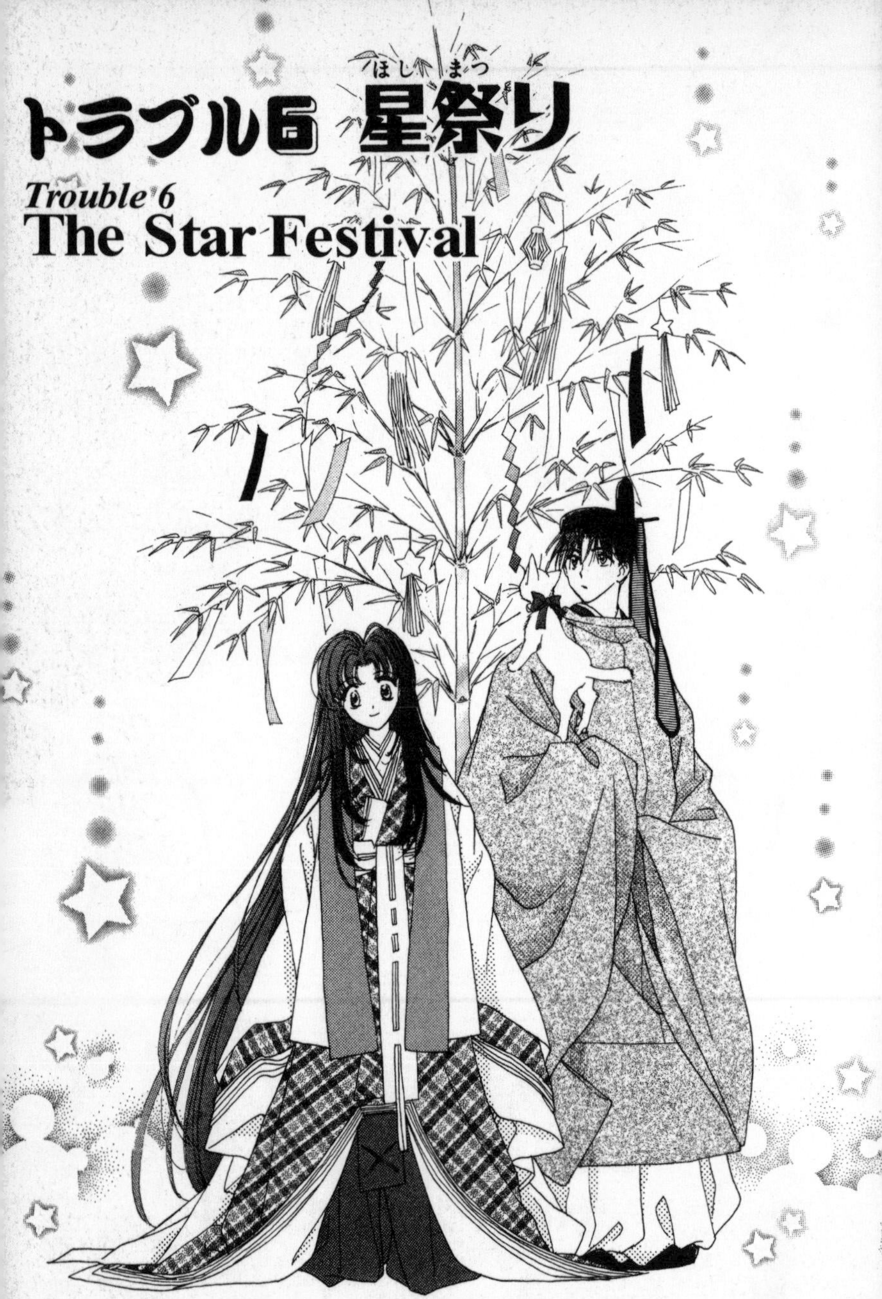

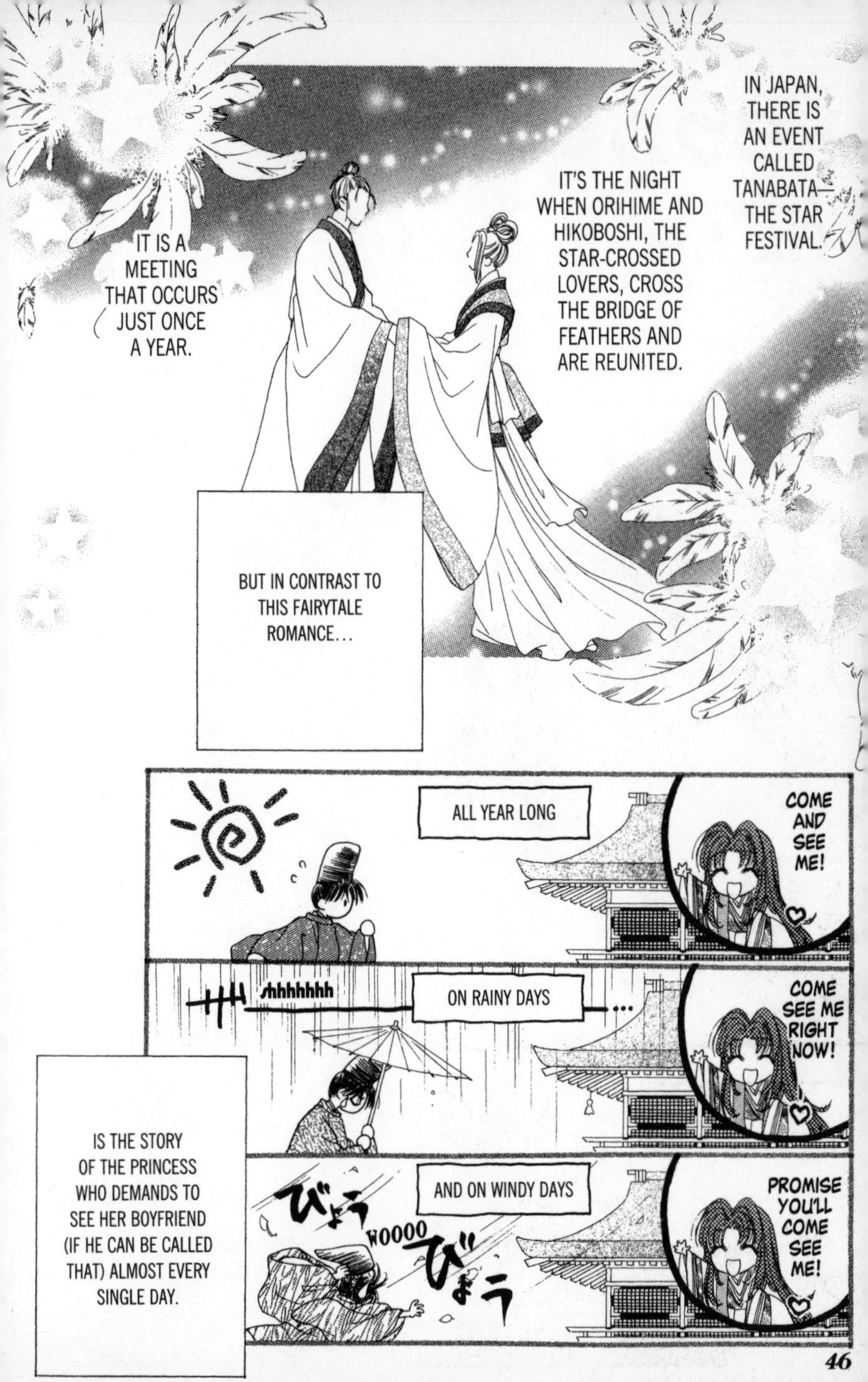
IN JAPAN, THERE IS AN EVENT CALLED TANABATA— THE STAR FESTIVAL.
IT'S THE NIGHT WHEN ORIHIME AND HIKOBOSHI, THE STAR-CROSSED LOVERS, CROSS THE BRIDGE OF FEATHERS AND ARE REUNITED.
IT IS A MEETING THAT OCCURS JUST ONCE A YEAR.
BUT IN CONTRAST TO THIS FAIRYTALE ROMANCE...
ALL YEAR LONG
COME AND SEE ME!
ON RAINY DAYS
shhhhhhh
COME SEE ME RIGHT NOW!
AND ON WINDY DAYS
PROMISE YOU'LL COME SEE ME!
びょう
WOOOO
びょう
IS THE STORY OF THE PRINCESS WHO DEMANDS TO SEE HER BOYFRIEND (IF HE CAN BE CALLED THAT) ALMOST EVERY SINGLE DAY.

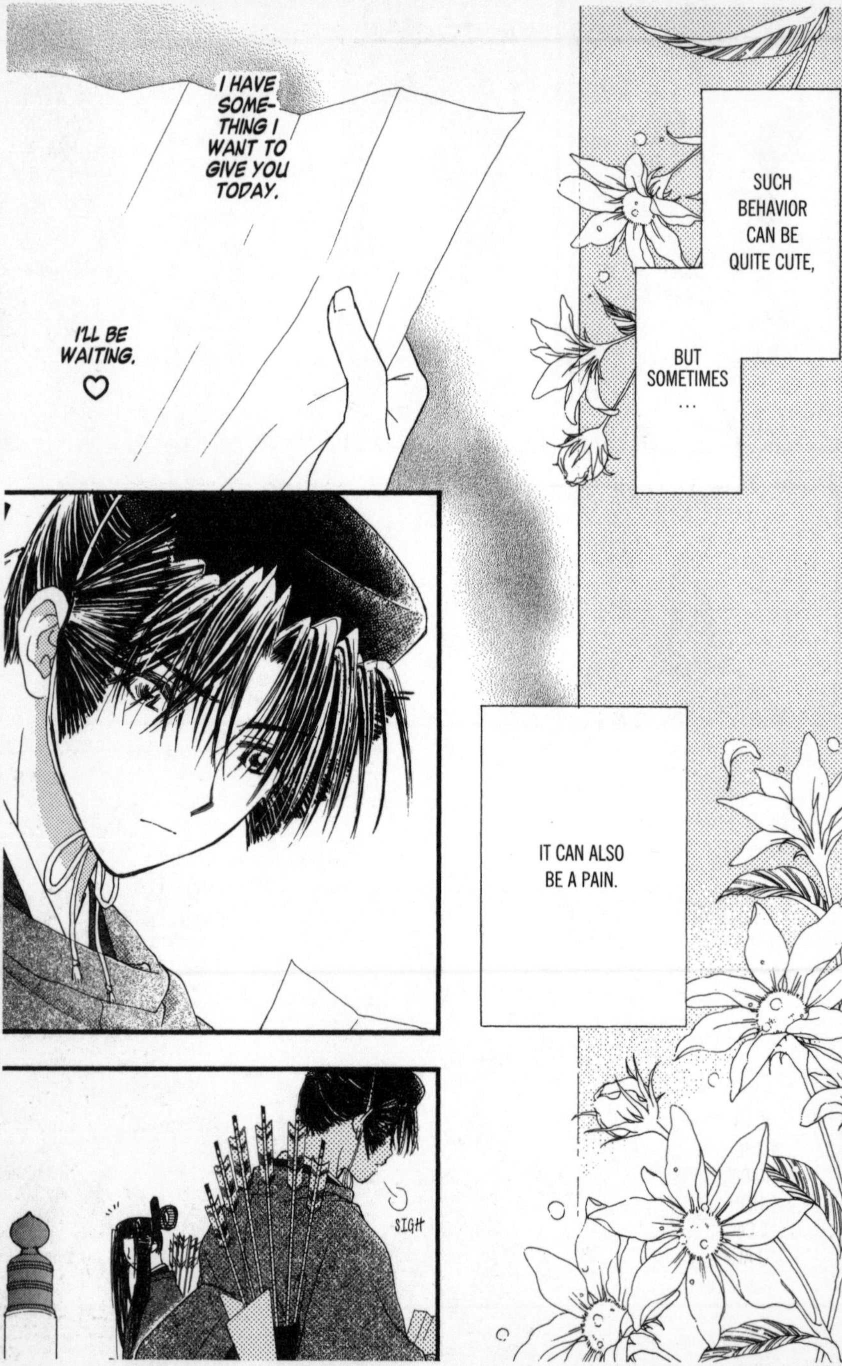
SUCH BEHAVIOR CAN BE QUITE CUTE,
BUT SOMETIMES ...
I HAVE SOMETHING I WANT TO GIVE YOU TODAY.
I'LL BE WAITING. ♡
IT CAN ALSO BE A PAIN.
SIGH

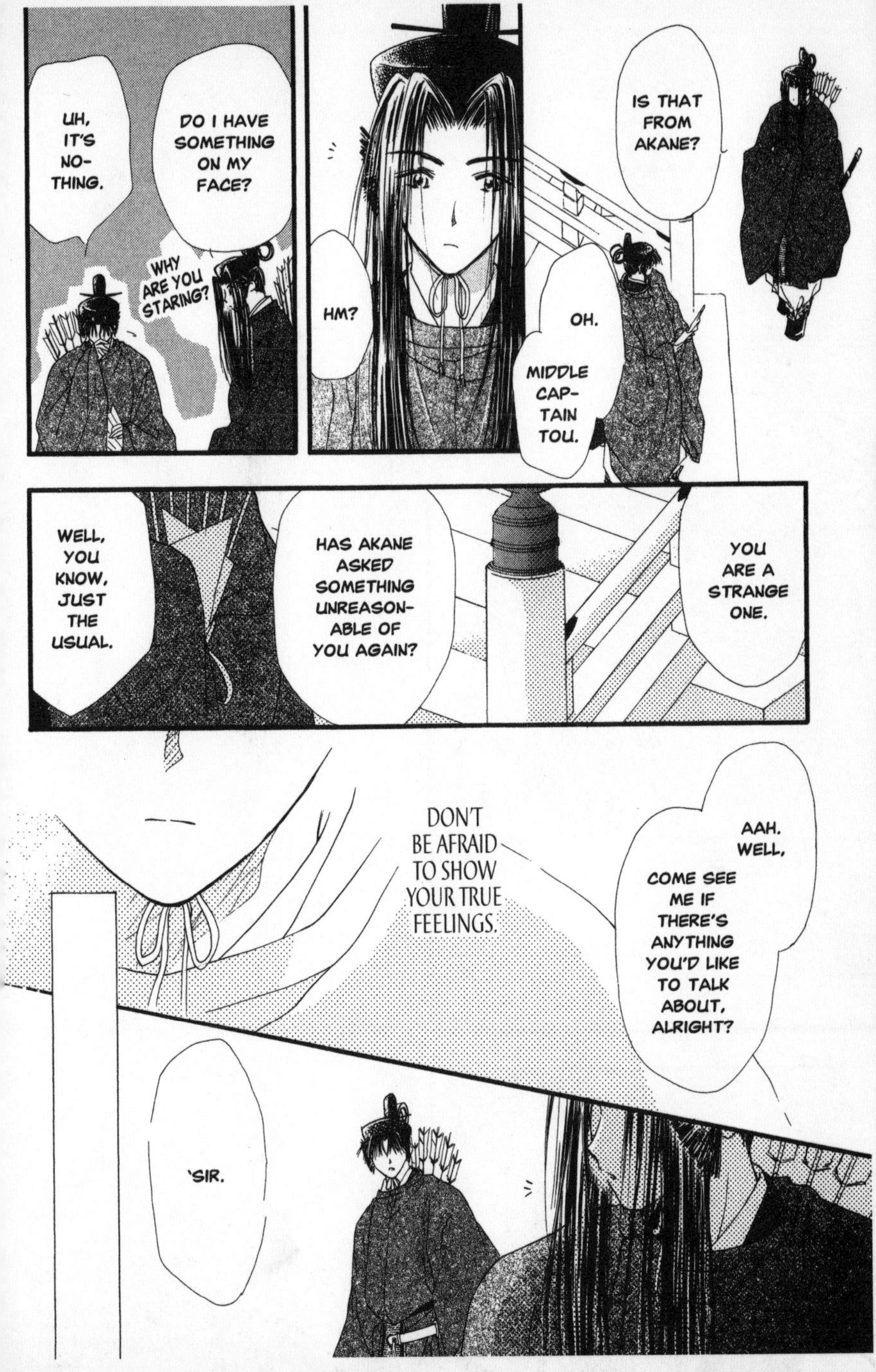
IS THAT FROM AKANE?
OH. MIDDLE CAPTAIN TOU.
HM?
DO I HAVE SOMETHING ON MY FACE?
WHY ARE YOU STARING?
UH, IT'S NOTHING.
YOU ARE A STRANGE ONE.
HAS AKANE ASKED SOMETHING UNREASONABLE OF YOU AGAIN?
WELL, YOU KNOW, JUST THE USUAL.
AAH. WELL, COME SEE ME IF THERE'S ANYTHING YOU'D LIKE TO TALK ABOUT, ALRIGHT?
DON'T BE AFRAID TO SHOW YOUR TRUE FEELINGS.
'SIR.

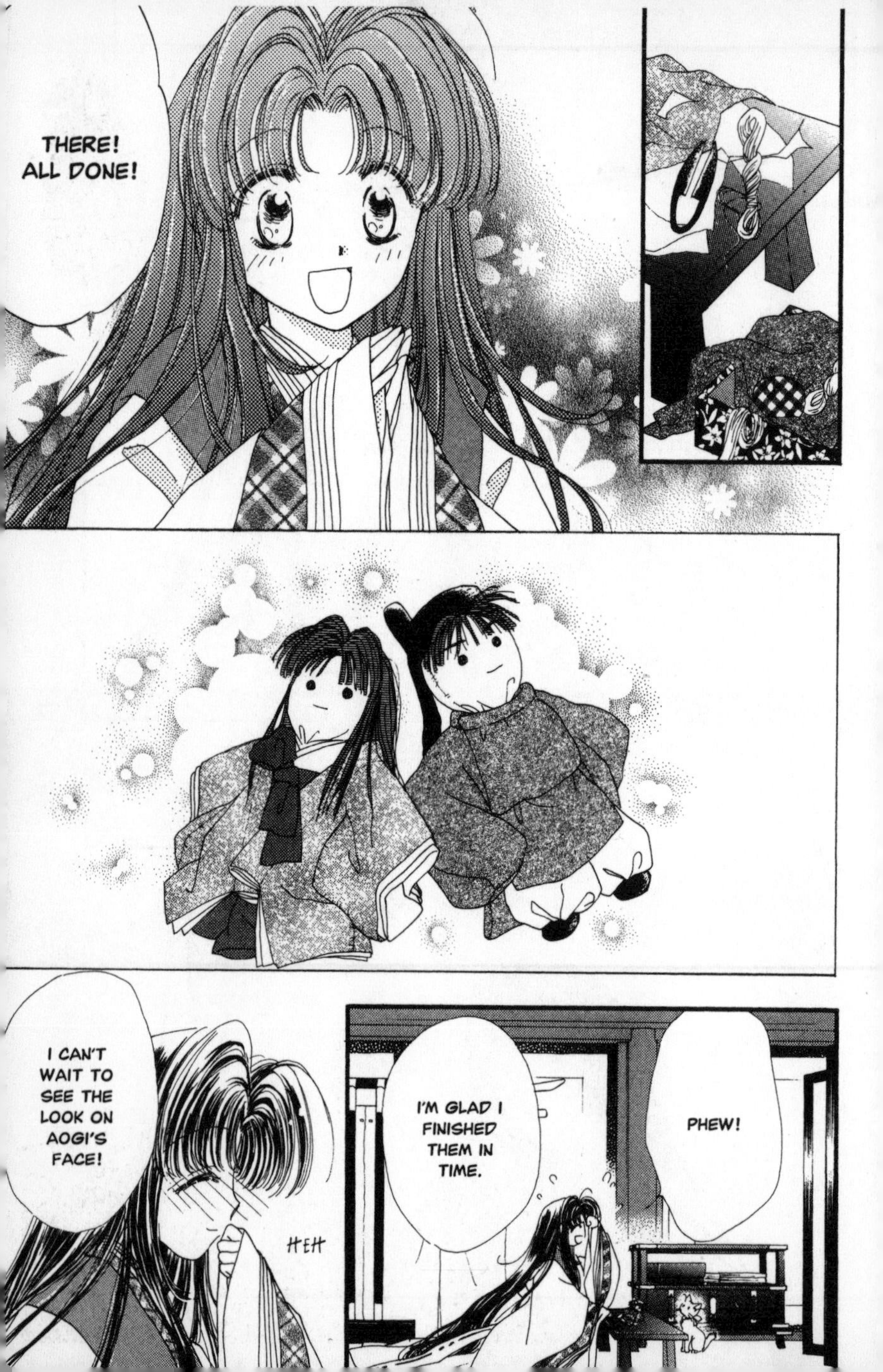
THERE! ALL DONE!
PHEW!
I'M GLAD I FINISHED THEM IN TIME.
I CAN'T WAIT TO SEE THE LOOK ON AOGI'S FACE!
HEH

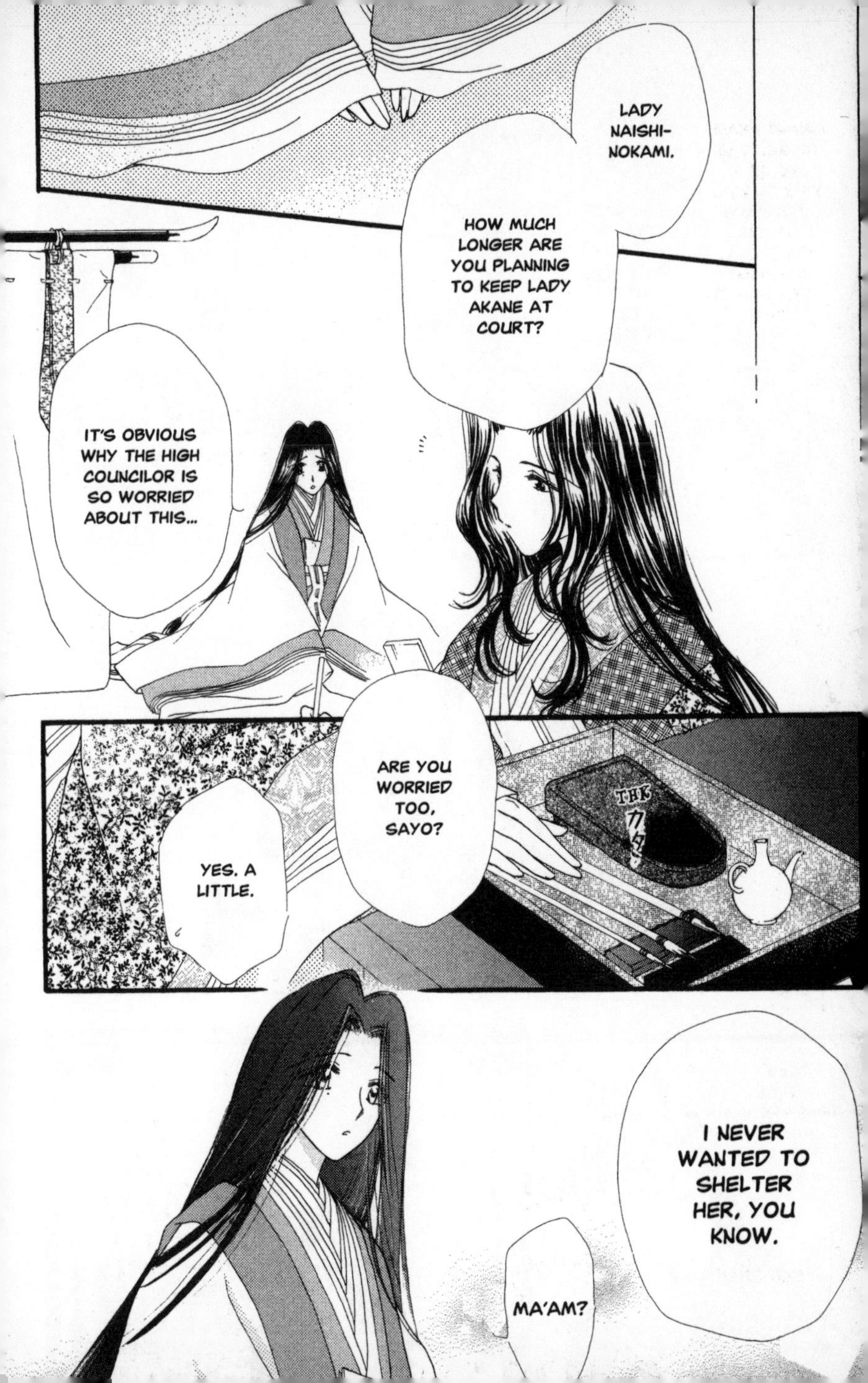
LADY NAISHI-NOKAMI.
HOW MUCH LONGER ARE YOU PLANNING TO KEEP LADY AKANE AT COURT?
IT'S OBVIOUS WHY THE HIGH COUNCILOR IS SO WORRIED ABOUT THIS...
ARE YOU WORRIED TOO, SAYO?
THK
カタ
YES. A LITTLE.
I NEVER WANTED TO SHELTER HER, YOU KNOW.
MA'AM?

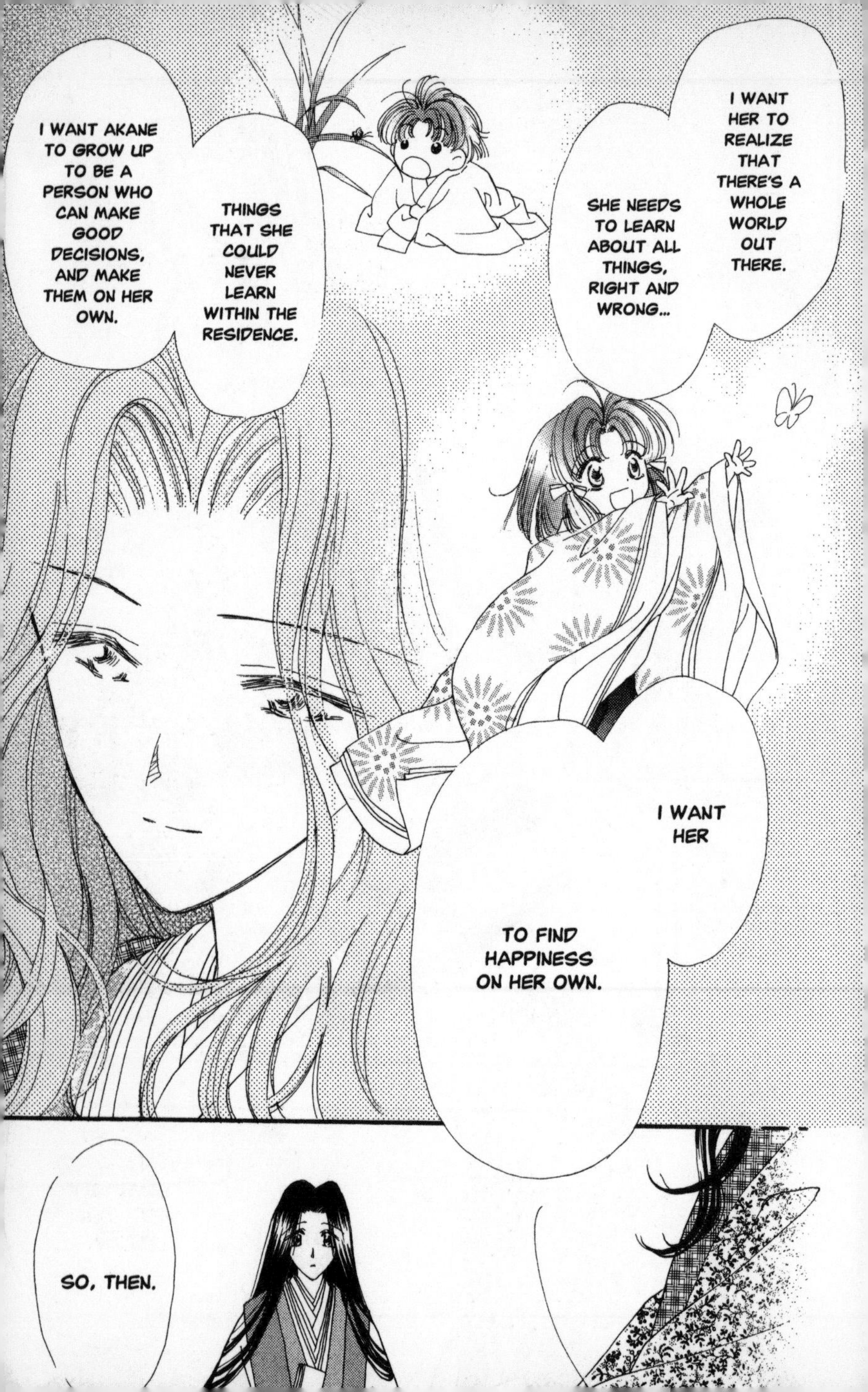
I WANT HER TO REALIZE THAT THERE'S A WHOLE WORLD OUT THERE.
SHE NEEDS TO LEARN ABOUT ALL THINGS, RIGHT AND WRONG...
THINGS THAT SHE COULD NEVER LEARN WITHIN THE RESIDENCE.
I WANT AKANE TO GROW UP TO BE A PERSON WHO CAN MAKE GOOD DECISIONS, AND MAKE THEM ON HER OWN.
I WANT HER
TO FIND HAPPINESS ON HER OWN.
SO, THEN.

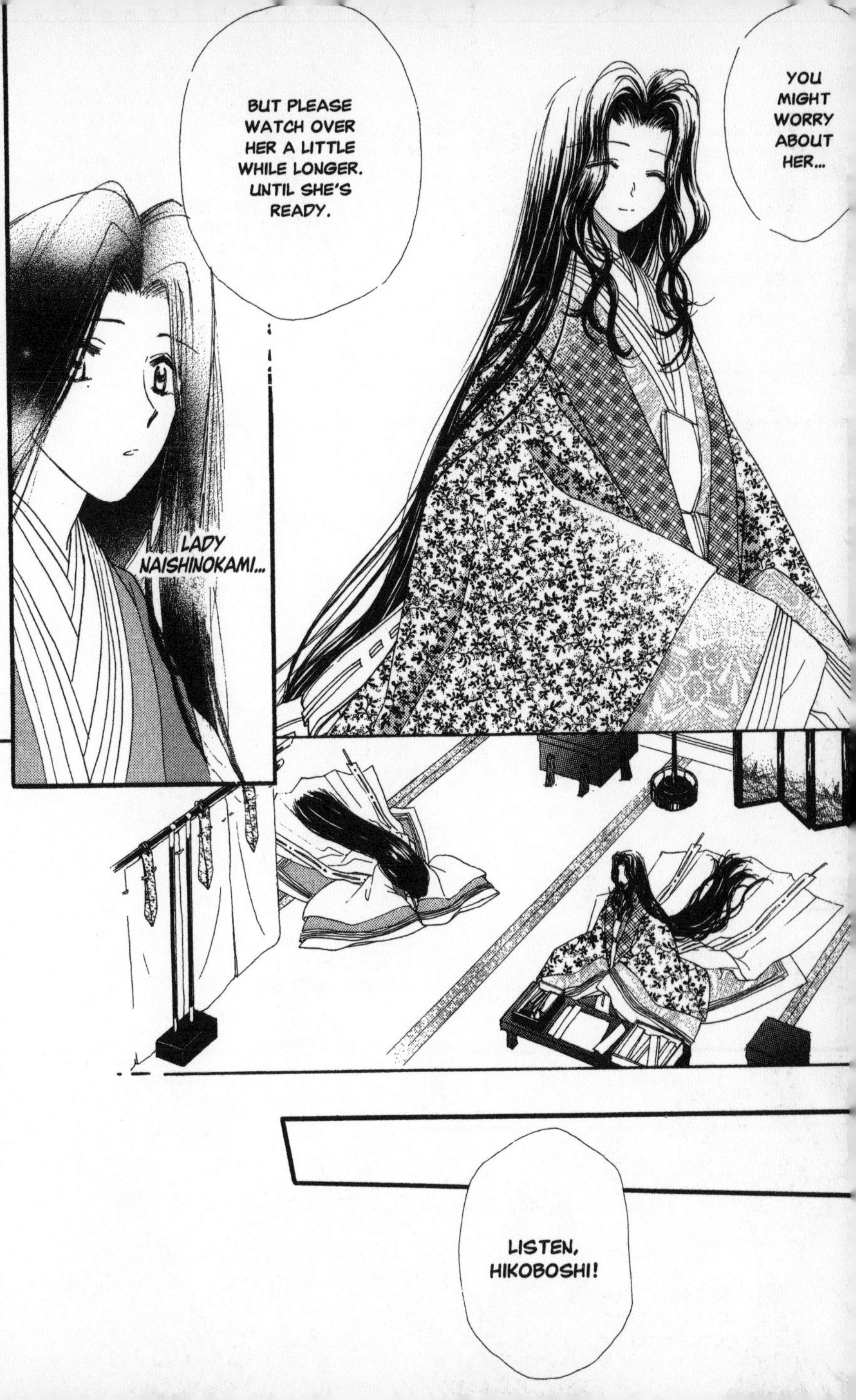
YOU MIGHT WORRY ABOUT HER...
BUT PLEASE WATCH OVER HER A LITTLE WHILE LONGER. UNTIL SHE'S READY.
LADY NAISHINOKAMI...
LISTEN, HIKOBOSHI!

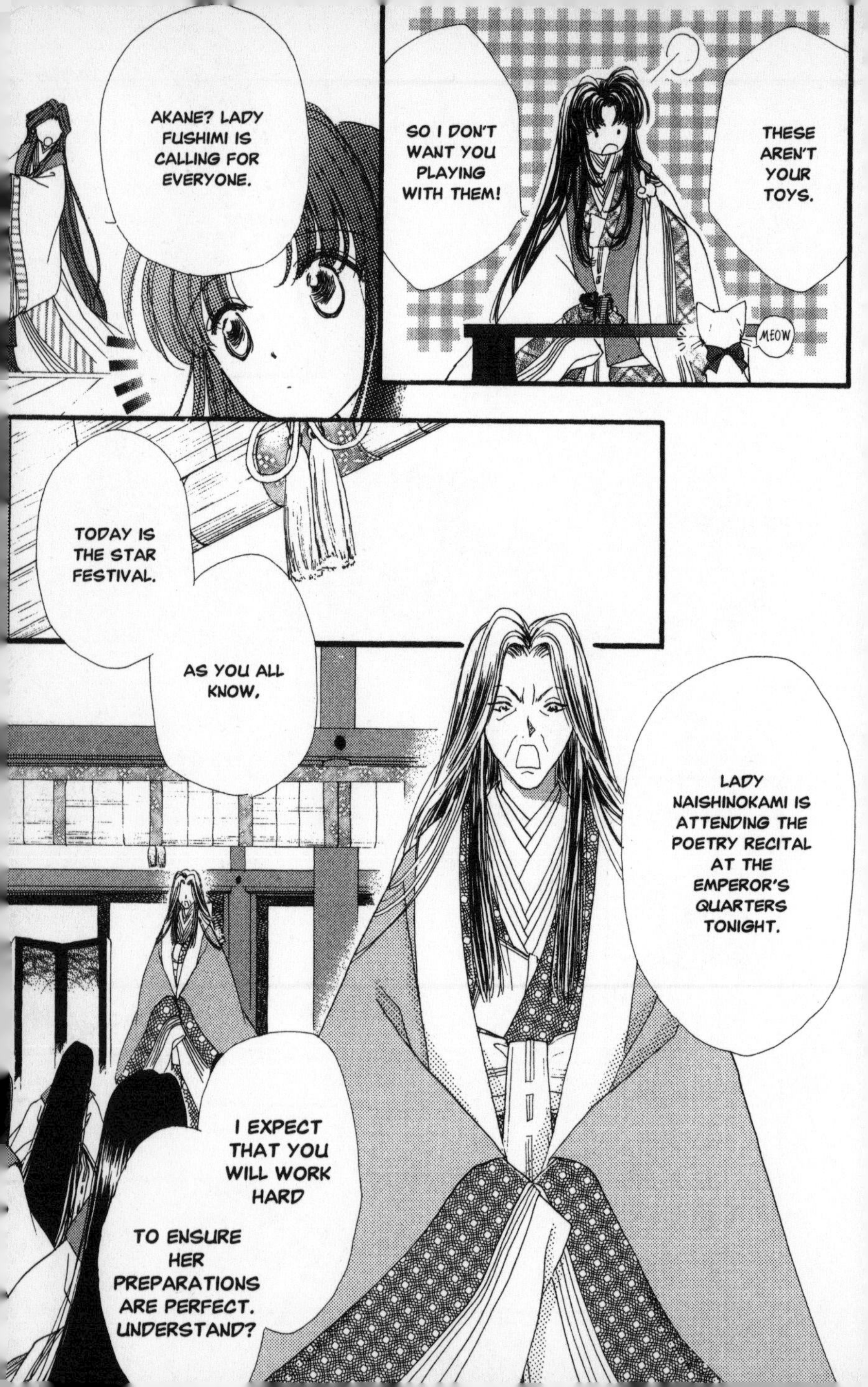
THESE AREN'T YOUR TOYS.
SO I DON'T WANT YOU PLAYING WITH THEM!
MEOW
AKANE? LADY FUSHIMI IS CALLING FOR EVERYONE.
TODAY IS THE STAR FESTIVAL.
AS YOU ALL KNOW,
LADY NAISHINOKAMI IS ATTENDING THE POETRY RECITAL AT THE EMPEROR'S QUARTERS TONIGHT.
I EXPECT THAT YOU WILL WORK HARD
TO ENSURE HER PREPARATIONS ARE PERFECT. UNDERSTAND?

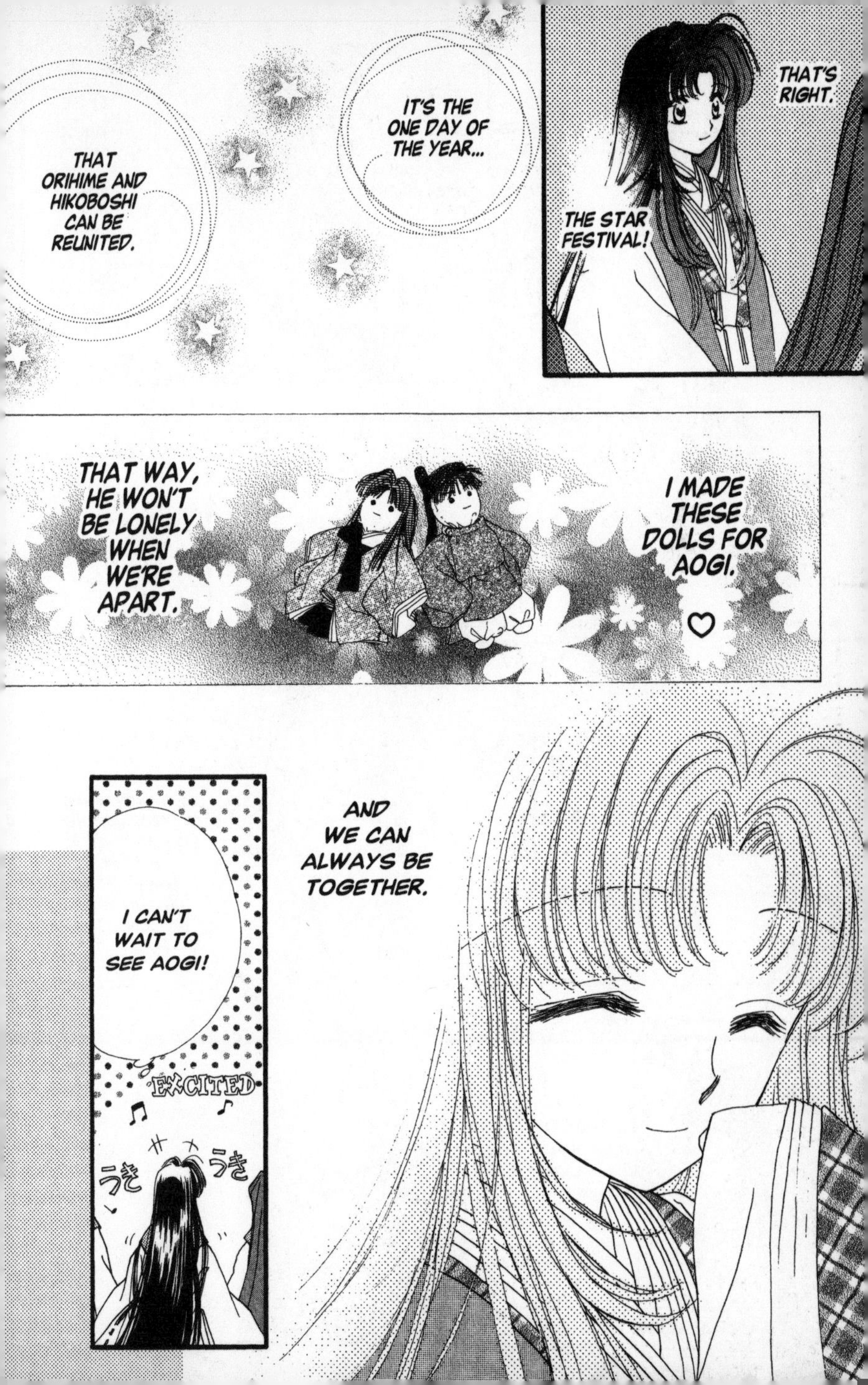
THAT'S RIGHT.
THE STAR FESTIVAL!
IT'S THE ONE DAY OF THE YEAR...
THAT ORIHIME AND HIKOBOSHI CAN BE REUNITED.
I MADE THESE DOLLS FOR AOGI.
THAT WAY, HE WON'T BE LONELY WHEN WE'RE APART.
AND WE CAN ALWAYS BE TOGETHER.
I CAN'T WAIT TO SEE AOGI!
EXCITED
うき うき

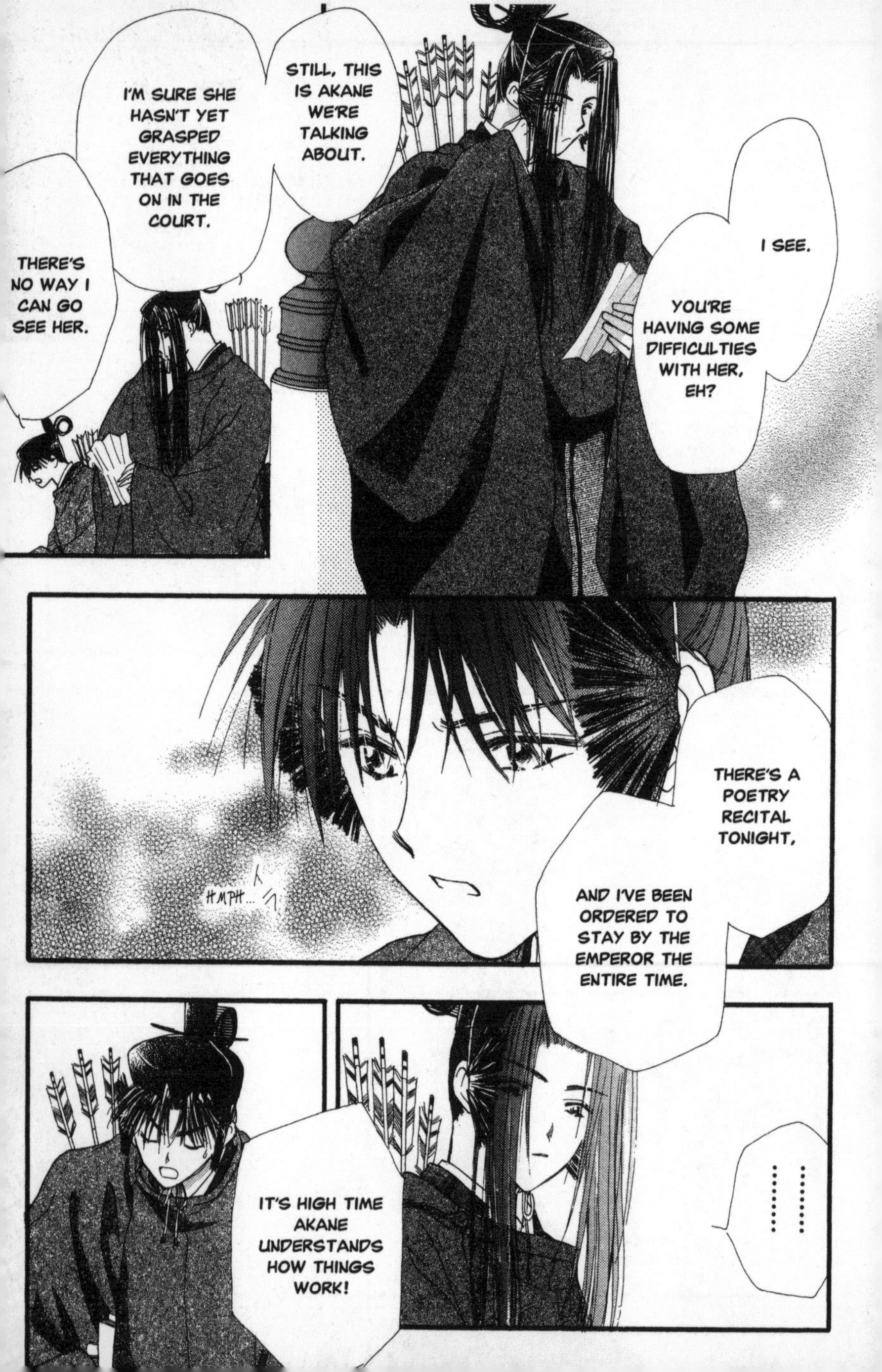
I SEE.
YOU'RE HAVING SOME DIFFICULTIES WITH HER, EH?
STILL, THIS IS AKANE WE'RE TALKING ABOUT.
I'M SURE SHE HASN'T YET GRASPED EVERYTHING THAT GOES ON IN THE COURT.
THERE'S NO WAY I CAN GO SEE HER.
THERE'S A POETRY RECITAL TONIGHT,
AND I'VE BEEN ORDERED TO STAY BY THE EMPEROR THE ENTIRE TIME.
HMPH...
......
IT'S HIGH TIME AKANE UNDERSTANDS HOW THINGS WORK!

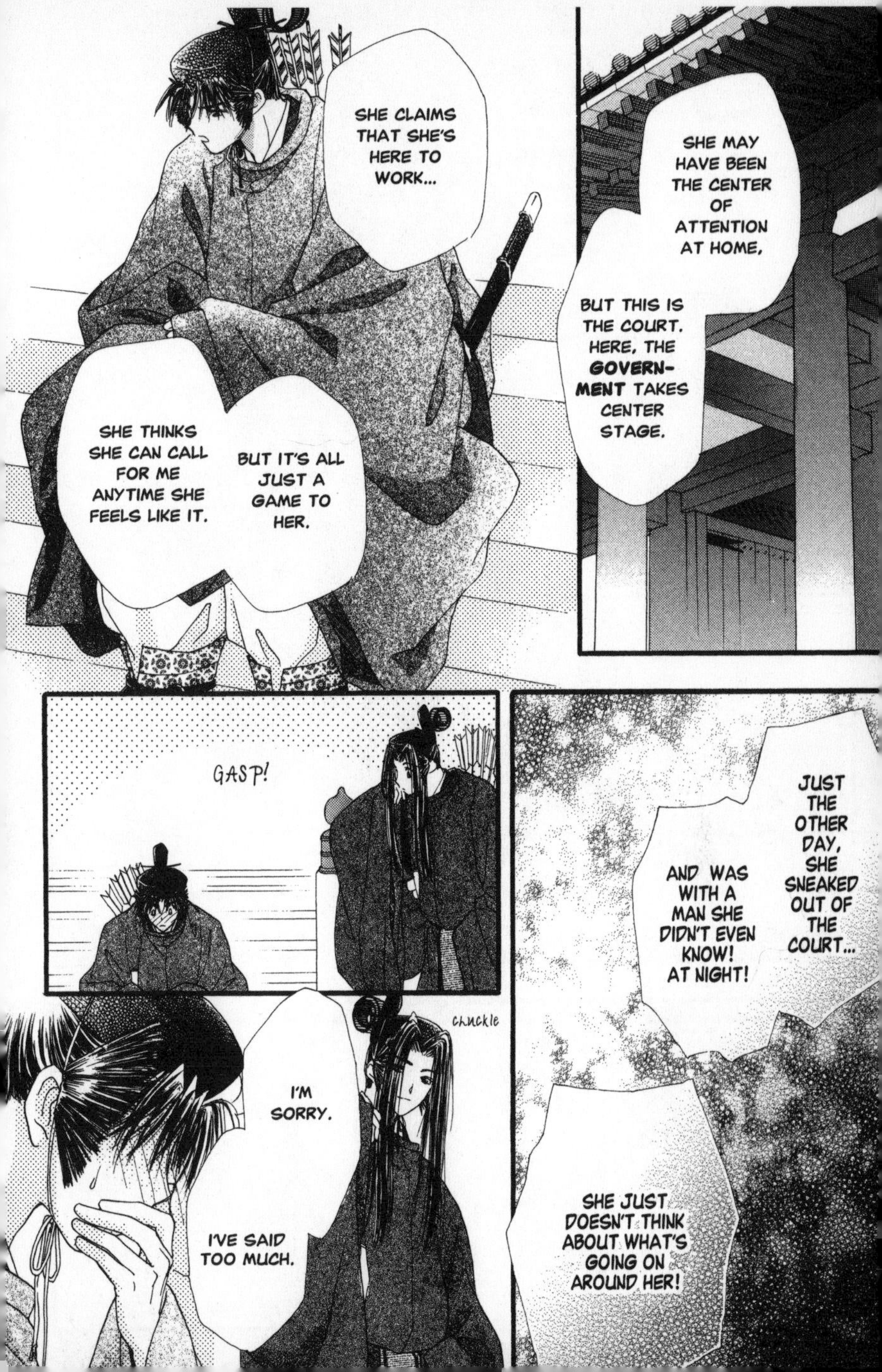
SHE MAY HAVE BEEN THE CENTER OF ATTENTION AT HOME,
BUT THIS IS THE COURT. HERE, THE **GOVERNMENT** TAKES CENTER STAGE.
SHE CLAIMS THAT SHE'S HERE TO WORK...
BUT IT'S ALL JUST A GAME TO HER.
SHE THINKS SHE CAN CALL FOR ME ANYTIME SHE FEELS LIKE IT.
JUST THE OTHER DAY, SHE SNEAKED OUT OF THE COURT...
AND WAS WITH A MAN SHE DIDN'T EVEN KNOW! AT NIGHT!
SHE JUST DOESN'T THINK ABOUT WHAT'S GOING ON AROUND HER!
GASP!
chuckle
I'M SORRY.
I'VE SAID TOO MUCH.

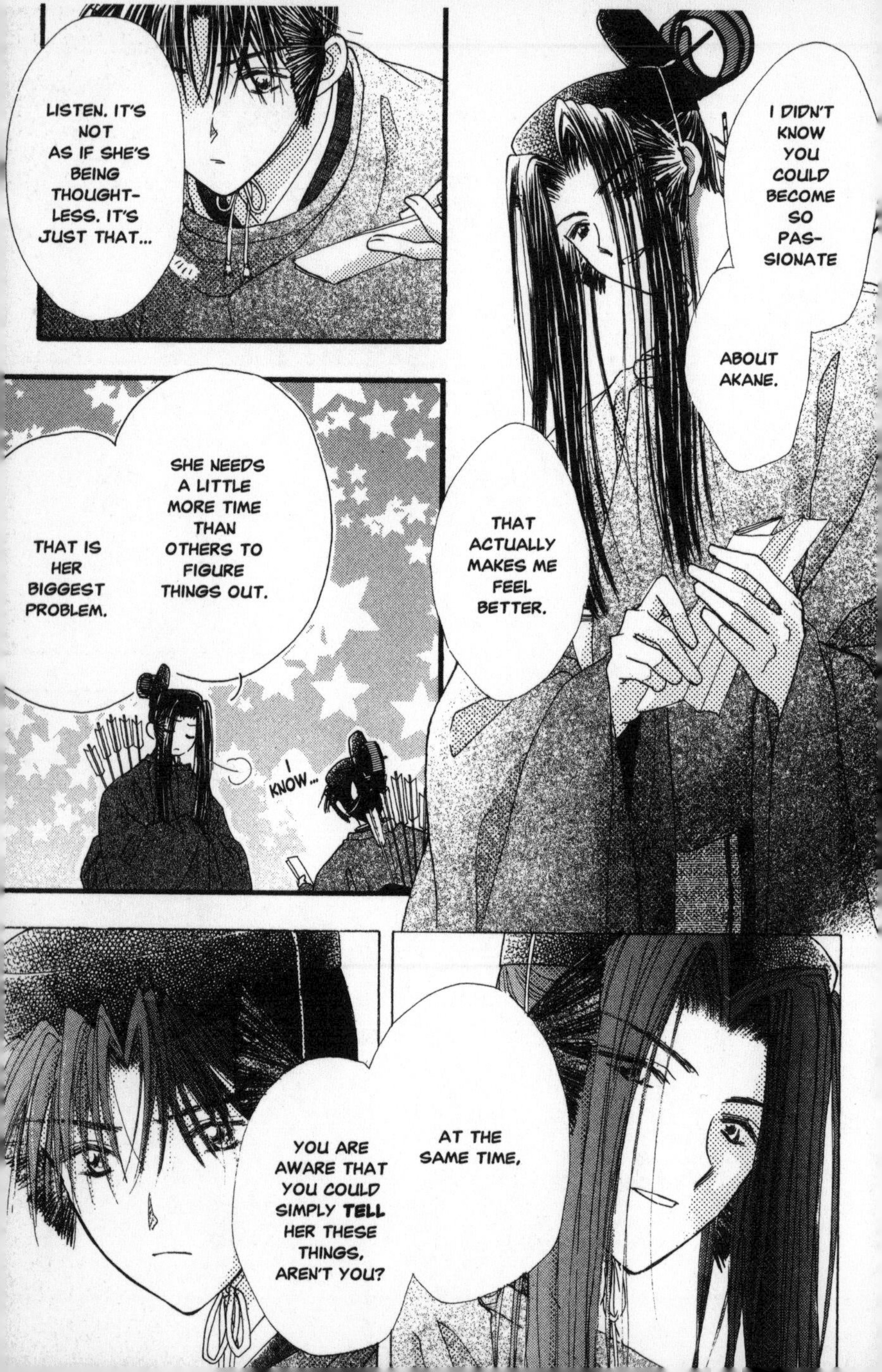
I DIDN'T KNOW YOU COULD BECOME SO PAS-SIONATE
ABOUT AKANE.
LISTEN. IT'S NOT AS IF SHE'S BEING THOUGHT-LESS. IT'S JUST THAT...
SHE NEEDS A LITTLE MORE TIME THAN OTHERS TO FIGURE THINGS OUT.
THAT IS HER BIGGEST PROBLEM.
I KNOW...
THAT ACTUALLY MAKES ME FEEL BETTER.
AT THE SAME TIME,
YOU ARE AWARE THAT YOU COULD SIMPLY **TELL** HER THESE THINGS, AREN'T YOU?

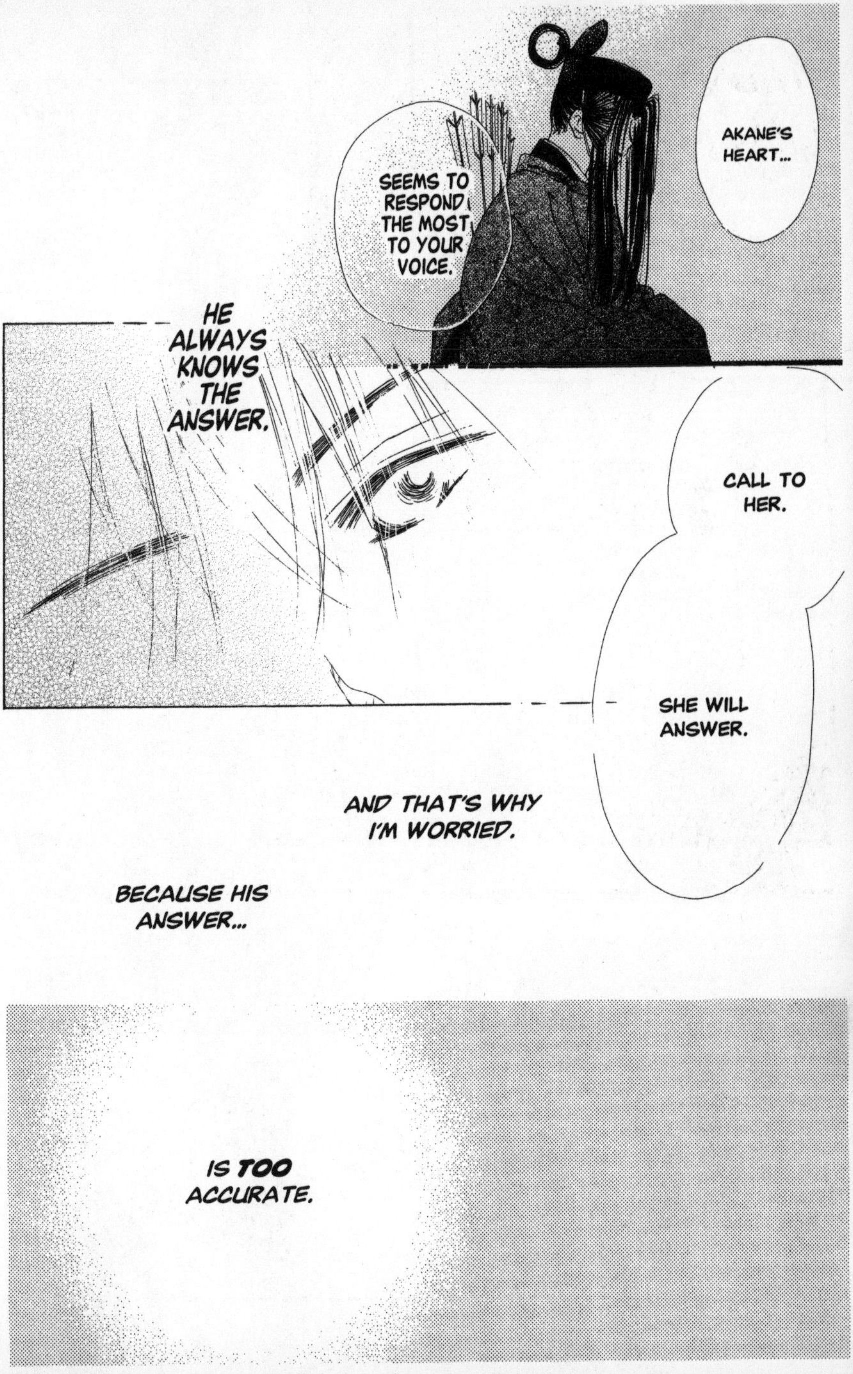
AKANE'S HEART...
SEEMS TO RESPOND THE MOST TO YOUR VOICE.
HE ALWAYS KNOWS THE ANSWER.
CALL TO HER.
SHE WILL ANSWER.
AND THAT'S WHY I'M WORRIED.
BECAUSE HIS ANSWER...
IS **TOO** ACCURATE.

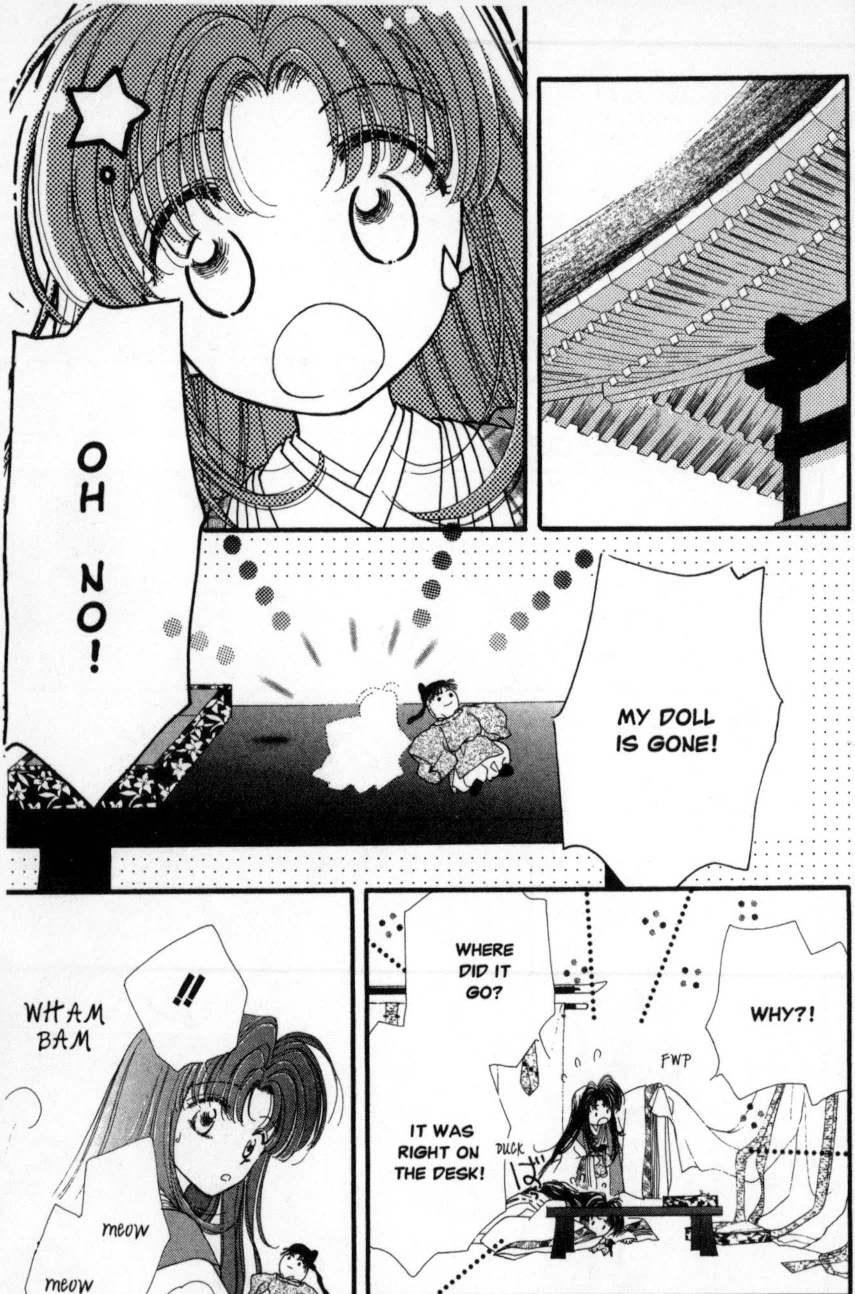
OH NO!
MY DOLL IS GONE!
WHY?!
WHERE DID IT GO?
FWP
IT WAS RIGHT ON THE DESK!
DUCK
!!
WHAM BAM
meow
meow

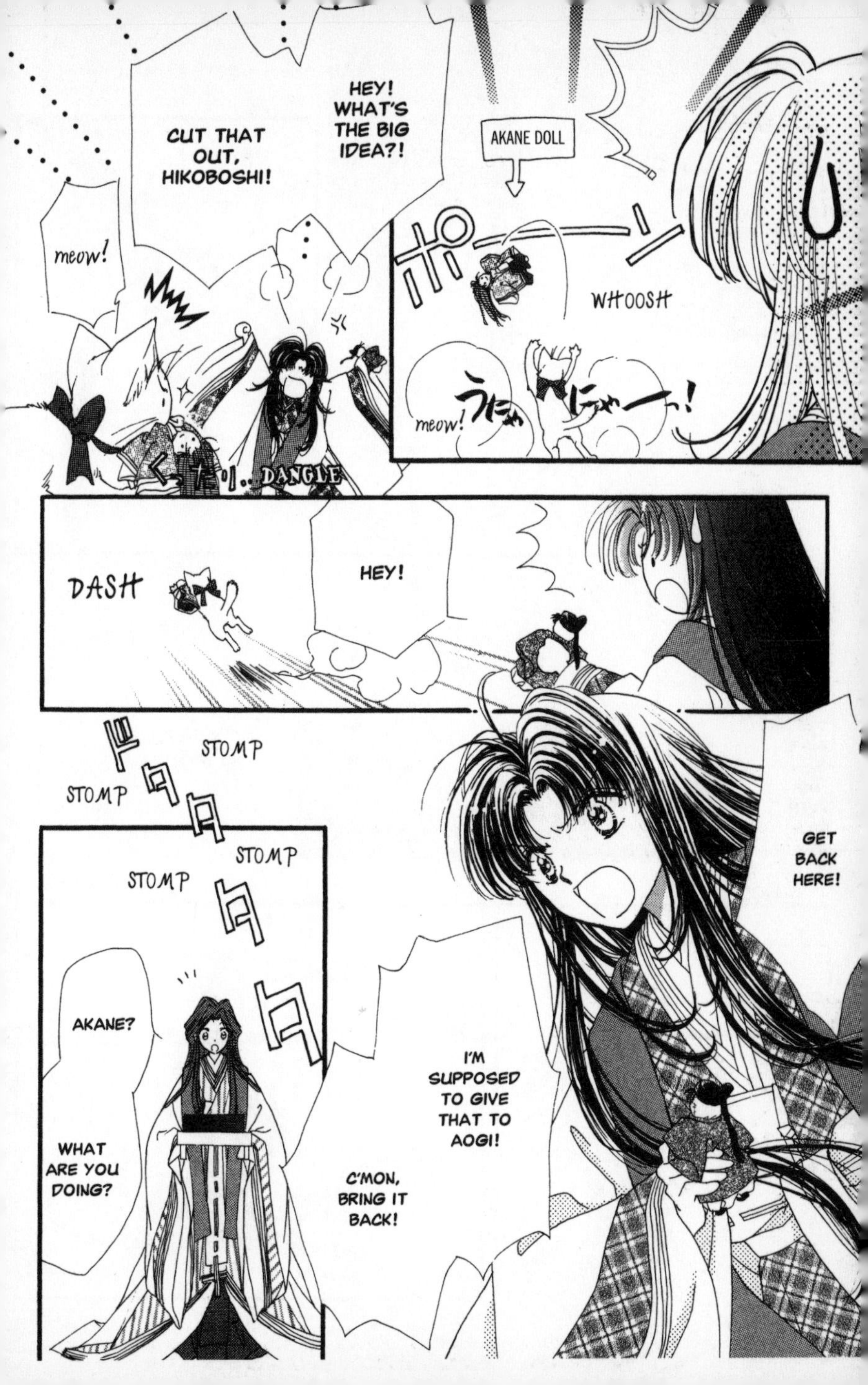

AKANE DOLL
WHOOSH
meow!
HEY! WHAT'S THE BIG IDEA?!
CUT THAT OUT, HIKOBOSHI!
meow!
DANGLE
HEY!
DASH
GET BACK HERE!
STOMP
STOMP
STOMP
STOMP
I'M SUPPOSED TO GIVE THAT TO AOGI!
C'MON, BRING IT BACK!
AKANE?
WHAT ARE YOU DOING?

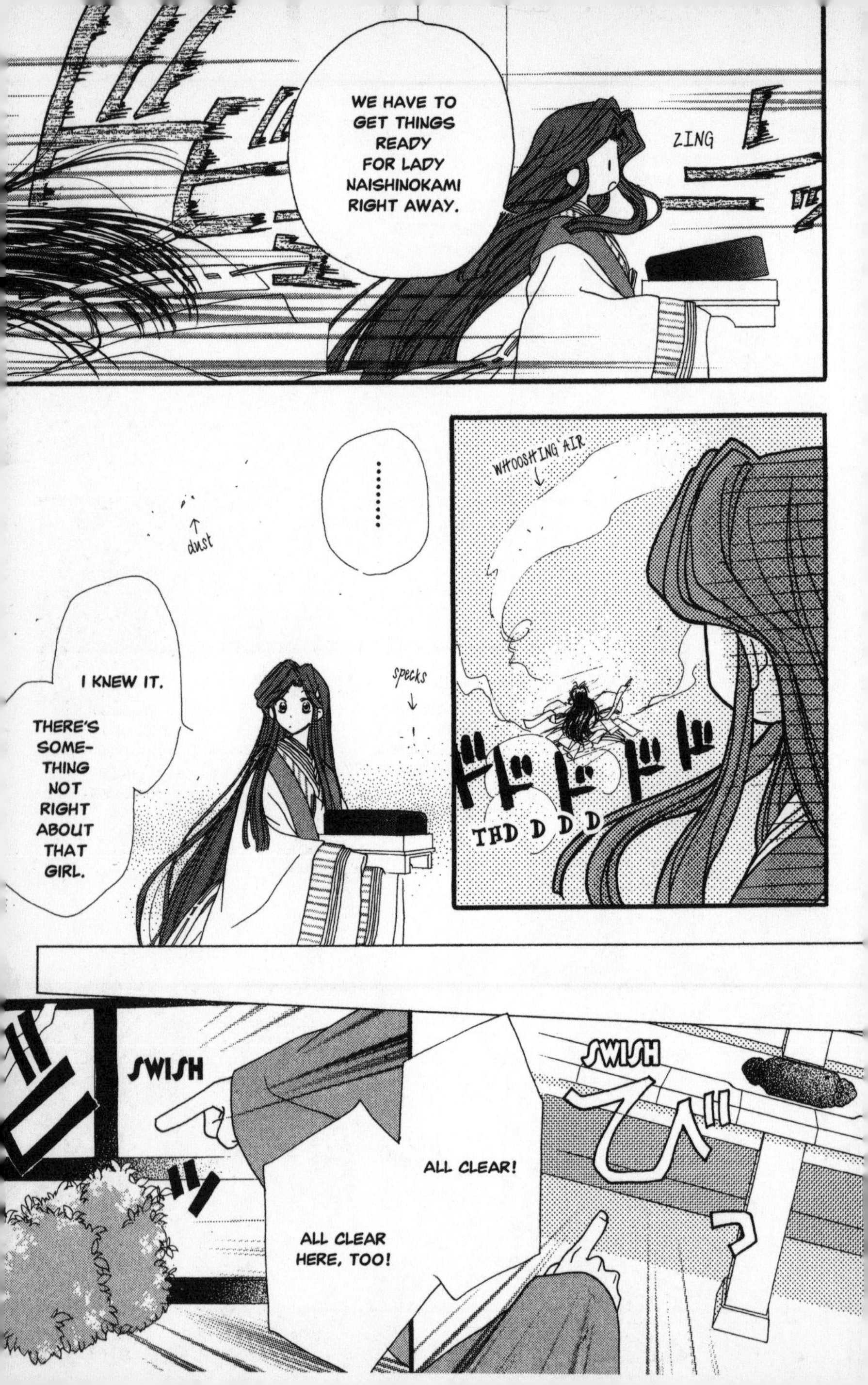
WE HAVE TO GET THINGS READY FOR LADY NAISHINOKAMI RIGHT AWAY.
ZING
WHOOSHING AIR
THD D D D
......
dust
specks
I KNEW IT.
THERE'S SOME-THING NOT RIGHT ABOUT THAT GIRL.
SWISH
SWISH
ALL CLEAR!
ALL CLEAR HERE, TOO!

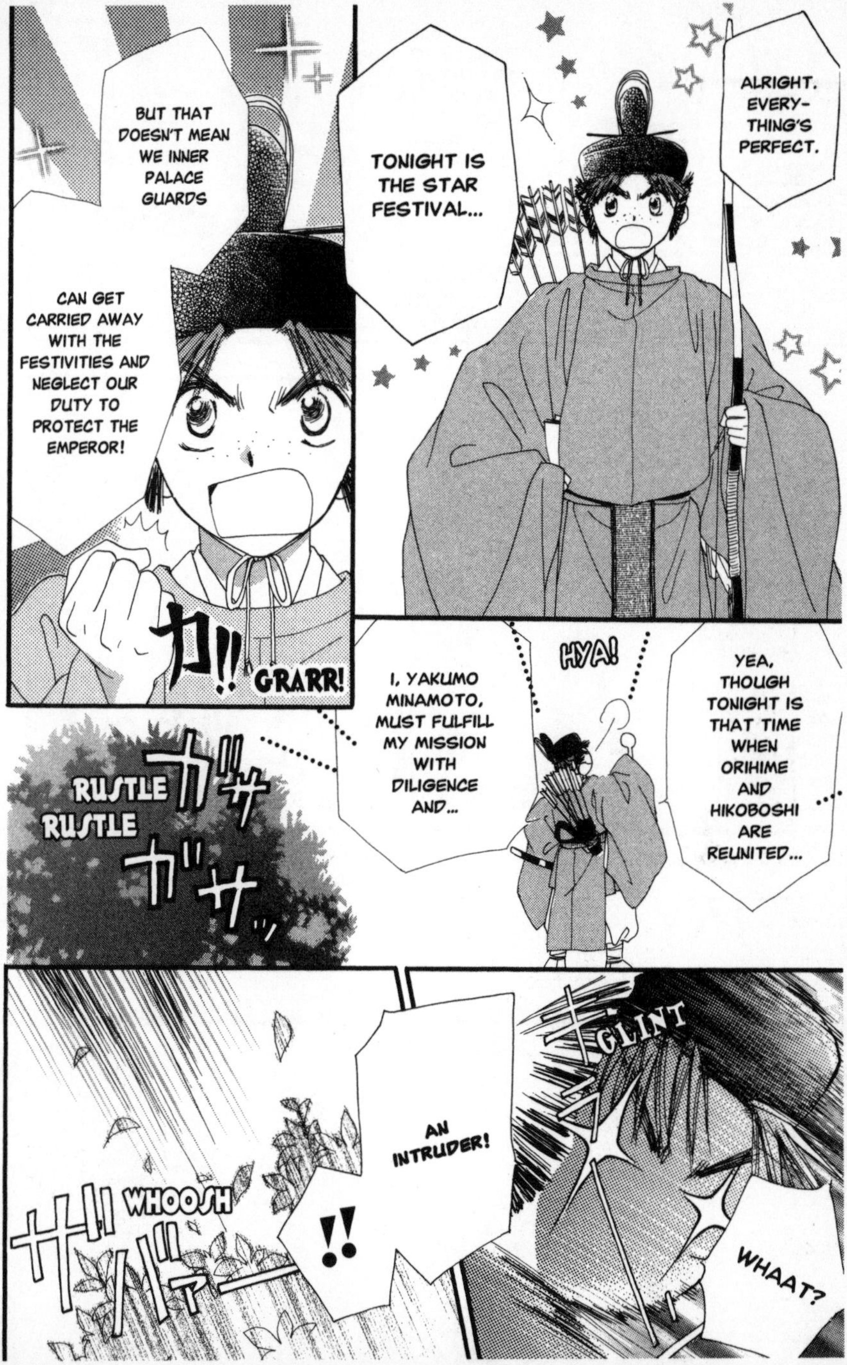
ALRIGHT. EVERY-THING'S PERFECT.
TONIGHT IS THE STAR FESTIVAL...
BUT THAT DOESN'T MEAN WE INNER PALACE GUARDS
CAN GET CARRIED AWAY WITH THE FESTIVITIES AND NEGLECT OUR DUTY TO PROTECT THE EMPEROR!
GRARR!
YEA, THOUGH TONIGHT IS THAT TIME WHEN ORIHIME AND HIKOBOSHI ARE REUNITED...
HYA!
I, YAKUMO MINAMOTO, MUST FULFILL MY MISSION WITH DILIGENCE AND...
RUSTLE RUSTLE
GLINT
WHAAT?
AN INTRUDER!
!!
WHOOSH

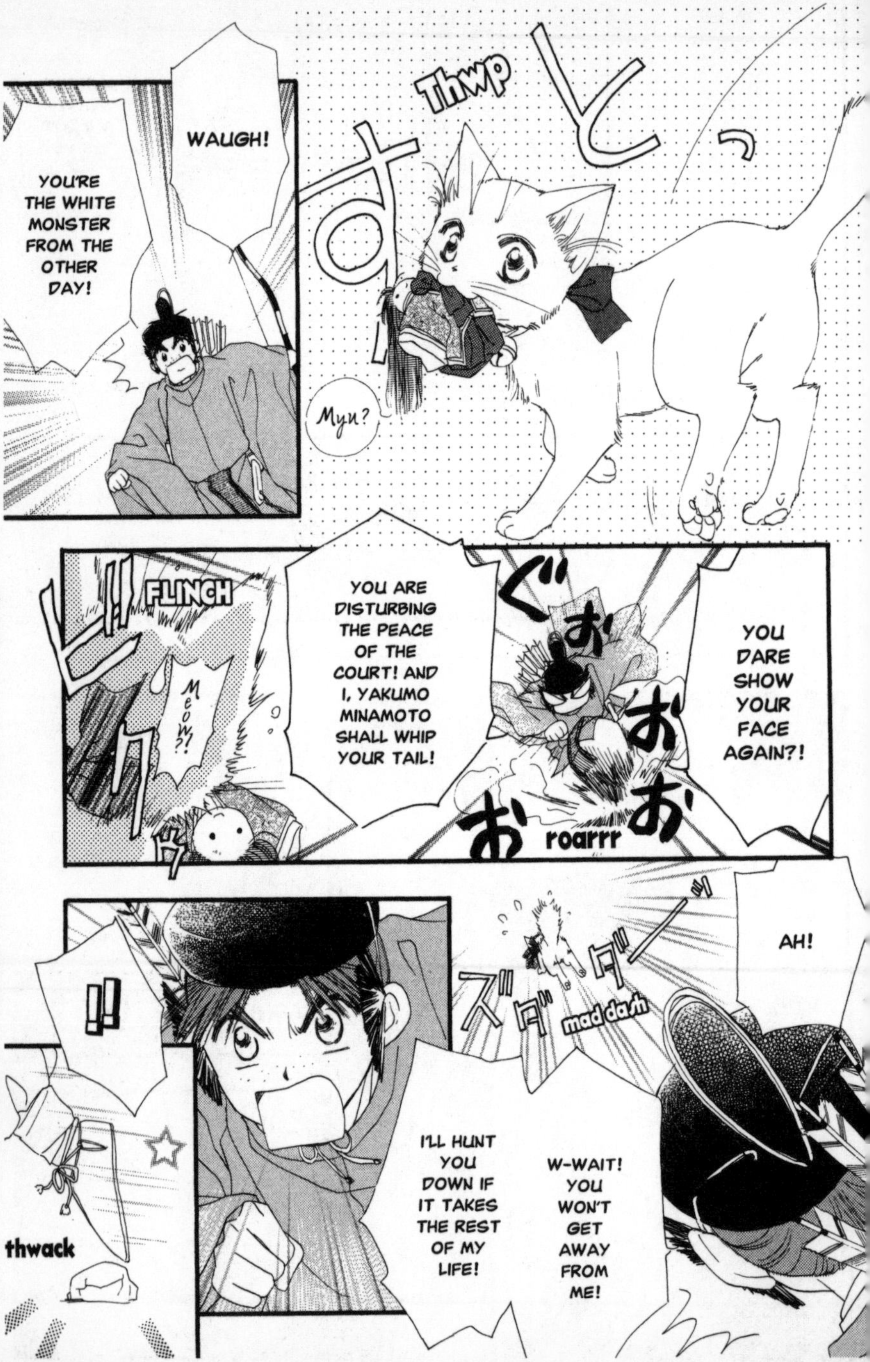

Thwp
Myu?
WAUGH!
YOU'RE THE WHITE MONSTER FROM THE OTHER DAY!
YOU DARE SHOW YOUR FACE AGAIN?!
roarrr
YOU ARE DISTURBING THE PEACE OF THE COURT! AND I, YAKUMO MINAMOTO SHALL WHIP YOUR TAIL!
FLINCH
Meow?!
AH!
mad dash
W-WAIT! YOU WON'T GET AWAY FROM ME!
I'LL HUNT YOU DOWN IF IT TAKES THE REST OF MY LIFE!
!!
thwack

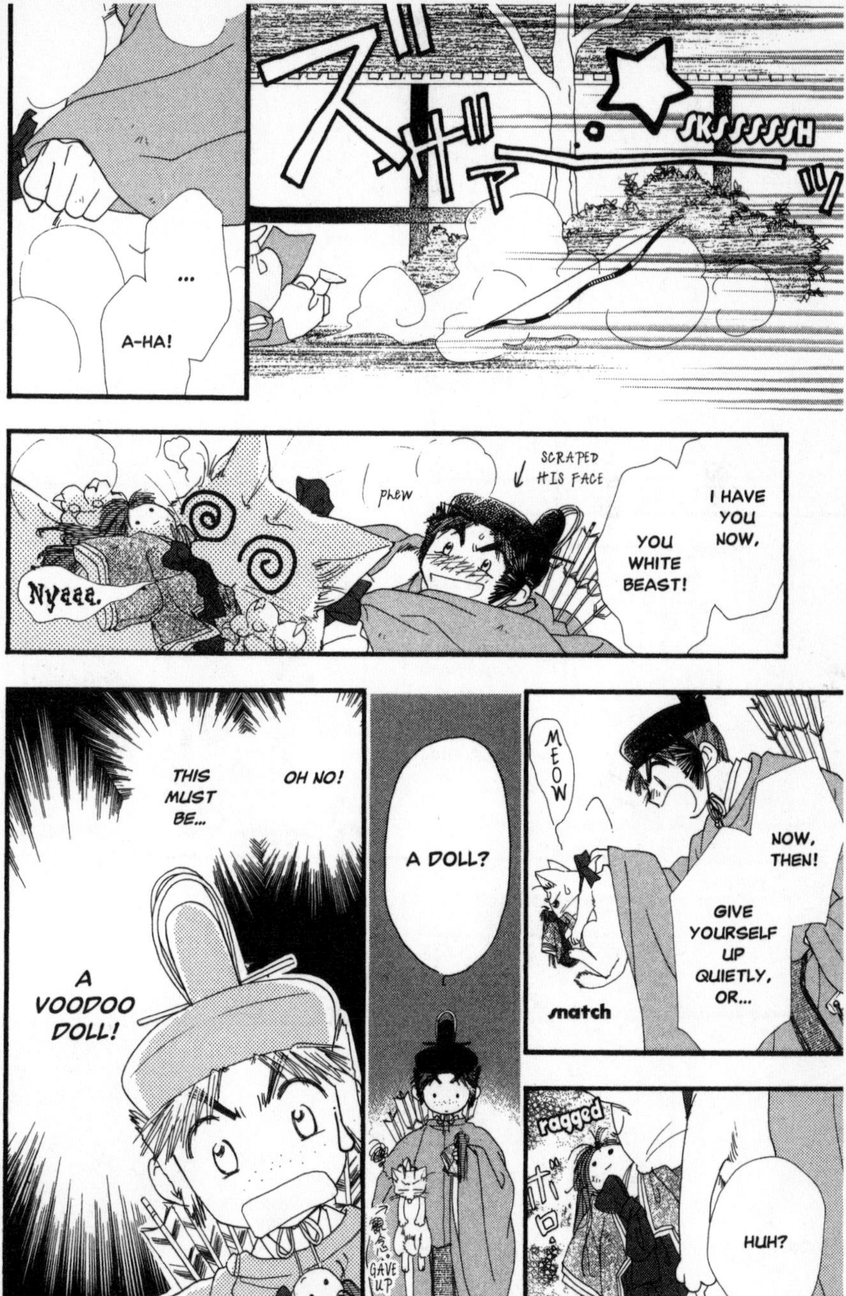
SKSSSSSH
...
A-HA!
I HAVE YOU NOW,
YOU WHITE BEAST!
SCRAPED HIS FACE
phew
Nyaaa.
MEOW
NOW, THEN!
GIVE YOURSELF UP QUIETLY, OR...
snatch
ragged
HUH?
A DOLL?
GAVE UP
OH NO!
THIS MUST BE...
A VOODOO DOLL!
DANGLE

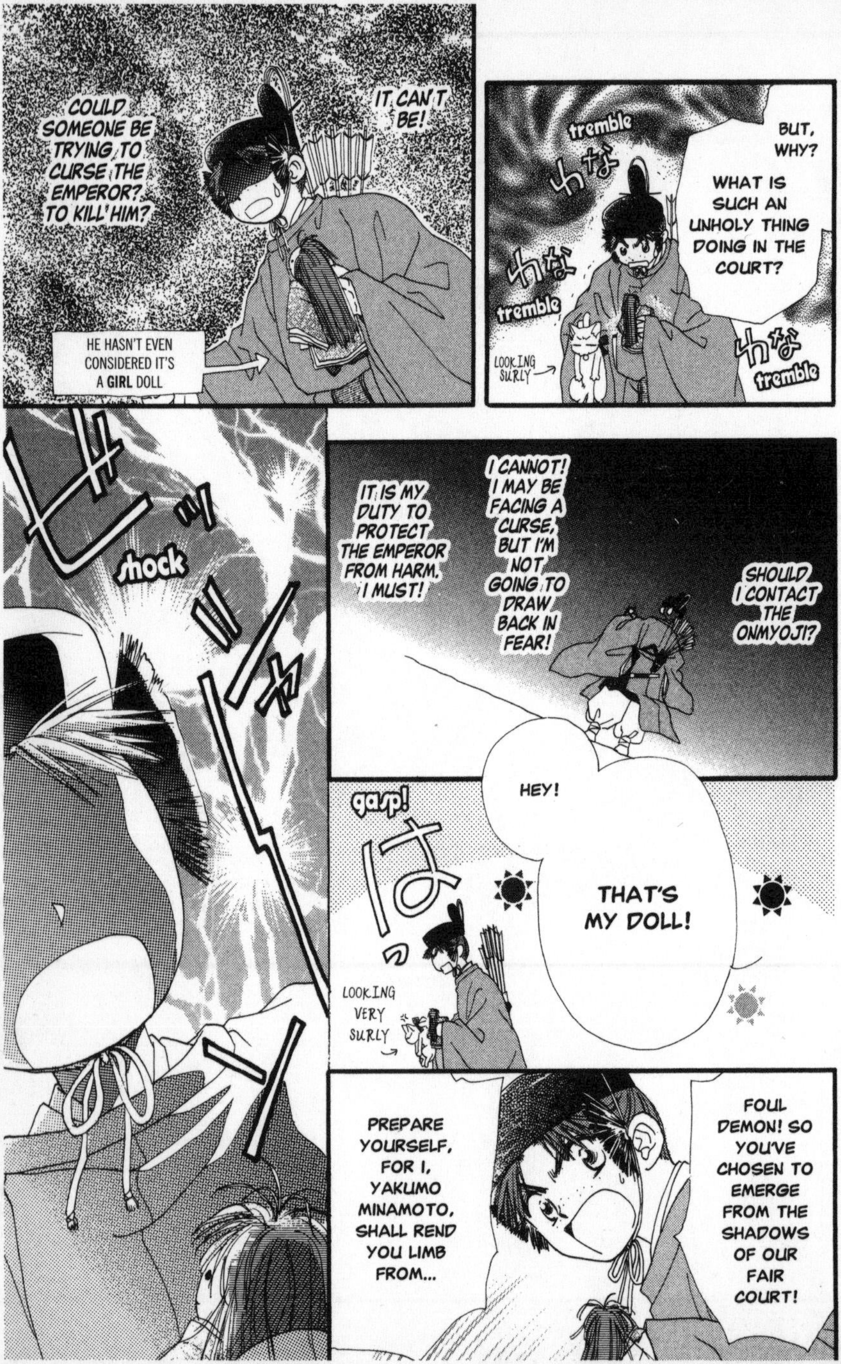

BUT, WHY?
WHAT IS SUCH AN UNHOLY THING DOING IN THE COURT?
tremble
tremble
tremble
LOOKING SURLY
IT CAN'T BE!
COULD SOMEONE BE TRYING TO CURSE THE EMPEROR? TO KILL HIM?
HE HASN'T EVEN CONSIDERED IT'S A GIRL DOLL
SHOULD I CONTACT THE ONMYOJI?
I CANNOT! I MAY BE FACING A CURSE, BUT I'M NOT GOING TO DRAW BACK IN FEAR!
IT IS MY DUTY TO PROTECT THE EMPEROR FROM HARM. I MUST!
HEY!
THAT'S MY DOLL!
gasp!
LOOKING VERY SURLY
shock
FOUL DEMON! SO YOU'VE CHOSEN TO EMERGE FROM THE SHADOWS OF OUR FAIR COURT!
PREPARE YOURSELF, FOR I, YAKUMO MINAMOTO, SHALL REND YOU LIMB FROM...

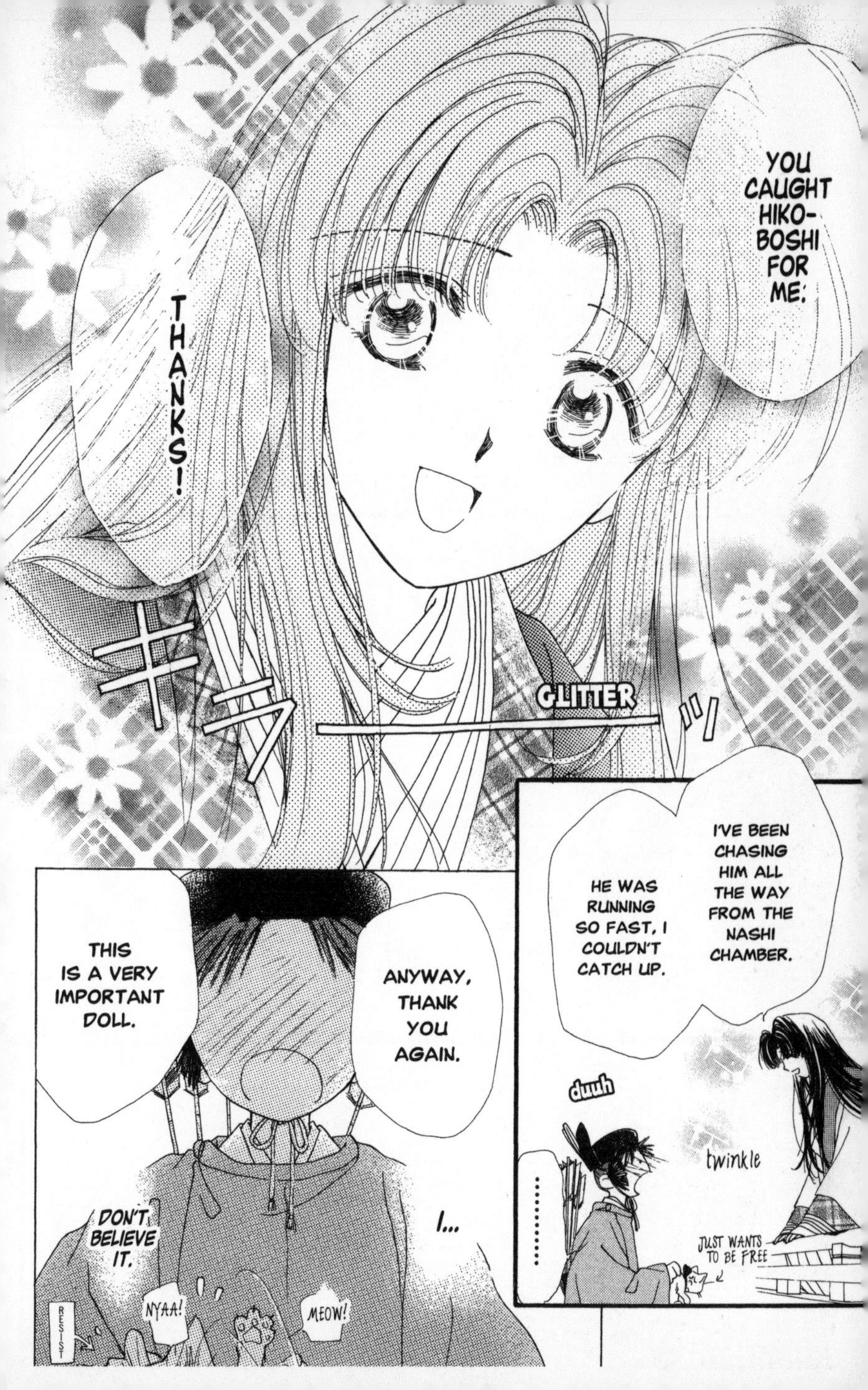

YOU CAUGHT HIKO-BOSHI FOR ME.
THANKS!
GLITTER
I'VE BEEN CHASING HIM ALL THE WAY FROM THE NASHI CHAMBER.
HE WAS RUNNING SO FAST, I COULDN'T CATCH UP.
duuh
twinkle
......
JUST WANTS TO BE FREE
ANYWAY, THANK YOU AGAIN.
THIS IS A VERY IMPORTANT DOLL.
I...
DON'T BELIEVE IT.
NYAA!
MEOW!
RESIST

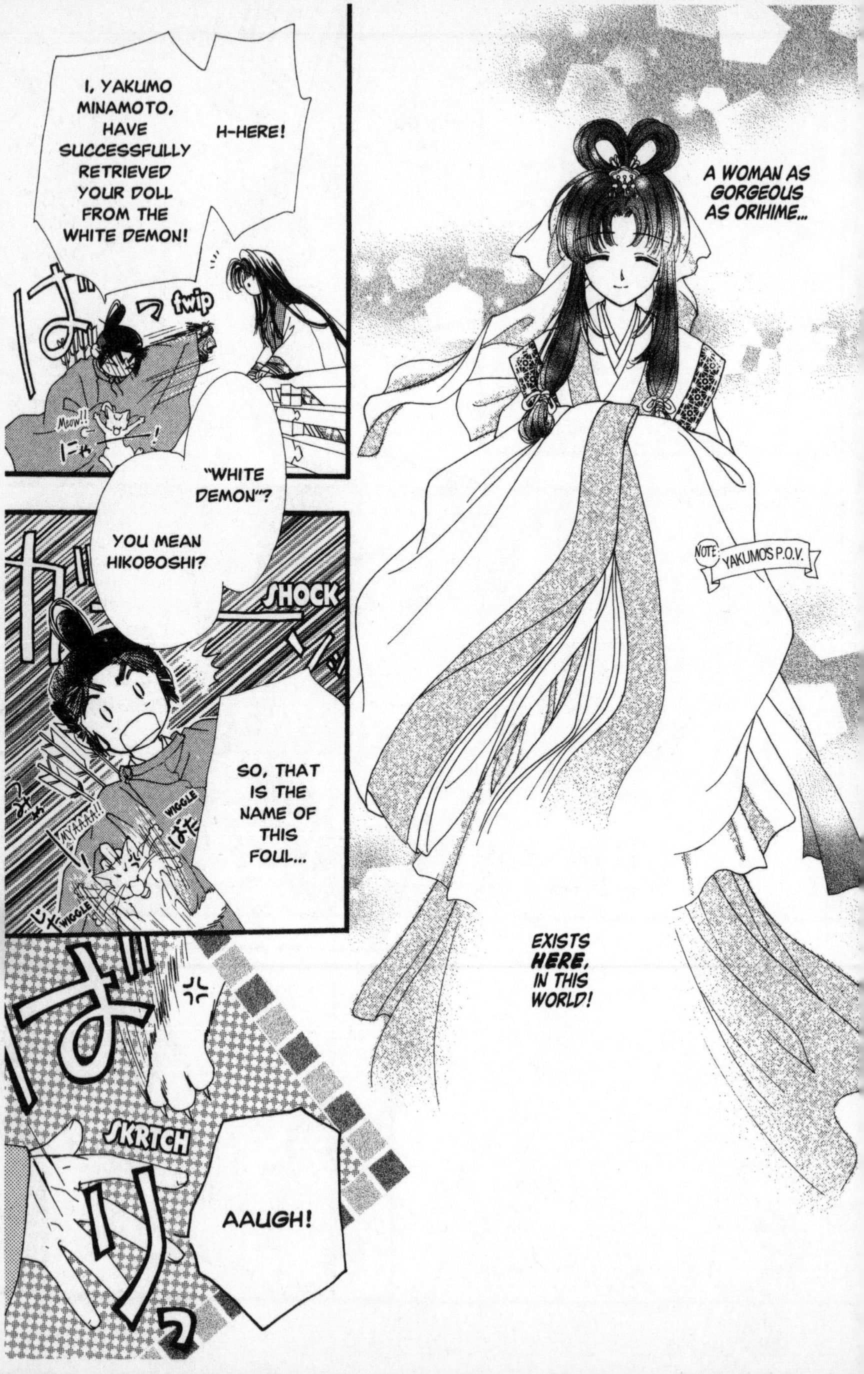
A WOMAN AS GORGEOUS AS ORIHIME...
NOTE: YAKUMO'S P.O.V.
EXISTS HERE, IN THIS WORLD!
H-HERE!
I, YAKUMO MINAMOTO, HAVE SUCCESSFULLY RETRIEVED YOUR DOLL FROM THE WHITE DEMON!
fwip
MEOW!!
"WHITE DEMON"?
YOU MEAN HIKOBOSHI?
SHOCK
SO, THAT IS THE NAME OF THIS FOUL...
WIGGLE
MYAAAA!!
WIGGLE
SKRTCH
AAUGH!

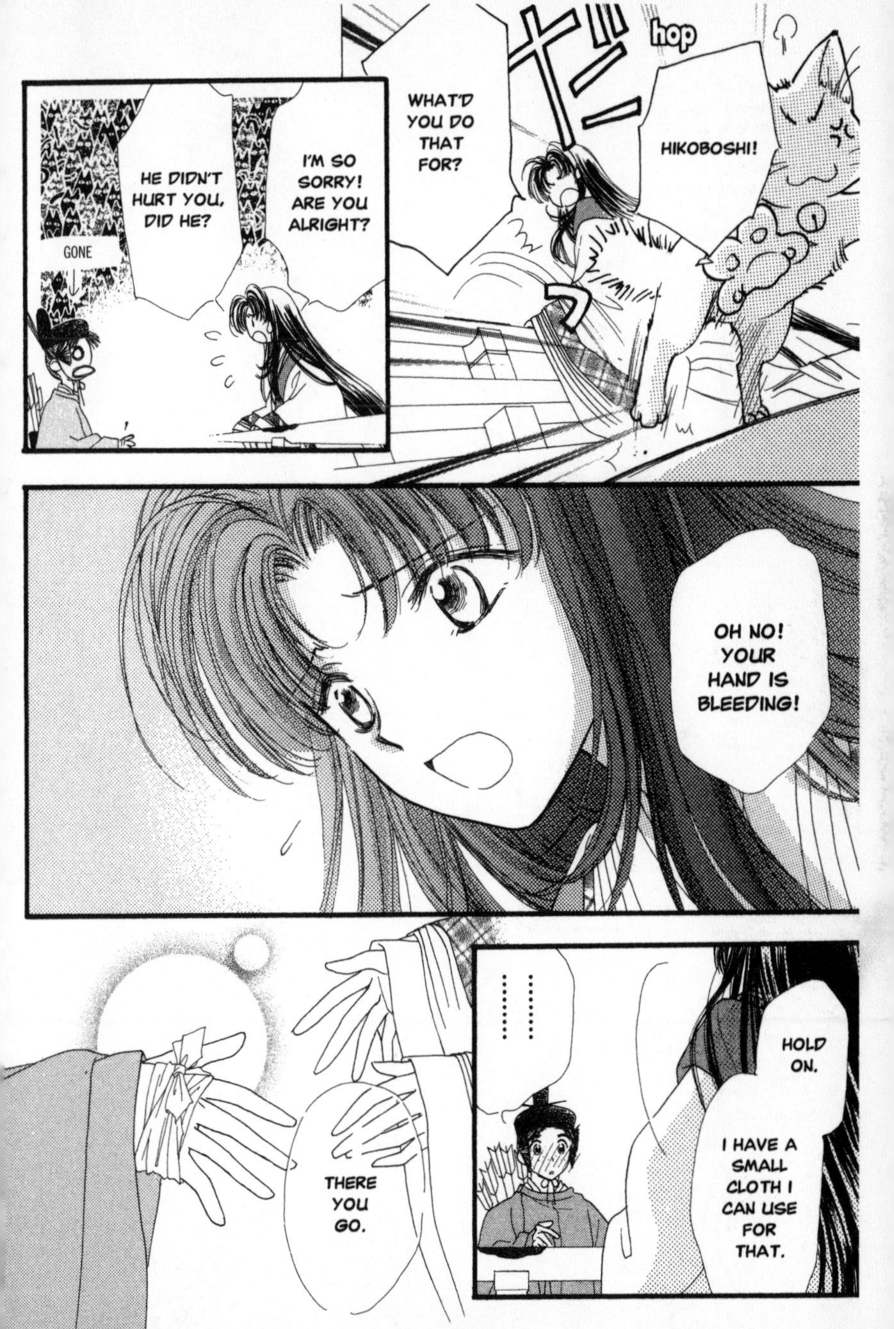
hop
HIKOBOSHI!
WHAT'D YOU DO THAT FOR?
I'M SO SORRY! ARE YOU ALRIGHT?
HE DIDN'T HURT YOU, DID HE?
GONE
OH NO! YOUR HAND IS BLEEDING!
HOLD ON.
I HAVE A SMALL CLOTH I CAN USE FOR THAT.
......
THERE YOU GO.

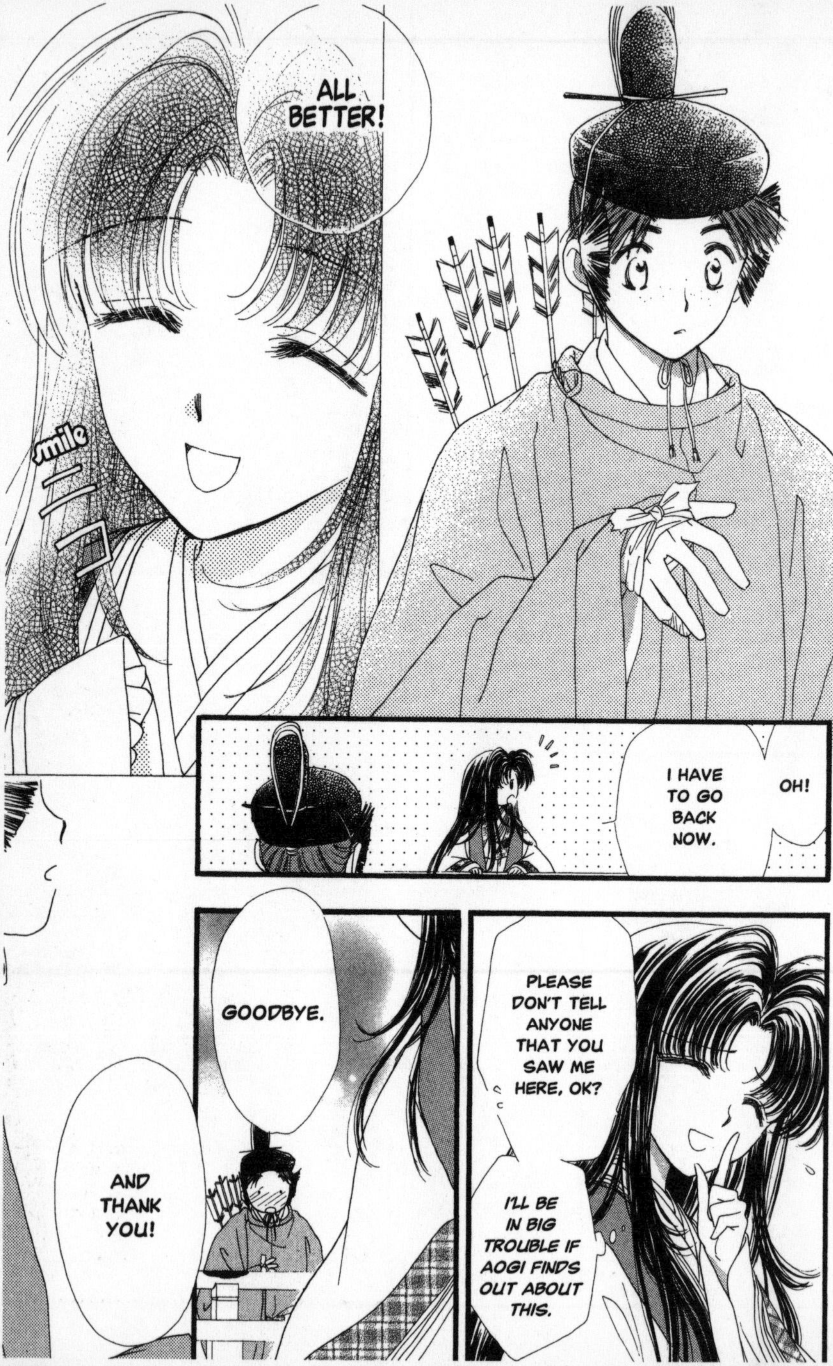
ALL BETTER!
smile
OH!
I HAVE TO GO BACK NOW.
PLEASE DON'T TELL ANYONE THAT YOU SAW ME HERE, OK?
I'LL BE IN BIG TROUBLE IF AOGI FINDS OUT ABOUT THIS.
GOODBYE.
AND THANK YOU!

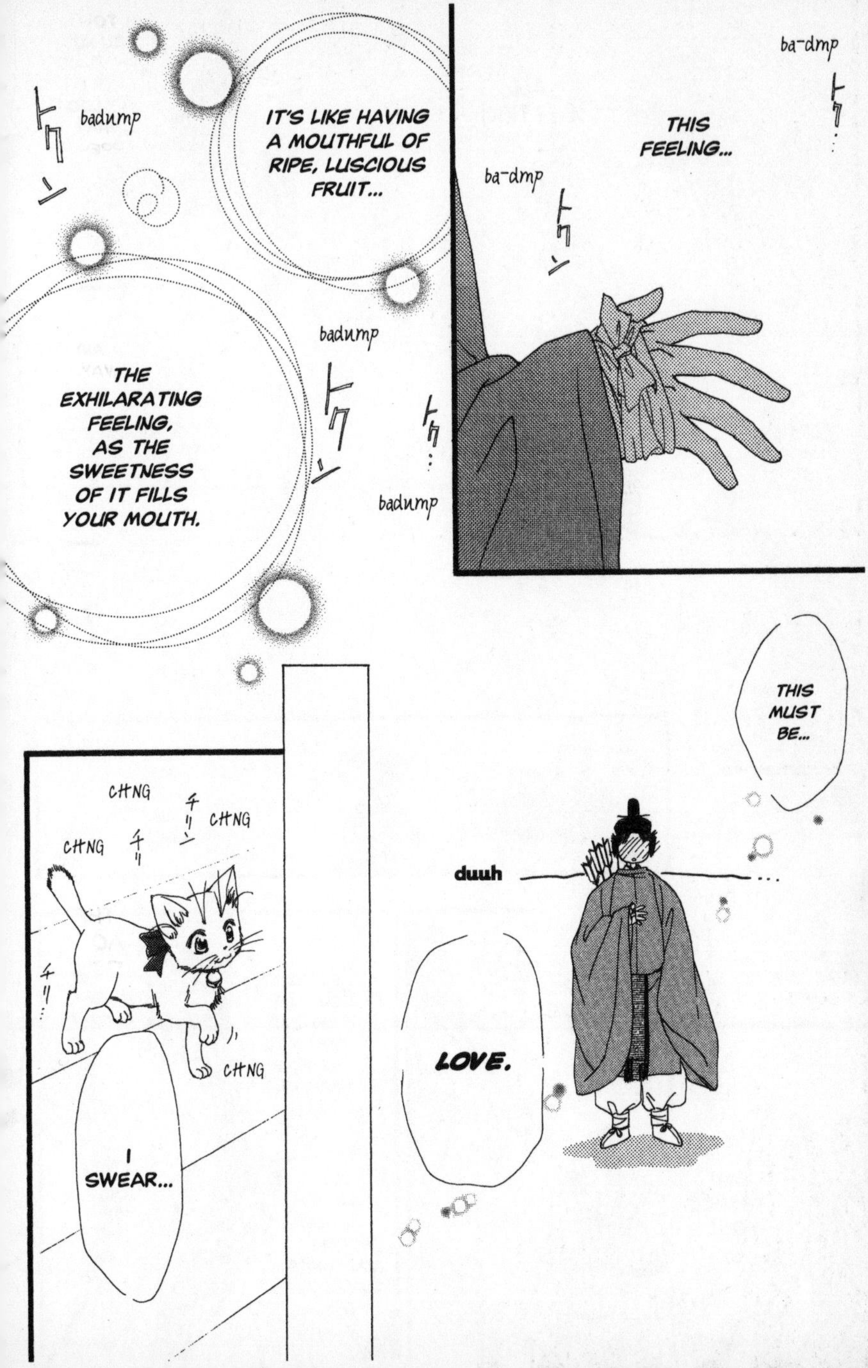
ba-dmp
THIS FEELING...
ba-dmp
IT'S LIKE HAVING A MOUTHFUL OF RIPE, LUSCIOUS FRUIT...
badump
badump
THE EXHILARATING FEELING, AS THE SWEETNESS OF IT FILLS YOUR MOUTH.
badump
THIS MUST BE...
duuh
LOVE.
CHNG
CHNG
CHNG
CHNG
I SWEAR...

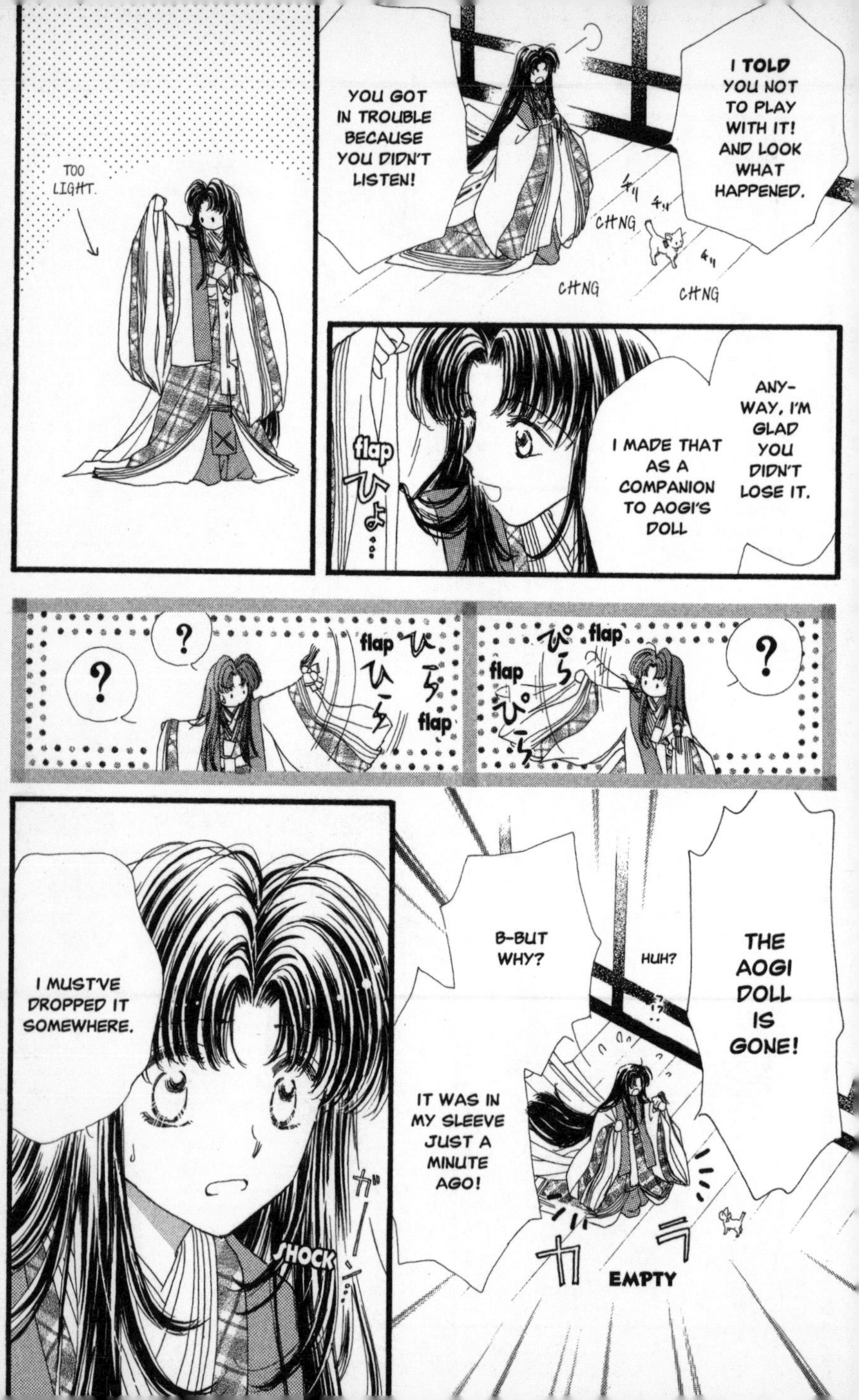
I TOLD YOU NOT TO PLAY WITH IT! AND LOOK WHAT HAPPENED.
YOU GOT IN TROUBLE BECAUSE YOU DIDN'T LISTEN!
CHNG
CHNG
CHNG
ANY-WAY, I'M GLAD YOU DIDN'T LOSE IT.
I MADE THAT AS A COMPANION TO AOGI'S DOLL
flap
TOO LIGHT.
?
flap
flap
?
?
flap
flap
THE AOGI DOLL IS GONE!
HUH?
B-BUT WHY?
IT WAS IN MY SLEEVE JUST A MINUTE AGO!
EMPTY
I MUST'VE DROPPED IT SOMEWHERE.
SHOCK

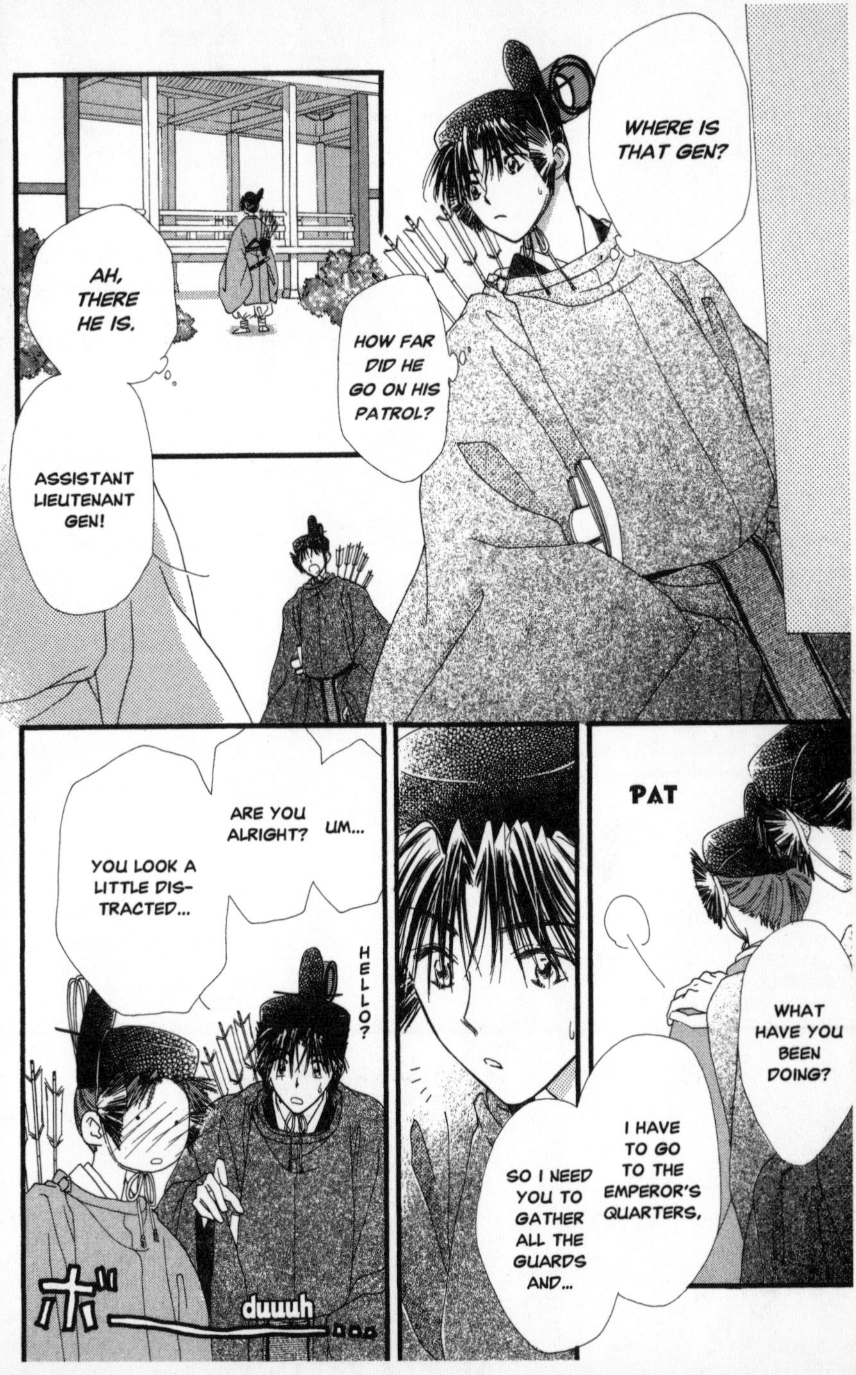
WHERE IS THAT GEN?
HOW FAR DID HE GO ON HIS PATROL?
AH, THERE HE IS.
ASSISTANT LIEUTENANT GEN!
PAT
WHAT HAVE YOU BEEN DOING?
I HAVE TO GO TO THE EMPEROR'S QUARTERS,
SO I NEED YOU TO GATHER ALL THE GUARDS AND...
UM...
ARE YOU ALRIGHT?
YOU LOOK A LITTLE DIS-TRACTED...
HELLO?
ボー
duuuh...

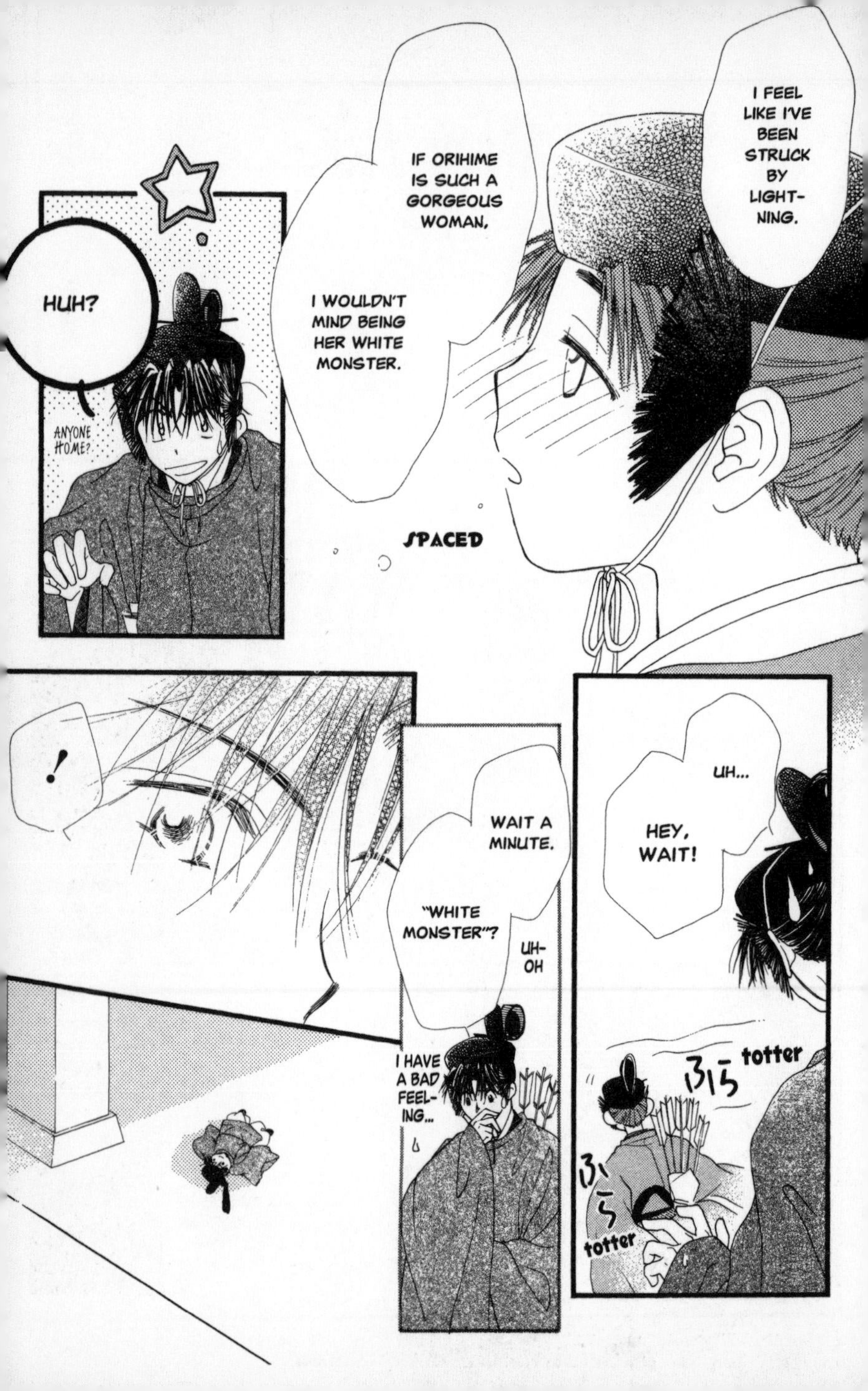
I FEEL LIKE I'VE BEEN STRUCK BY LIGHT-NING.
IF ORIHIME IS SUCH A GORGEOUS WOMAN,
I WOULDN'T MIND BEING HER WHITE MONSTER.
SPACED
HUH?
ANYONE HOME?
UH...
HEY, WAIT!
ふらー totter
ふらー totter
WAIT A MINUTE.
"WHITE MONSTER"?
UH-OH
I HAVE A BAD FEEL-ING...
!

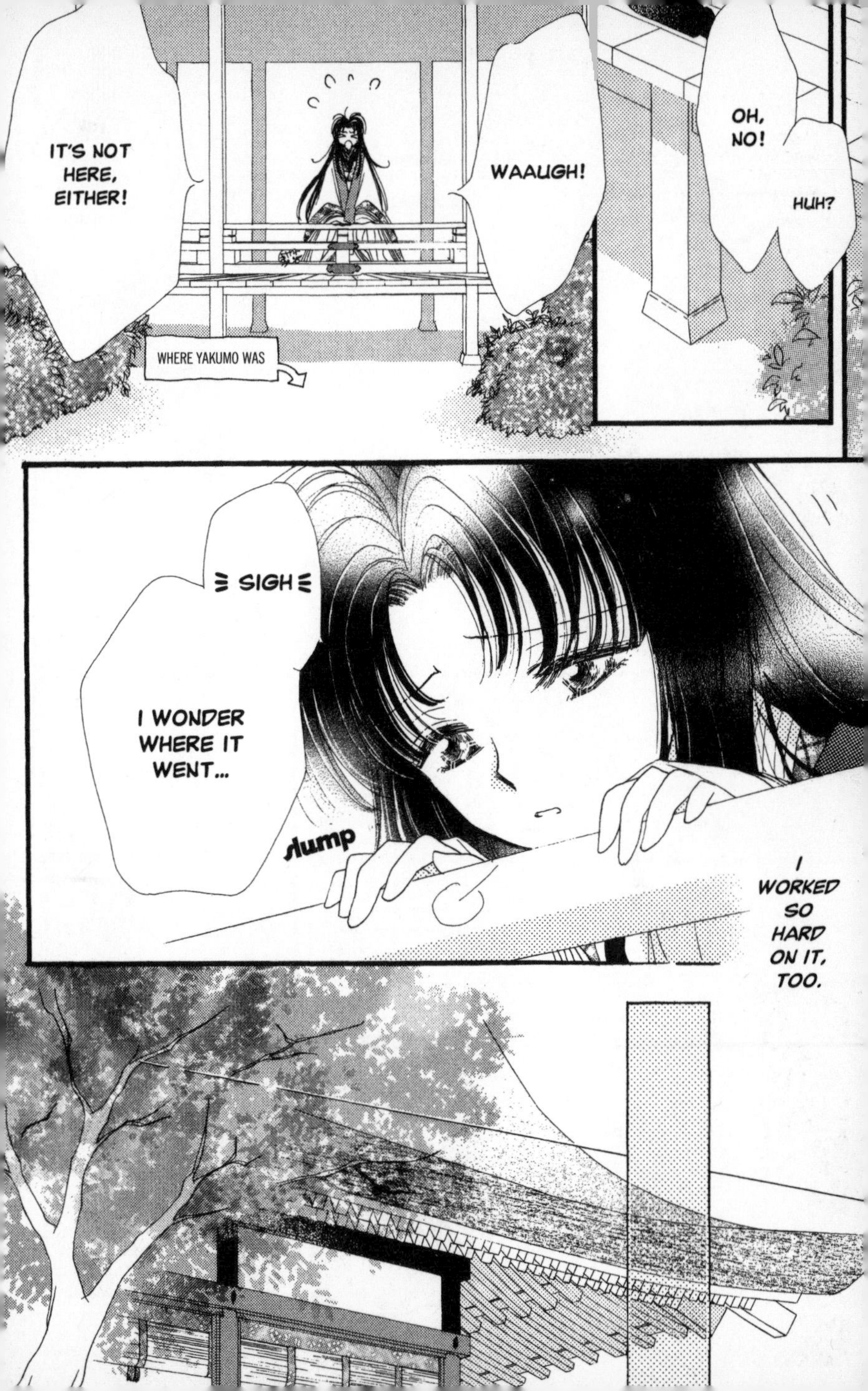

OH, NO!
HUH?
WAAUGH!
IT'S NOT HERE, EITHER!
WHERE YAKUMO WAS
SIGH
I WONDER WHERE IT WENT...
slump
I WORKED SO HARD ON IT, TOO.

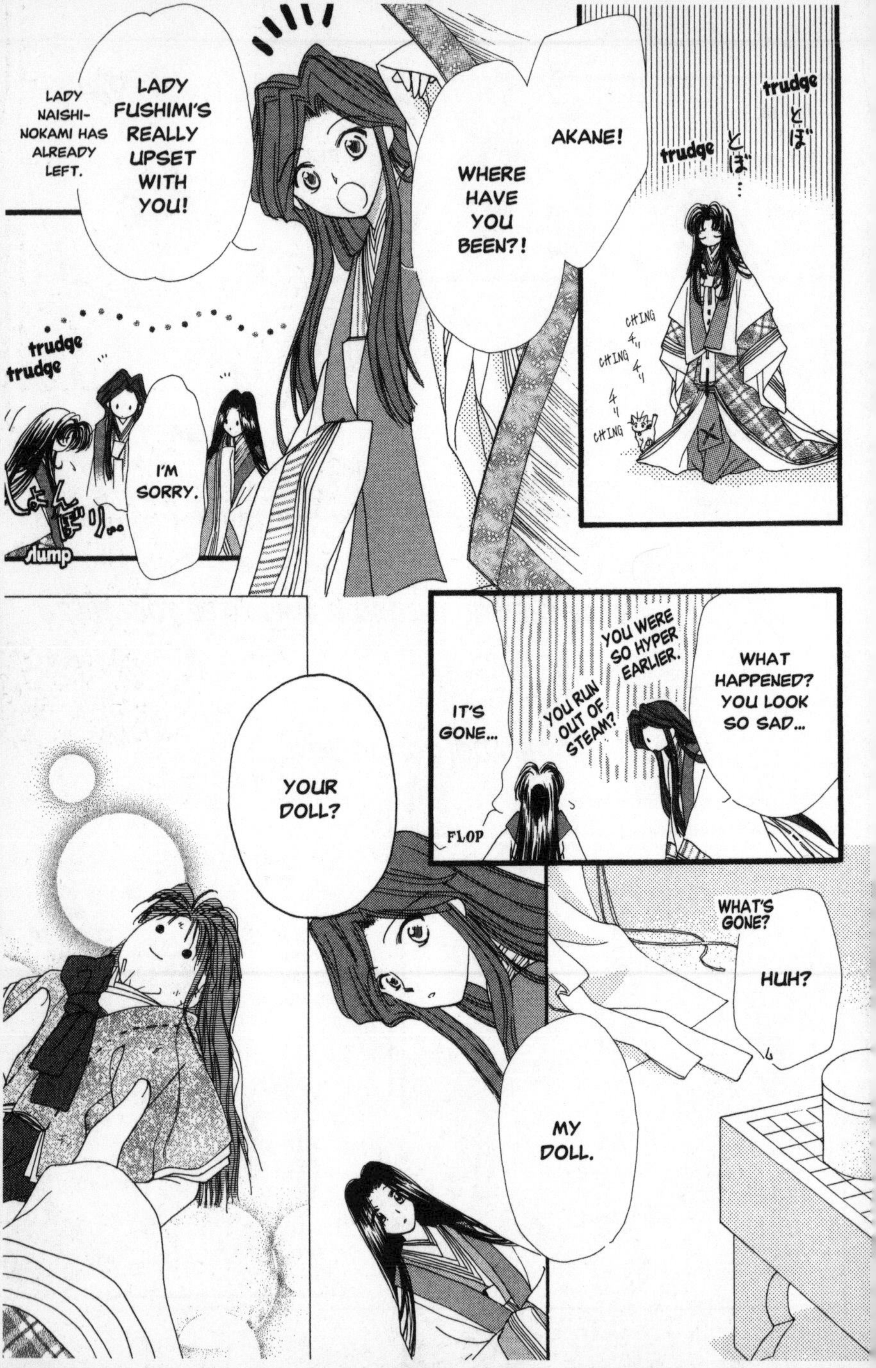
trudge
とぼ とぼ…
trudge
CHING
CHING
CHING
AKANE!
WHERE HAVE YOU BEEN?!
LADY FUSHIMI'S REALLY UPSET WITH YOU!
LADY NAISHI-NOKAMI HAS ALREADY LEFT.
trudge
trudge
I'M SORRY.
slump
WHAT HAPPENED? YOU LOOK SO SAD...
YOU WERE SO HYPER EARLIER.
YOU RUN OUT OF STEAM?
IT'S GONE...
FLOP
WHAT'S GONE?
HUH?
MY DOLL.
YOUR DOLL?

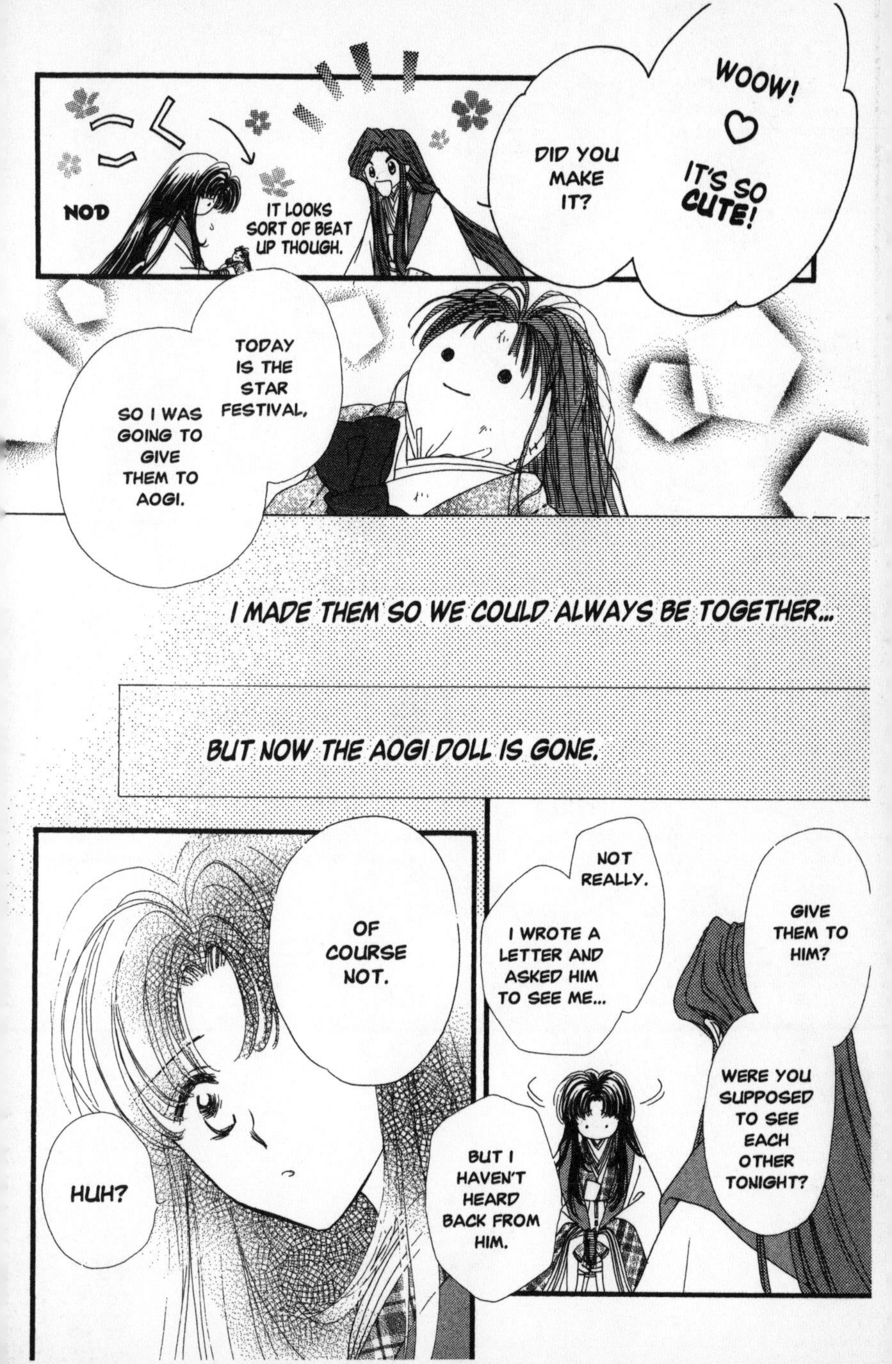
WOOW! ♡ IT'S SO CUTE!
DID YOU MAKE IT?
IT LOOKS SORT OF BEAT UP THOUGH.
NOD
TODAY IS THE STAR FESTIVAL,
SO I WAS GOING TO GIVE THEM TO AOGI.
I MADE THEM SO WE COULD ALWAYS BE TOGETHER...
BUT NOW THE AOGI DOLL IS GONE.
GIVE THEM TO HIM?
WERE YOU SUPPOSED TO SEE EACH OTHER TONIGHT?
NOT REALLY.
I WROTE A LETTER AND ASKED HIM TO SEE ME...
BUT I HAVEN'T HEARD BACK FROM HIM.
OF COURSE NOT.
HUH?

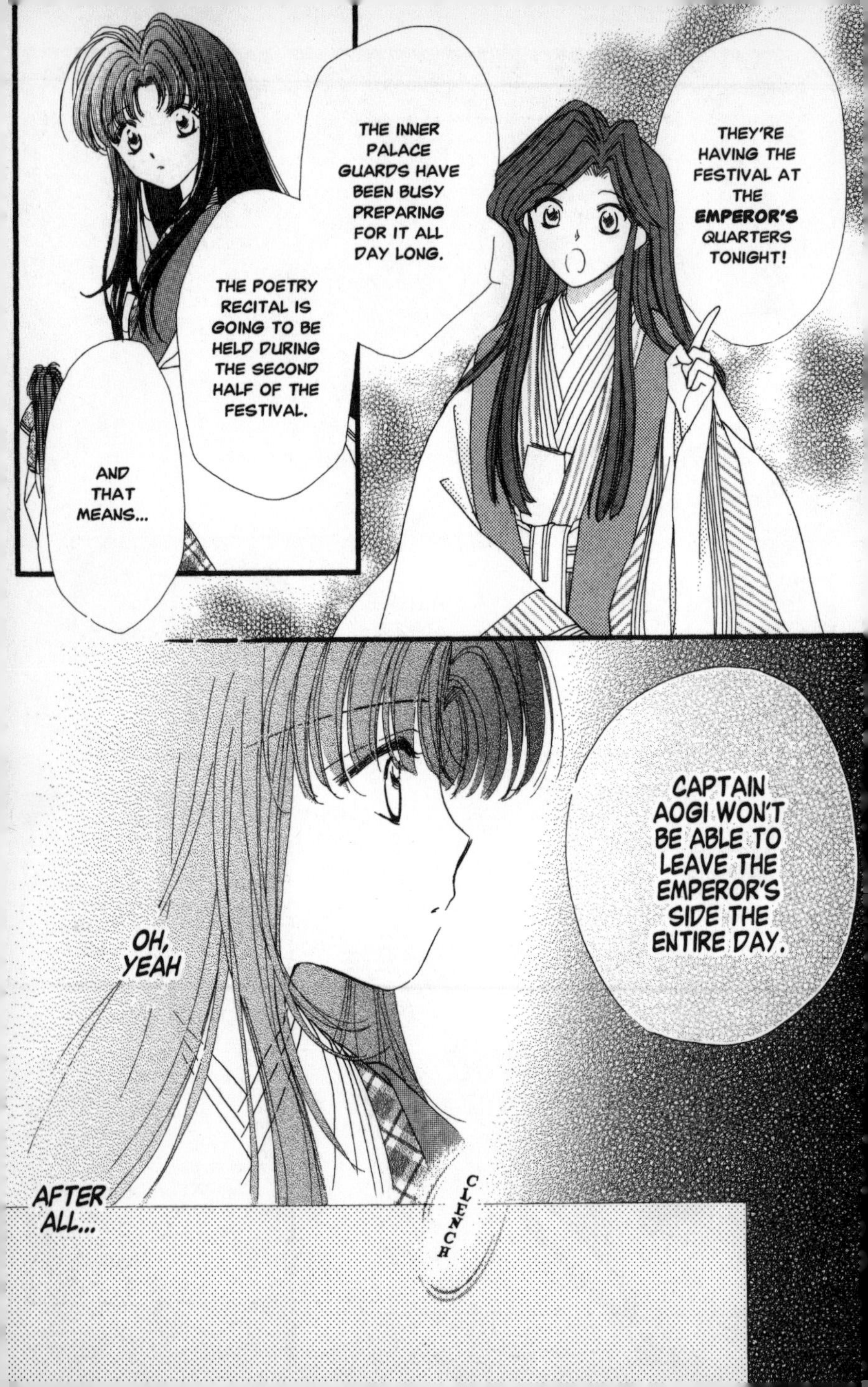
THEY'RE HAVING THE FESTIVAL AT THE **EMPEROR'S** QUARTERS TONIGHT!
THE INNER PALACE GUARDS HAVE BEEN BUSY PREPARING FOR IT ALL DAY LONG.
THE POETRY RECITAL IS GOING TO BE HELD DURING THE SECOND HALF OF THE FESTIVAL.
AND THAT MEANS...
CAPTAIN AOGI WON'T BE ABLE TO LEAVE THE EMPEROR'S SIDE THE ENTIRE DAY.
OH, YEAH
CLENCH
AFTER ALL...

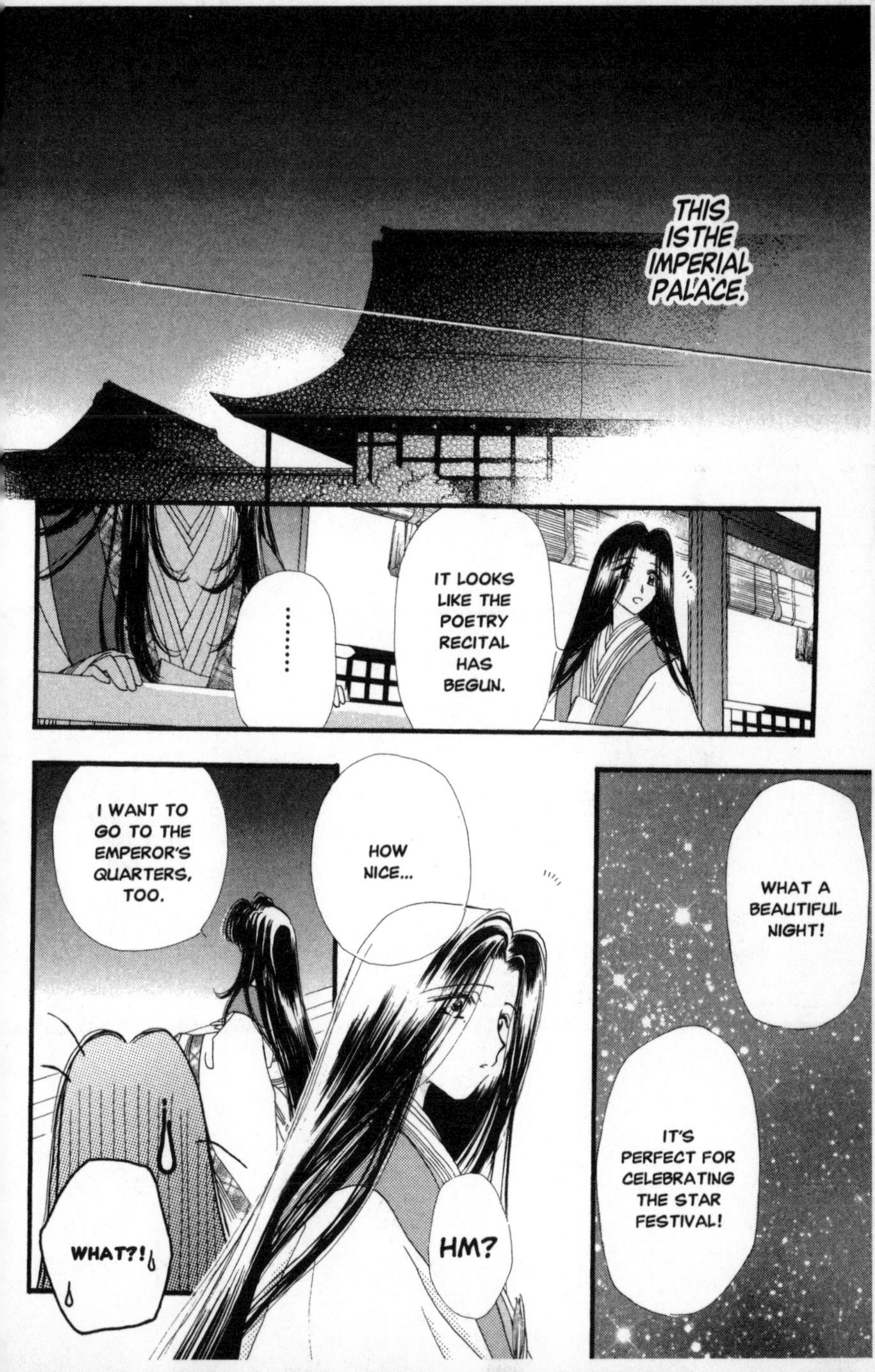
THIS IS THE IMPERIAL PALACE.
IT LOOKS LIKE THE POETRY RECITAL HAS BEGUN.
....
WHAT A BEAUTIFUL NIGHT!
IT'S PERFECT FOR CELEBRATING THE STAR FESTIVAL!
HOW NICE...
I WANT TO GO TO THE EMPEROR'S QUARTERS, TOO.
HM?
WHAT?!

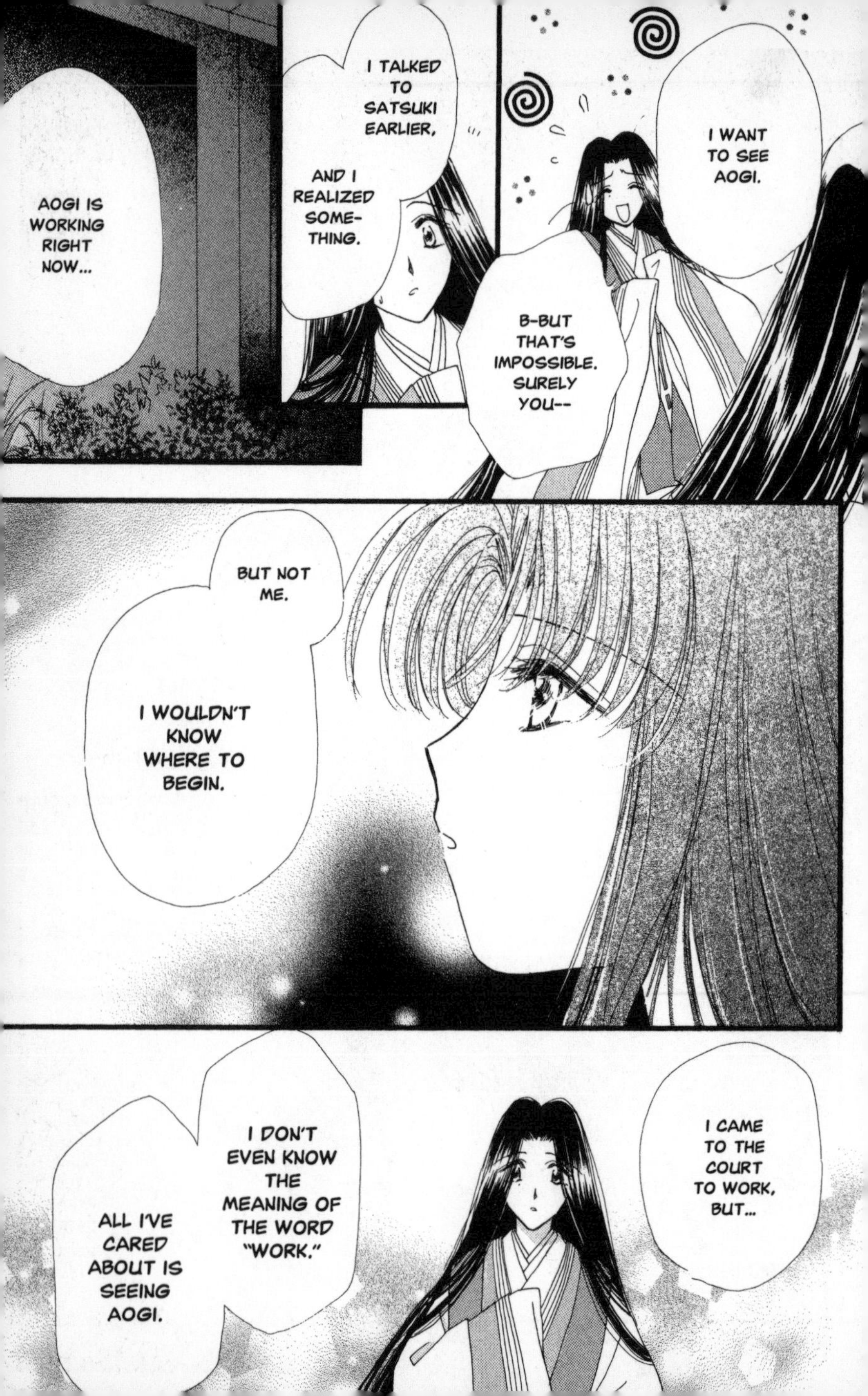

I WANT TO SEE AOGI.
B-BUT THAT'S IMPOSSIBLE. SURELY YOU--
I TALKED TO SATSUKI EARLIER,
AND I REALIZED SOME-THING.
AOGI IS WORKING RIGHT NOW...
BUT NOT ME.
I WOULDN'T KNOW WHERE TO BEGIN.
I CAME TO THE COURT TO WORK, BUT...
I DON'T EVEN KNOW THE MEANING OF THE WORD "WORK."
ALL I'VE CARED ABOUT IS SEEING AOGI.

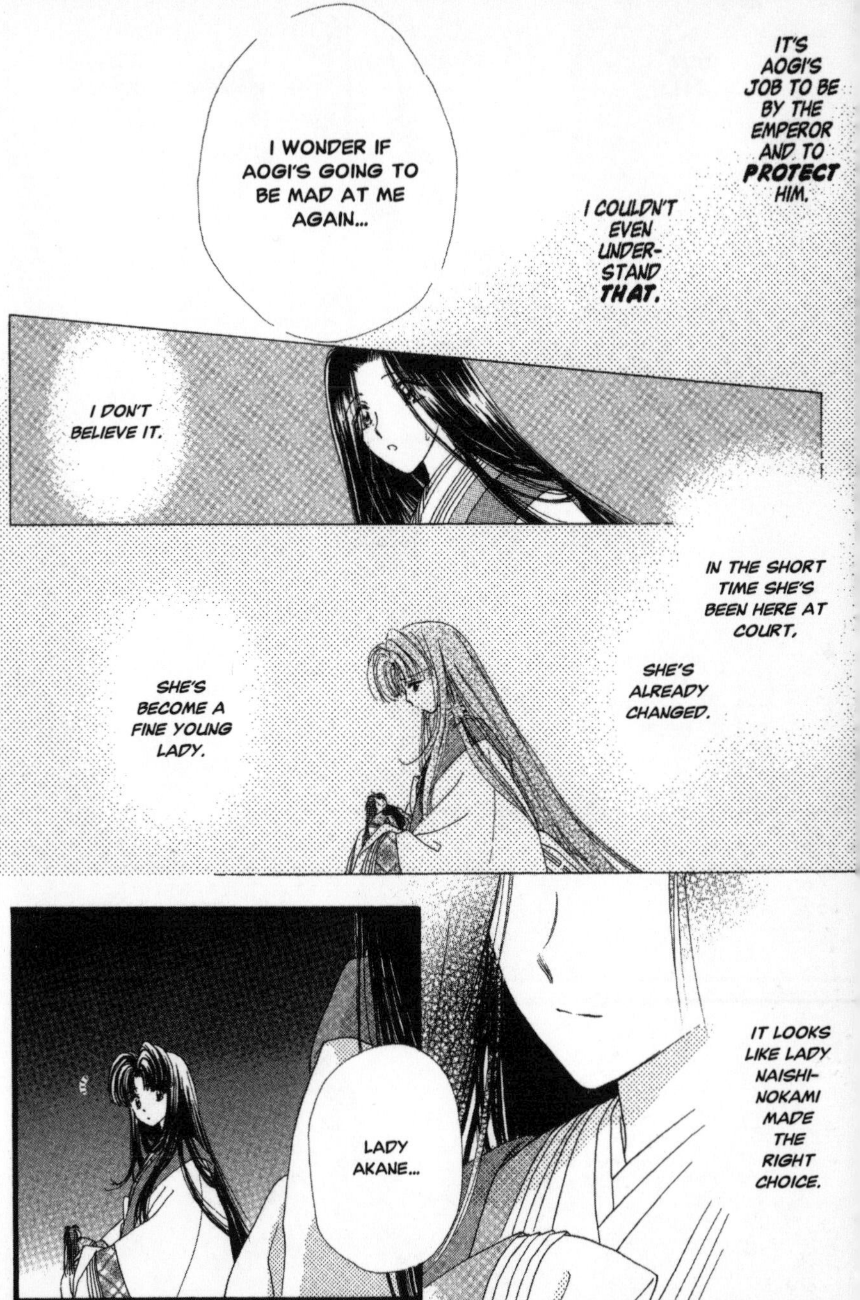
IT'S AOGI'S JOB TO BE BY THE EMPEROR AND TO **PROTECT** HIM.
I COULDN'T EVEN UNDERSTAND **THAT.**
I WONDER IF AOGI'S GOING TO BE MAD AT ME AGAIN...
I DON'T BELIEVE IT.
IN THE SHORT TIME SHE'S BEEN HERE AT COURT,
SHE'S ALREADY CHANGED.
SHE'S BECOME A FINE YOUNG LADY.
IT LOOKS LIKE LADY NAISHI-NOKAMI MADE THE RIGHT CHOICE.
LADY AKANE...

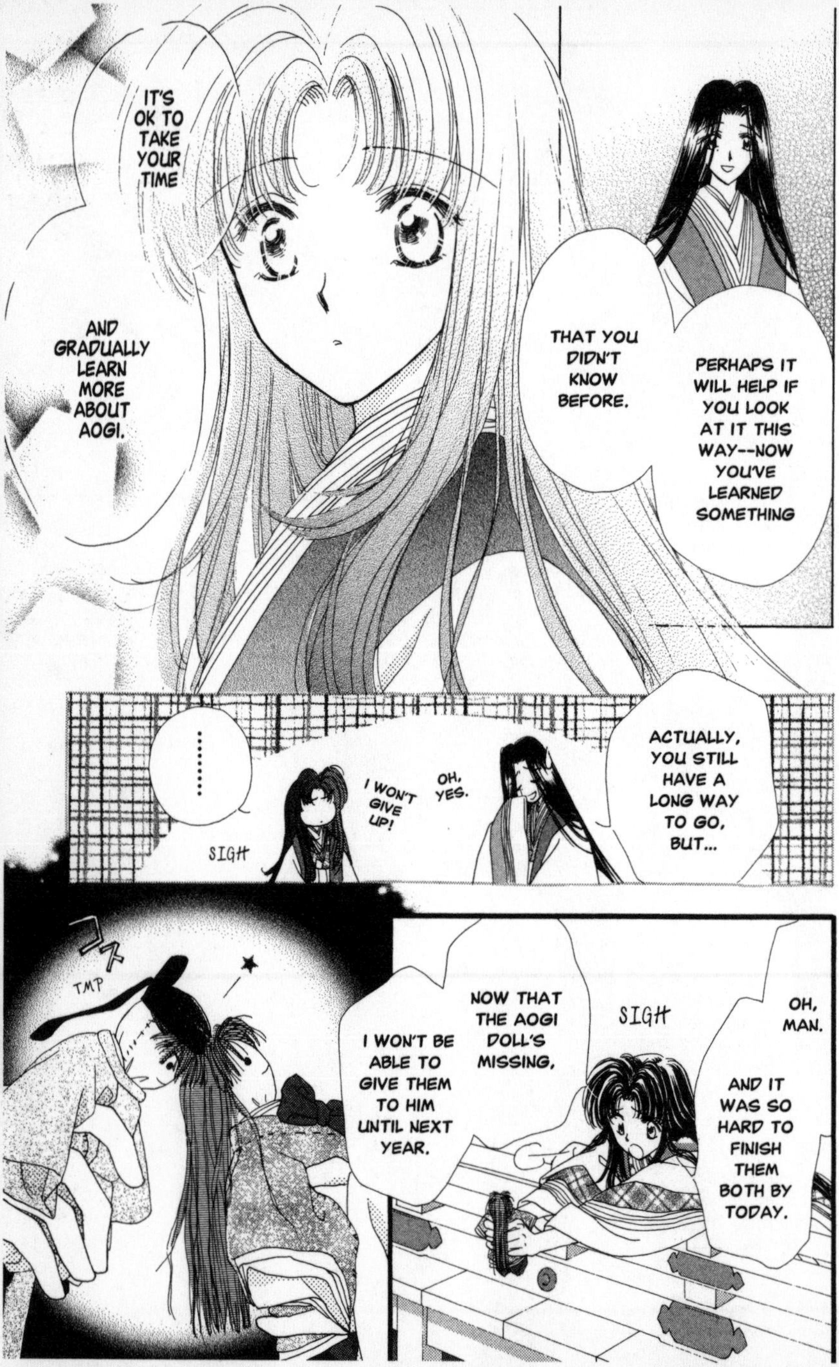
PERHAPS IT WILL HELP IF YOU LOOK AT IT THIS WAY--NOW YOU'VE LEARNED SOMETHING
THAT YOU DIDN'T KNOW BEFORE.
IT'S OK TO TAKE YOUR TIME
AND GRADUALLY LEARN MORE ABOUT AOGI.
ACTUALLY, YOU STILL HAVE A LONG WAY TO GO, BUT...
OH, YES.
I WON'T GIVE UP!
SIGH
....
OH, MAN.
AND IT WAS SO HARD TO FINISH THEM BOTH BY TODAY.
SIGH
NOW THAT THE AOGI DOLL'S MISSING,
I WON'T BE ABLE TO GIVE THEM TO HIM UNTIL NEXT YEAR.
コツ
TMP

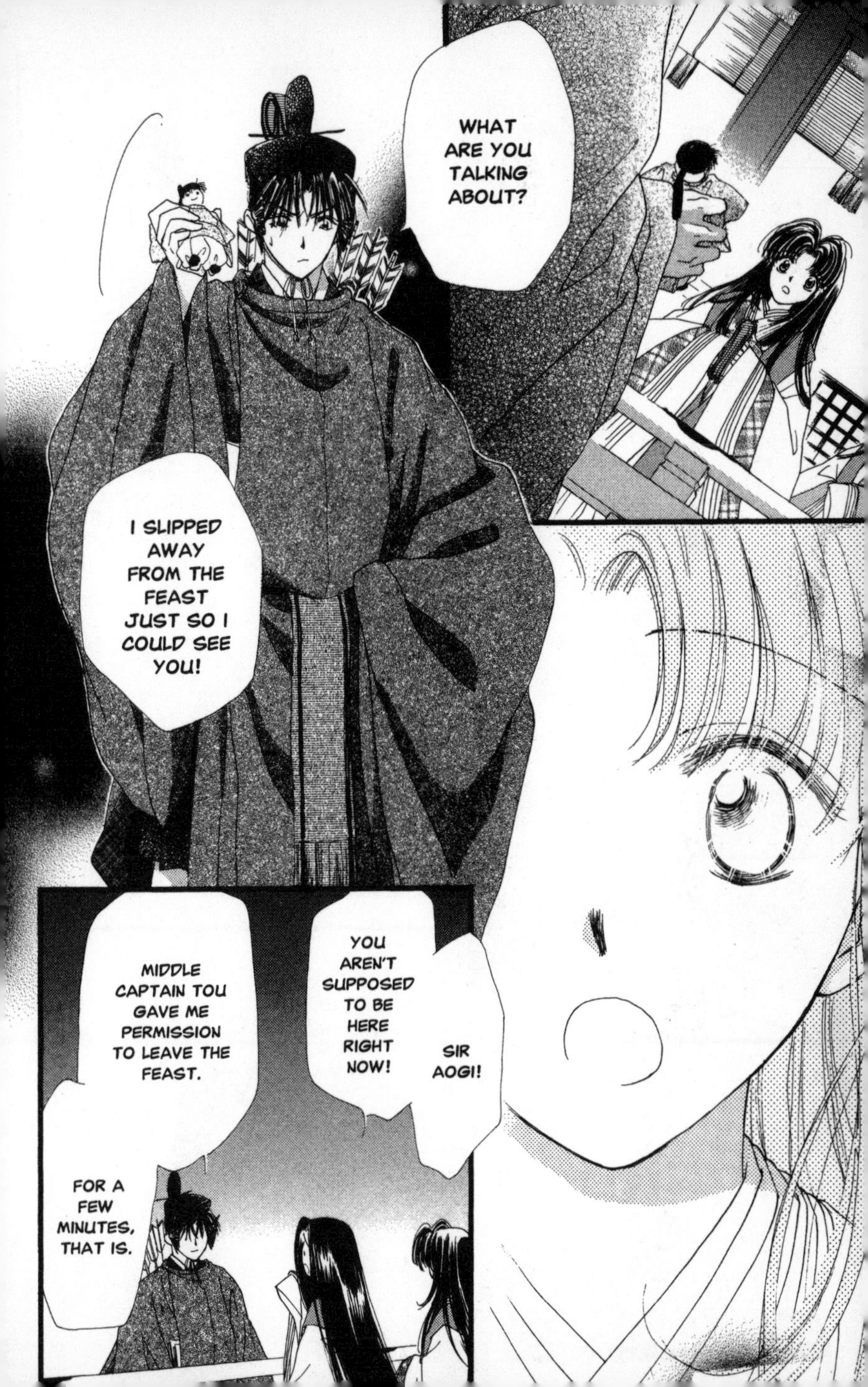
WHAT ARE YOU TALKING ABOUT?
I SLIPPED AWAY FROM THE FEAST JUST SO I COULD SEE YOU!
SIR AOGI!
YOU AREN'T SUPPOSED TO BE HERE RIGHT NOW!
MIDDLE CAPTAIN TOU GAVE ME PERMISSION TO LEAVE THE FEAST.
FOR A FEW MINUTES, THAT IS.

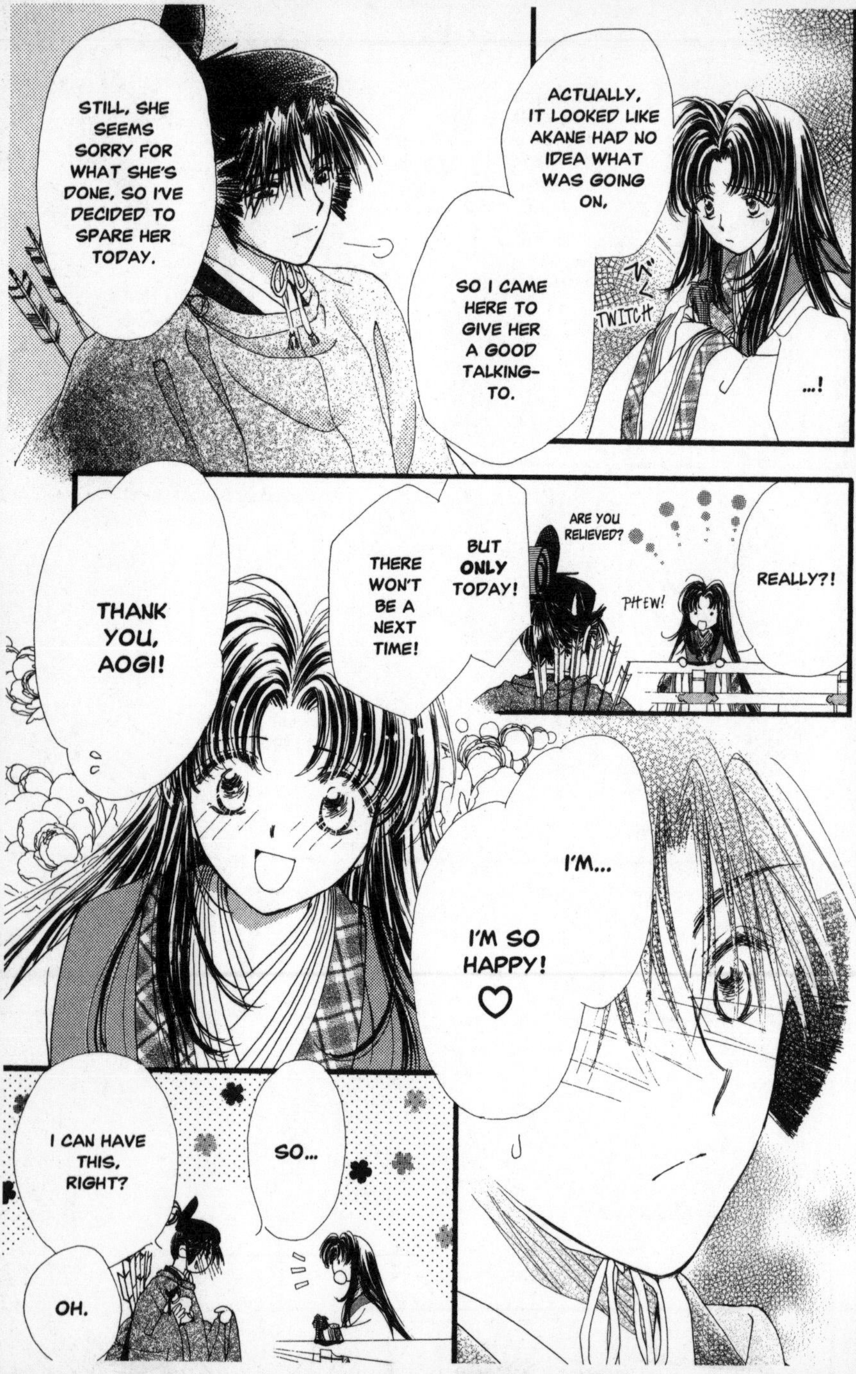
ACTUALLY, IT LOOKED LIKE AKANE HAD NO IDEA WHAT WAS GOING ON,
SO I CAME HERE TO GIVE HER A GOOD TALKING-TO.
びく
TWITCH
...!
STILL, SHE SEEMS SORRY FOR WHAT SHE'S DONE, SO I'VE DECIDED TO SPARE HER TODAY.
REALLY?!
ARE YOU RELIEVED?
PHEW!
BUT ONLY TODAY!
THERE WON'T BE A NEXT TIME!
THANK YOU, AOGI!
I'M...
I'M SO HAPPY! ♡
SO...
I CAN HAVE THIS, RIGHT?
OH.

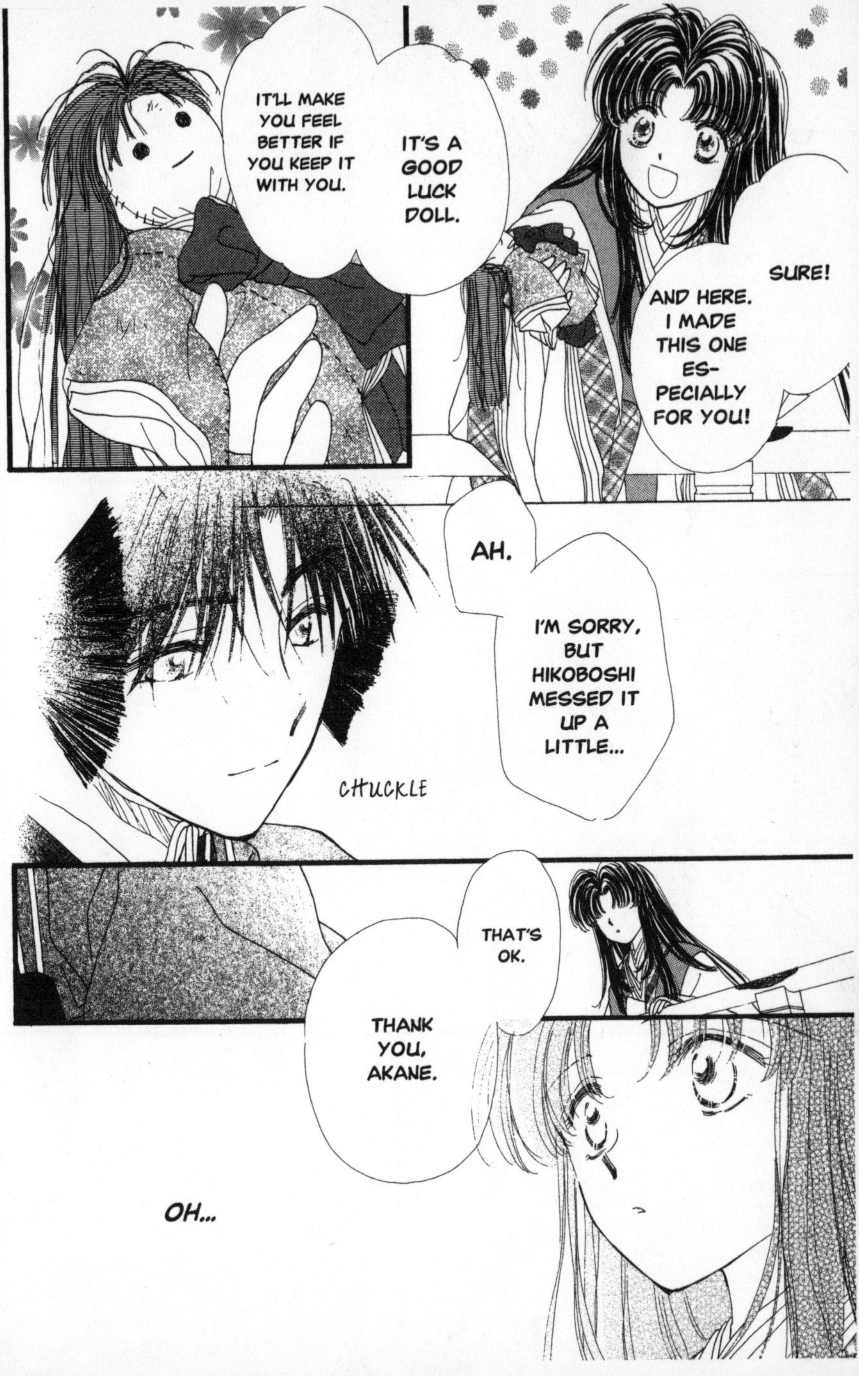
SURE!
AND HERE. I MADE THIS ONE ES-PECIALLY FOR YOU!
IT'S A GOOD LUCK DOLL.
IT'LL MAKE YOU FEEL BETTER IF YOU KEEP IT WITH YOU.
AH.
I'M SORRY, BUT HIKOBOSHI MESSED IT UP A LITTLE...
CHUCKLE
THAT'S OK.
THANK YOU, AKANE.
OH...

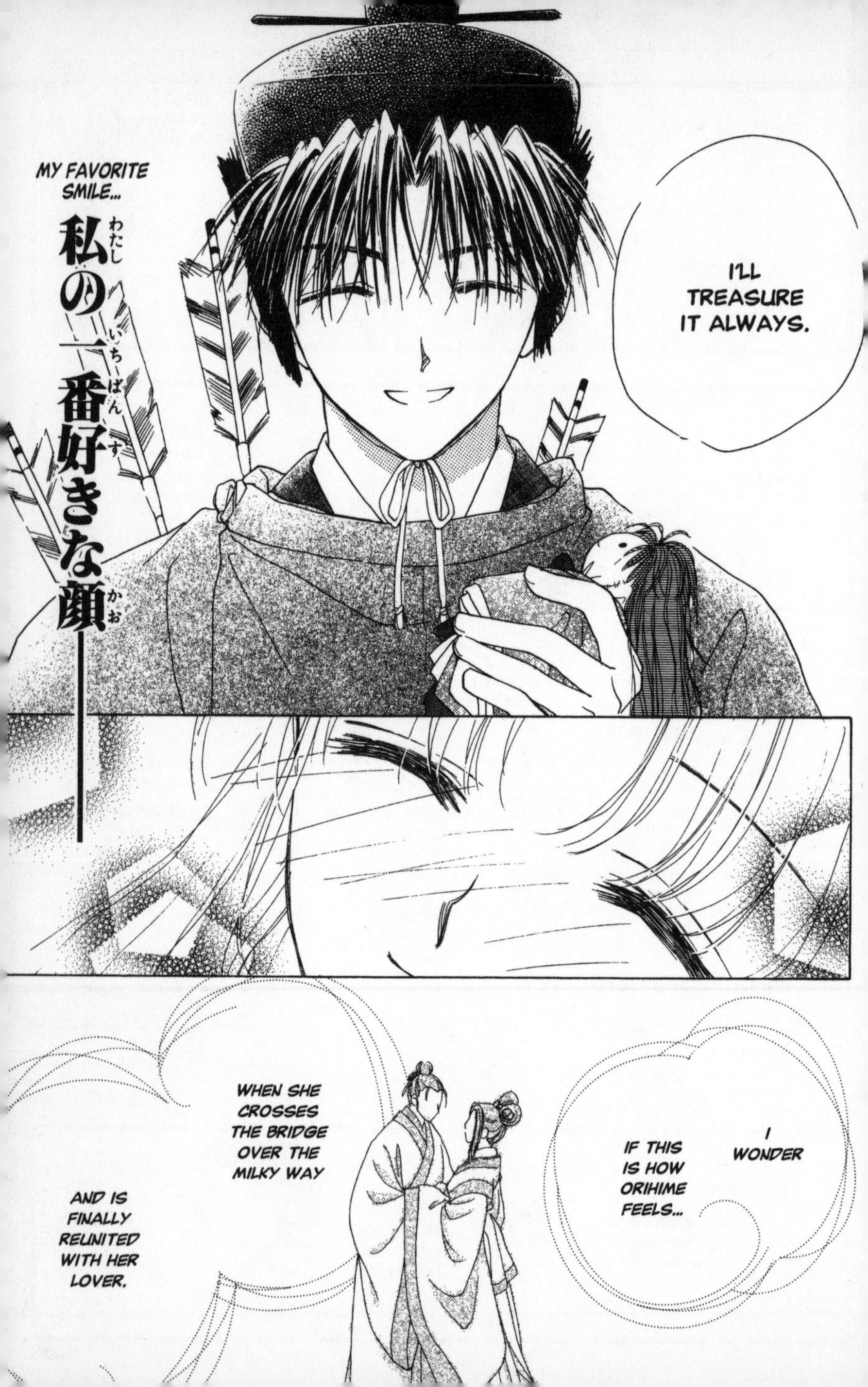
I'LL TREASURE IT ALWAYS.
MY FAVORITE SMILE...
私の一番好きな顔——
I WONDER
IF THIS IS HOW ORIHIME FEELS...
WHEN SHE CROSSES THE BRIDGE OVER THE MILKY WAY
AND IS FINALLY REUNITED WITH HER LOVER.

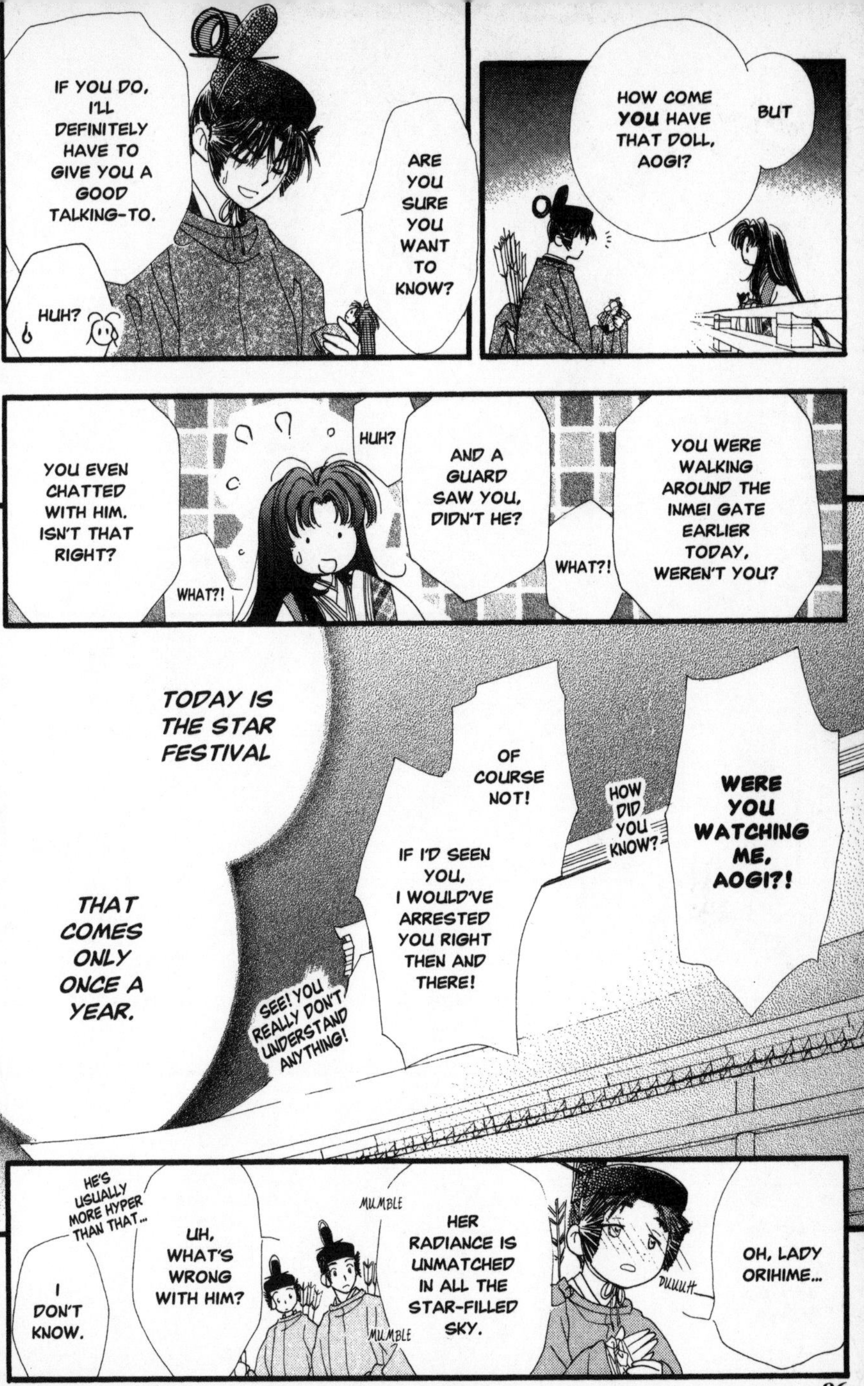
BUT
HOW COME YOU HAVE THAT DOLL, AOGI?
ARE YOU SURE YOU WANT TO KNOW?
IF YOU DO, I'LL DEFINITELY HAVE TO GIVE YOU A GOOD TALKING-TO.
HUH?
YOU WERE WALKING AROUND THE INMEI GATE EARLIER TODAY, WEREN'T YOU?
WHAT?!
AND A GUARD SAW YOU, DIDN'T HE?
HUH?
YOU EVEN CHATTED WITH HIM. ISN'T THAT RIGHT?
WHAT?!
WERE YOU WATCHING ME, AOGI?!
HOW DID YOU KNOW?
OF COURSE NOT!
IF I'D SEEN YOU, I WOULD'VE ARRESTED YOU RIGHT THEN AND THERE!
SEE! YOU REALLY DON'T UNDERSTAND ANYTHING!
TODAY IS THE STAR FESTIVAL
THAT COMES ONLY ONCE A YEAR.
OH, LADY ORIHIME...
DUUUH
HER RADIANCE IS UNMATCHED IN ALL THE STAR-FILLED SKY.
MUMBLE
MUMBLE
UH, WHAT'S WRONG WITH HIM?
HE'S USUALLY MORE HYPER THAN THAT...
I DON'T KNOW.

トラブル7 お友達(ともだち) Trouble 7 Friends

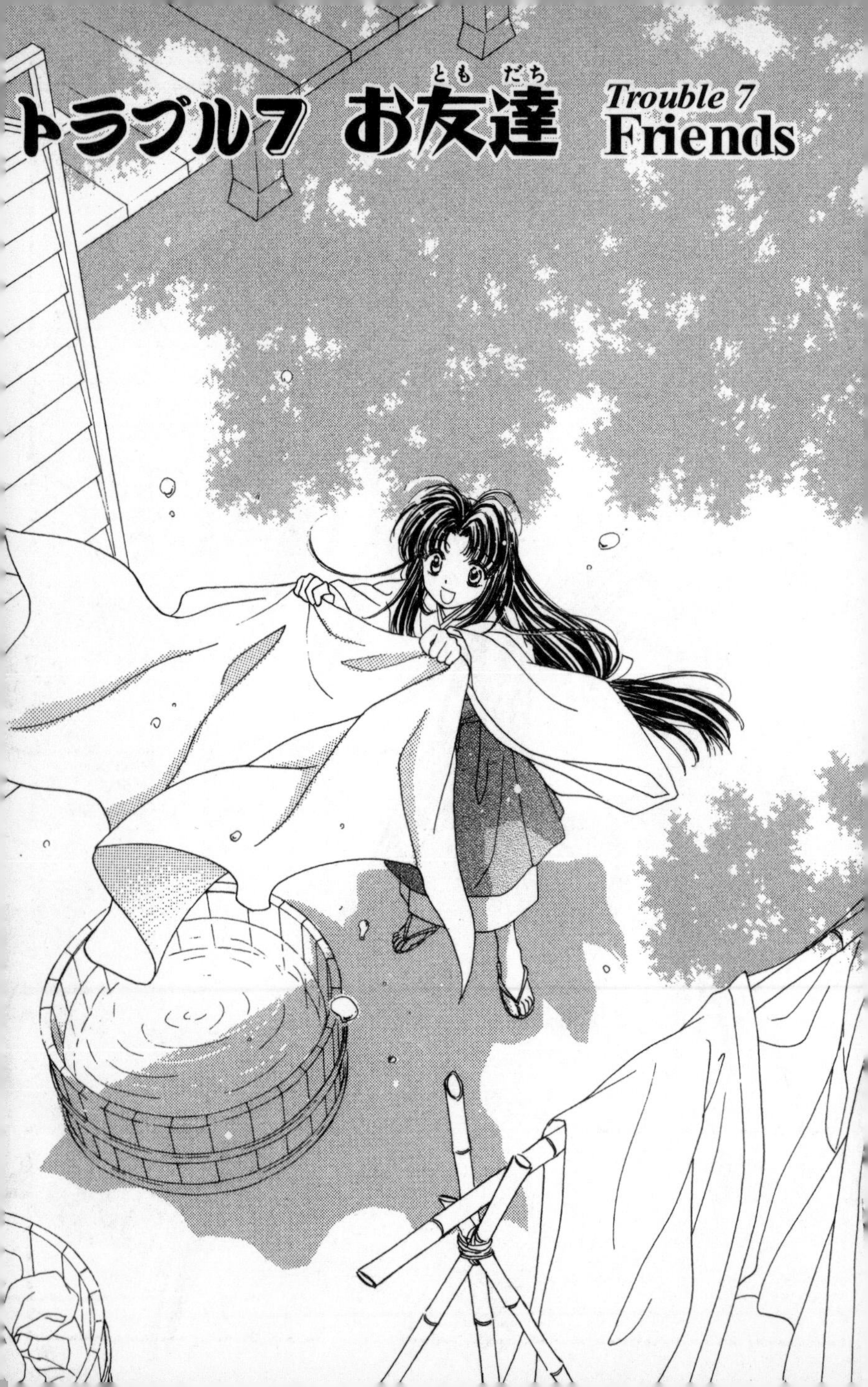

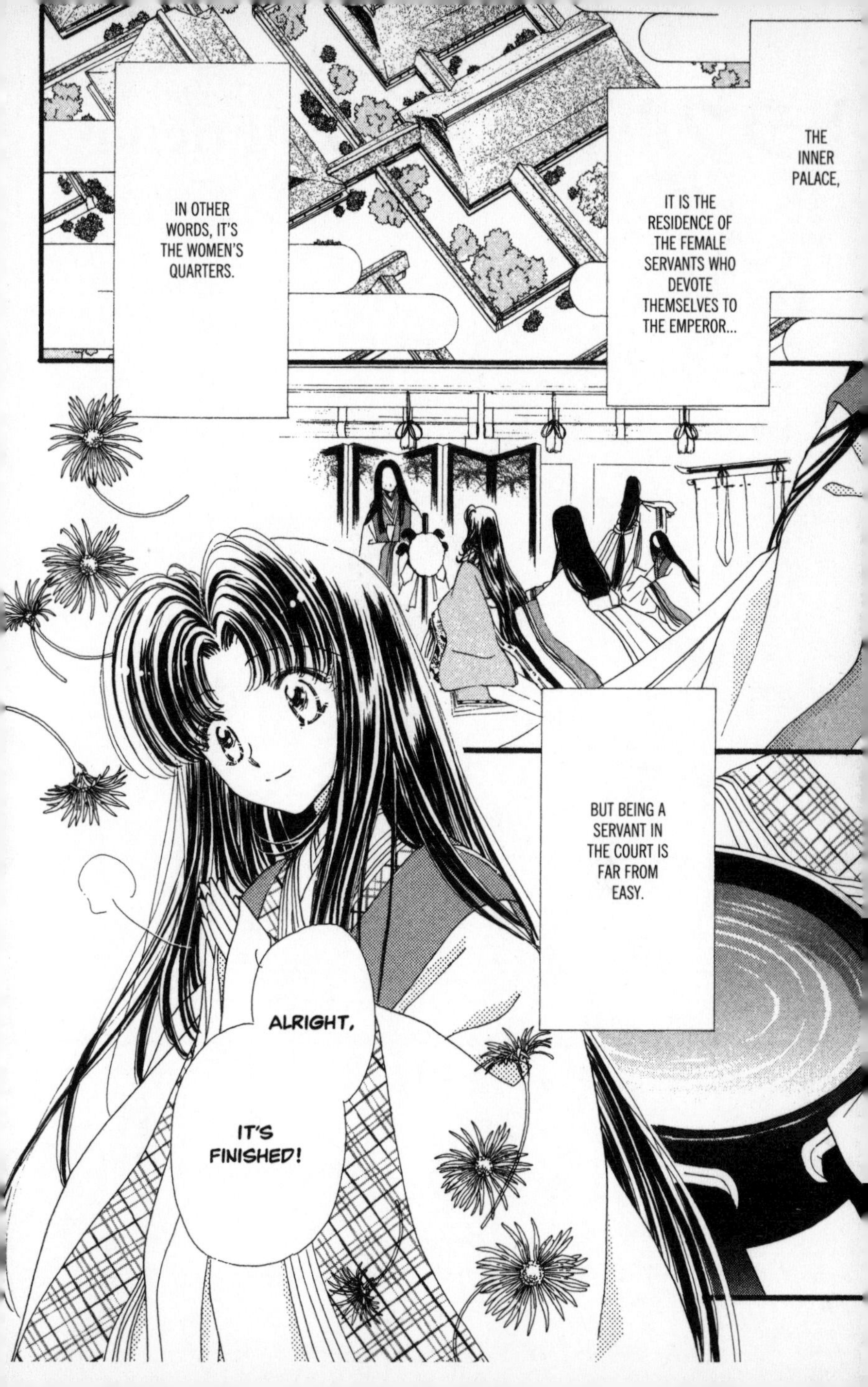
THE INNER PALACE,
IT IS THE RESIDENCE OF THE FEMALE SERVANTS WHO DEVOTE THEMSELVES TO THE EMPEROR...
IN OTHER WORDS, IT'S THE WOMEN'S QUARTERS.
BUT BEING A SERVANT IN THE COURT IS FAR FROM EASY.
ALRIGHT,
IT'S FINISHED!

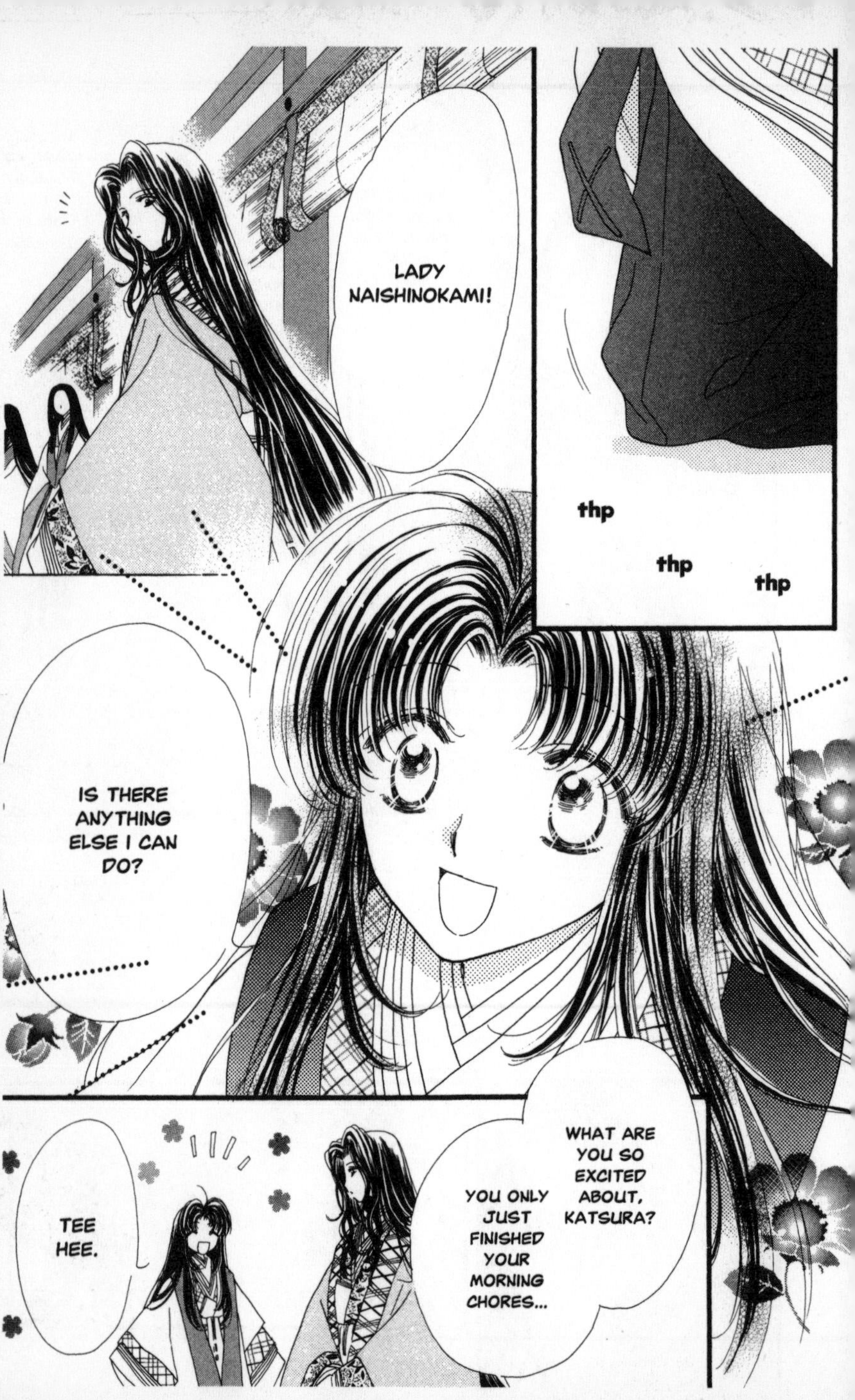
thp
thp
thp
LADY NAISHINOKAMI!
IS THERE ANYTHING ELSE I CAN DO?
WHAT ARE YOU SO EXCITED ABOUT, KATSURA?
YOU ONLY JUST FINISHED YOUR MORNING CHORES...
TEE HEE.

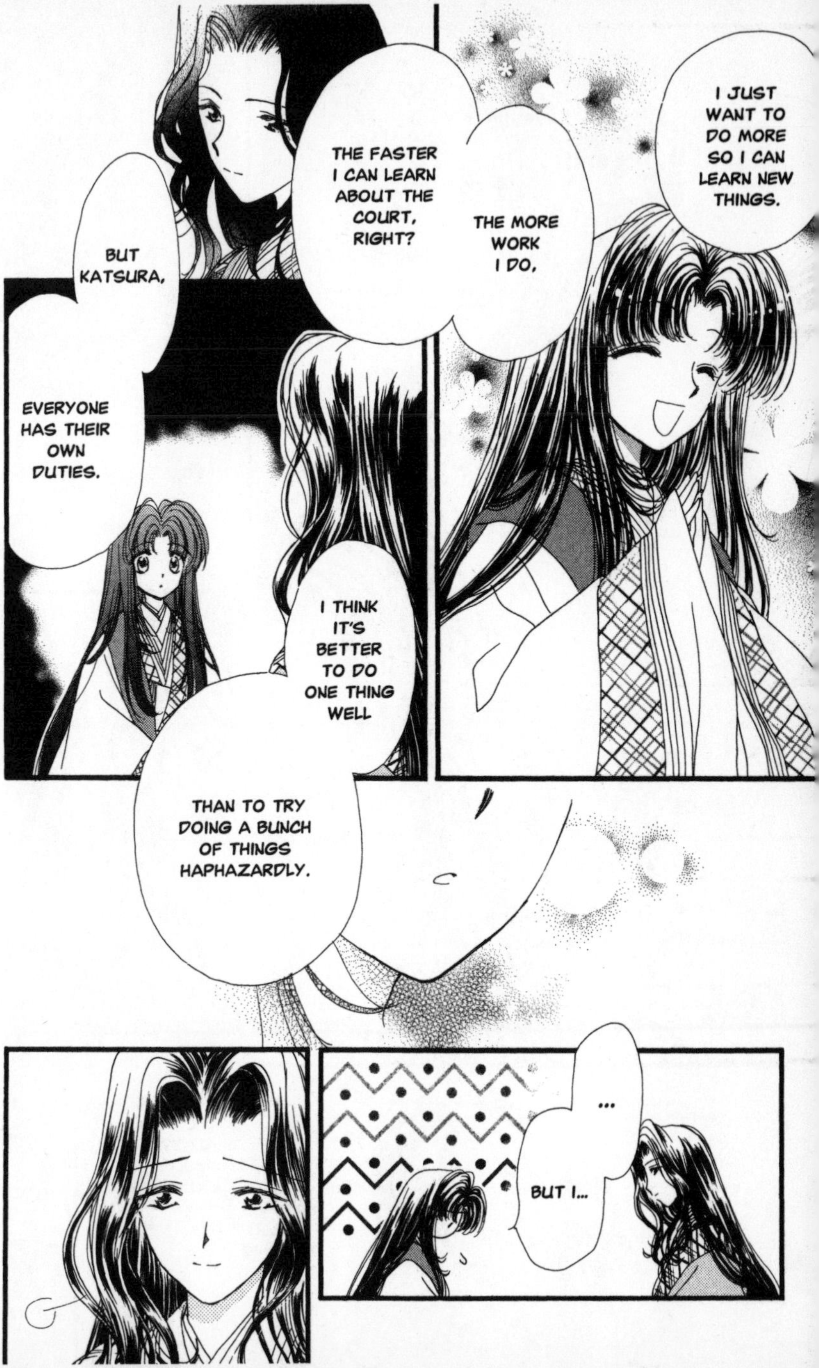
I JUST WANT TO DO MORE SO I CAN LEARN NEW THINGS.
THE MORE WORK I DO,
THE FASTER I CAN LEARN ABOUT THE COURT, RIGHT?
BUT KATSURA,
EVERYONE HAS THEIR OWN DUTIES.
I THINK IT'S BETTER TO DO ONE THING WELL
THAN TO TRY DOING A BUNCH OF THINGS HAPHAZARDLY.
...
BUT I...

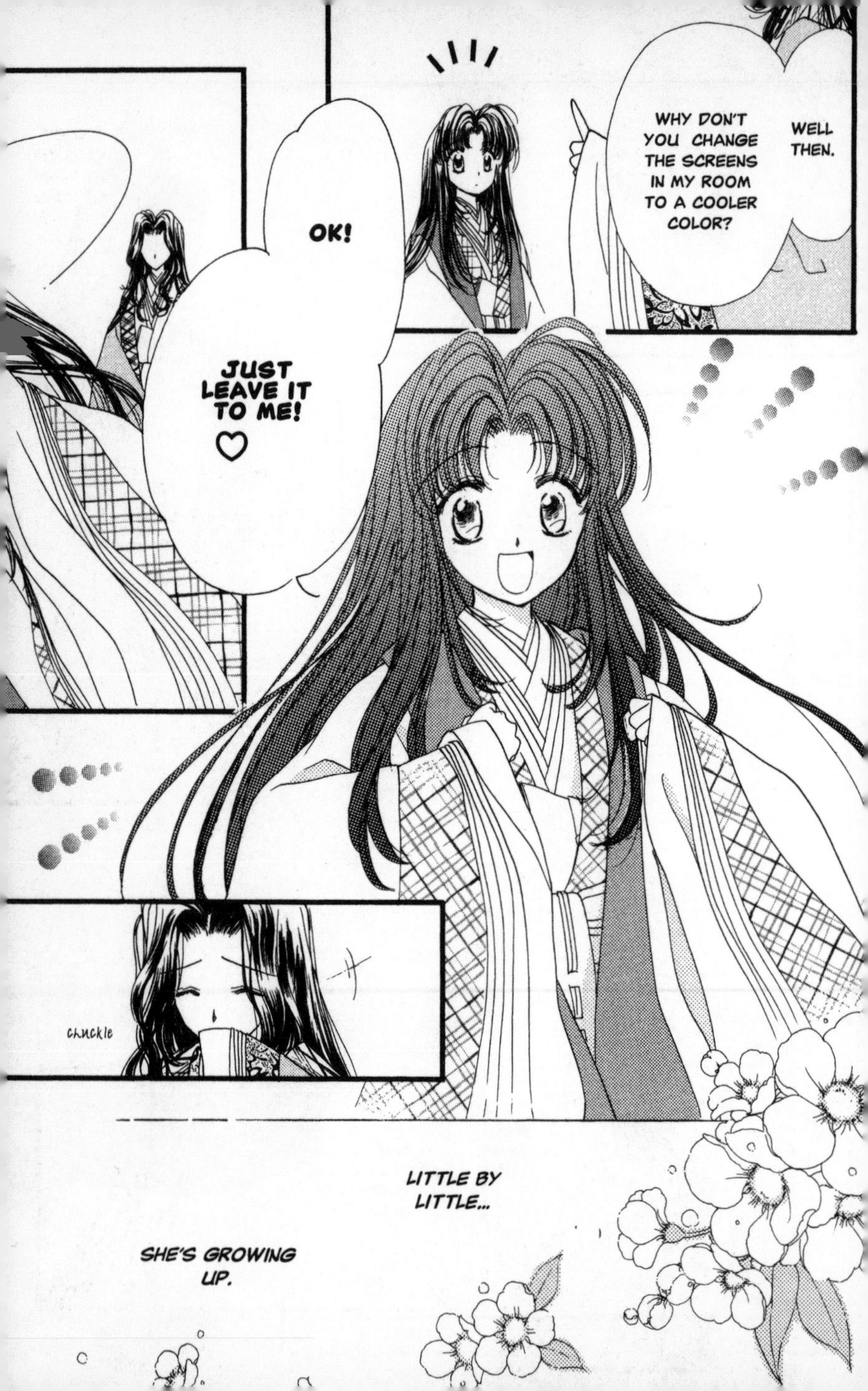
WELL THEN.
WHY DON'T YOU CHANGE THE SCREENS IN MY ROOM TO A COOLER COLOR?
OK!
JUST LEAVE IT TO ME! ♡
chuckle
LITTLE BY LITTLE...
SHE'S GROWING UP.

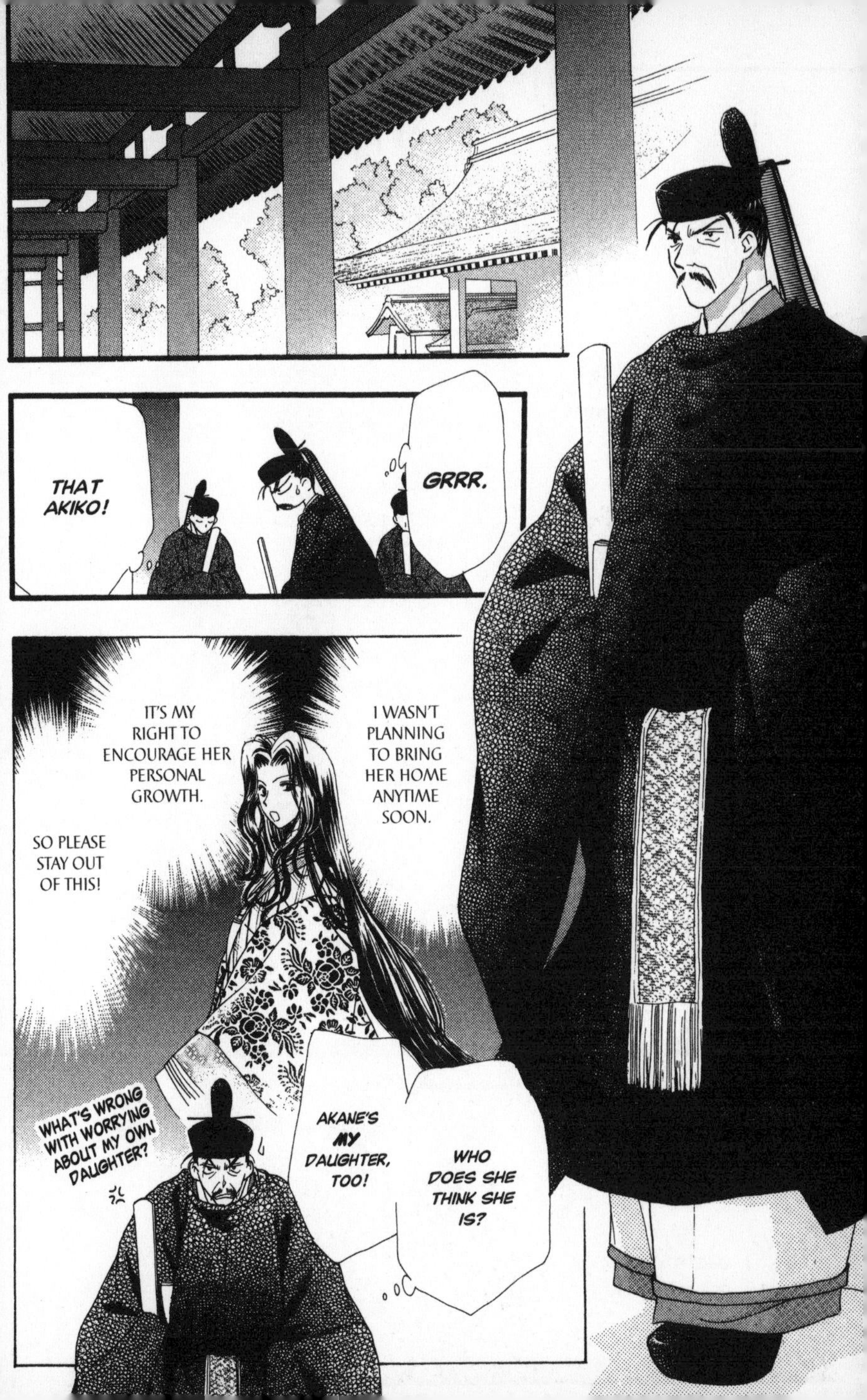
GRRR.
THAT AKIKO!
I WASN'T PLANNING TO BRING HER HOME ANYTIME SOON.
IT'S MY RIGHT TO ENCOURAGE HER PERSONAL GROWTH.
SO PLEASE STAY OUT OF THIS!
WHO DOES SHE THINK SHE IS?
AKANE'S MY DAUGHTER, TOO!
WHAT'S WRONG WITH WORRYING ABOUT MY OWN DAUGHTER?

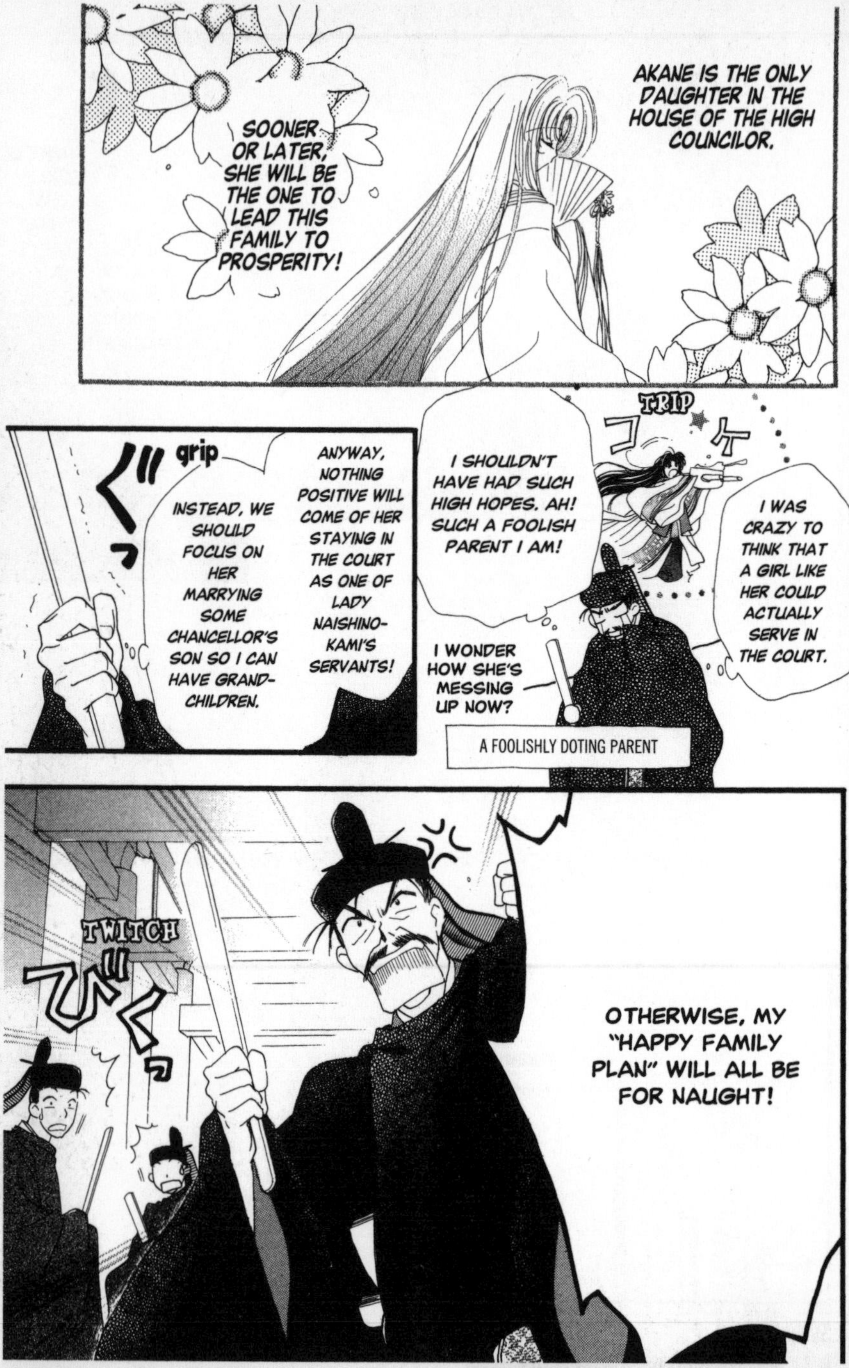
AKANE IS THE ONLY DAUGHTER IN THE HOUSE OF THE HIGH COUNCILOR.
SOONER OR LATER, SHE WILL BE THE ONE TO LEAD THIS FAMILY TO PROSPERITY!
TRIP
I WAS CRAZY TO THINK THAT A GIRL LIKE HER COULD ACTUALLY SERVE IN THE COURT.
I SHOULDN'T HAVE HAD SUCH HIGH HOPES. AH! SUCH A FOOLISH PARENT I AM!
I WONDER HOW SHE'S MESSING UP NOW?
A FOOLISHLY DOTING PARENT
ANYWAY, NOTHING POSITIVE WILL COME OF HER STAYING IN THE COURT AS ONE OF LADY NAISHINO-KAMI'S SERVANTS!
INSTEAD, WE SHOULD FOCUS ON HER MARRYING SOME CHANCELLOR'S SON SO I CAN HAVE GRAND-CHILDREN.
grip
OTHERWISE, MY "HAPPY FAMILY PLAN" WILL ALL BE FOR NAUGHT!
TWITCH

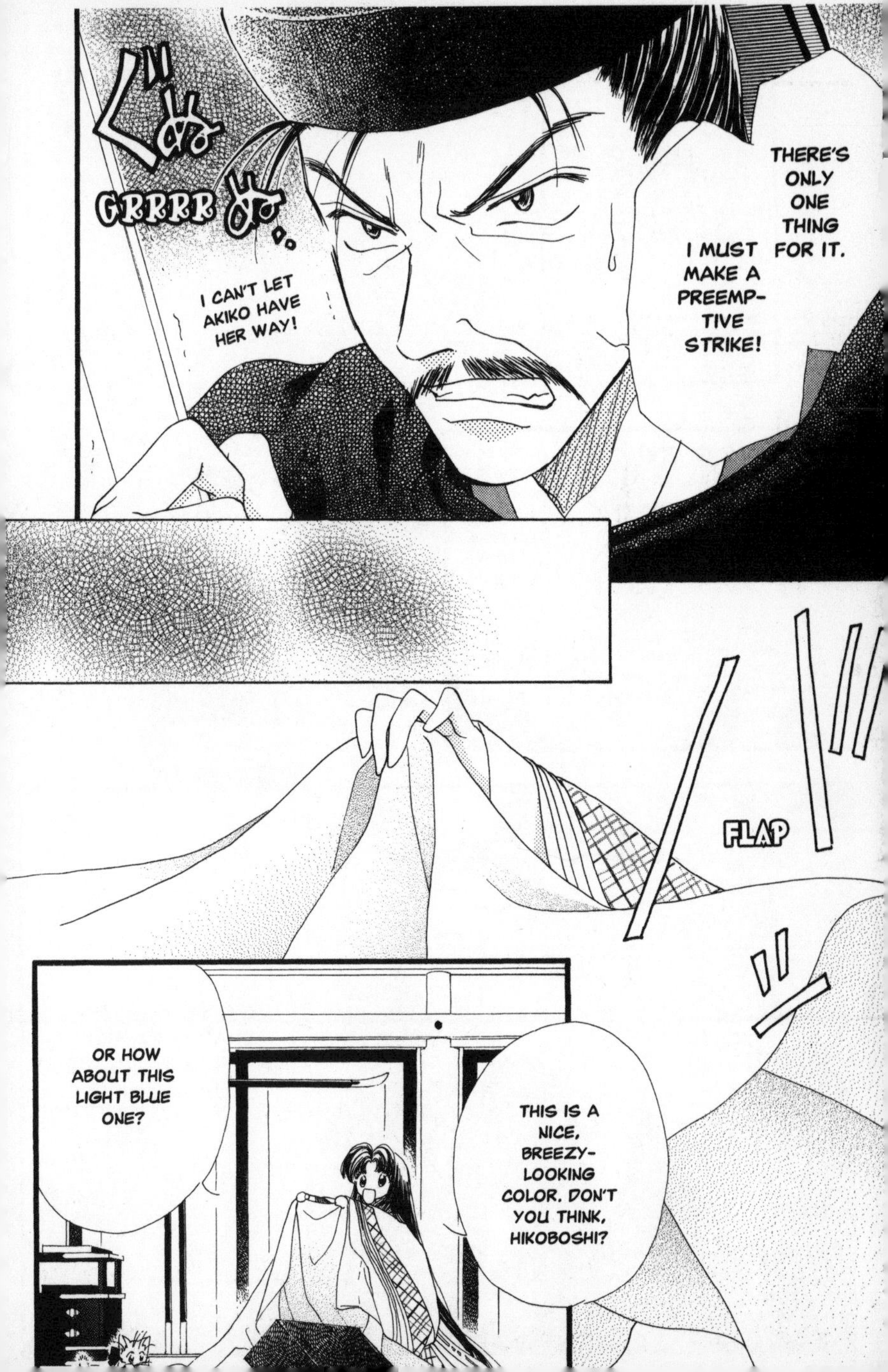
GRRRR
THERE'S ONLY ONE THING FOR IT.
I MUST MAKE A PREEMP-TIVE STRIKE!
I CAN'T LET AKIKO HAVE HER WAY!
FLAP
THIS IS A NICE, BREEZY-LOOKING COLOR. DON'T YOU THINK, HIKOBOSHI?
OR HOW ABOUT THIS LIGHT BLUE ONE?

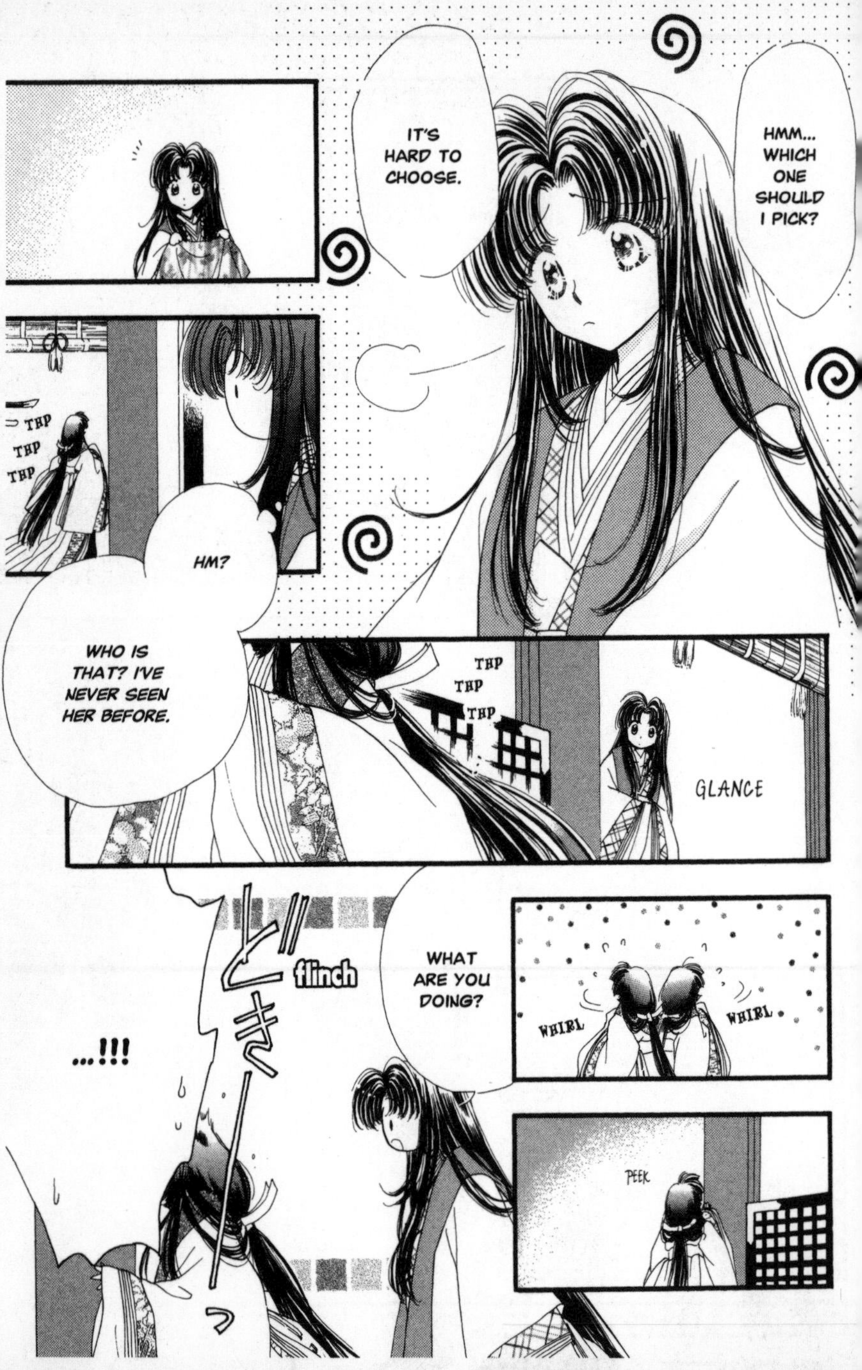
HMM... WHICH ONE SHOULD I PICK?
IT'S HARD TO CHOOSE.
TBP
TBP
TBP
HM?
WHO IS THAT? I'VE NEVER SEEN HER BEFORE.
TBP
TBP
TBP
GLANCE
WHIRL
WHIRL
PEEK
WHAT ARE YOU DOING?
どきーっ
flinch
...!!!

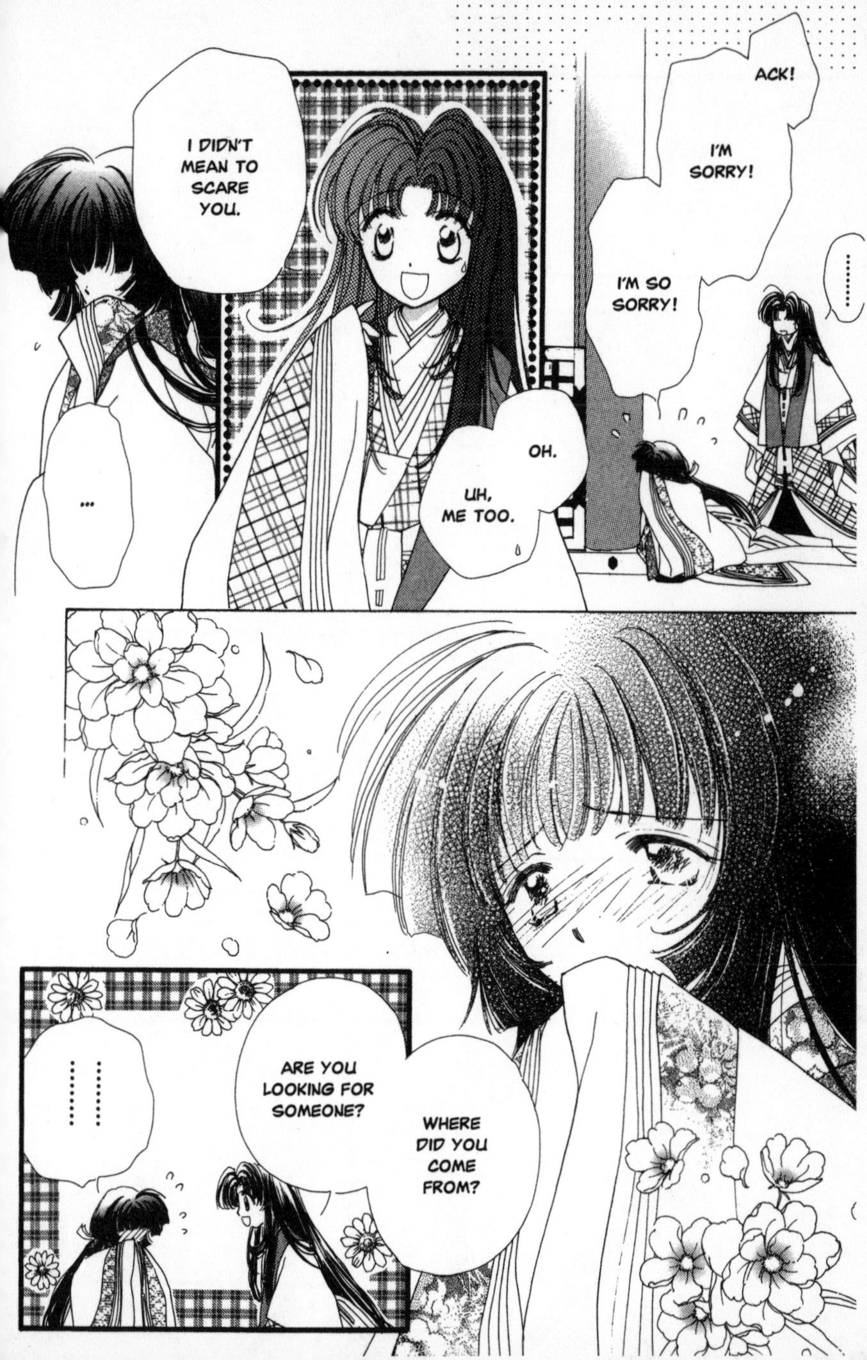
ACK!
I'M SORRY!
I'M SO SORRY!
......
OH.
UH, ME TOO.
I DIDN'T MEAN TO SCARE YOU.
...
WHERE DID YOU COME FROM?
ARE YOU LOOKING FOR SOMEONE?
......

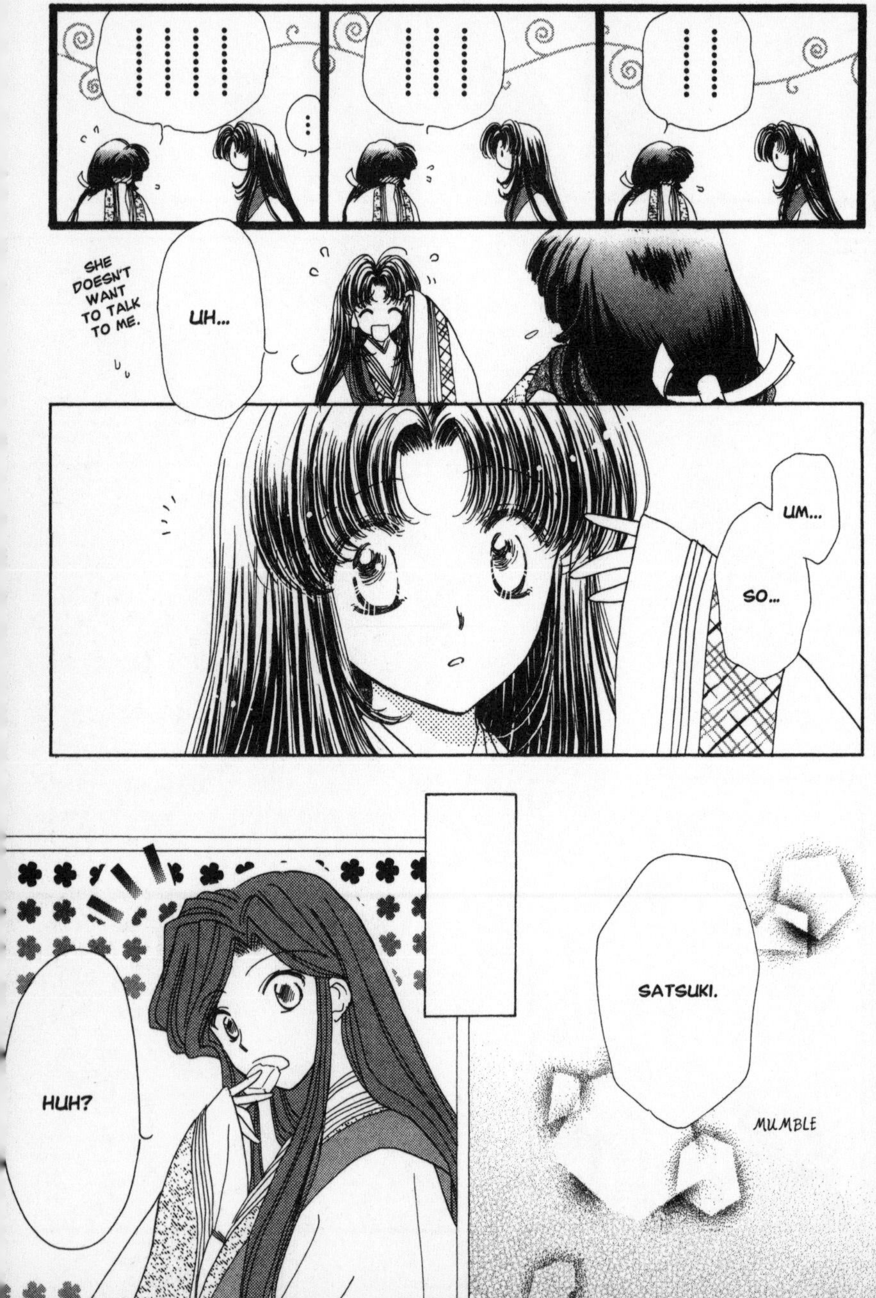

UH...
SHE DOESN'T WANT TO TALK TO ME.
UM...
SO...
SATSUKI.
MUMBLE
HUH?

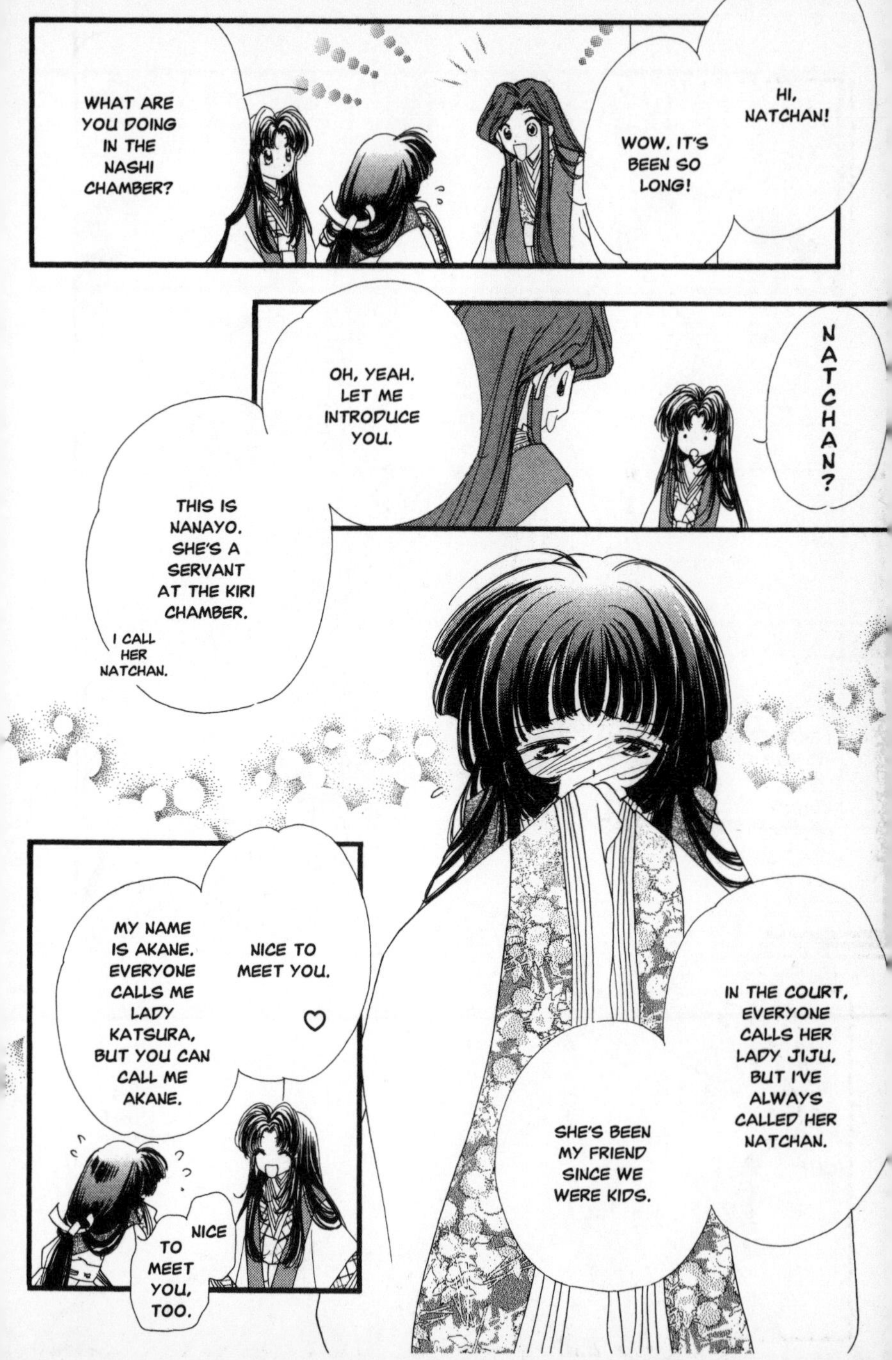
HI, NATCHAN!
WOW. IT'S BEEN SO LONG!
WHAT ARE YOU DOING IN THE NASHI CHAMBER?
NATCHAN?
OH, YEAH. LET ME INTRODUCE YOU.
THIS IS NANAYO. SHE'S A SERVANT AT THE KIRI CHAMBER.
I CALL HER NATCHAN.
IN THE COURT, EVERYONE CALLS HER LADY JIJU, BUT I'VE ALWAYS CALLED HER NATCHAN.
SHE'S BEEN MY FRIEND SINCE WE WERE KIDS.
NICE TO MEET YOU. ♡
MY NAME IS AKANE. EVERYONE CALLS ME LADY KATSURA, BUT YOU CAN CALL ME AKANE.
NICE TO MEET YOU, TOO.

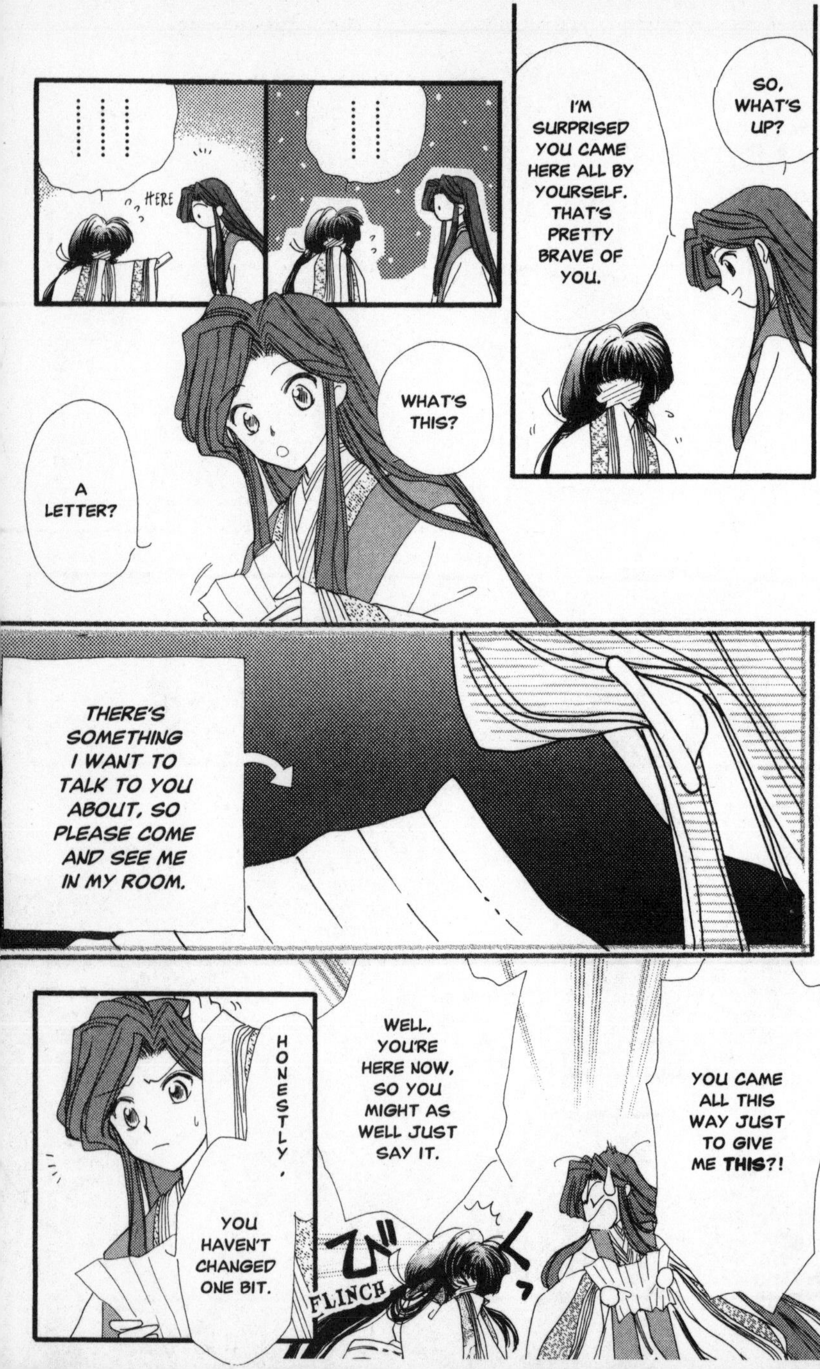
SO, WHAT'S UP?
I'M SURPRISED YOU CAME HERE ALL BY YOURSELF. THAT'S PRETTY BRAVE OF YOU.
......
......
HERE
WHAT'S THIS?
A LETTER?
THERE'S SOMETHING I WANT TO TALK TO YOU ABOUT, SO PLEASE COME AND SEE ME IN MY ROOM.
YOU CAME ALL THIS WAY JUST TO GIVE ME **THIS**?!
FLINCH
WELL, YOU'RE HERE NOW, SO YOU MIGHT AS WELL JUST SAY IT.
HONESTLY,
YOU HAVEN'T CHANGED ONE BIT.

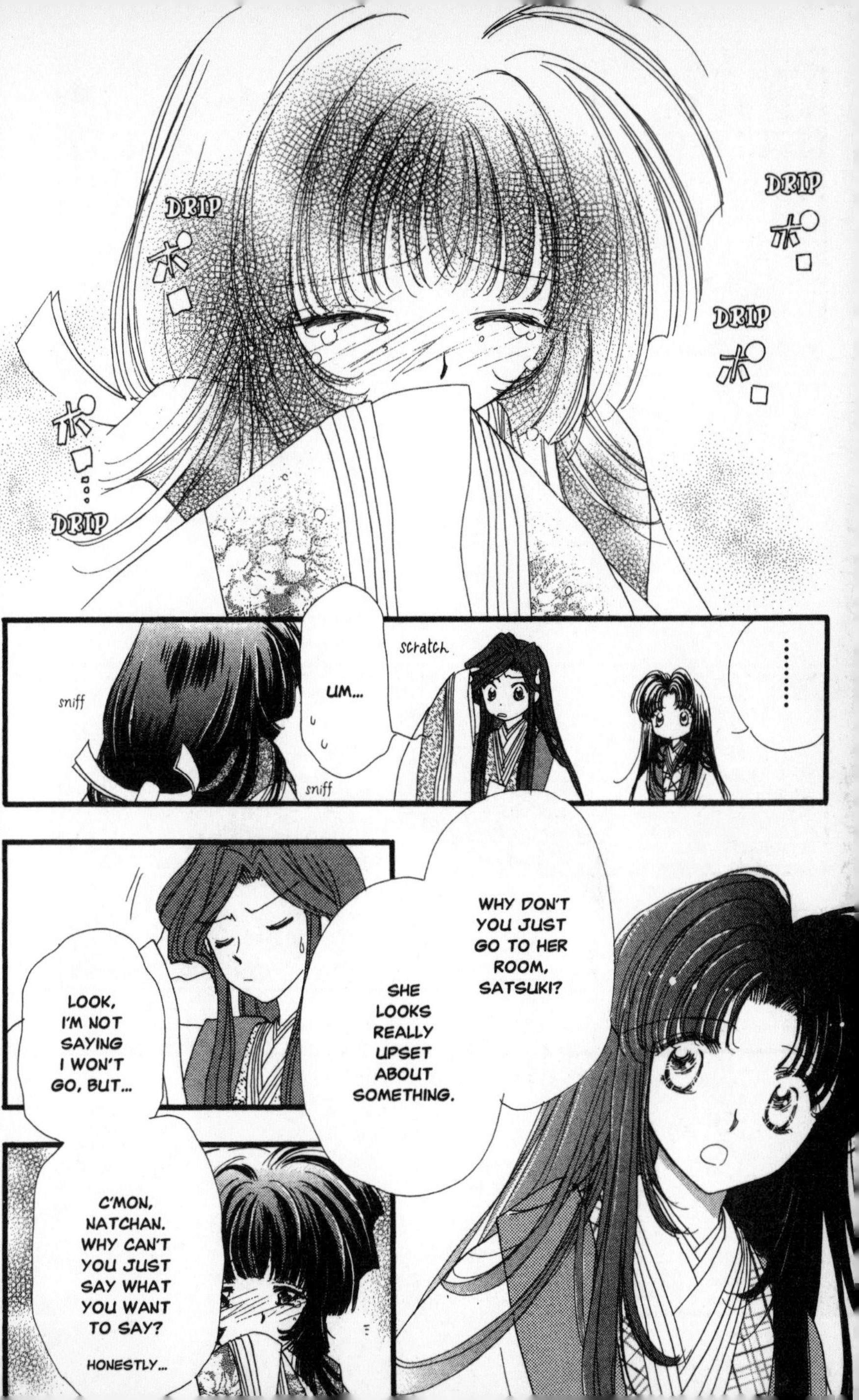
DRIP
ポロ
DRIP
ポロ
DRIP
ポロ
DRIP
ポロ...
DRIP
......
scratch
UM...
sniff
sniff
WHY DON'T YOU JUST GO TO HER ROOM, SATSUKI?
SHE LOOKS REALLY UPSET ABOUT SOMETHING.
LOOK, I'M NOT SAYING I WON'T GO, BUT...
C'MON, NATCHAN. WHY CAN'T YOU JUST SAY WHAT YOU WANT TO SAY?
HONESTLY...

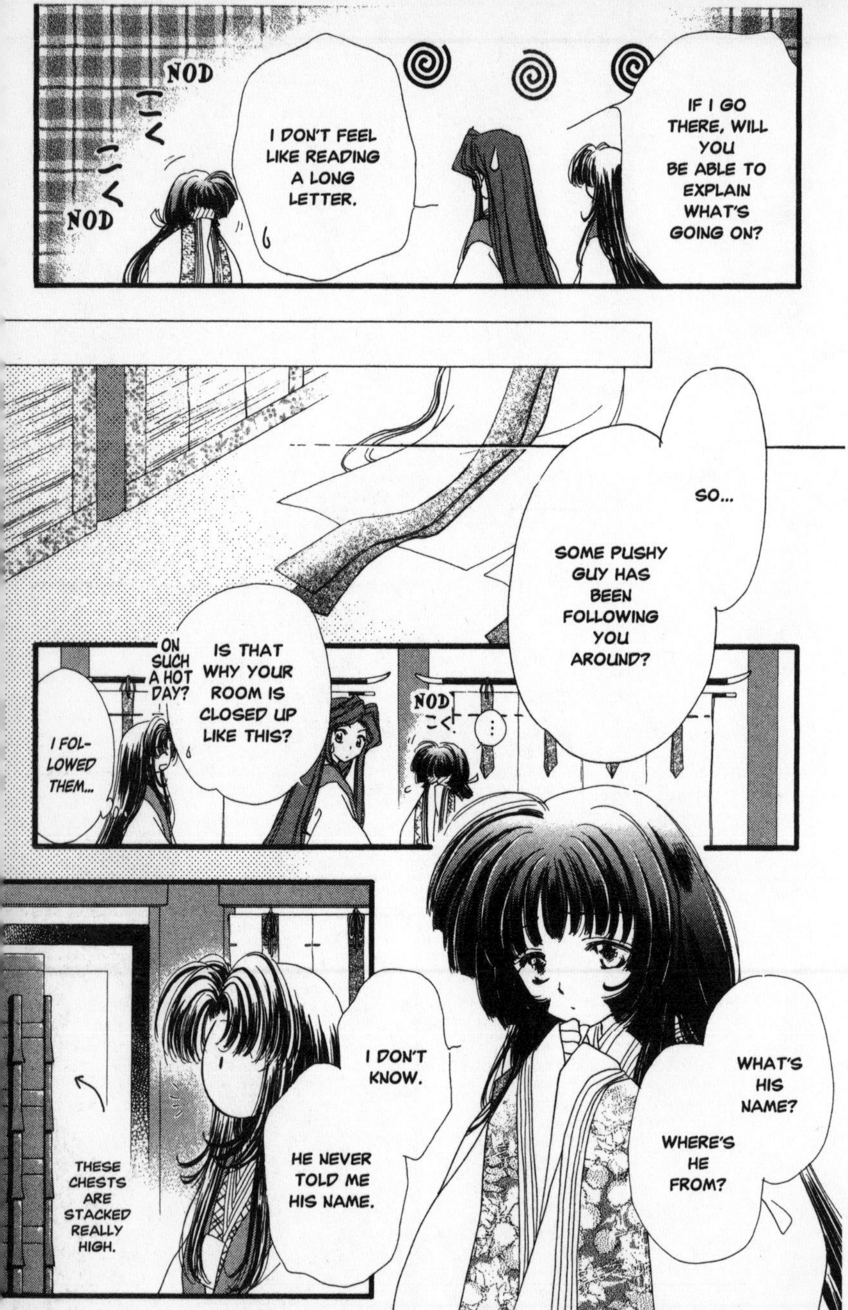
IF I GO THERE, WILL YOU BE ABLE TO EXPLAIN WHAT'S GOING ON?
I DON'T FEEL LIKE READING A LONG LETTER.
NOD
こく
こく
NOD
SO...
SOME PUSHY GUY HAS BEEN FOLLOWING YOU AROUND?
NOD
こく
...
IS THAT WHY YOUR ROOM IS CLOSED UP LIKE THIS?
ON SUCH A HOT DAY?
I FOL-LOWED THEM...
WHAT'S HIS NAME?
WHERE'S HE FROM?
I DON'T KNOW.
HE NEVER TOLD ME HIS NAME.
THESE CHESTS ARE STACKED REALLY HIGH.

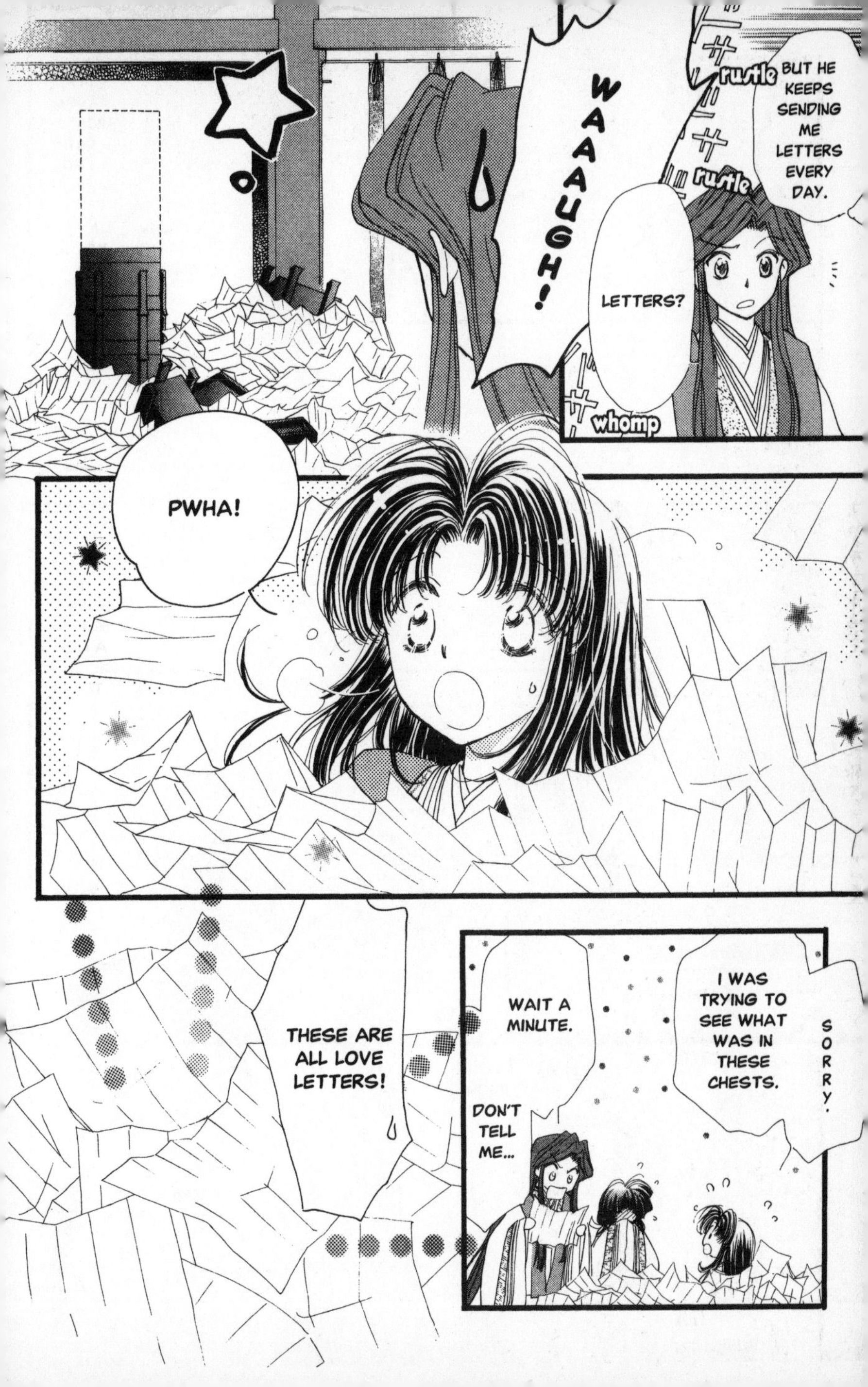
rustle
rustle
BUT HE KEEPS SENDING ME LETTERS EVERY DAY.
LETTERS?
WAAAAUGH!
whomp
PWHA!
I WAS TRYING TO SEE WHAT WAS IN THESE CHESTS.
SORRY.
WAIT A MINUTE.
DON'T TELL ME...
THESE ARE ALL LOVE LETTERS!

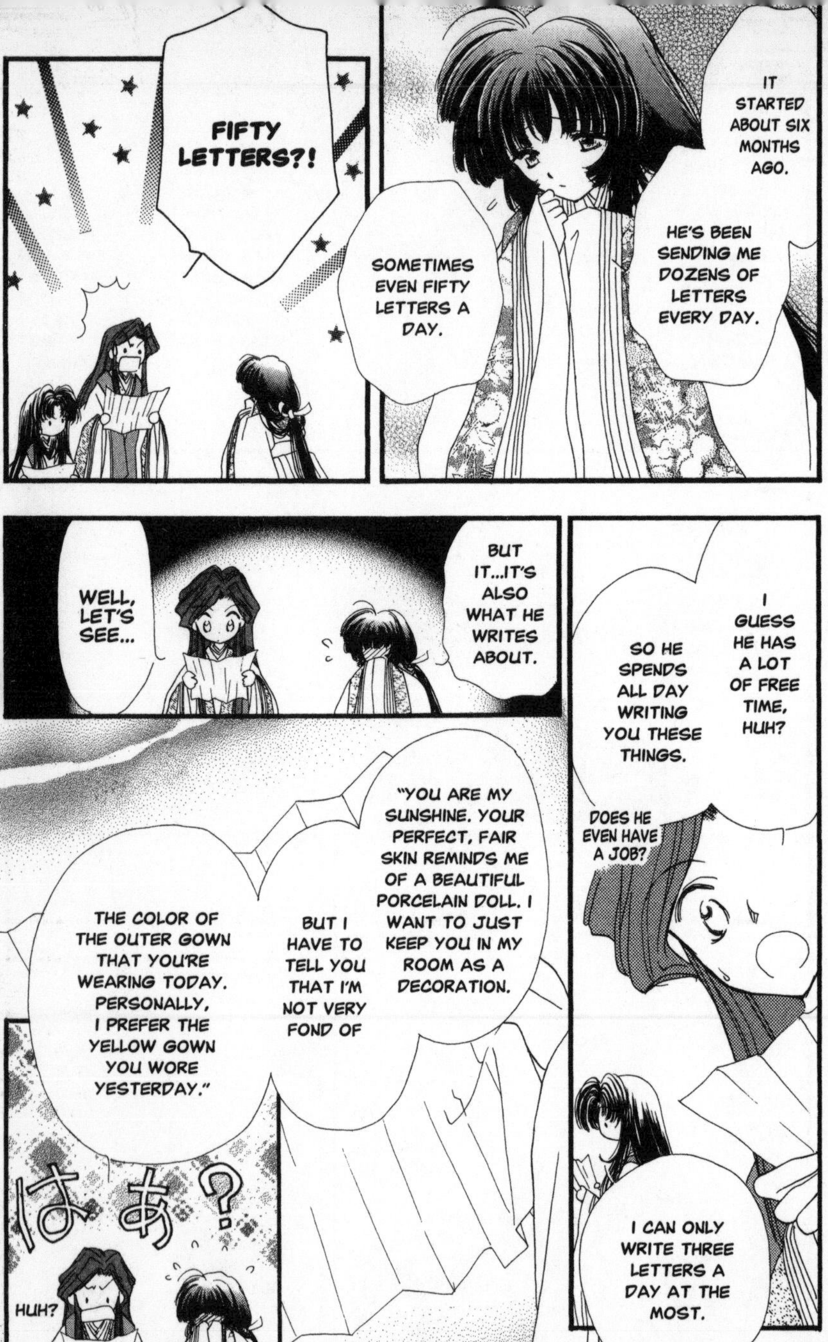
IT STARTED ABOUT SIX MONTHS AGO.
HE'S BEEN SENDING ME DOZENS OF LETTERS EVERY DAY.
SOMETIMES EVEN FIFTY LETTERS A DAY.
FIFTY LETTERS?!
I GUESS HE HAS A LOT OF FREE TIME, HUH?
SO HE SPENDS ALL DAY WRITING YOU THESE THINGS.
DOES HE EVEN HAVE A JOB?
I CAN ONLY WRITE THREE LETTERS A DAY AT THE MOST.
BUT IT...IT'S ALSO WHAT HE WRITES ABOUT.
WELL, LET'S SEE...
"YOU ARE MY SUNSHINE. YOUR PERFECT, FAIR SKIN REMINDS ME OF A BEAUTIFUL PORCELAIN DOLL. I WANT TO JUST KEEP YOU IN MY ROOM AS A DECORATION.
BUT I HAVE TO TELL YOU THAT I'M NOT VERY FOND OF
THE COLOR OF THE OUTER GOWN THAT YOU'RE WEARING TODAY. PERSONALLY, I PREFER THE YELLOW GOWN YOU WORE YESTERDAY."
はあ?
HUH?

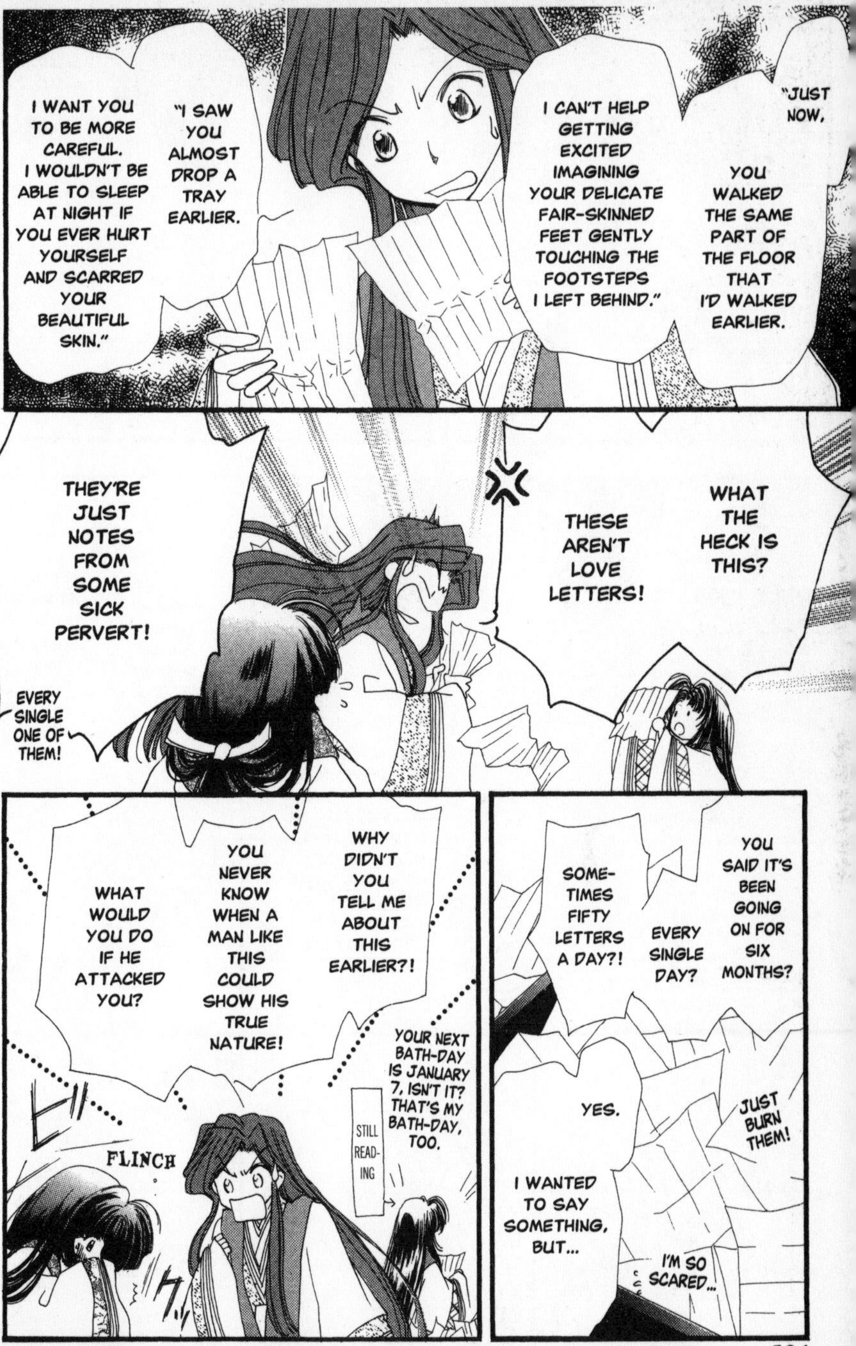
"JUST NOW, YOU WALKED THE SAME PART OF THE FLOOR THAT I'D WALKED EARLIER.
I CAN'T HELP GETTING EXCITED IMAGINING YOUR DELICATE FAIR-SKINNED FEET GENTLY TOUCHING THE FOOTSTEPS I LEFT BEHIND."
"I SAW YOU ALMOST DROP A TRAY EARLIER.
I WANT YOU TO BE MORE CAREFUL. I WOULDN'T BE ABLE TO SLEEP AT NIGHT IF YOU EVER HURT YOURSELF AND SCARRED YOUR BEAUTIFUL SKIN."
WHAT THE HECK IS THIS?
THESE AREN'T LOVE LETTERS!
THEY'RE JUST NOTES FROM SOME SICK PERVERT!
EVERY SINGLE ONE OF THEM!
YOU SAID IT'S BEEN GOING ON FOR SIX MONTHS?
EVERY SINGLE DAY?
SOME-TIMES FIFTY LETTERS A DAY?!
JUST BURN THEM!
YES.
I WANTED TO SAY SOMETHING, BUT...
I'M SO SCARED...
WHY DIDN'T YOU TELL ME ABOUT THIS EARLIER?!
YOU NEVER KNOW WHEN A MAN LIKE THIS COULD SHOW HIS TRUE NATURE!
WHAT WOULD YOU DO IF HE ATTACKED YOU?
YOUR NEXT BATH-DAY IS JANUARY 7, ISN'T IT? THAT'S MY BATH-DAY, TOO.
STILL READ-ING
FLINCH

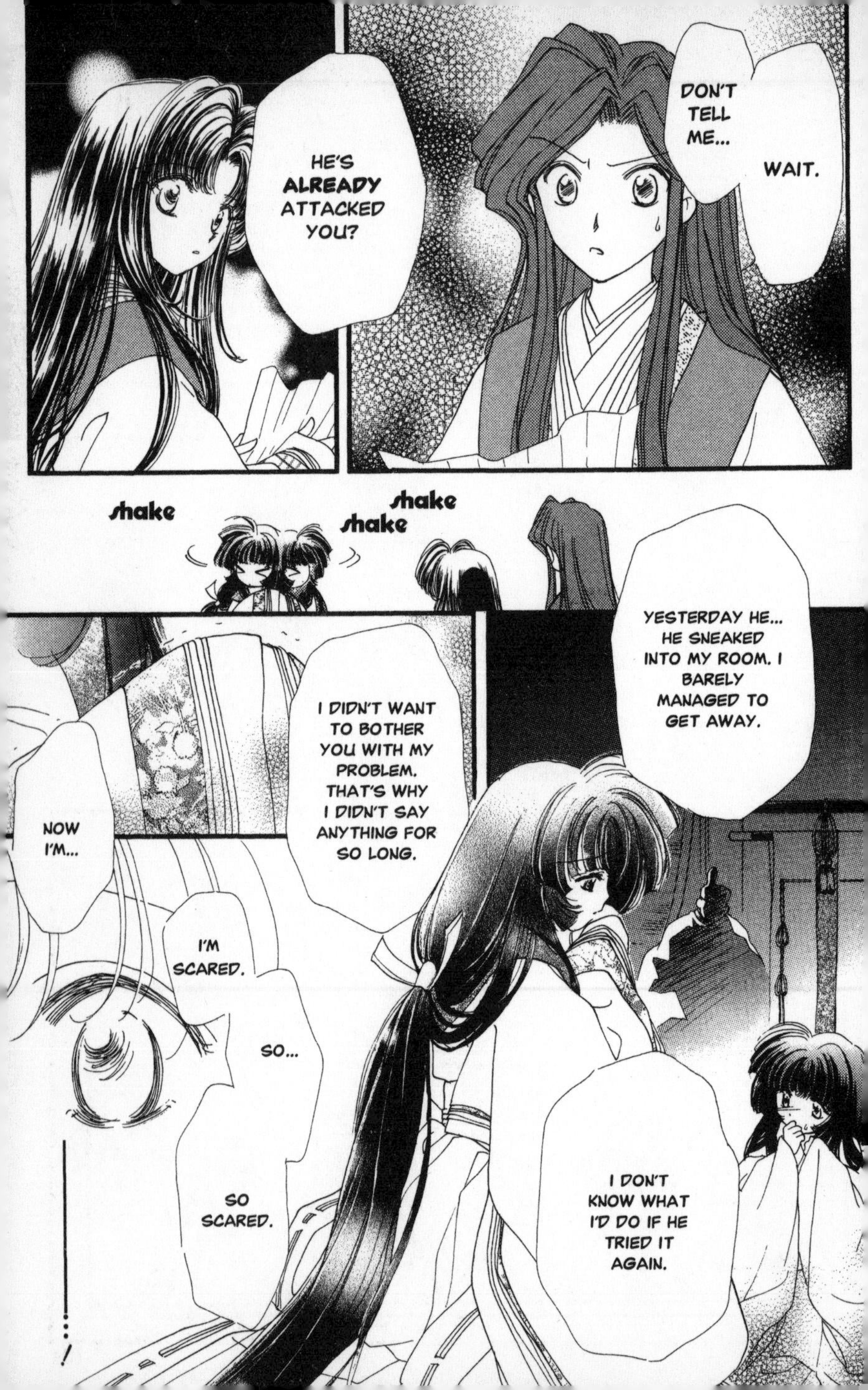
DON'T TELL ME...
WAIT.
HE'S ALREADY ATTACKED YOU?
shake
shake
shake
YESTERDAY HE... HE SNEAKED INTO MY ROOM. I BARELY MANAGED TO GET AWAY.
I DIDN'T WANT TO BOTHER YOU WITH MY PROBLEM. THAT'S WHY I DIDN'T SAY ANYTHING FOR SO LONG.
NOW I'M...
I'M SCARED.
SO...
SO SCARED.
I DON'T KNOW WHAT I'D DO IF HE TRIED IT AGAIN.
......!

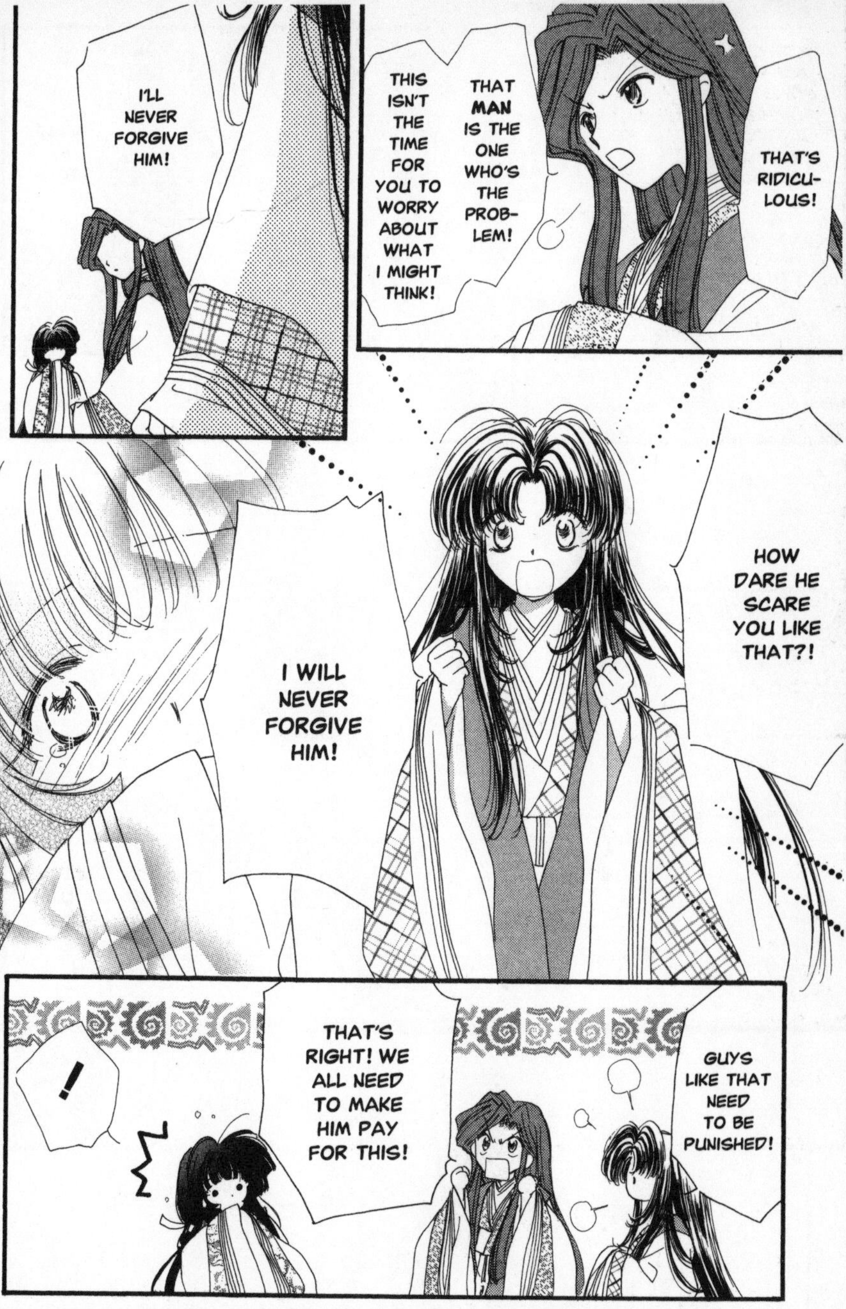
THAT'S RIDICULOUS!
THAT MAN IS THE ONE WHO'S THE PROBLEM!
THIS ISN'T THE TIME FOR YOU TO WORRY ABOUT WHAT I MIGHT THINK!
I'LL NEVER FORGIVE HIM!
HOW DARE HE SCARE YOU LIKE THAT?!
I WILL NEVER FORGIVE HIM!
GUYS LIKE THAT NEED TO BE PUNISHED!
THAT'S RIGHT! WE ALL NEED TO MAKE HIM PAY FOR THIS!
!

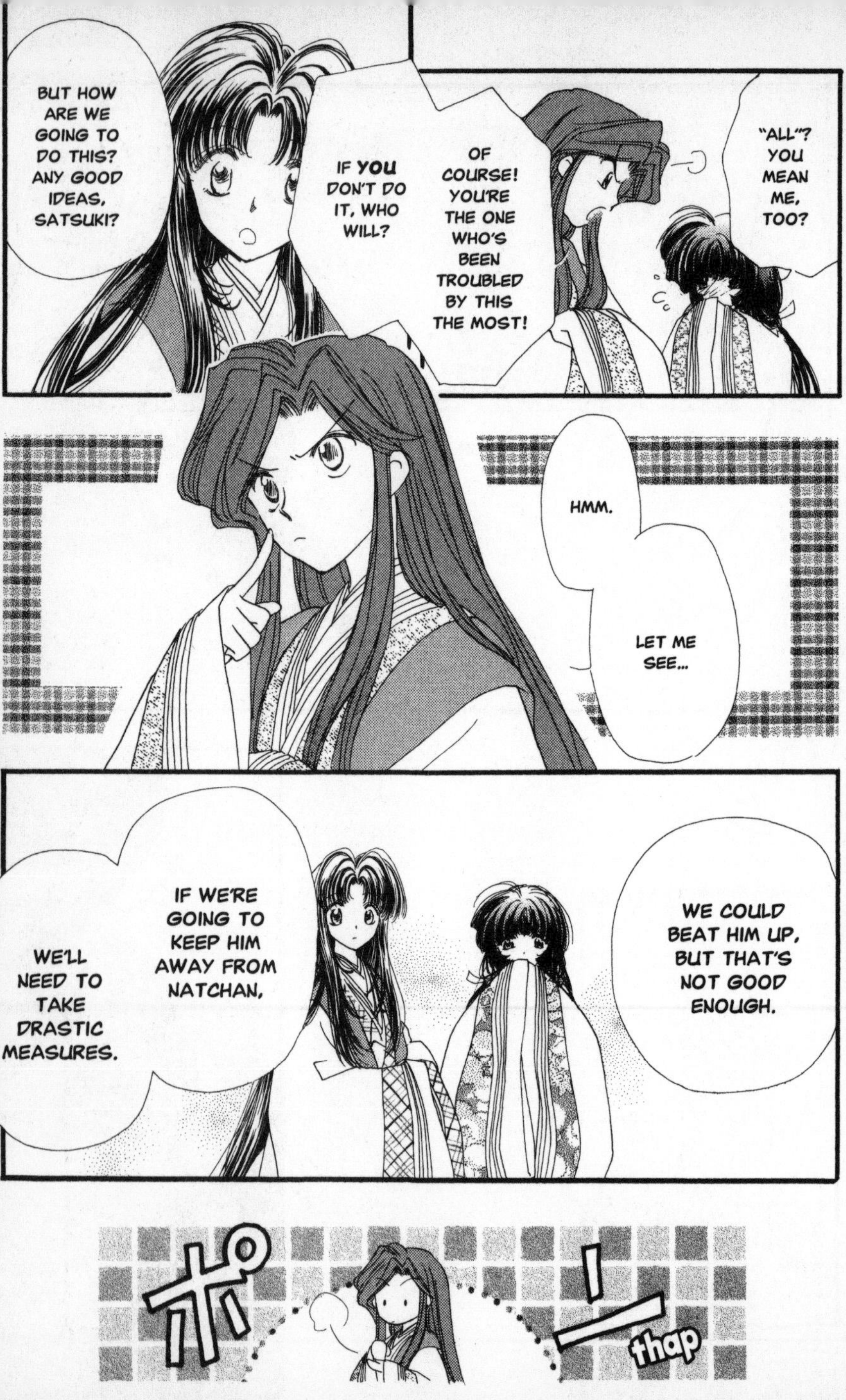
"ALL"? YOU MEAN ME, TOO?
OF COURSE! YOU'RE THE ONE WHO'S BEEN TROUBLED BY THIS THE MOST!
IF **YOU** DON'T DO IT, WHO WILL?
BUT HOW ARE WE GOING TO DO THIS? ANY GOOD IDEAS, SATSUKI?
HMM.
LET ME SEE...
WE COULD BEAT HIM UP, BUT THAT'S NOT GOOD ENOUGH.
IF WE'RE GOING TO KEEP HIM AWAY FROM NATCHAN,
WE'LL NEED TO TAKE DRASTIC MEASURES.
ポ
ー
thap

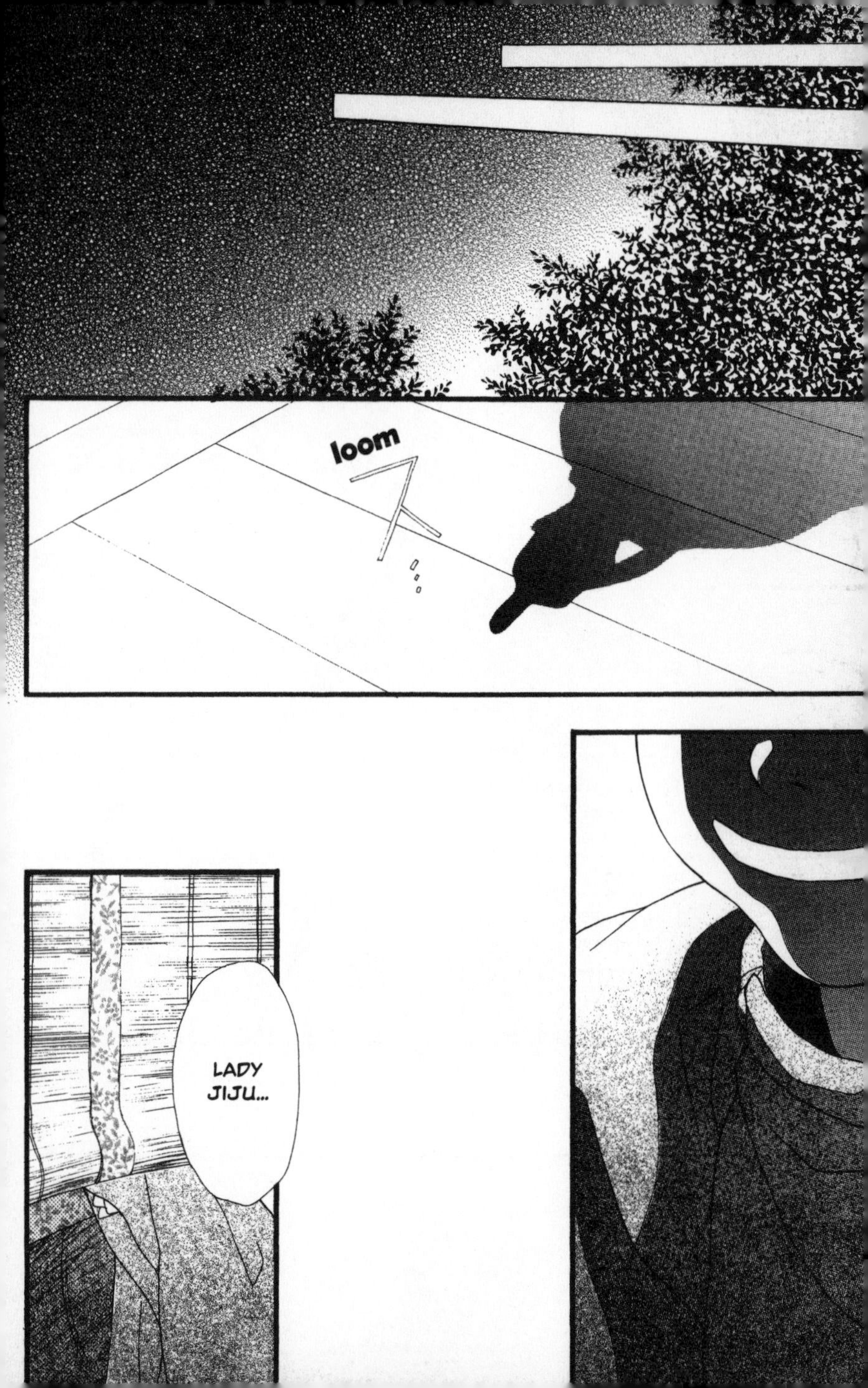
loom
LADY JIJU...

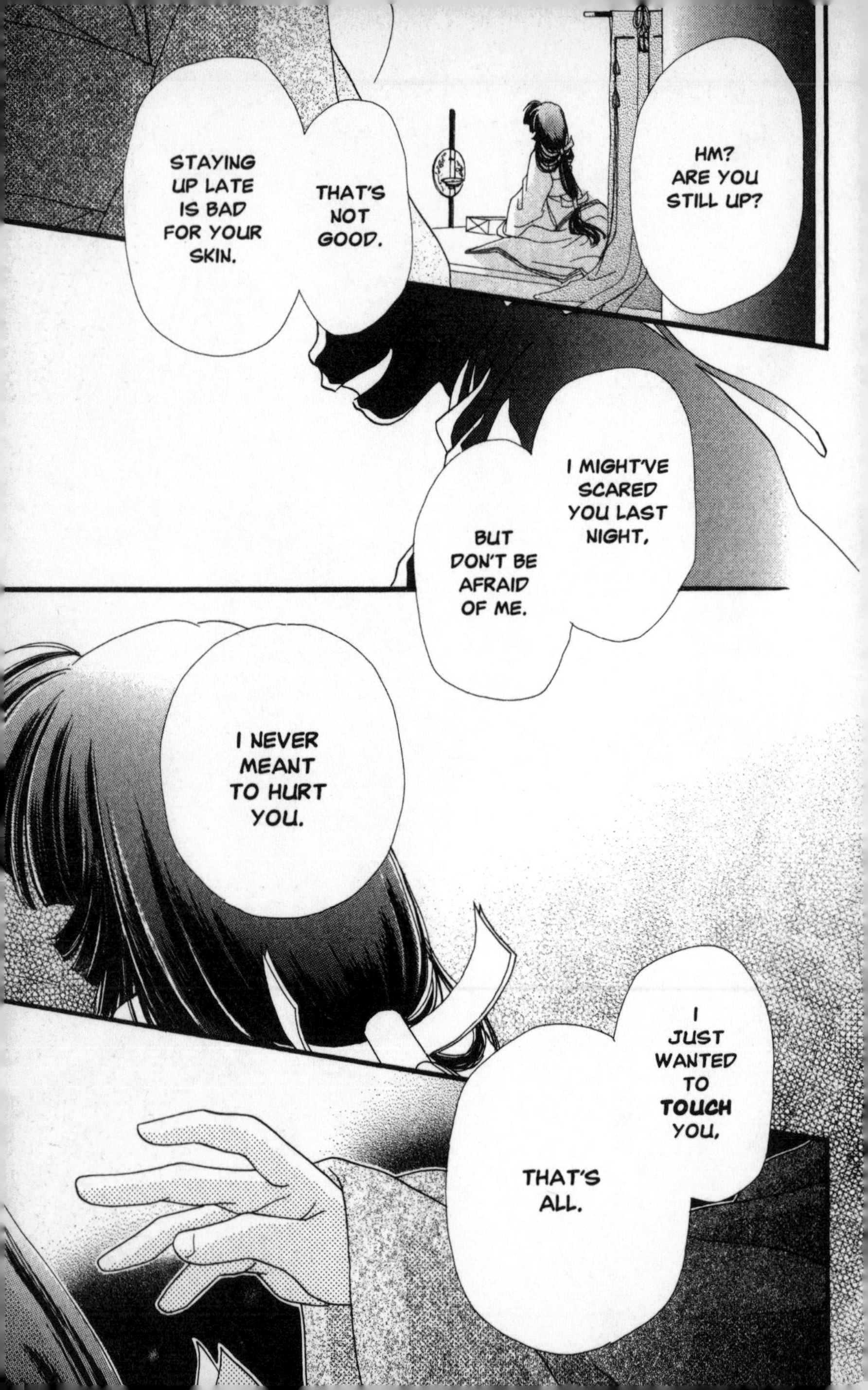
HM? ARE YOU STILL UP?
THAT'S NOT GOOD.
STAYING UP LATE IS BAD FOR YOUR SKIN.
I MIGHT'VE SCARED YOU LAST NIGHT,
BUT DON'T BE AFRAID OF ME.
I NEVER MEANT TO HURT YOU.
I JUST WANTED TO **TOUCH** YOU,
THAT'S ALL.

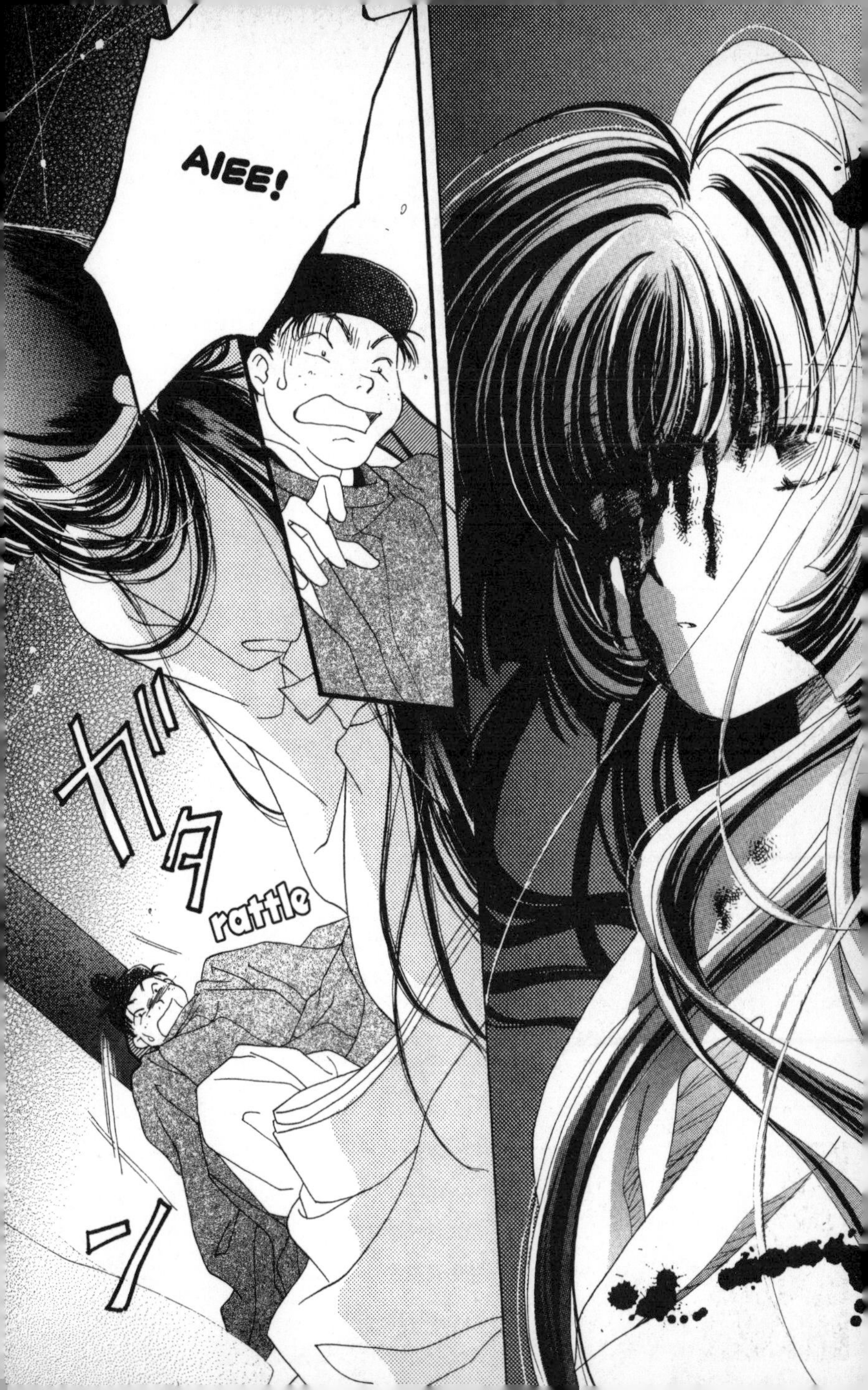
AIEE!
rattle

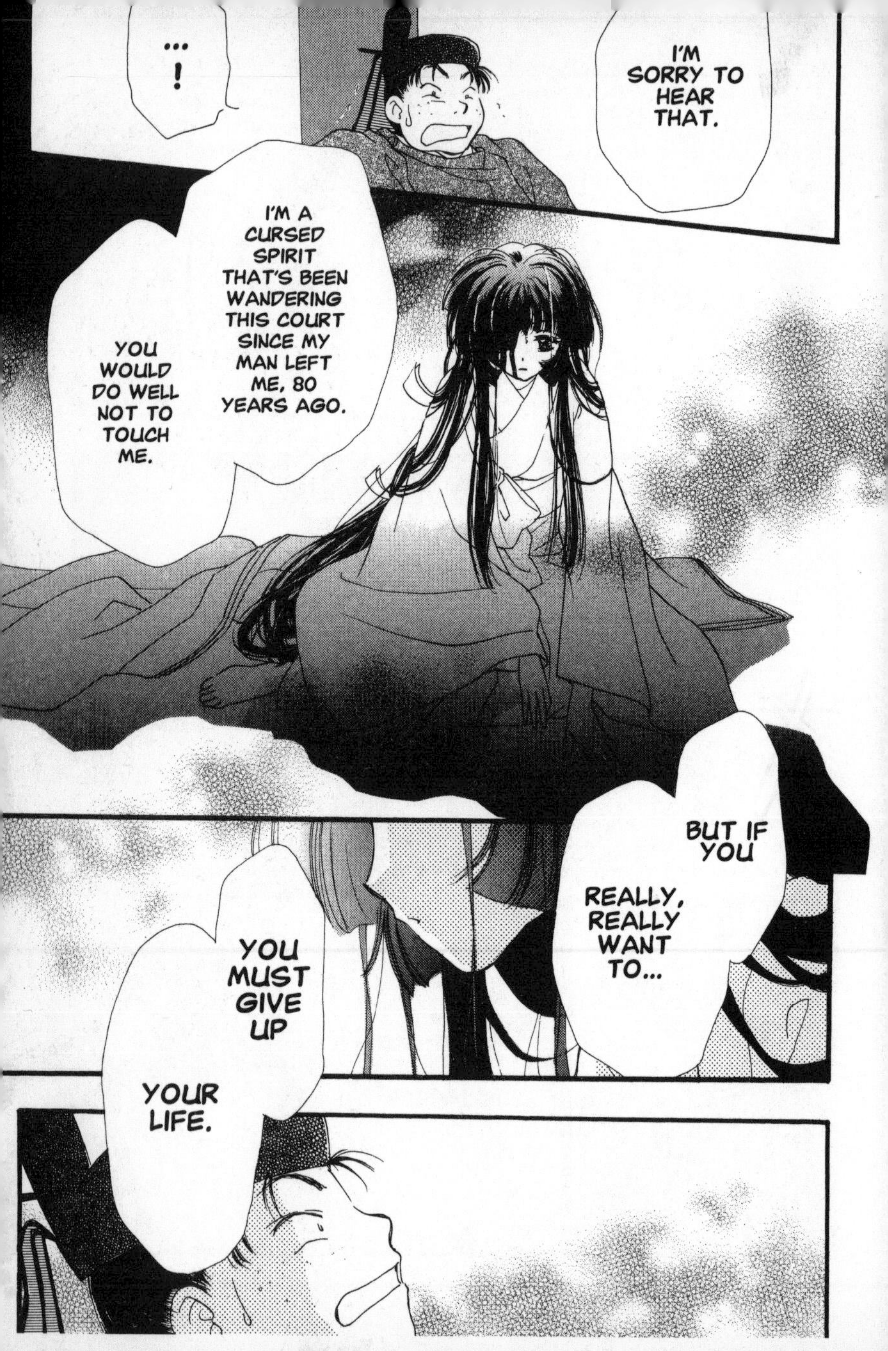
I'M SORRY TO HEAR THAT.
...!
I'M A CURSED SPIRIT THAT'S BEEN WANDERING THIS COURT SINCE MY MAN LEFT ME, 80 YEARS AGO.
YOU WOULD DO WELL NOT TO TOUCH ME.
BUT IF YOU
REALLY, REALLY WANT TO...
YOU MUST GIVE UP
YOUR LIFE.

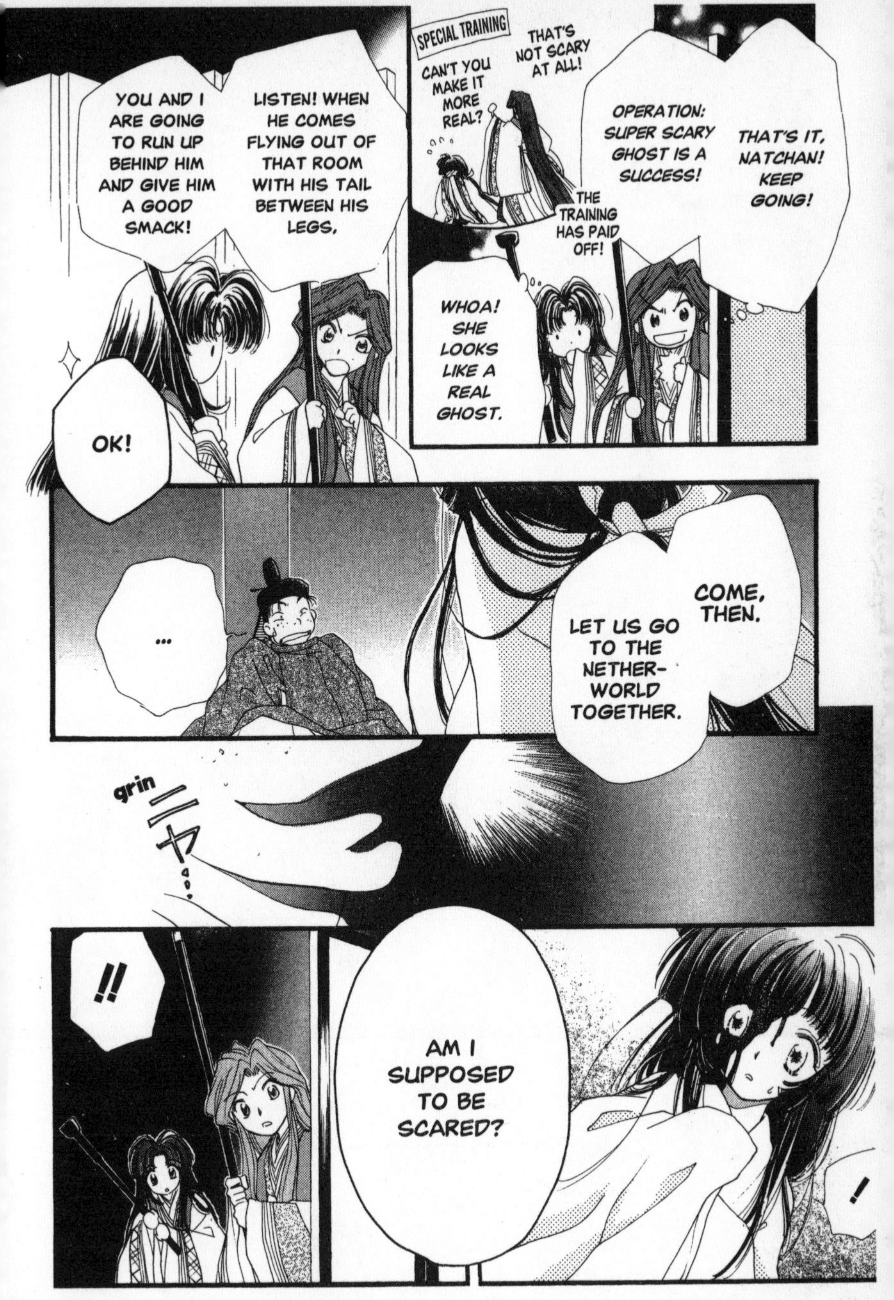

THAT'S IT, NATCHAN! KEEP GOING!
OPERATION: SUPER SCARY GHOST IS A SUCCESS!
THE TRAINING HAS PAID OFF!
SPECIAL TRAINING
THAT'S NOT SCARY AT ALL!
CAN'T YOU MAKE IT MORE REAL?
WHOA! SHE LOOKS LIKE A REAL GHOST.
LISTEN! WHEN HE COMES FLYING OUT OF THAT ROOM WITH HIS TAIL BETWEEN HIS LEGS,
YOU AND I ARE GOING TO RUN UP BEHIND HIM AND GIVE HIM A GOOD SMACK!
OK!
COME, THEN.
LET US GO TO THE NETHER-WORLD TOGETHER.
...
grin
ニヤ
!
AM I SUPPOSED TO BE SCARED?
!!

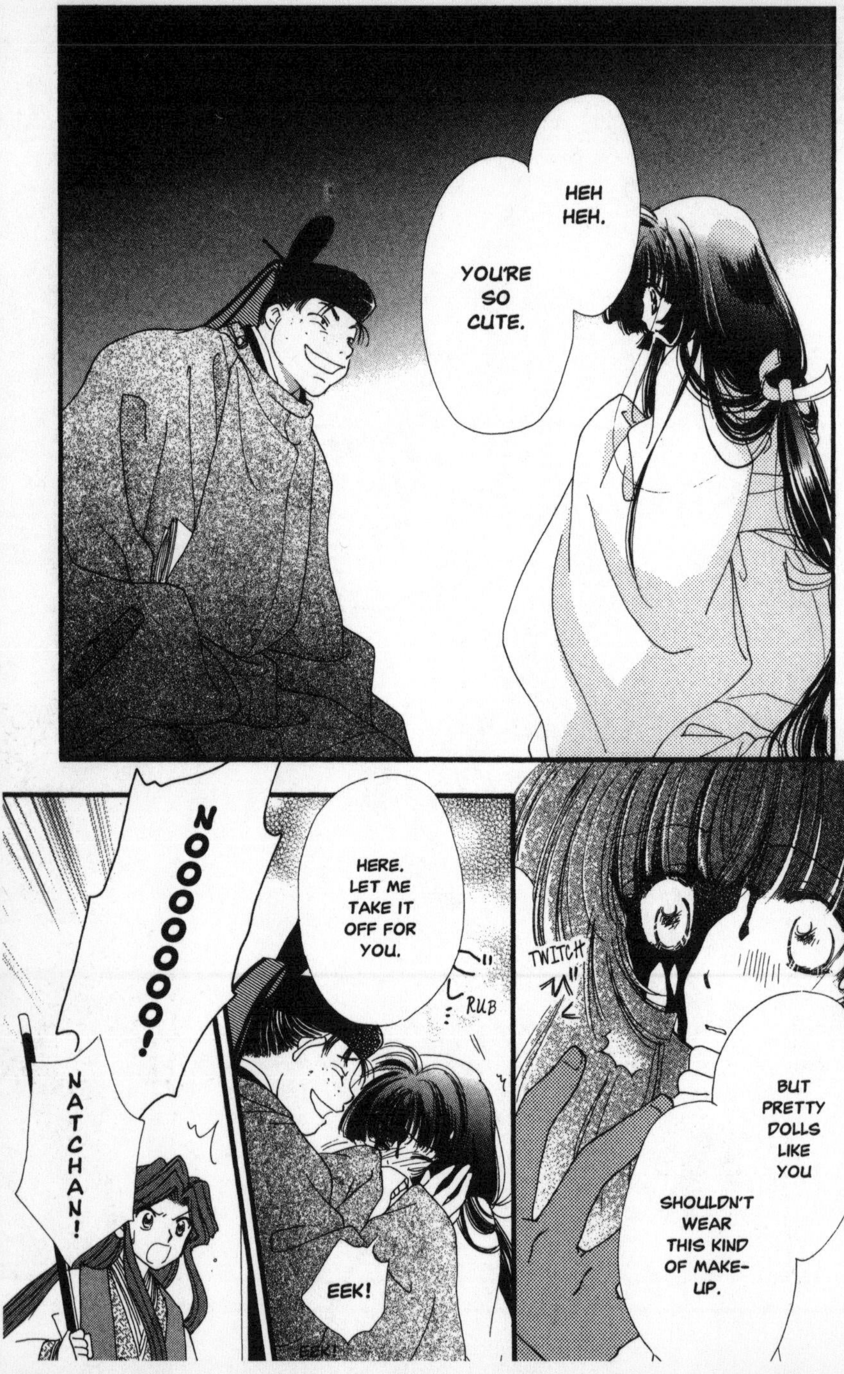

HEH HEH.
YOU'RE SO CUTE.
TWITCH
BUT PRETTY DOLLS LIKE YOU
SHOULDN'T WEAR THIS KIND OF MAKE-UP.
HERE. LET ME TAKE IT OFF FOR YOU.
RUB
EEK!
EEK!
NOOOOOOOOO!
NATCHAN!

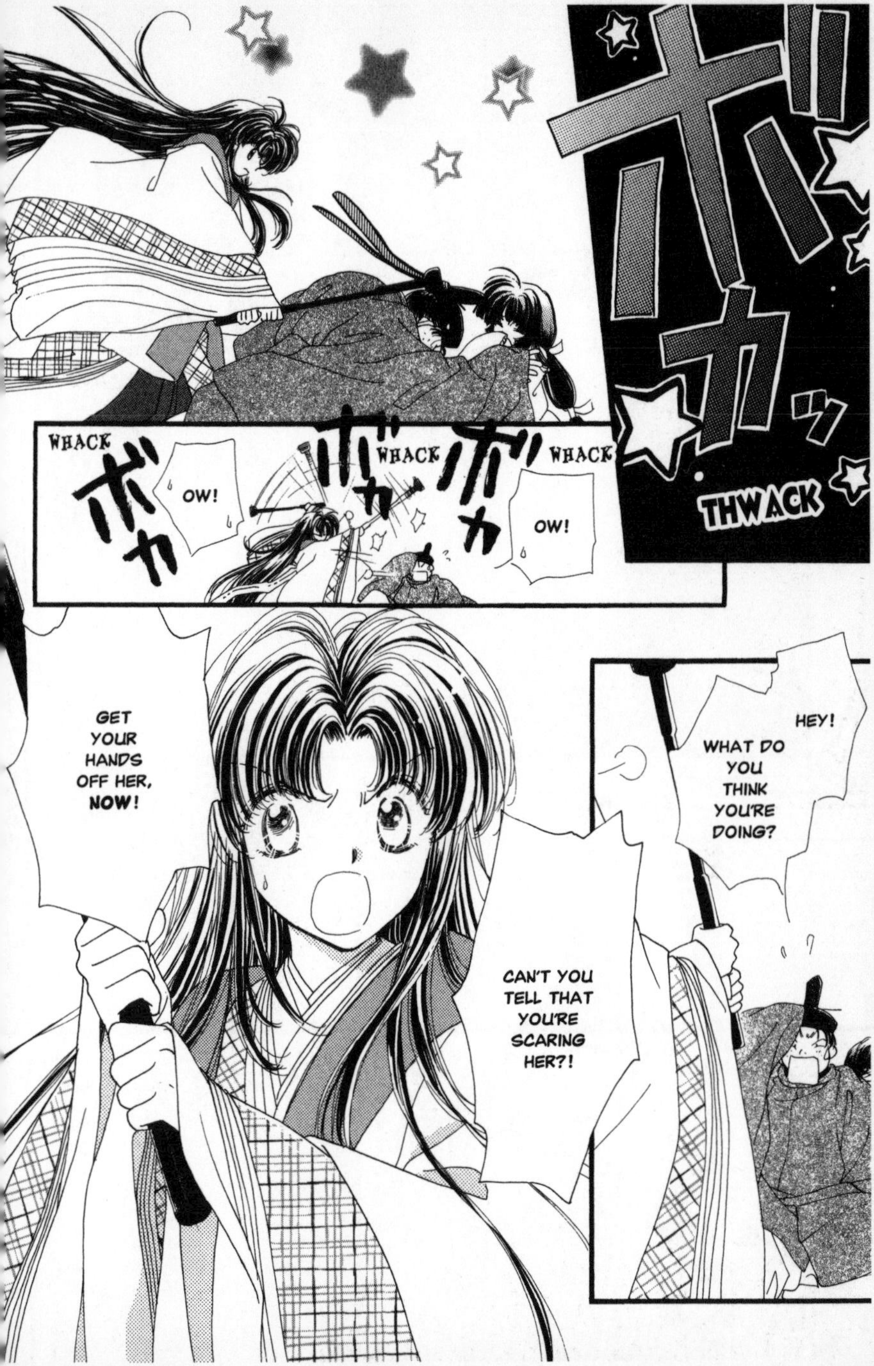
ボカッ
THWACK
ボカ
WHACK
OW!
ボカ
WHACK
ボカ
WHACK
OW!
HEY!
WHAT DO YOU THINK YOU'RE DOING?
GET YOUR HANDS OFF HER, NOW!
CAN'T YOU TELL THAT YOU'RE SCARING HER?!

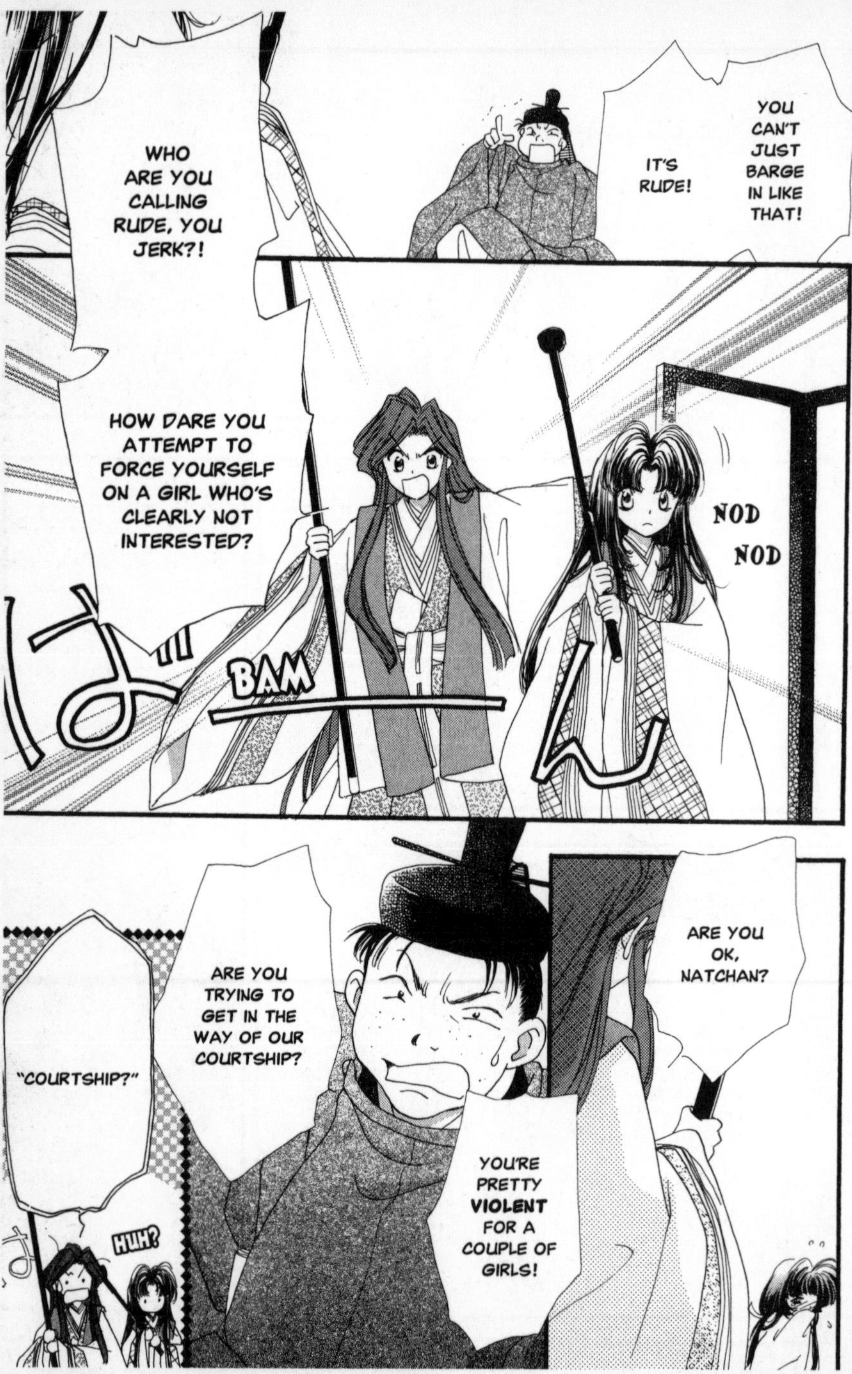

YOU CAN'T JUST BARGE IN LIKE THAT!
IT'S RUDE!
WHO ARE YOU CALLING RUDE, YOU JERK?!
NOD NOD
HOW DARE YOU ATTEMPT TO FORCE YOURSELF ON A GIRL WHO'S CLEARLY NOT INTERESTED?
BAM
ARE YOU OK, NATCHAN?
ARE YOU TRYING TO GET IN THE WAY OF OUR COURTSHIP?
YOU'RE PRETTY **VIOLENT** FOR A COUPLE OF GIRLS!
"COURTSHIP?"
HUH?

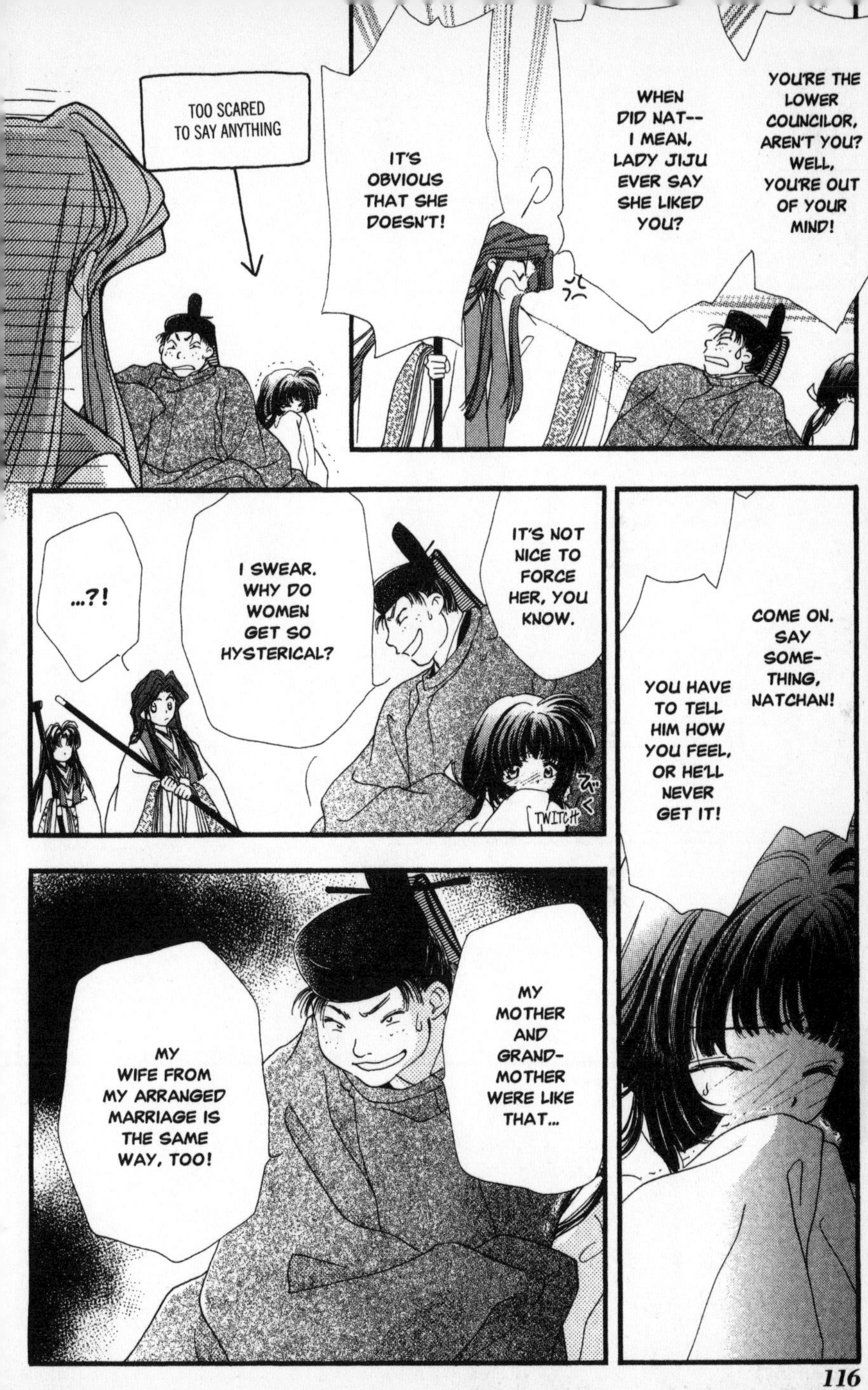
YOU'RE THE LOWER COUNCILOR, AREN'T YOU? WELL, YOU'RE OUT OF YOUR MIND!
WHEN DID NAT-- I MEAN, LADY JIJU EVER SAY SHE LIKED YOU?
IT'S OBVIOUS THAT SHE DOESN'T!
TOO SCARED TO SAY ANYTHING
COME ON. SAY SOME-THING, NATCHAN!
YOU HAVE TO TELL HIM HOW YOU FEEL, OR HE'LL NEVER GET IT!
IT'S NOT NICE TO FORCE HER, YOU KNOW.
I SWEAR. WHY DO WOMEN GET SO HYSTERICAL?
...?!
びく
TWITCH
MY MOTHER AND GRAND-MOTHER WERE LIKE THAT...
MY WIFE FROM MY ARRANGED MARRIAGE IS THE SAME WAY, TOO!

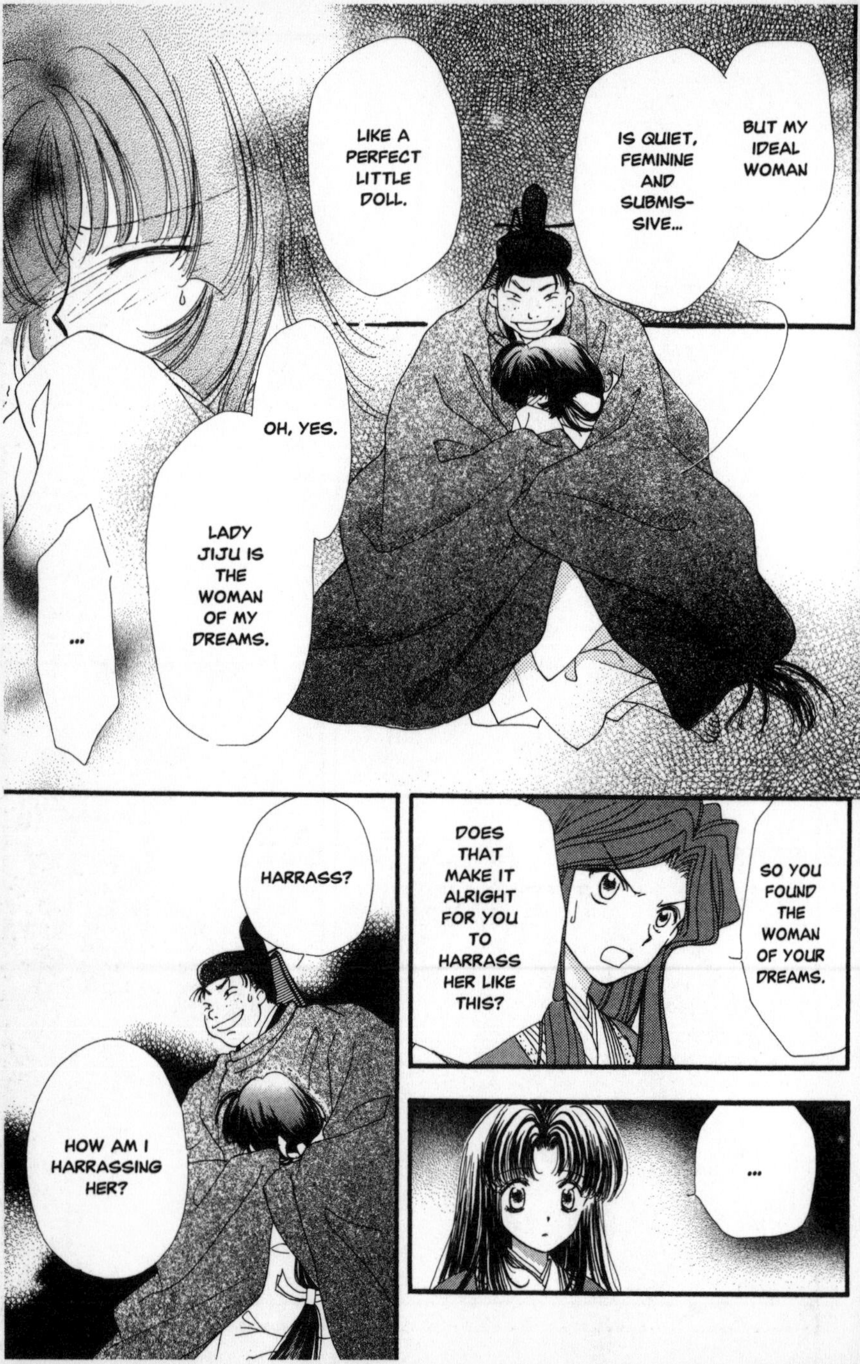
BUT MY IDEAL WOMAN
IS QUIET, FEMININE AND SUBMIS-SIVE...
LIKE A PERFECT LITTLE DOLL.
OH, YES.
LADY JIJU IS THE WOMAN OF MY DREAMS.
...
SO YOU FOUND THE WOMAN OF YOUR DREAMS.
DOES THAT MAKE IT ALRIGHT FOR YOU TO HARRASS HER LIKE THIS?
HARRASS?
HOW AM I HARRASSING HER?
...

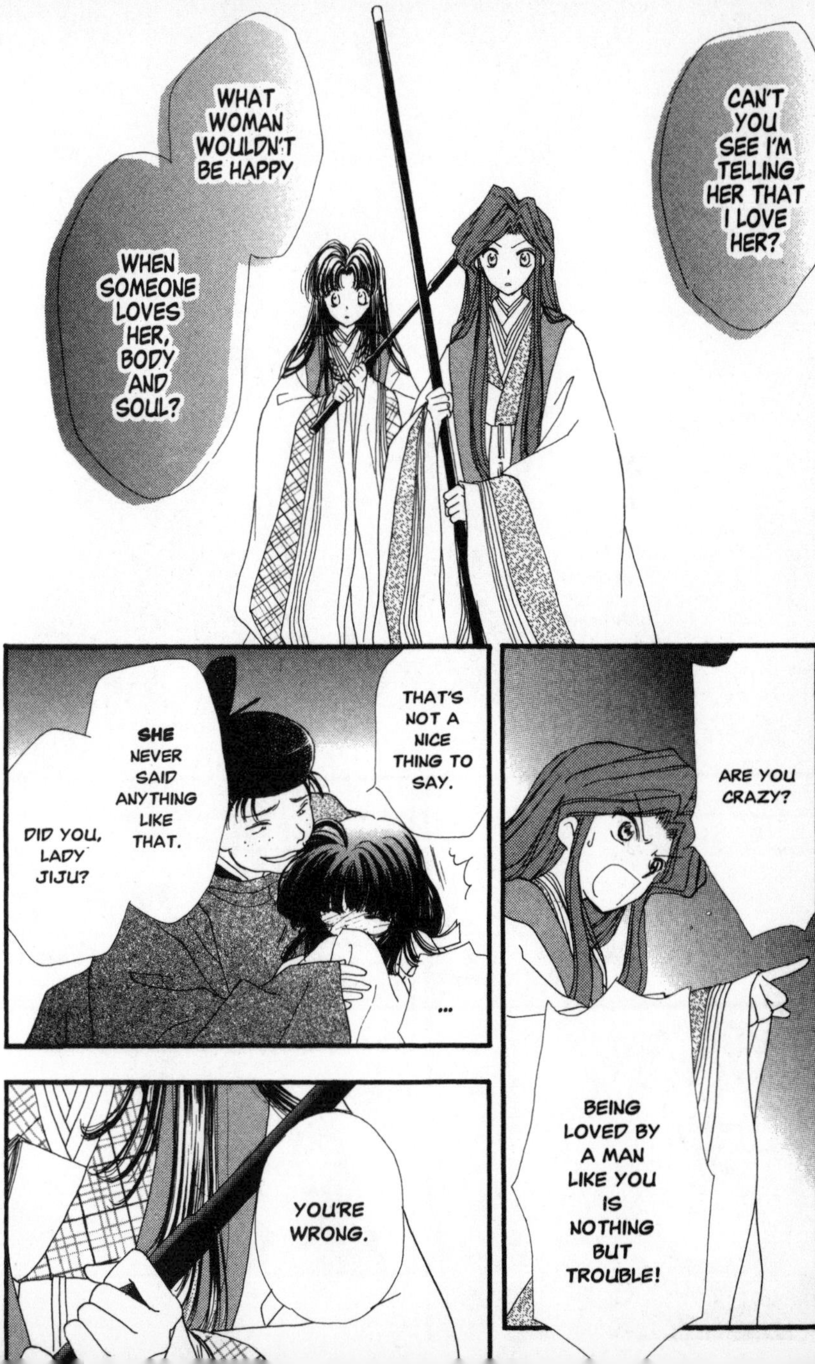
CAN'T YOU SEE I'M TELLING HER THAT I LOVE HER?
WHAT WOMAN WOULDN'T BE HAPPY
WHEN SOMEONE LOVES HER, BODY AND SOUL?
ARE YOU CRAZY?
BEING LOVED BY A MAN LIKE YOU IS NOTHING BUT TROUBLE!
THAT'S NOT A NICE THING TO SAY.
SHE NEVER SAID ANYTHING LIKE THAT.
DID YOU, LADY JIJU?
...
YOU'RE WRONG.

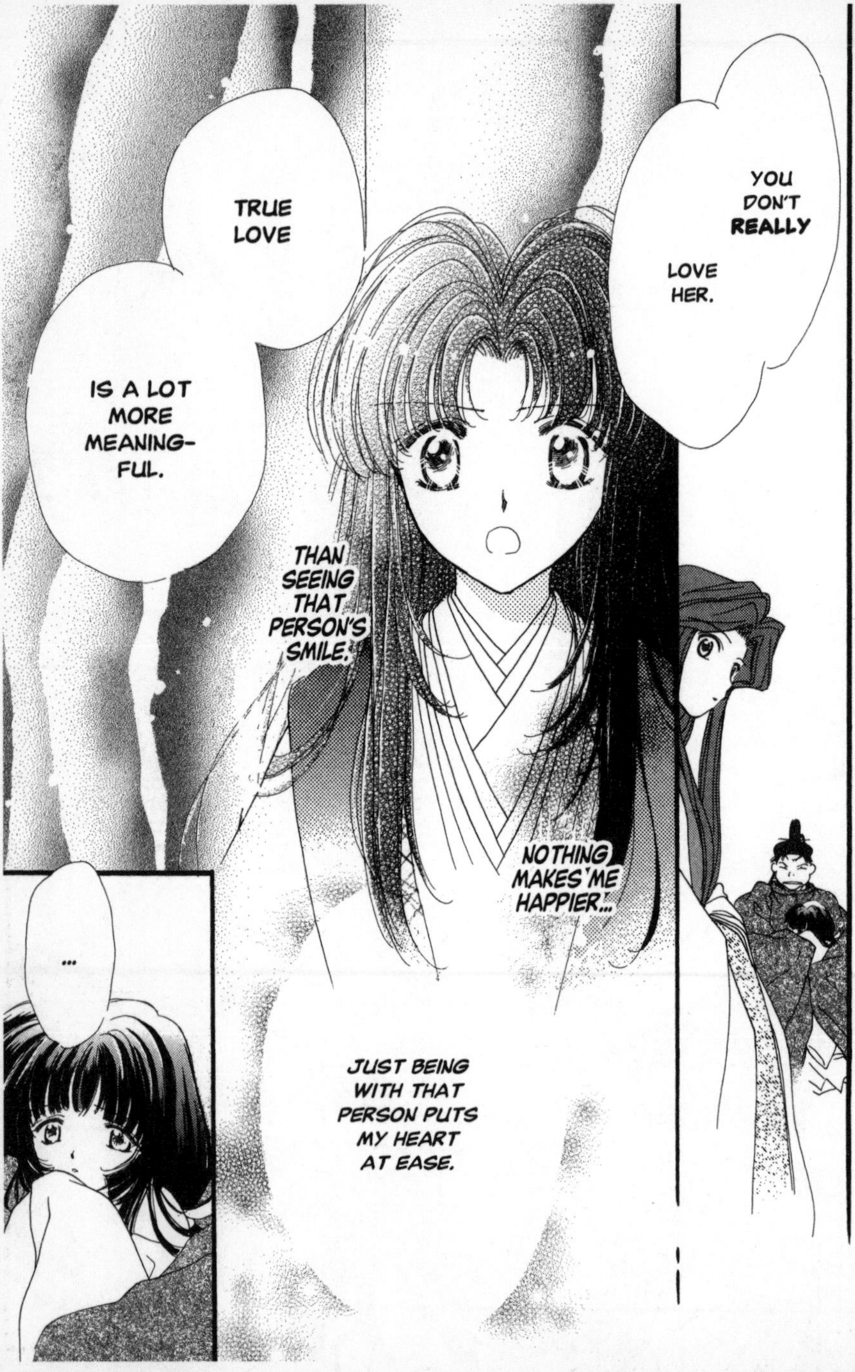
YOU DON'T REALLY
LOVE HER.
NOTHING MAKES ME HAPPIER...
THAN SEEING THAT PERSON'S SMILE.
TRUE LOVE
IS A LOT MORE MEANING-FUL.
JUST BEING WITH THAT PERSON PUTS MY HEART AT EASE.
...

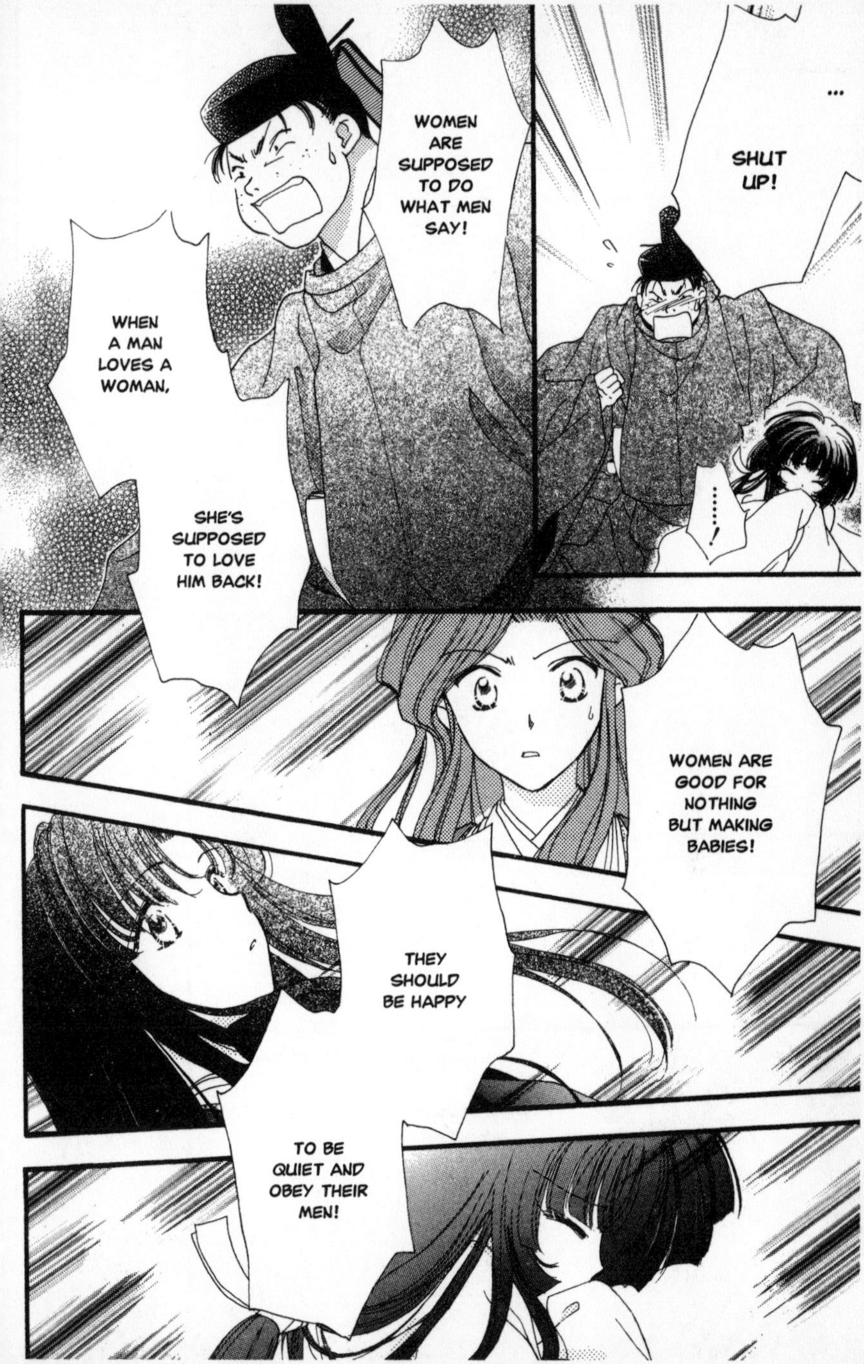
...
SHUT UP!
......!
WOMEN ARE SUPPOSED TO DO WHAT MEN SAY!
WHEN A MAN LOVES A WOMAN,
SHE'S SUPPOSED TO LOVE HIM BACK!
WOMEN ARE GOOD FOR NOTHING BUT MAKING BABIES!
THEY SHOULD BE HAPPY
TO BE QUIET AND OBEY THEIR MEN!

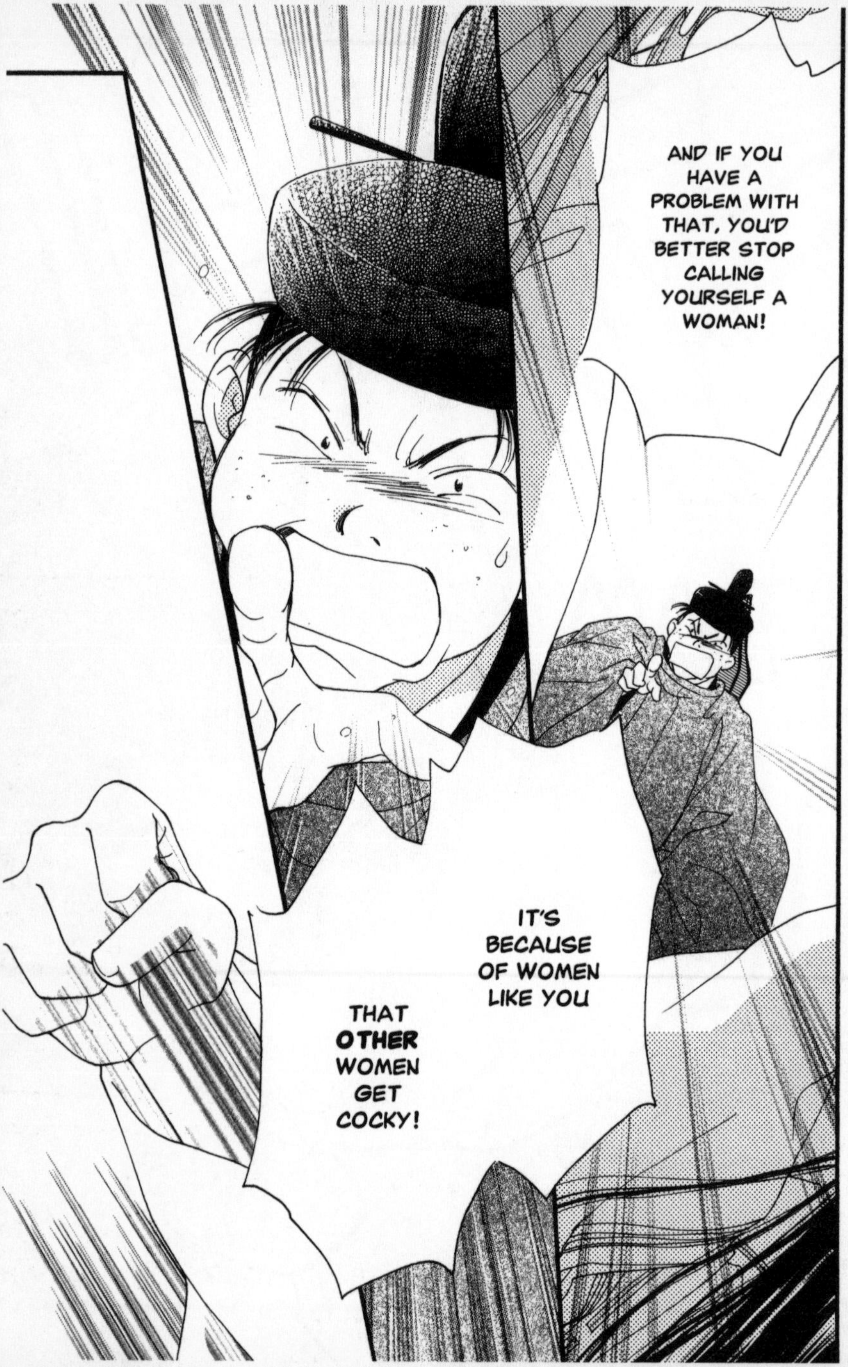
AND IF YOU HAVE A PROBLEM WITH THAT, YOU'D BETTER STOP CALLING YOURSELF A WOMAN!
IT'S BECAUSE OF WOMEN LIKE YOU
THAT **OTHER** WOMEN GET COCKY!

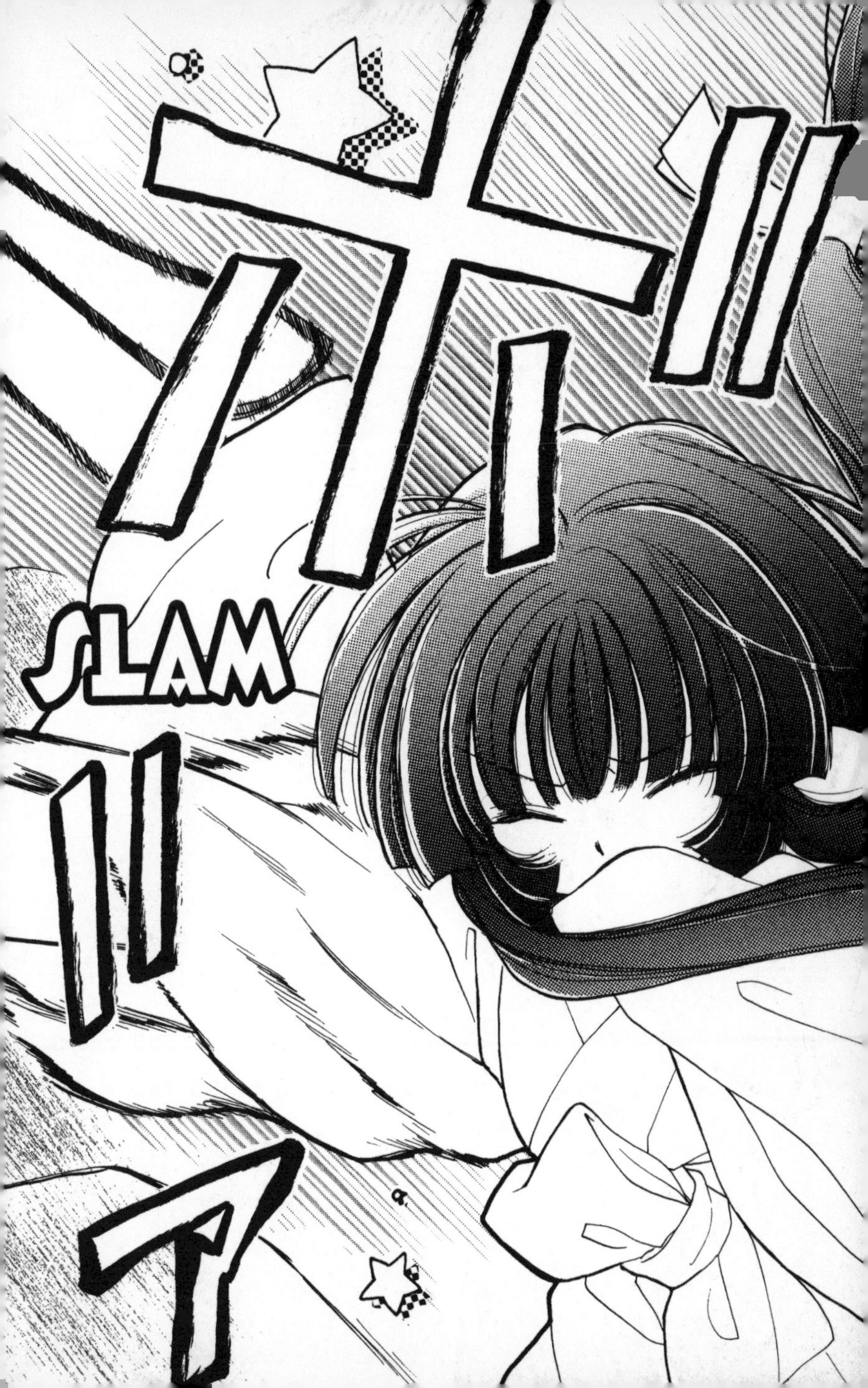
SLAM

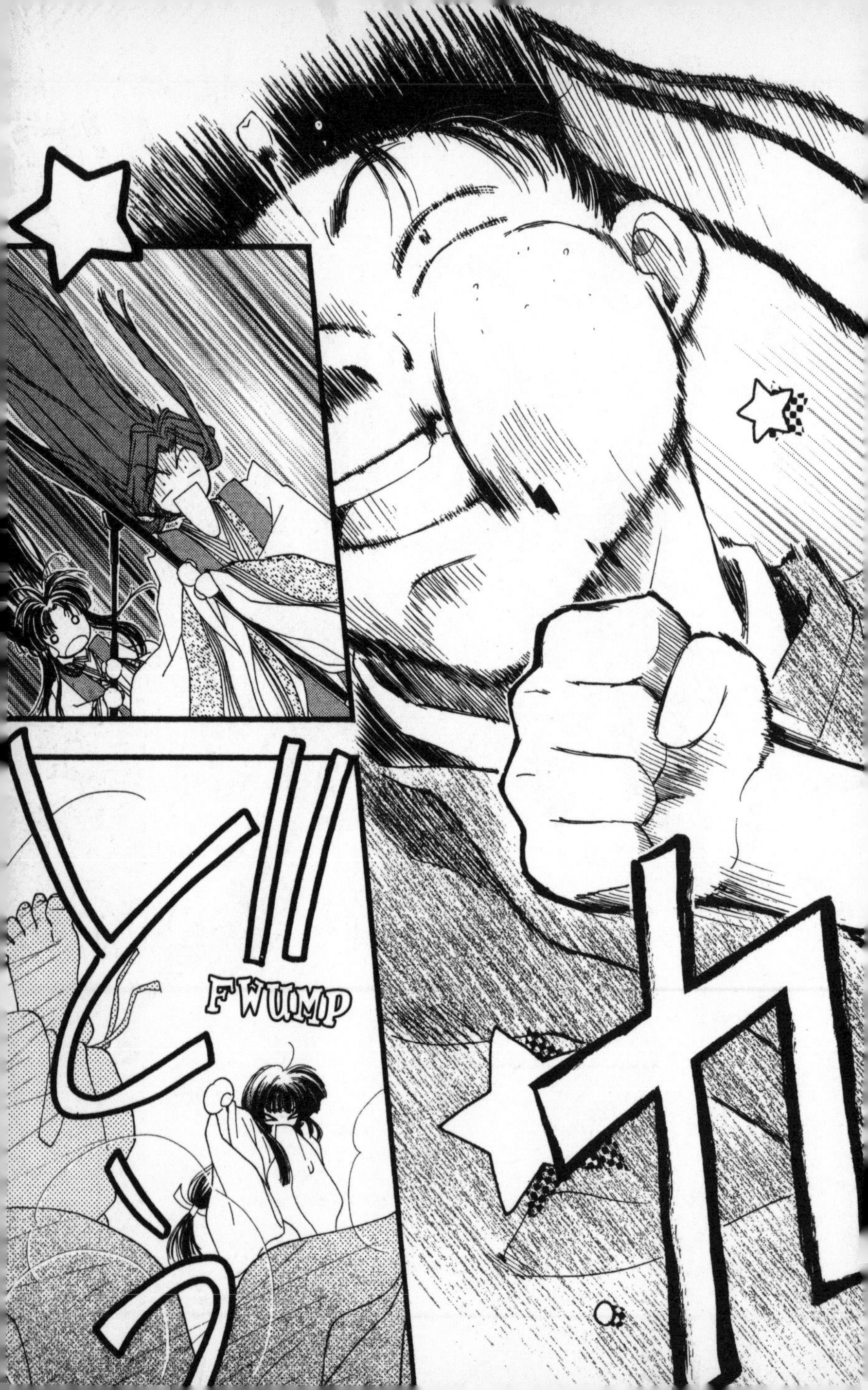
FWUMP

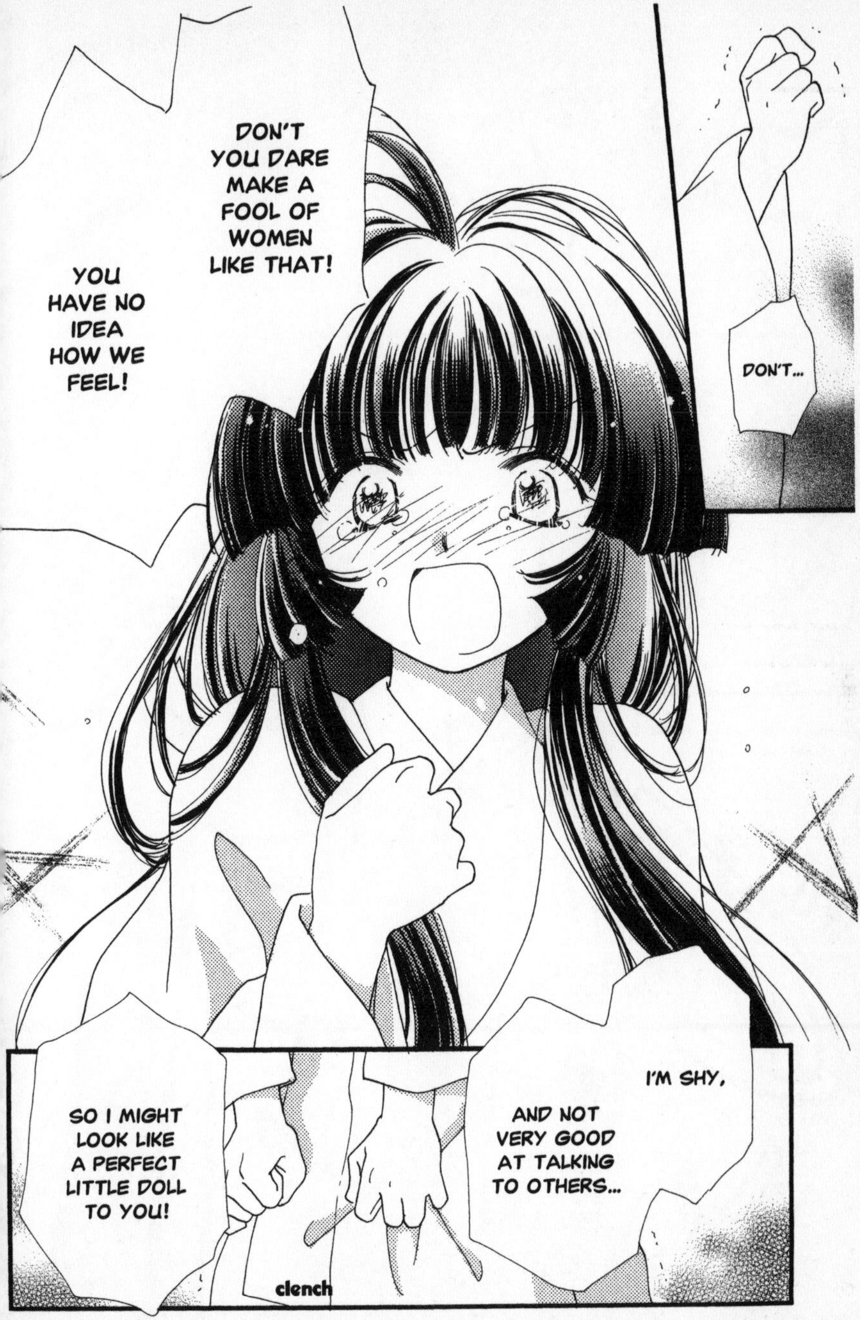
DON'T...
DON'T YOU DARE MAKE A FOOL OF WOMEN LIKE THAT!
YOU HAVE NO IDEA HOW WE FEEL!
I'M SHY,
AND NOT VERY GOOD AT TALKING TO OTHERS...
SO I MIGHT LOOK LIKE A PERFECT LITTLE DOLL TO YOU!
clench

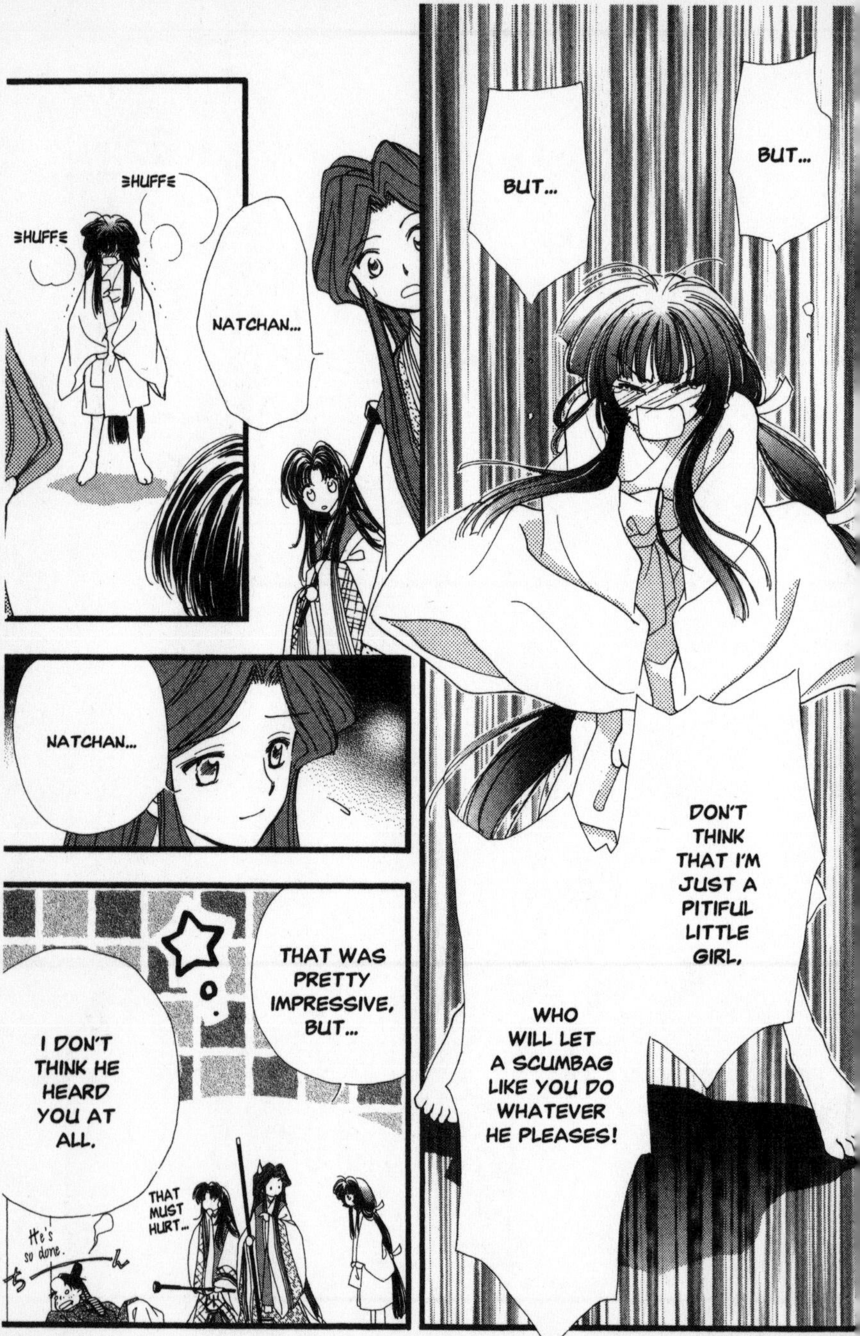
BUT...
BUT...
DON'T THINK THAT I'M JUST A PITIFUL LITTLE GIRL,
WHO WILL LET A SCUMBAG LIKE YOU DO WHATEVER HE PLEASES!
NATCHAN...
HUFF
HUFF
NATCHAN...
THAT WAS PRETTY IMPRESSIVE, BUT...
I DON'T THINK HE HEARD YOU AT ALL.
THAT MUST HURT...
He's so done.

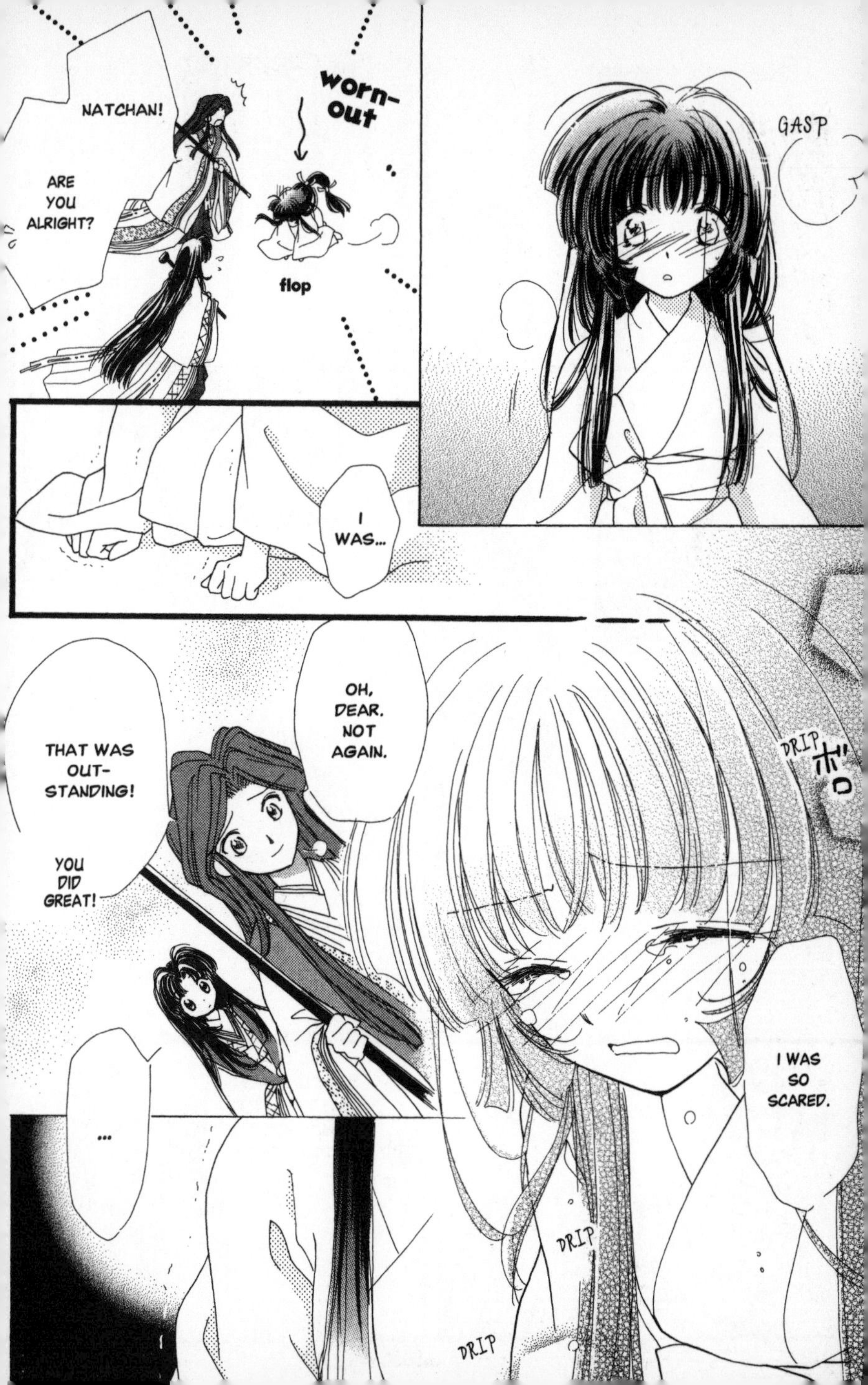

worn-out
flop
NATCHAN!
ARE YOU ALRIGHT?
GASP
I WAS...
DRIP ボロ
OH, DEAR. NOT AGAIN.
THAT WAS OUT-STANDING!
YOU DID GREAT!
I WAS SO SCARED.
...
DRIP
DRIP

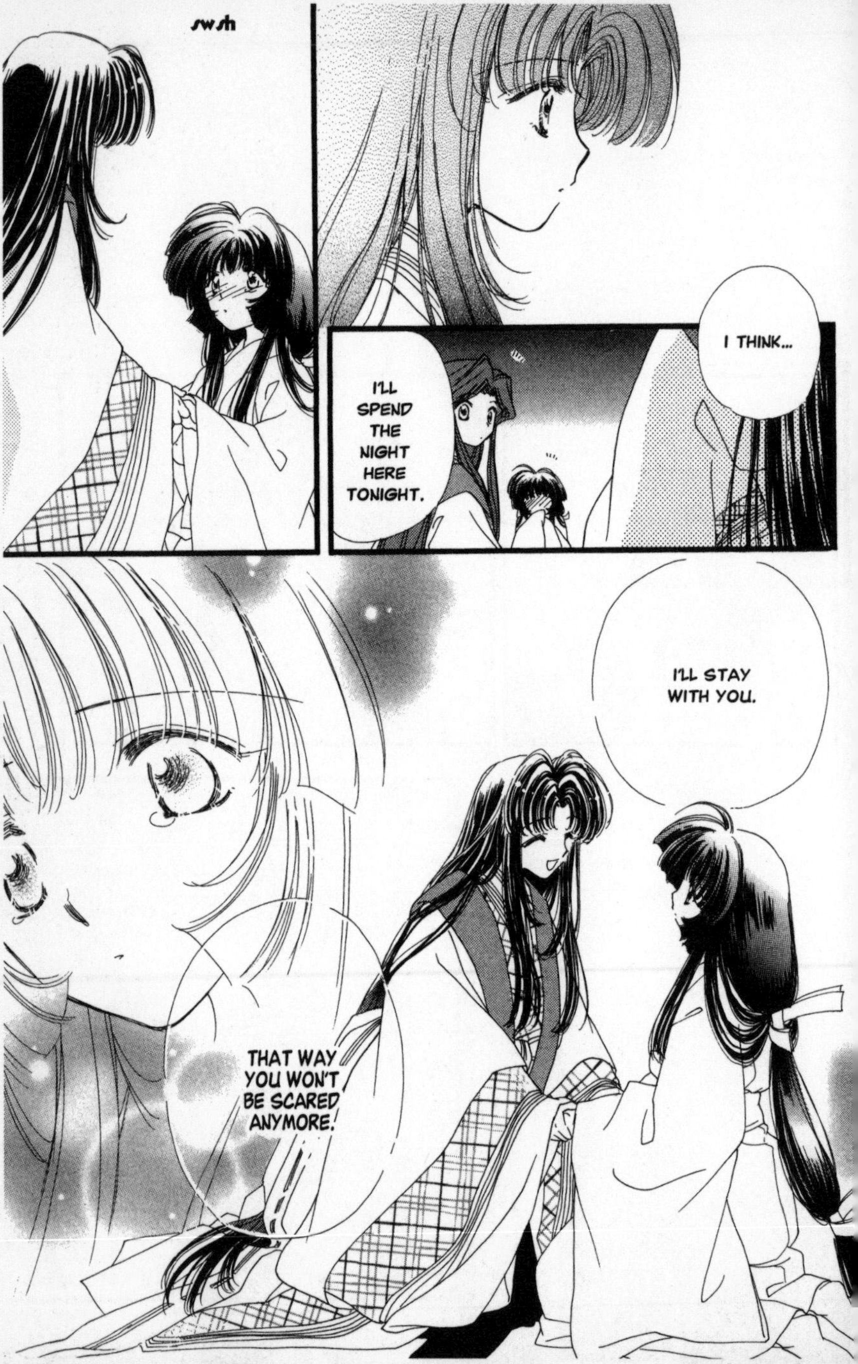
swsh
I THINK...
I'LL SPEND THE NIGHT HERE TONIGHT.
I'LL STAY WITH YOU.
THAT WAY YOU WON'T BE SCARED ANYMORE.

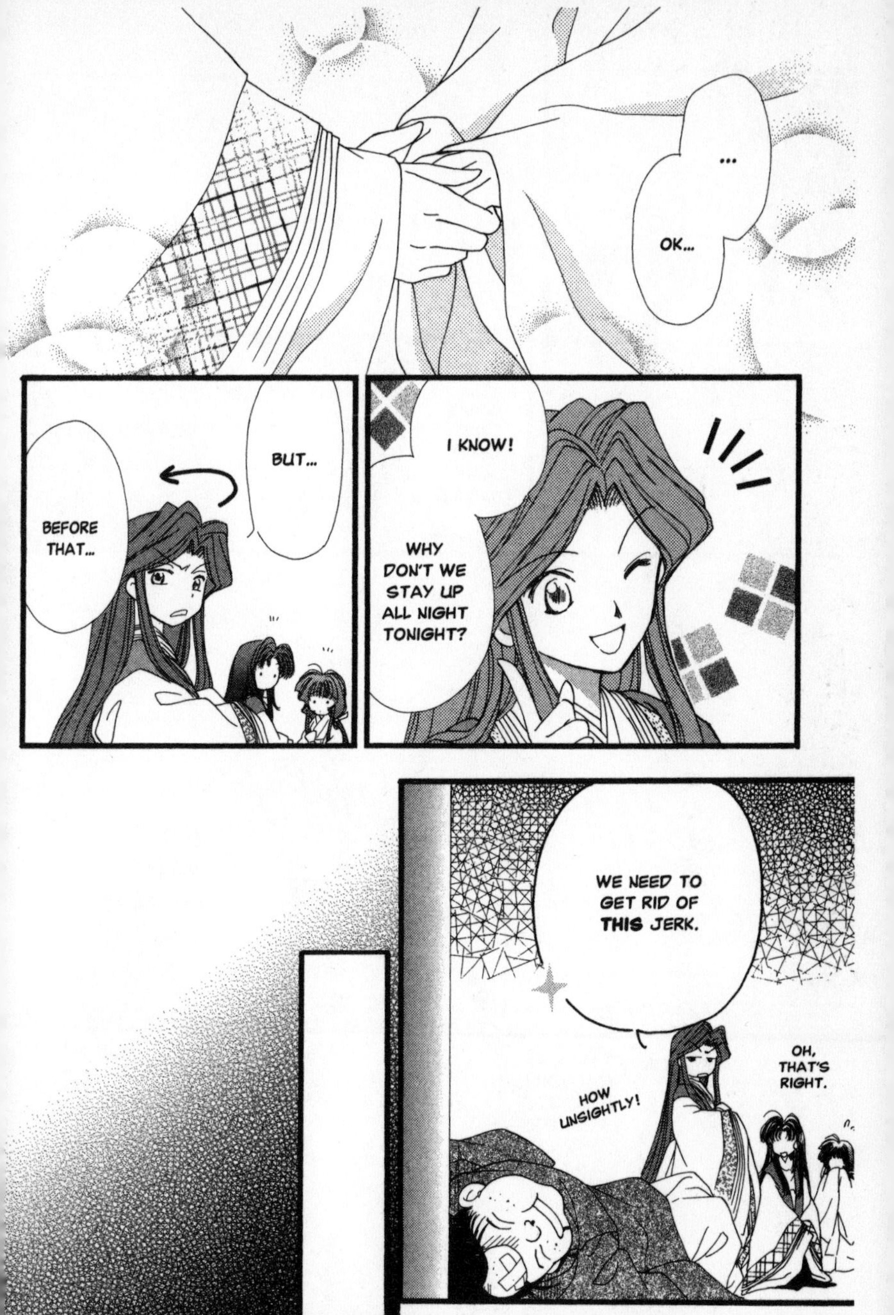
...
OK...
I KNOW!
WHY DON'T WE STAY UP ALL NIGHT TONIGHT?
BUT...
BEFORE THAT...
WE NEED TO GET RID OF THIS JERK.
OH, THAT'S RIGHT.
HOW UNSIGHTLY!

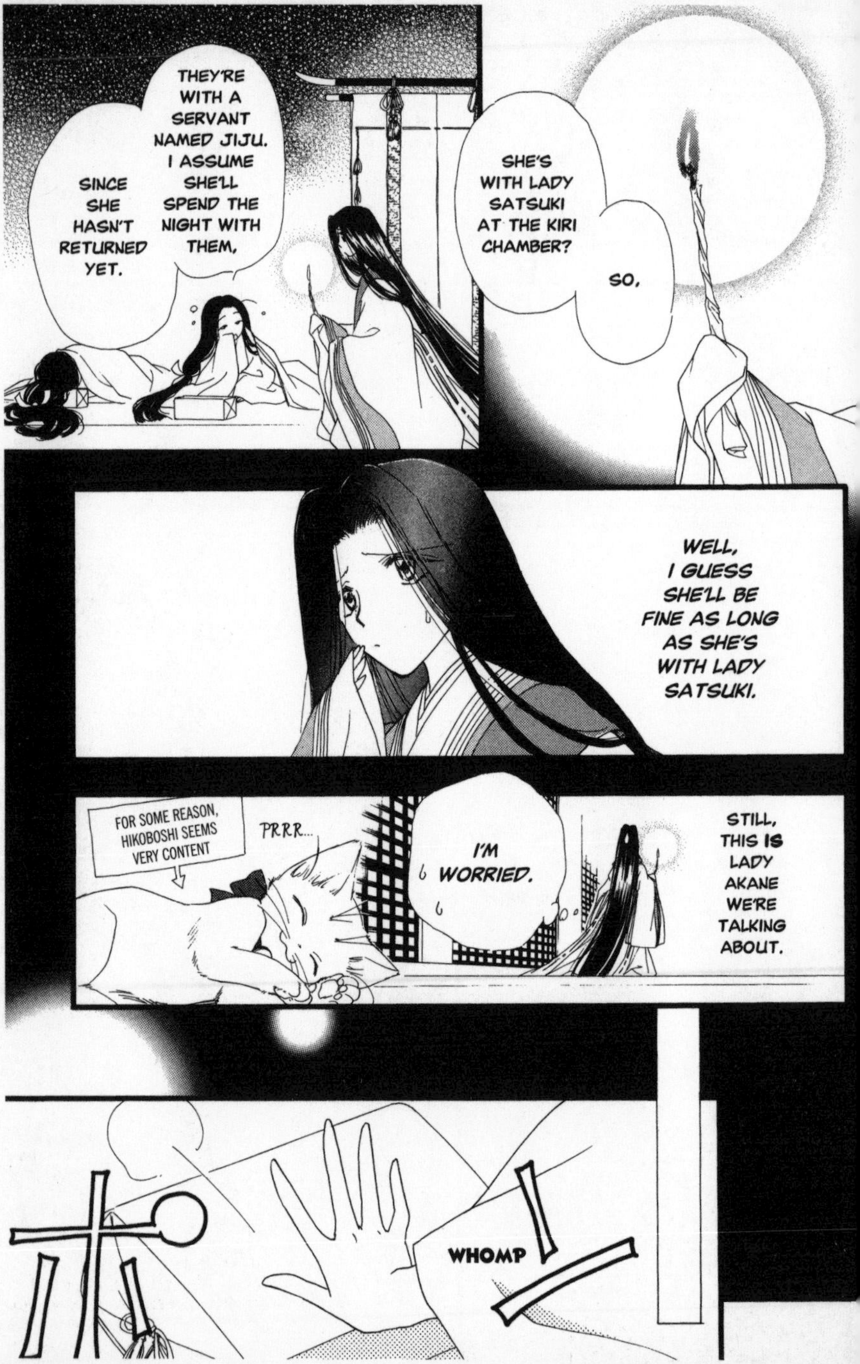
SHE'S WITH LADY SATSUKI AT THE KIRI CHAMBER?
SO,
THEY'RE WITH A SERVANT NAMED JIJU. I ASSUME SHE'LL SPEND THE NIGHT WITH THEM,
SINCE SHE HASN'T RETURNED YET.
WELL, I GUESS SHE'LL BE FINE AS LONG AS SHE'S WITH LADY SATSUKI.
STILL, THIS IS LADY AKANE WE'RE TALKING ABOUT.
I'M WORRIED.
PRRR...
FOR SOME REASON, HIKOBOSHI SEEMS VERY CONTENT
WHOMP

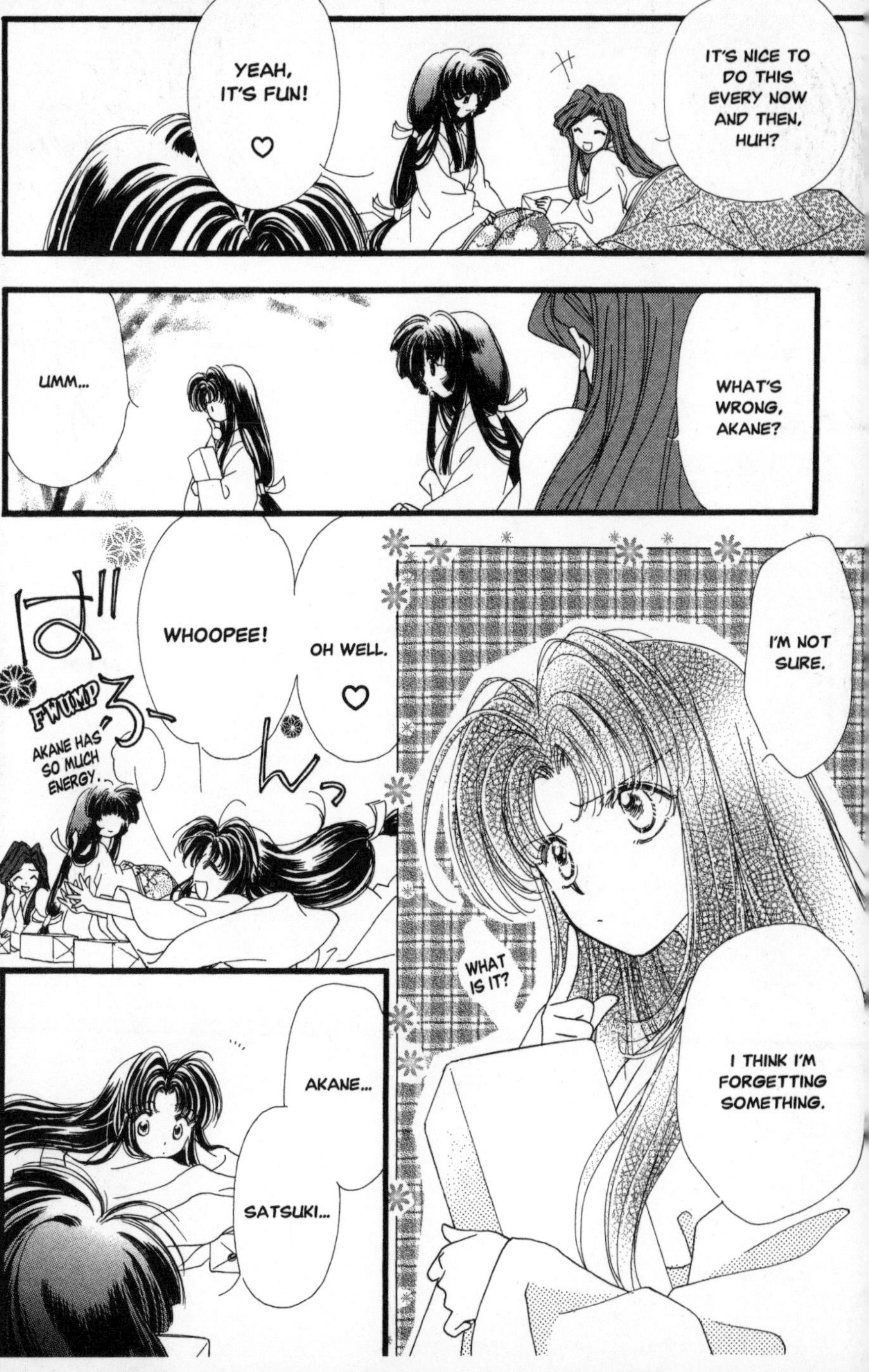
IT'S NICE TO DO THIS EVERY NOW AND THEN, HUH?
YEAH, IT'S FUN! ♡
WHAT'S WRONG, AKANE?
UMM...
I'M NOT SURE.
I THINK I'M FORGETTING SOMETHING.
WHAT IS IT?
OH WELL. ♡
WHOOPEE!
FWUMP
AKANE HAS SO MUCH ENERGY...
AKANE...
SATSUKI...

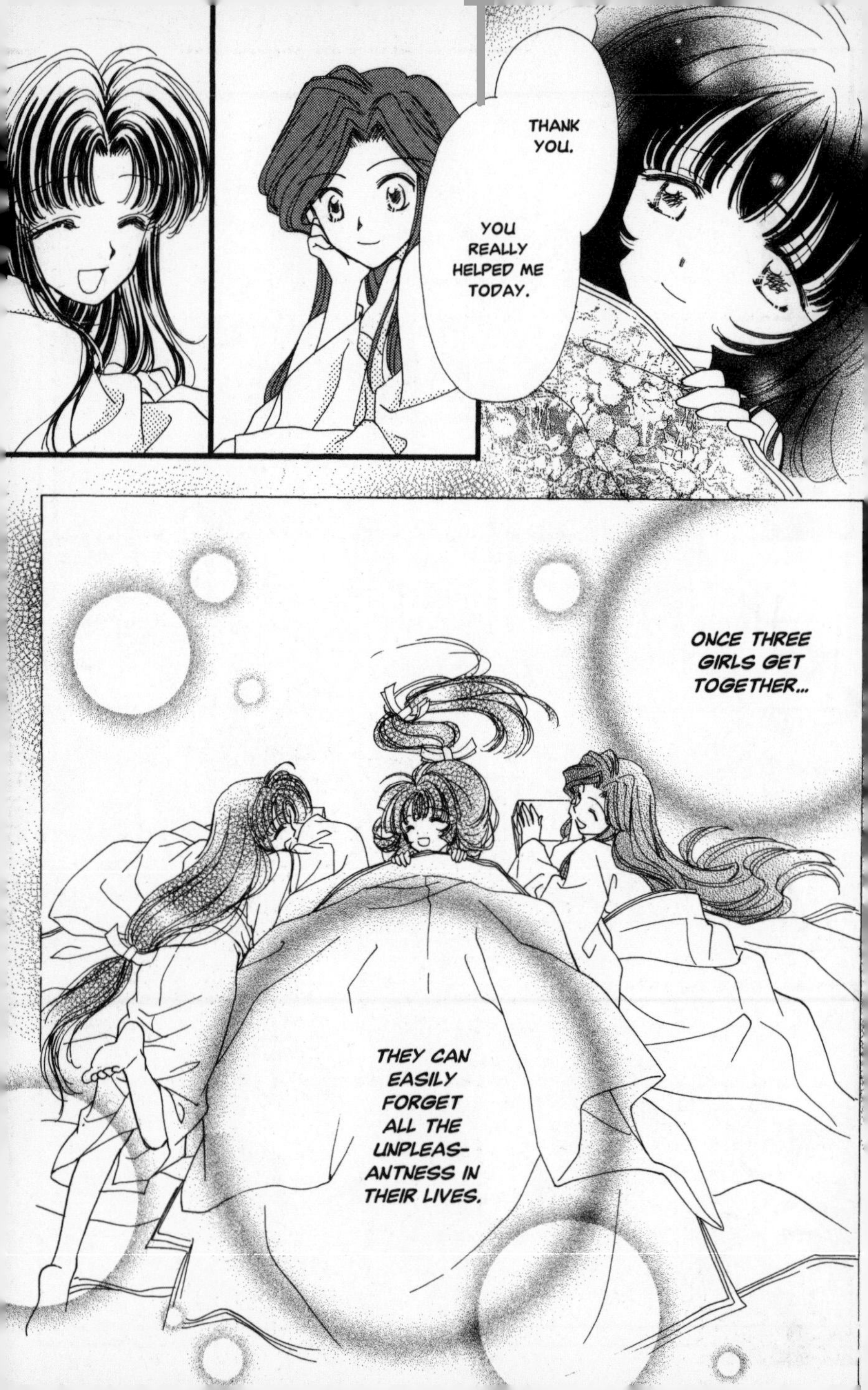
THANK YOU.
YOU REALLY HELPED ME TODAY.
ONCE THREE GIRLS GET TOGETHER...
THEY CAN EASILY FORGET ALL THE UNPLEAS-ANTNESS IN THEIR LIVES.

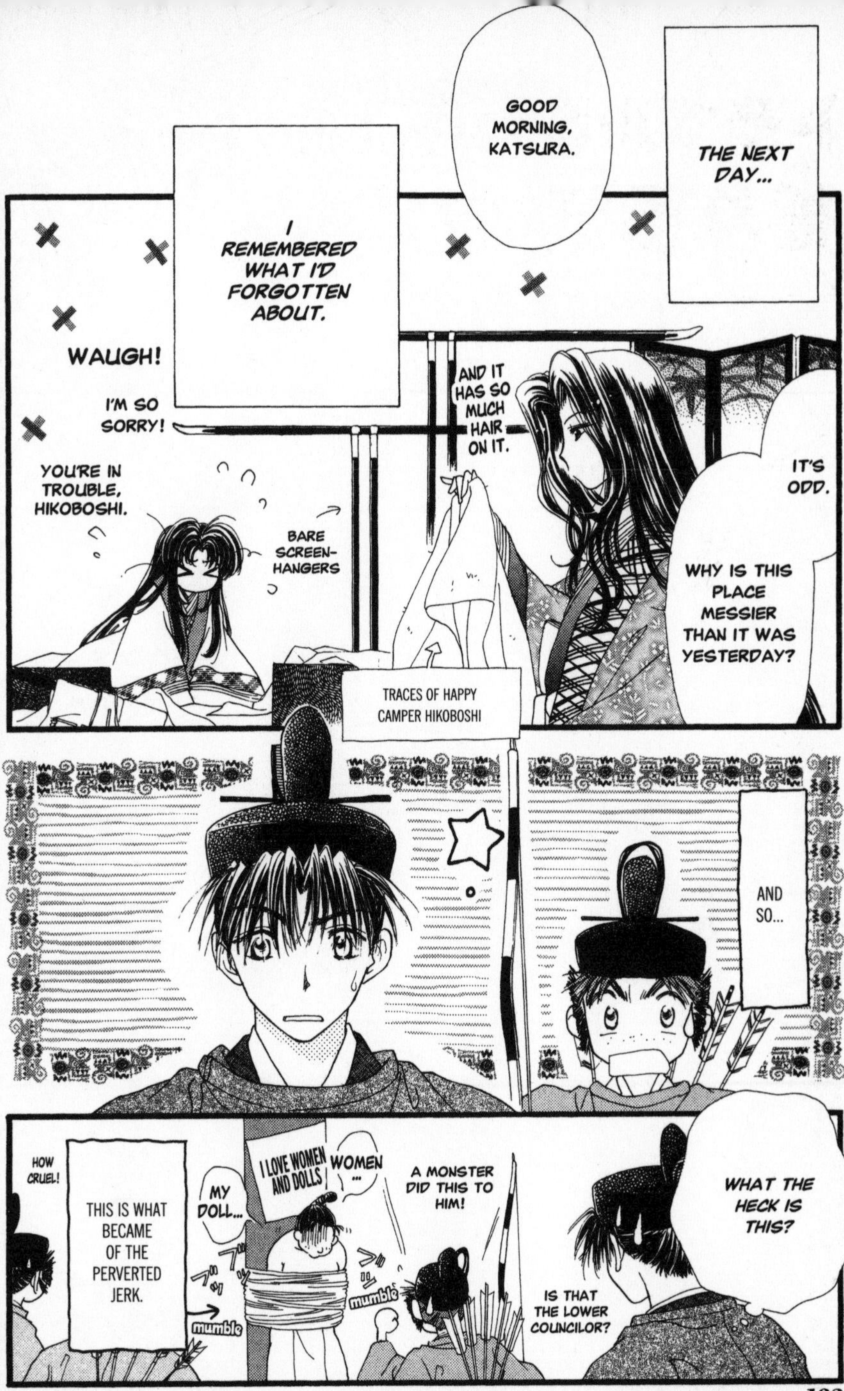
THE NEXT DAY...
GOOD MORNING, KATSURA.
I REMEMBERED WHAT I'D FORGOTTEN ABOUT.
IT'S ODD.
WHY IS THIS PLACE MESSIER THAN IT WAS YESTERDAY?
AND IT HAS SO MUCH HAIR ON IT.
BARE SCREEN-HANGERS
TRACES OF HAPPY CAMPER HIKOBOSHI
WAUGH!
I'M SO SORRY!
YOU'RE IN TROUBLE, HIKOBOSHI.
AND SO...
WHAT THE HECK IS THIS?
IS THAT THE LOWER COUNCILOR?
A MONSTER DID THIS TO HIM!
WOMEN...
I LOVE WOMEN AND DOLLS
MY DOLL...
mumble
mumble
THIS IS WHAT BECAME OF THE PERVERTED JERK.
HOW CRUEL!

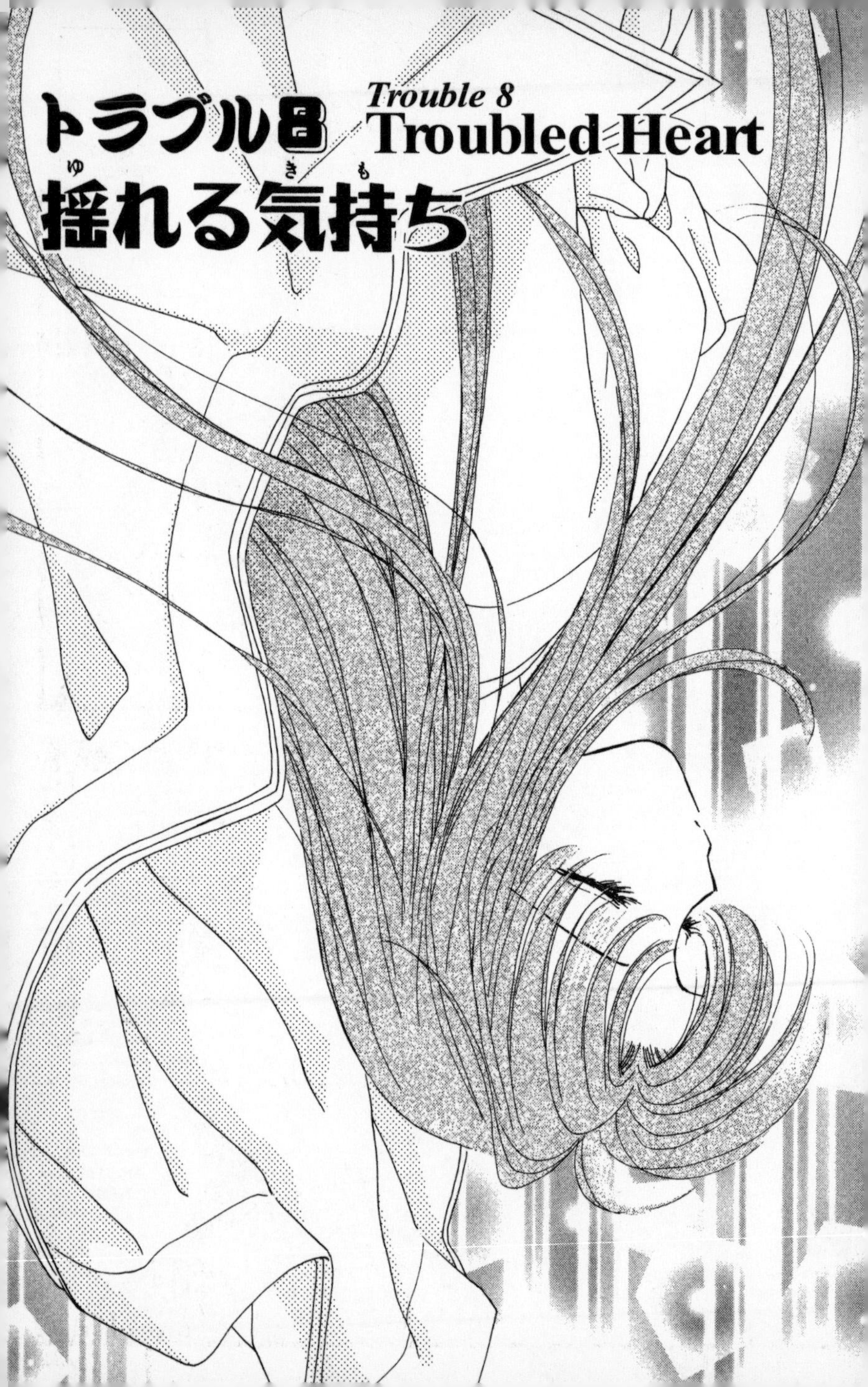
トラブル8
揺れる気持ち
Trouble 8
Troubled Heart

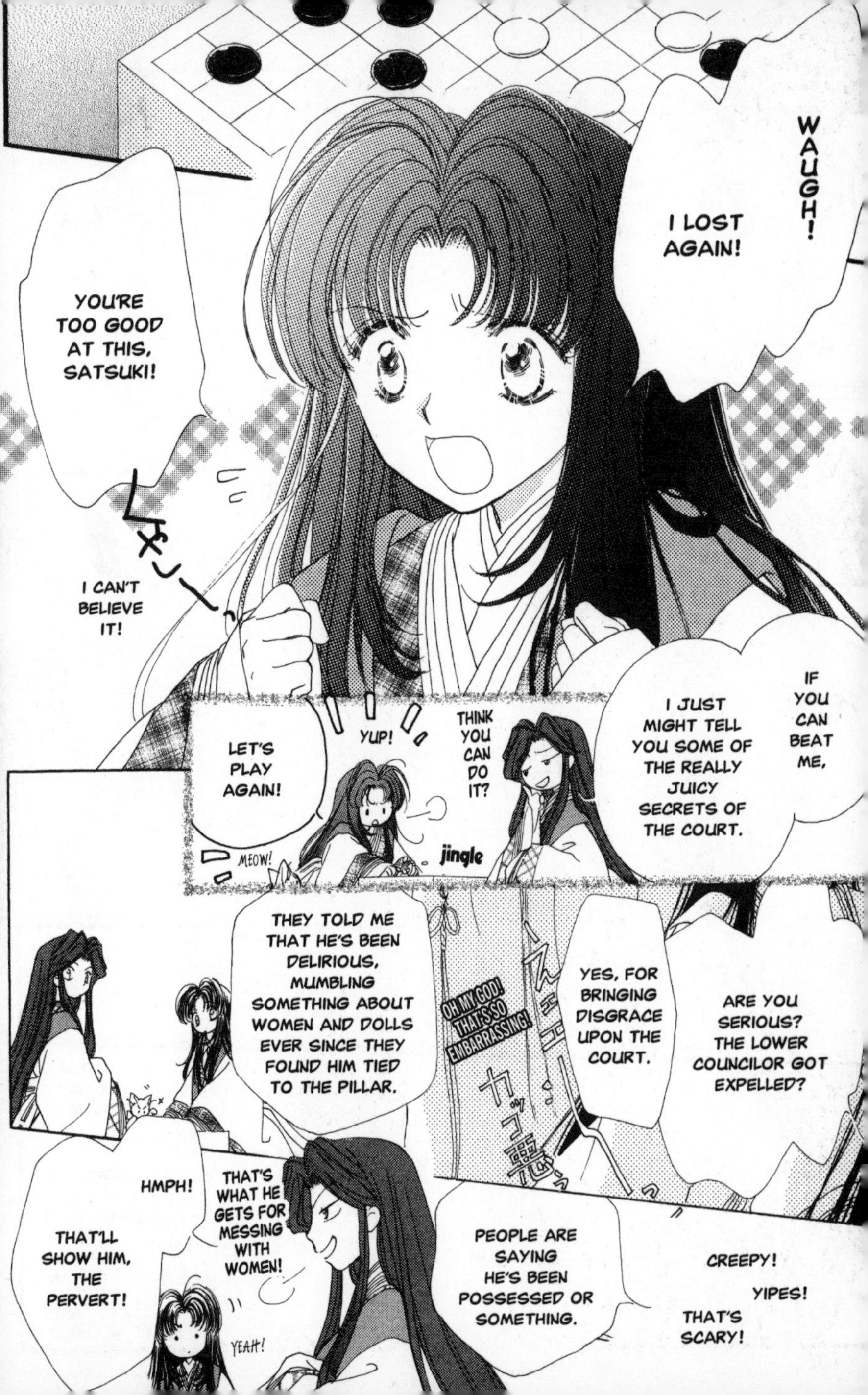
WAUGH!
I LOST AGAIN!
YOU'RE TOO GOOD AT THIS, SATSUKI!
I CAN'T BELIEVE IT!
IF YOU CAN BEAT ME,
I JUST MIGHT TELL YOU SOME OF THE REALLY JUICY SECRETS OF THE COURT.
THINK YOU CAN DO IT?
jingle
YUP!
LET'S PLAY AGAIN!
MEOW!
ARE YOU SERIOUS? THE LOWER COUNCILOR GOT EXPELLED?
YES, FOR BRINGING DISGRACE UPON THE COURT.
OH MY GOD! THAT'S SO EMBARRASSING!
THEY TOLD ME THAT HE'S BEEN DELIRIOUS, MUMBLING SOMETHING ABOUT WOMEN AND DOLLS EVER SINCE THEY FOUND HIM TIED TO THE PILLAR.
CREEPY!
YIPES!
THAT'S SCARY!
PEOPLE ARE SAYING HE'S BEEN POSSESSED OR SOMETHING.
THAT'S WHAT HE GETS FOR MESSING WITH WOMEN!
HMPH!
THAT'LL SHOW HIM, THE PERVERT!
YEAH!

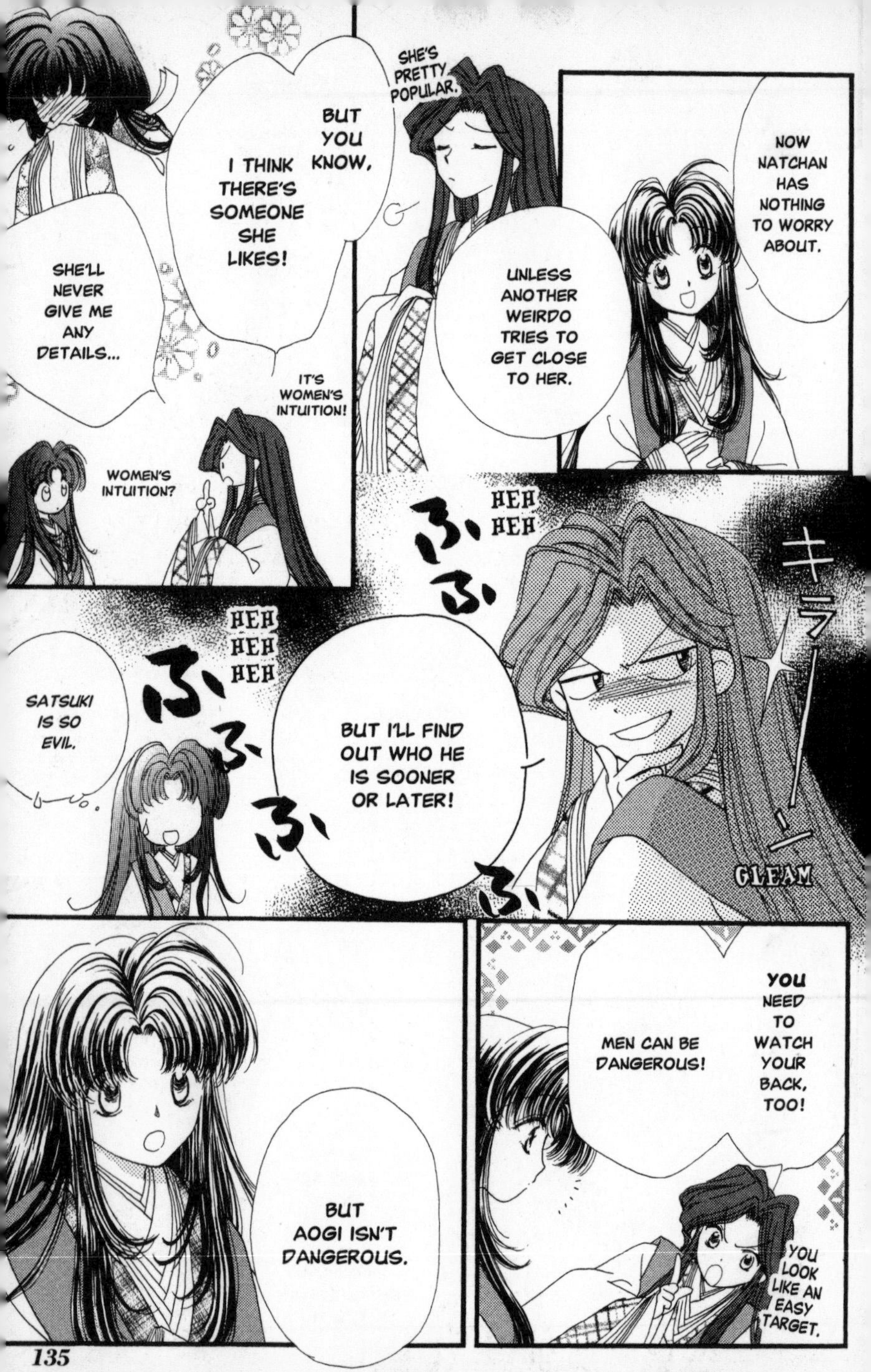
NOW NATCHAN HAS NOTHING TO WORRY ABOUT.
UNLESS ANOTHER WEIRDO TRIES TO GET CLOSE TO HER.
SHE'S PRETTY POPULAR.
BUT YOU KNOW,
I THINK THERE'S SOMEONE SHE LIKES!
SHE'LL NEVER GIVE ME ANY DETAILS...
IT'S WOMEN'S INTUITION!
WOMEN'S INTUITION?
ふふ
HEH HEH
キラーン
GLEAM
BUT I'LL FIND OUT WHO HE IS SOONER OR LATER!
ふふふ
HEH HEH HEH
SATSUKI IS SO EVIL.
YOU NEED TO WATCH YOUR BACK, TOO!
MEN CAN BE DANGEROUS!
YOU LOOK LIKE AN EASY TARGET.
BUT AOGI ISN'T DANGEROUS.

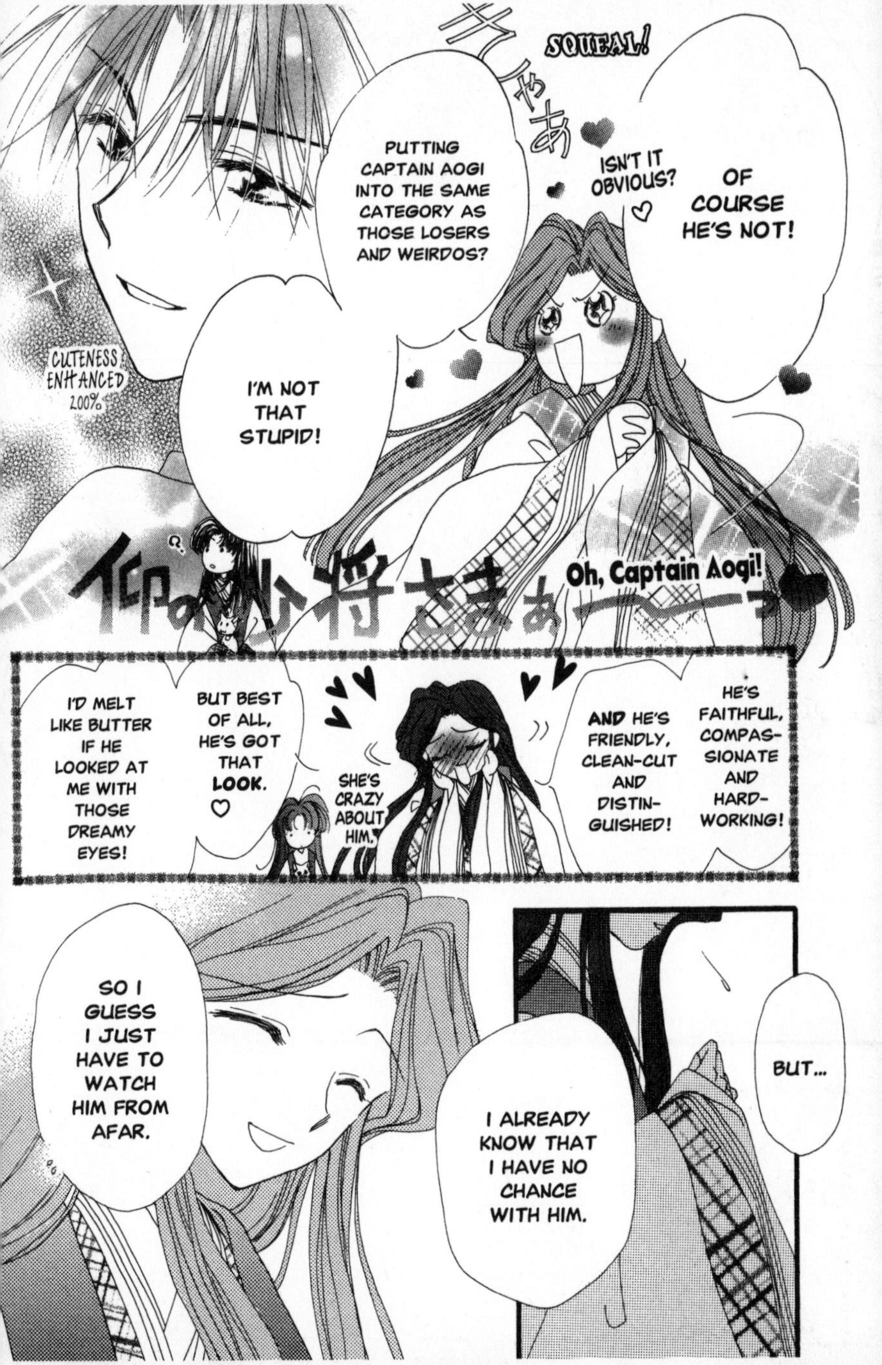
SQUEAL!
OF COURSE HE'S NOT!
ISN'T IT OBVIOUS?
PUTTING CAPTAIN AOGI INTO THE SAME CATEGORY AS THOSE LOSERS AND WEIRDOS?
I'M NOT THAT STUPID!
CUTENESS ENHANCED 200%
Oh, Captain Aogi!
HE'S FAITHFUL, COMPASSIONATE AND HARD-WORKING!
AND HE'S FRIENDLY, CLEAN-CUT AND DISTINGUISHED!
SHE'S CRAZY ABOUT HIM.
BUT BEST OF ALL, HE'S GOT THAT LOOK. ♡
I'D MELT LIKE BUTTER IF HE LOOKED AT ME WITH THOSE DREAMY EYES!
BUT...
I ALREADY KNOW THAT I HAVE NO CHANCE WITH HIM.
SO I GUESS I JUST HAVE TO WATCH HIM FROM AFAR.

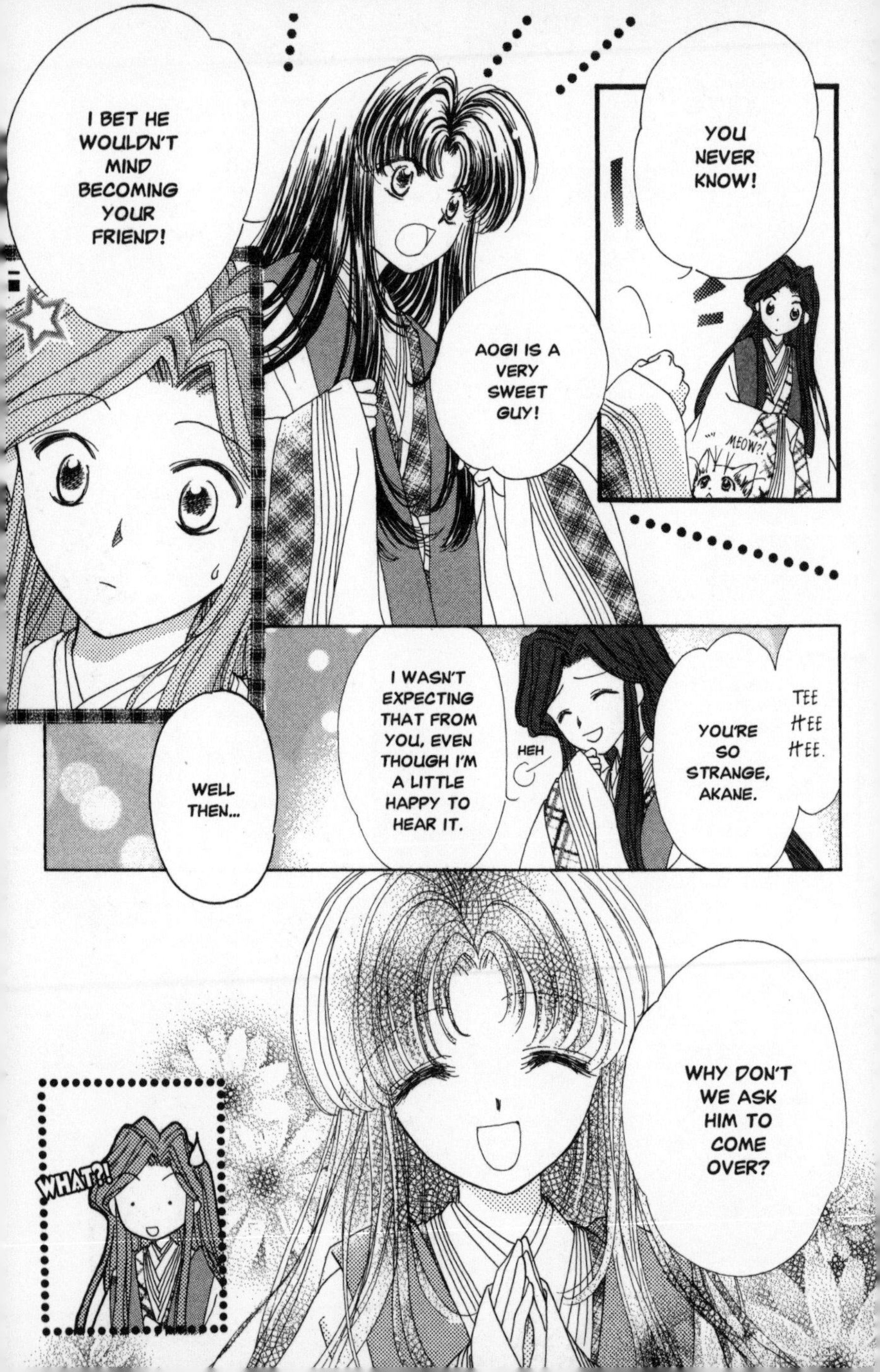
YOU NEVER KNOW!
MEOW?!
AOGI IS A VERY SWEET GUY!
I BET HE WOULDN'T MIND BECOMING YOUR FRIEND!
TEE HEE HEE.
YOU'RE SO STRANGE, AKANE.
HEH
I WASN'T EXPECTING THAT FROM YOU, EVEN THOUGH I'M A LITTLE HAPPY TO HEAR IT.
WELL THEN...
WHY DON'T WE ASK HIM TO COME OVER?
WHAT?!

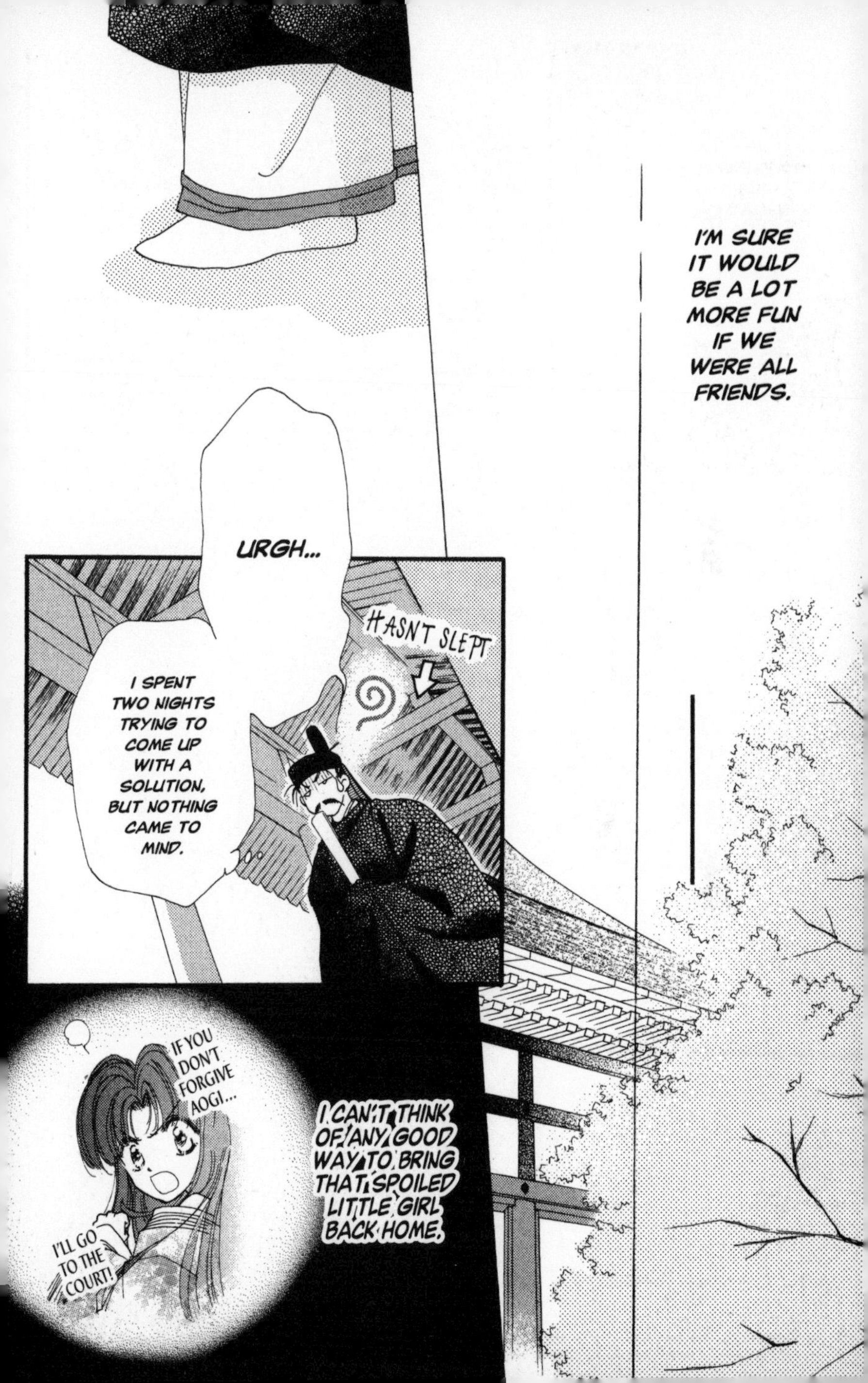
I'M SURE IT WOULD BE A LOT MORE FUN IF WE WERE ALL FRIENDS.
URGH...
I SPENT TWO NIGHTS TRYING TO COME UP WITH A SOLUTION, BUT NOTHING CAME TO MIND.
HASN'T SLEPT
I CAN'T THINK OF ANY GOOD WAY TO BRING THAT SPOILED LITTLE GIRL BACK HOME.
IF YOU DON'T FORGIVE AOGI...
I'LL GO TO THE COURT!

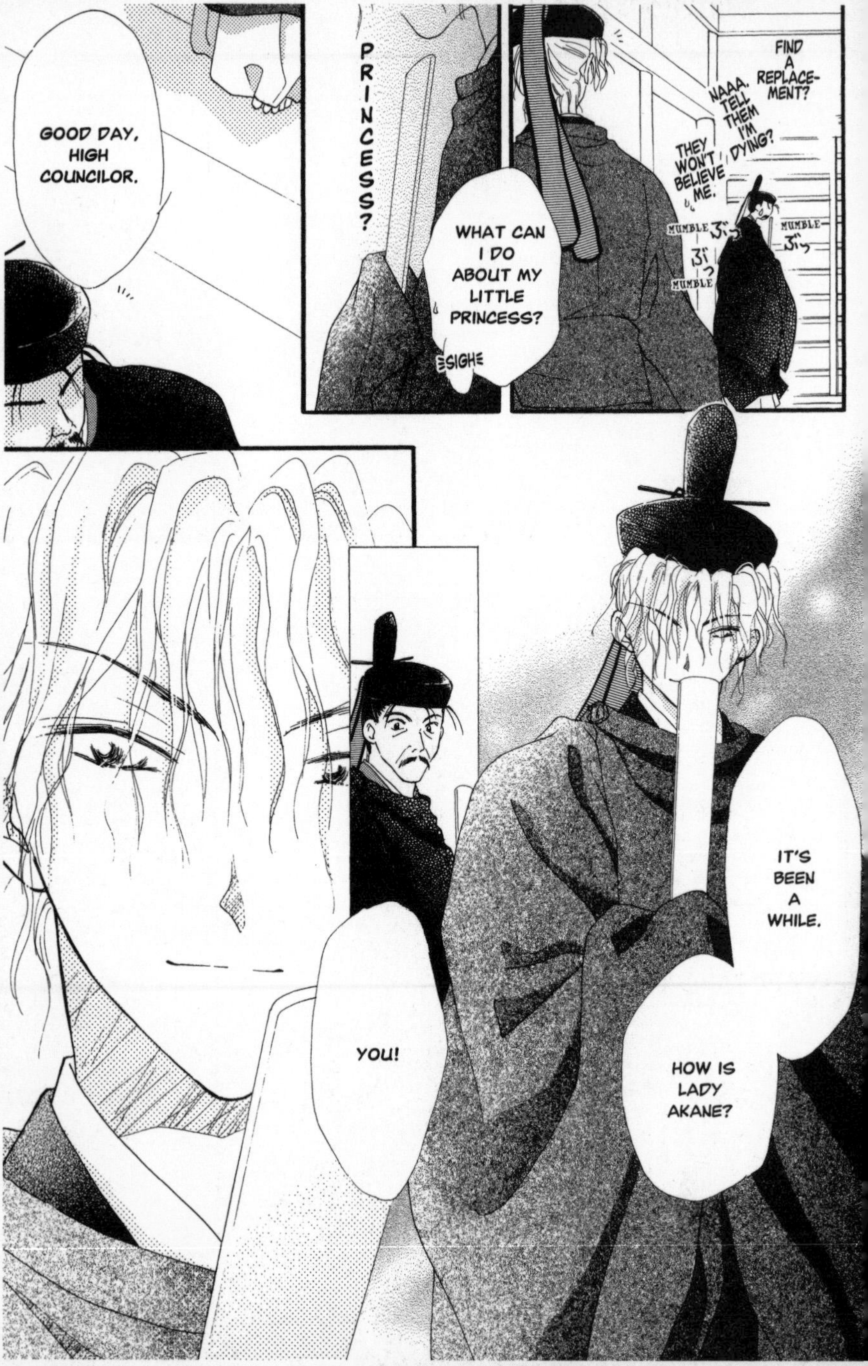
FIND A REPLACEMENT?
NAAA. TELL THEM I'M DYING?
THEY WON'T BELIEVE ME.
MUMBLE ぶつ
MUMBLE ぶつ
MUMBLE ぶつ
WHAT CAN I DO ABOUT MY LITTLE PRINCESS?
SIGH
PRINCESS?
GOOD DAY, HIGH COUNCILOR.
IT'S BEEN A WHILE.
HOW IS LADY AKANE?
YOU!

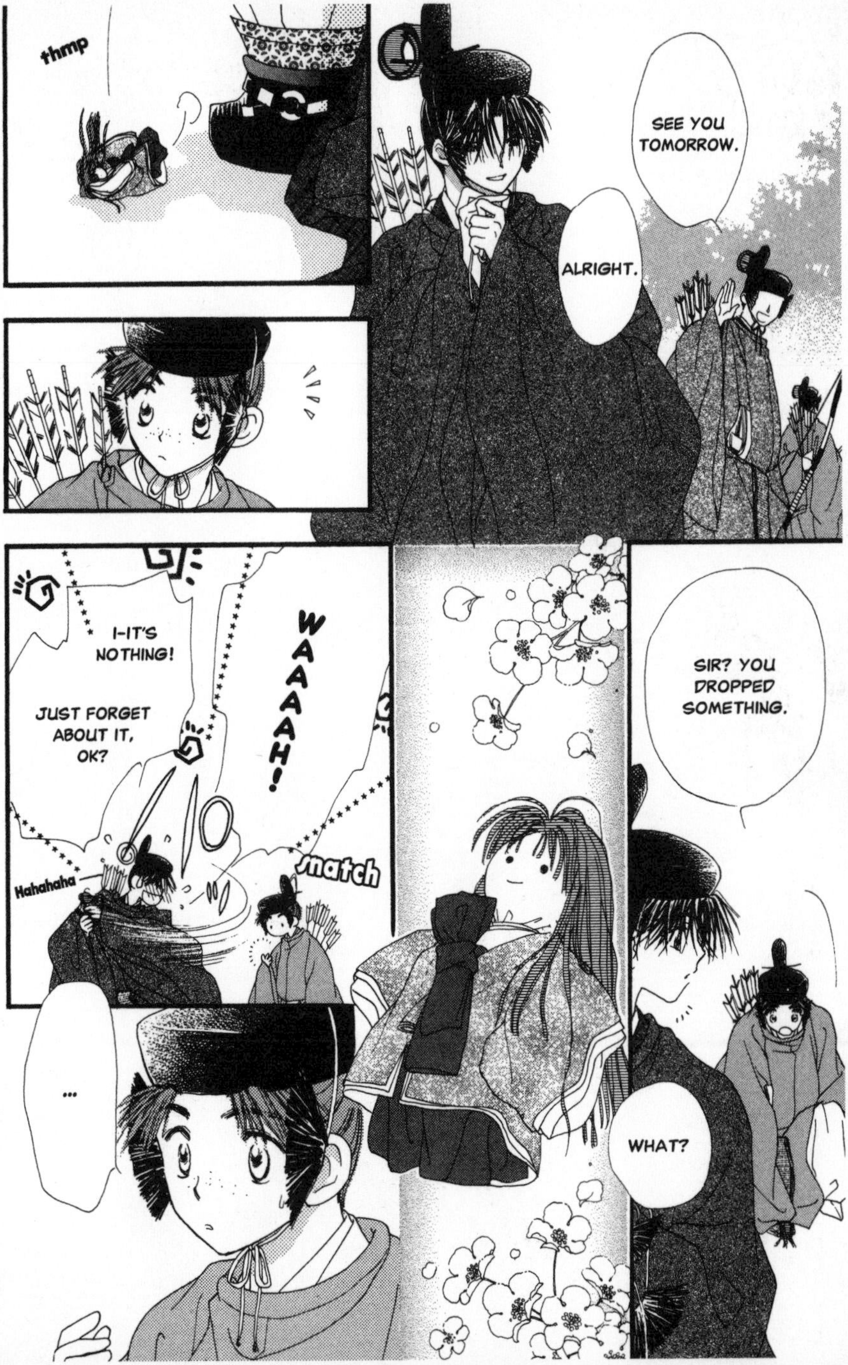
SEE YOU TOMORROW.
ALRIGHT.
thmp
SIR? YOU DROPPED SOMETHING.
WHAT?
WAAAAAH!
I-IT'S NOTHING!
JUST FORGET ABOUT IT, OK?
snatch
Hahahaha
...

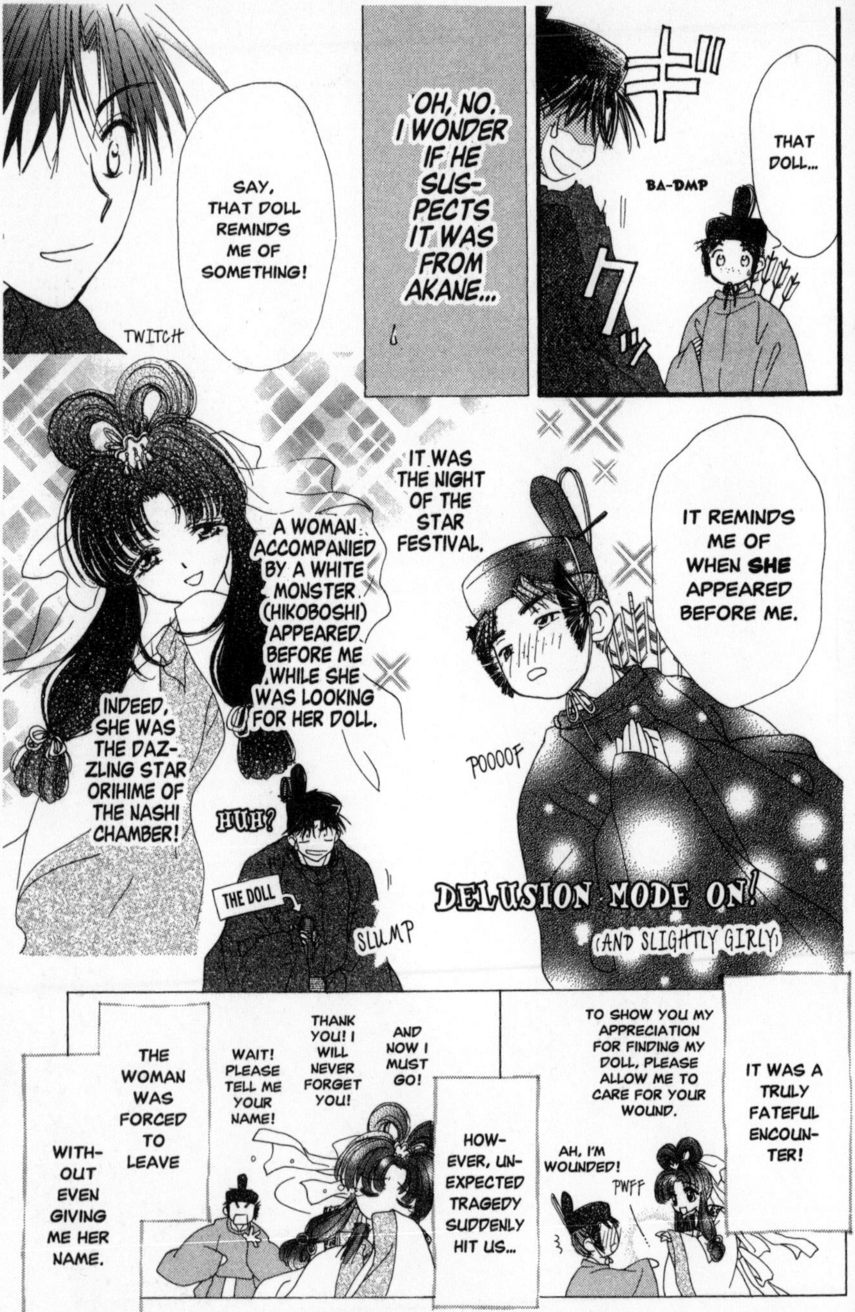
THAT DOLL...
BA-DMP
OH, NO. I WONDER IF HE SUS-PECTS IT WAS FROM AKANE...
SAY, THAT DOLL REMINDS ME OF SOMETHING!
TWITCH
IT REMINDS ME OF WHEN SHE APPEARED BEFORE ME.
IT WAS THE NIGHT OF THE STAR FESTIVAL.
A WOMAN ACCOMPANIED BY A WHITE MONSTER (HIKOBOSHI) APPEARED BEFORE ME WHILE SHE WAS LOOKING FOR HER DOLL.
INDEED, SHE WAS THE DAZ-ZLING STAR ORIHIME OF THE NASHI CHAMBER!
POOOOF
DELUSION MODE ON!
(AND SLIGHTLY GIRLY)
HUH?
THE DOLL
SLUMP
IT WAS A TRULY FATEFUL ENCOUN-TER!
TO SHOW YOU MY APPRECIATION FOR FINDING MY DOLL, PLEASE ALLOW ME TO CARE FOR YOUR WOUND.
AH, I'M WOUNDED!
PWFF
HOW-EVER, UN-EXPECTED TRAGEDY SUDDENLY HIT US...
AND NOW I MUST GO!
THANK YOU! I WILL NEVER FORGET YOU!
WAIT! PLEASE TELL ME YOUR NAME!
THE WOMAN WAS FORCED TO LEAVE
WITH-OUT EVEN GIVING ME HER NAME.

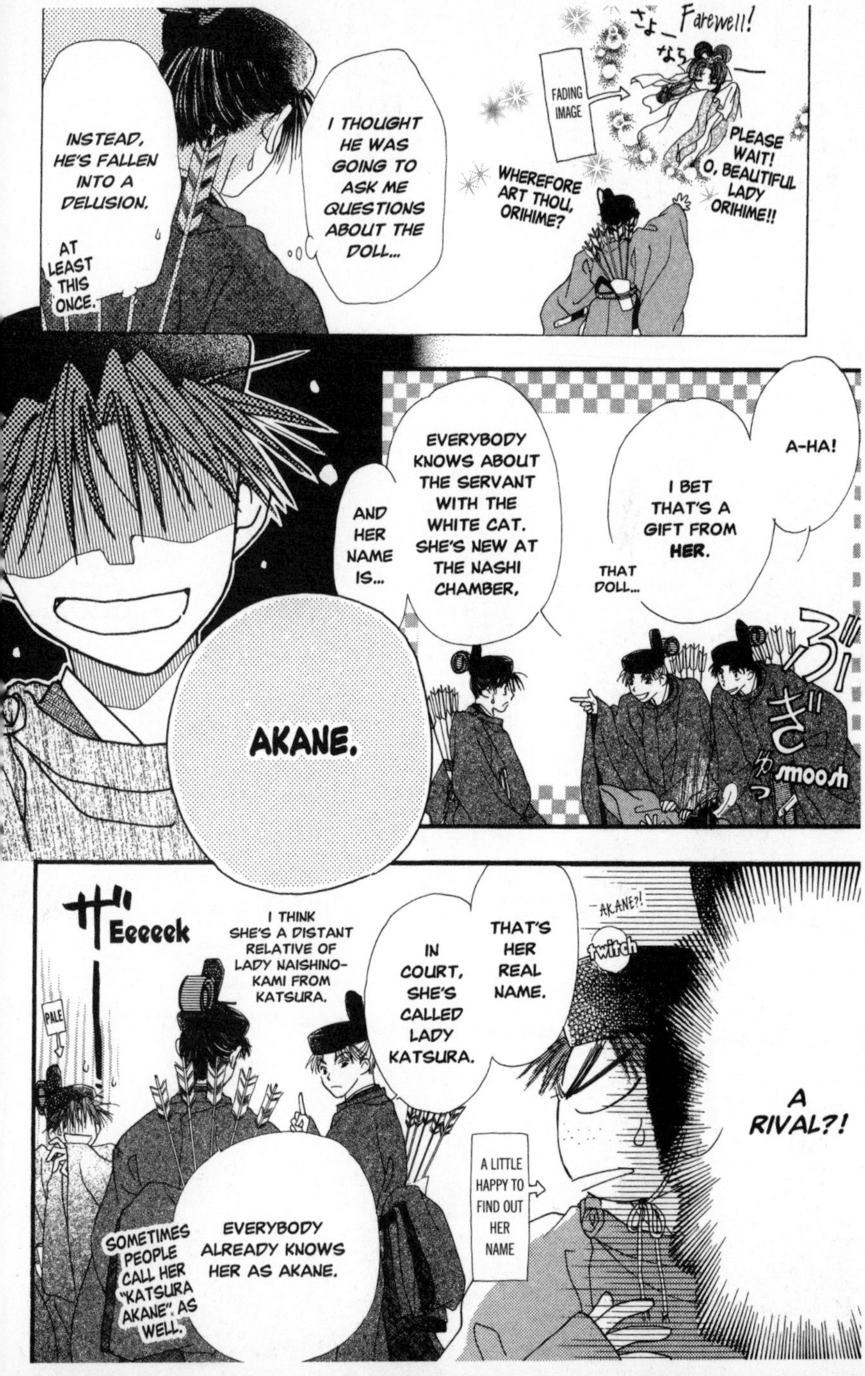
さよー なら Farewell!
FADING IMAGE
PLEASE WAIT! O, BEAUTIFUL LADY ORIHIME!!
WHEREFORE ART THOU, ORIHIME?
I THOUGHT HE WAS GOING TO ASK ME QUESTIONS ABOUT THE DOLL...
INSTEAD, HE'S FALLEN INTO A DELUSION.
AT LEAST THIS ONCE.
A-HA!
I BET THAT'S A GIFT FROM HER.
THAT DOLL...
smoosh
EVERYBODY KNOWS ABOUT THE SERVANT WITH THE WHITE CAT. SHE'S NEW AT THE NASHI CHAMBER,
AND HER NAME IS...
AKANE.
A RIVAL?!
—AKANE?!
twitch
A LITTLE HAPPY TO FIND OUT HER NAME
THAT'S HER REAL NAME.
IN COURT, SHE'S CALLED LADY KATSURA.
I THINK SHE'S A DISTANT RELATIVE OF LADY NAISHINO-KAMI FROM KATSURA.
EVERYBODY ALREADY KNOWS HER AS AKANE.
SOMETIMES PEOPLE CALL HER "KATSURA AKANE" AS WELL.
Eeeeek
PALE

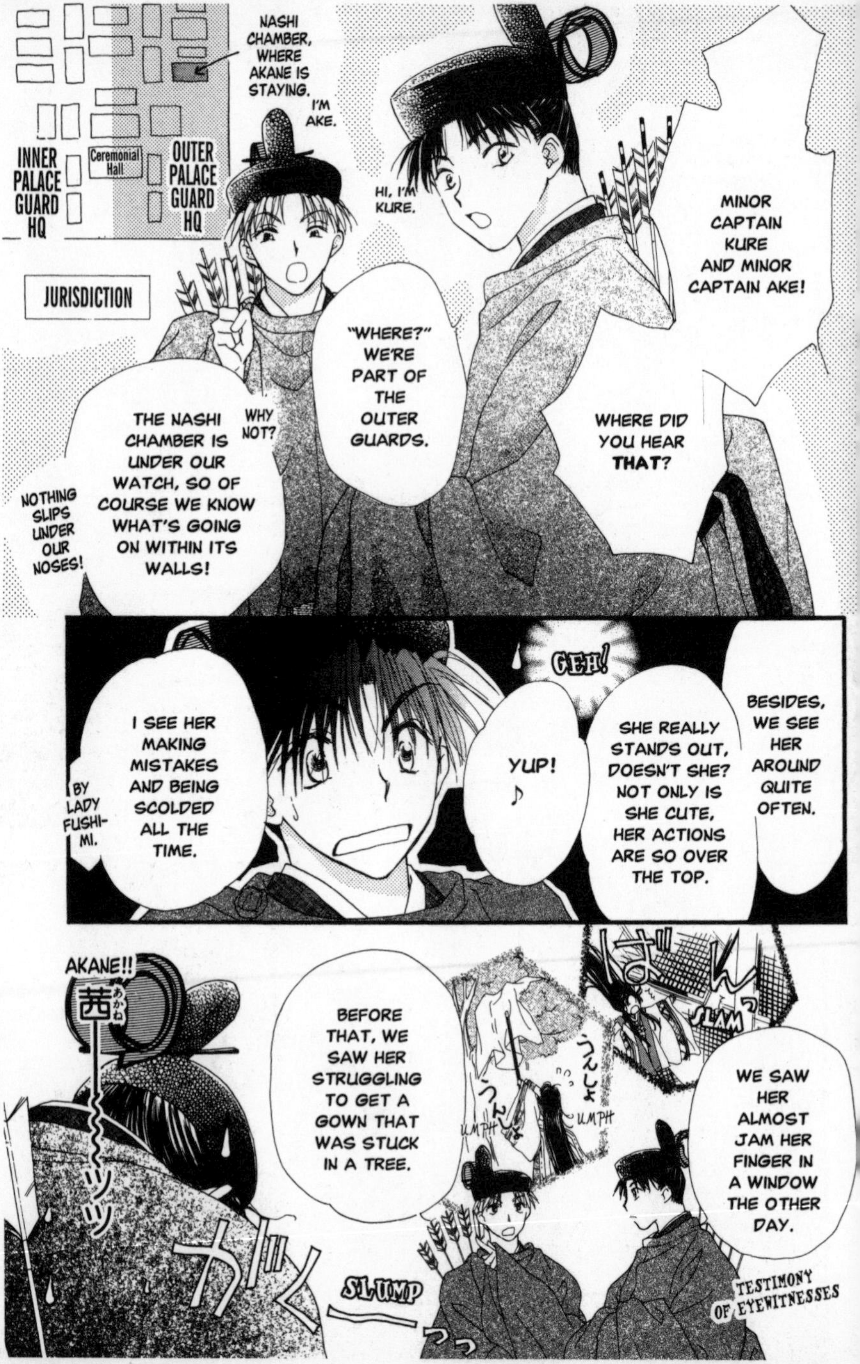
MINOR CAPTAIN KURE AND MINOR CAPTAIN AKE!
WHERE DID YOU HEAR THAT?
HI, I'M KURE.
I'M AKE.
NASHI CHAMBER, WHERE AKANE IS STAYING.
INNER PALACE GUARD HQ
Ceremonial Hall
OUTER PALACE GUARD HQ
JURISDICTION
"WHERE?" WE'RE PART OF THE OUTER GUARDS.
WHY NOT?
THE NASHI CHAMBER IS UNDER OUR WATCH, SO OF COURSE WE KNOW WHAT'S GOING ON WITHIN ITS WALLS!
NOTHING SLIPS UNDER OUR NOSES!
BESIDES, WE SEE HER AROUND QUITE OFTEN.
SHE REALLY STANDS OUT, DOESN'T SHE? NOT ONLY IS SHE CUTE, HER ACTIONS ARE SO OVER THE TOP.
YUP! ♪
GEH!
I SEE HER MAKING MISTAKES AND BEING SCOLDED ALL THE TIME.
BY LADY FUSHIMI.
SLAM
WE SAW HER ALMOST JAM HER FINGER IN A WINDOW THE OTHER DAY.
うんしょ
UMPH
うんしょ
UMPH
BEFORE THAT, WE SAW HER STRUGGLING TO GET A GOWN THAT WAS STUCK IN A TREE.
AKANE!!
茜
SLUMP
TESTIMONY OF EYEWITNESSES

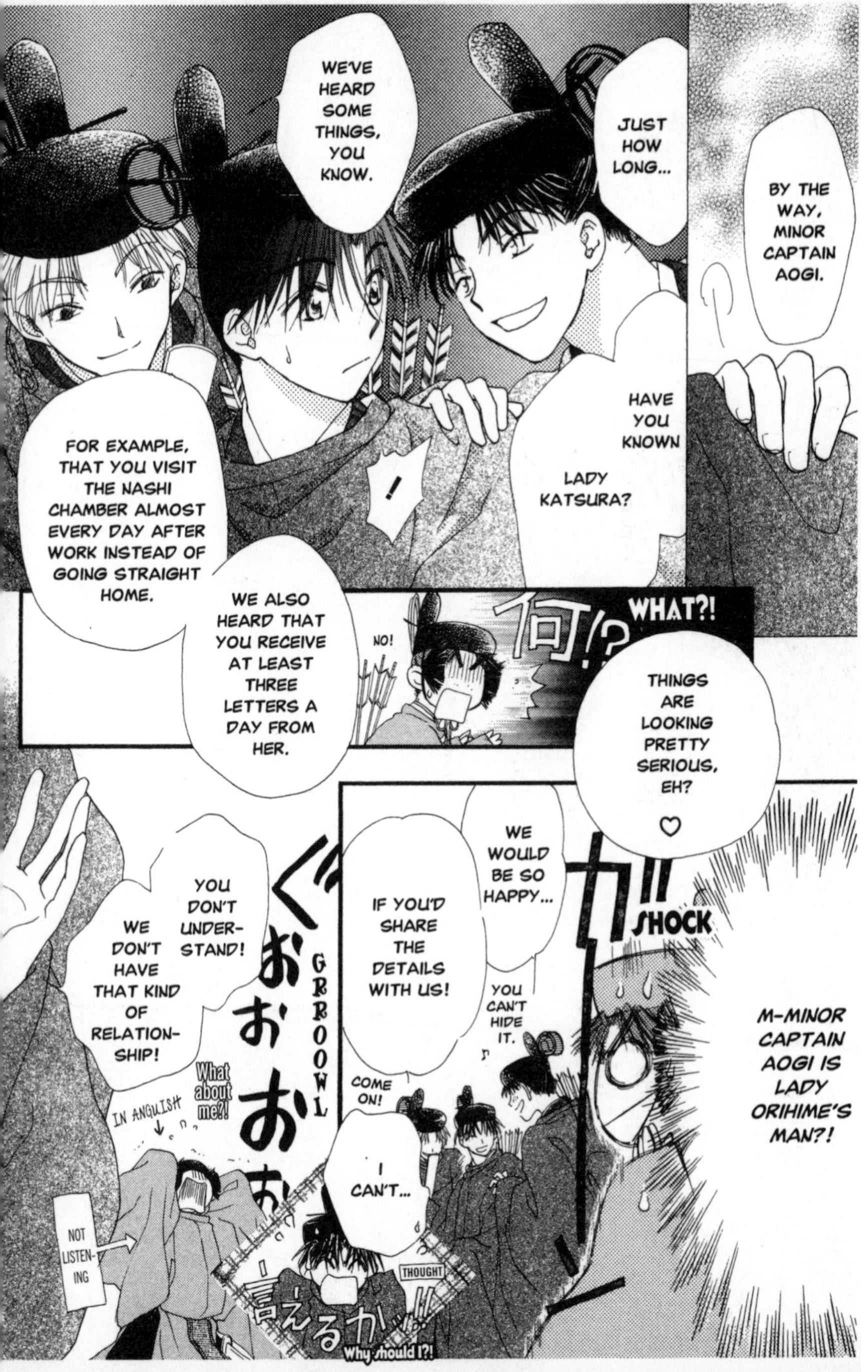
BY THE WAY, MINOR CAPTAIN AOGI.
JUST HOW LONG...
HAVE YOU KNOWN
LADY KATSURA?
WE'VE HEARD SOME THINGS, YOU KNOW.
!
FOR EXAMPLE, THAT YOU VISIT THE NASHI CHAMBER ALMOST EVERY DAY AFTER WORK INSTEAD OF GOING STRAIGHT HOME.
THINGS ARE LOOKING PRETTY SERIOUS, EH? ♡
何!?
WHAT?!
NO!
WE ALSO HEARD THAT YOU RECEIVE AT LEAST THREE LETTERS A DAY FROM HER.
ガ
SHOCK
M-MINOR CAPTAIN AOGI IS LADY ORIHIME'S MAN?!
WE WOULD BE SO HAPPY...
IF YOU'D SHARE THE DETAILS WITH US!
YOU CAN'T HIDE IT.
COME ON!
I CAN'T...
THOUGHT
言えるか!!
Why should I?!
ぐおおおお
GRROOOWL
YOU DON'T UNDER-STAND!
WE DON'T HAVE THAT KIND OF RELATION-SHIP!
What about me?!
IN ANGUISH
NOT LISTEN-ING

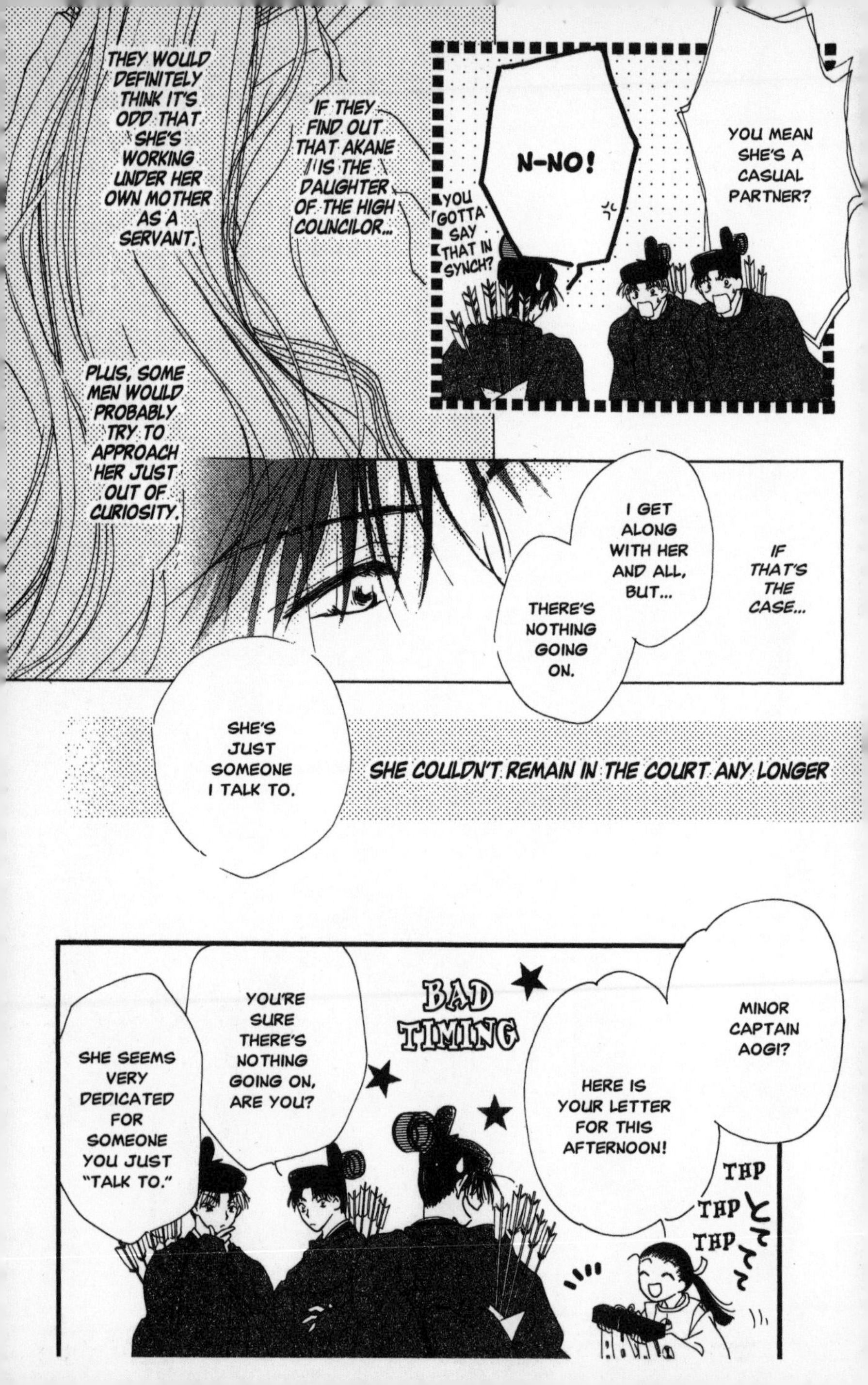

YOU MEAN SHE'S A CASUAL PARTNER?
N-NO!
YOU GOTTA SAY THAT IN SYNCH?
IF THEY FIND OUT THAT AKANE IS THE DAUGHTER OF THE HIGH COUNCILOR...
THEY WOULD DEFINITELY THINK IT'S ODD THAT SHE'S WORKING UNDER HER OWN MOTHER AS A SERVANT.
PLUS, SOME MEN WOULD PROBABLY TRY TO APPROACH HER JUST OUT OF CURIOSITY.
IF THAT'S THE CASE...
SHE COULDN'T REMAIN IN THE COURT ANY LONGER
I GET ALONG WITH HER AND ALL, BUT...
THERE'S NOTHING GOING ON.
SHE'S JUST SOMEONE I TALK TO.
MINOR CAPTAIN AOGI?
HERE IS YOUR LETTER FOR THIS AFTERNOON!
THP THP THP
BAD TIMING
YOU'RE SURE THERE'S NOTHING GOING ON, ARE YOU?
SHE SEEMS VERY DEDICATED FOR SOMEONE YOU JUST "TALK TO."

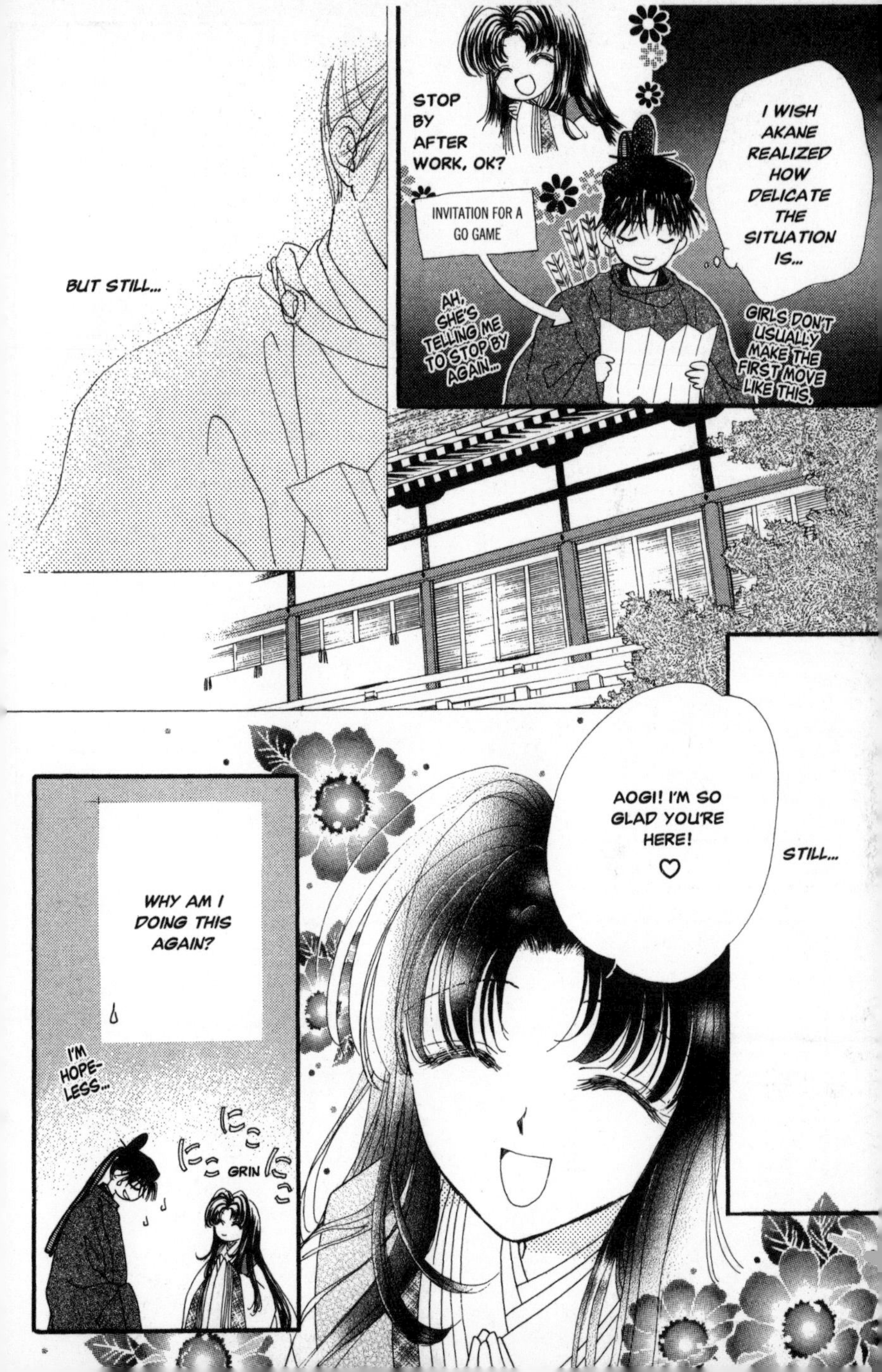

I WISH AKANE REALIZED HOW DELICATE THE SITUATION IS...
GIRLS DON'T USUALLY MAKE THE FIRST MOVE LIKE THIS.
STOP BY AFTER WORK, OK?
INVITATION FOR A GO GAME
AH, SHE'S TELLING ME TO STOP BY AGAIN...
BUT STILL...
STILL...
AOGI! I'M SO GLAD YOU'RE HERE! ♡
WHY AM I DOING THIS AGAIN?
I'M HOPE-LESS...
GRIN

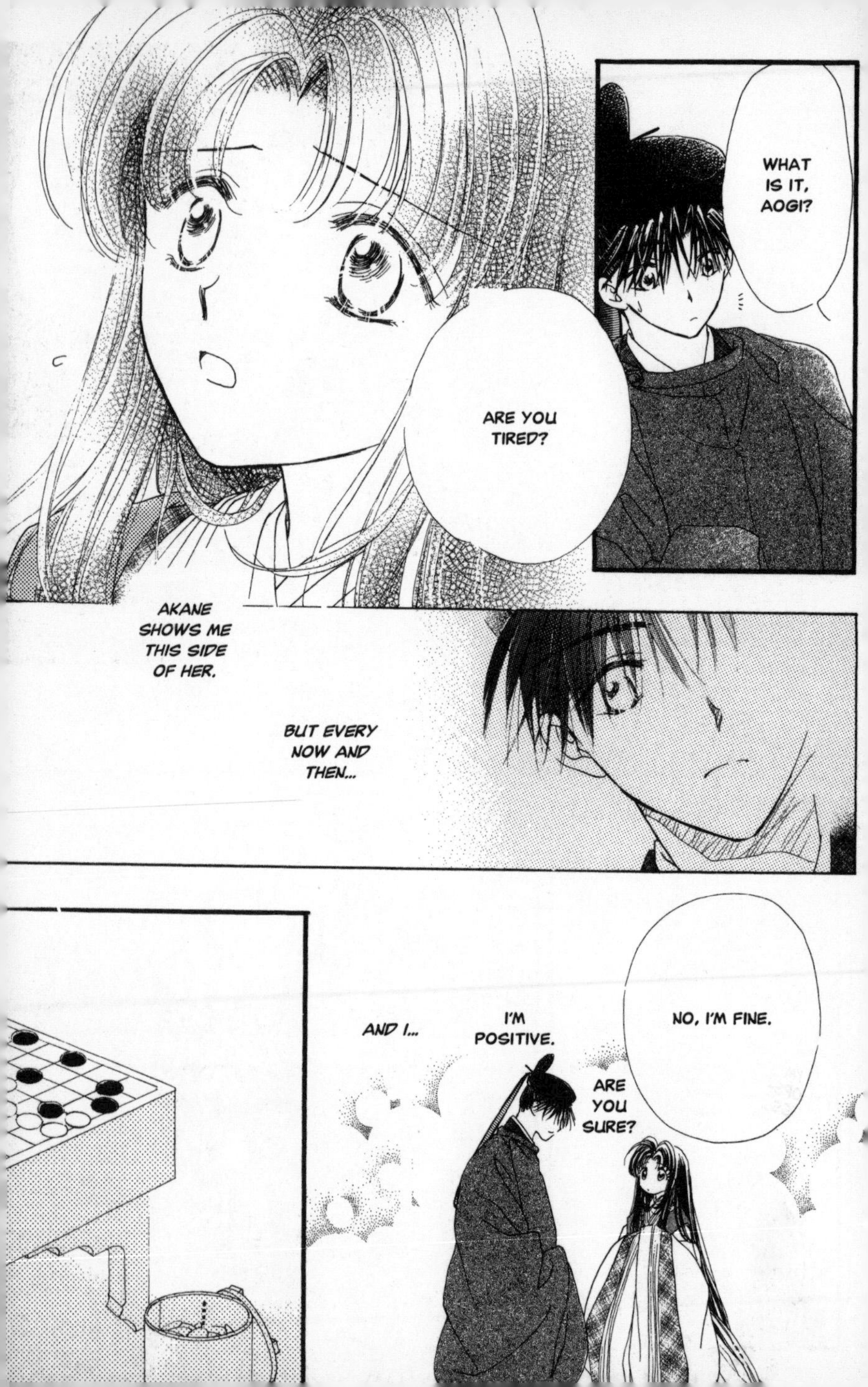
WHAT IS IT, AOGI?
ARE YOU TIRED?
BUT EVERY NOW AND THEN...
AKANE SHOWS ME THIS SIDE OF HER.
NO, I'M FINE.
ARE YOU SURE?
I'M POSITIVE.
AND I...

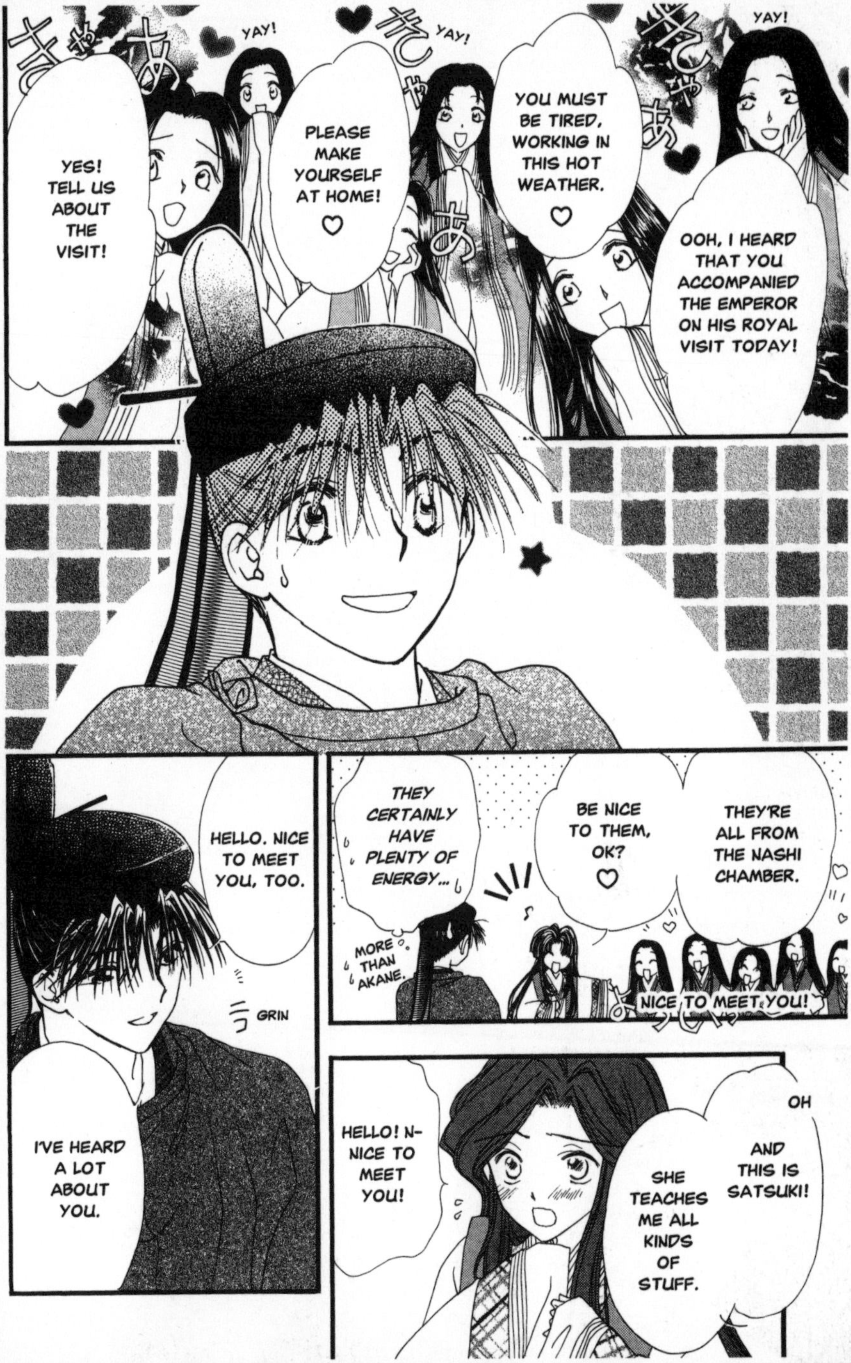
YAY!
OOH, I HEARD THAT YOU ACCOMPANIED THE EMPEROR ON HIS ROYAL VISIT TODAY!
YOU MUST BE TIRED, WORKING IN THIS HOT WEATHER. ♡
YAY!
PLEASE MAKE YOURSELF AT HOME! ♡
YAY!
YES! TELL US ABOUT THE VISIT!
THEY'RE ALL FROM THE NASHI CHAMBER.
BE NICE TO THEM, OK? ♡
NICE TO MEET YOU!
THEY CERTAINLY HAVE PLENTY OF ENERGY...
MORE THAN AKANE.
OH
AND THIS IS SATSUKI!
SHE TEACHES ME ALL KINDS OF STUFF.
HELLO! N-NICE TO MEET YOU!
HELLO. NICE TO MEET YOU, TOO.
GRIN
I'VE HEARD A LOT ABOUT YOU.

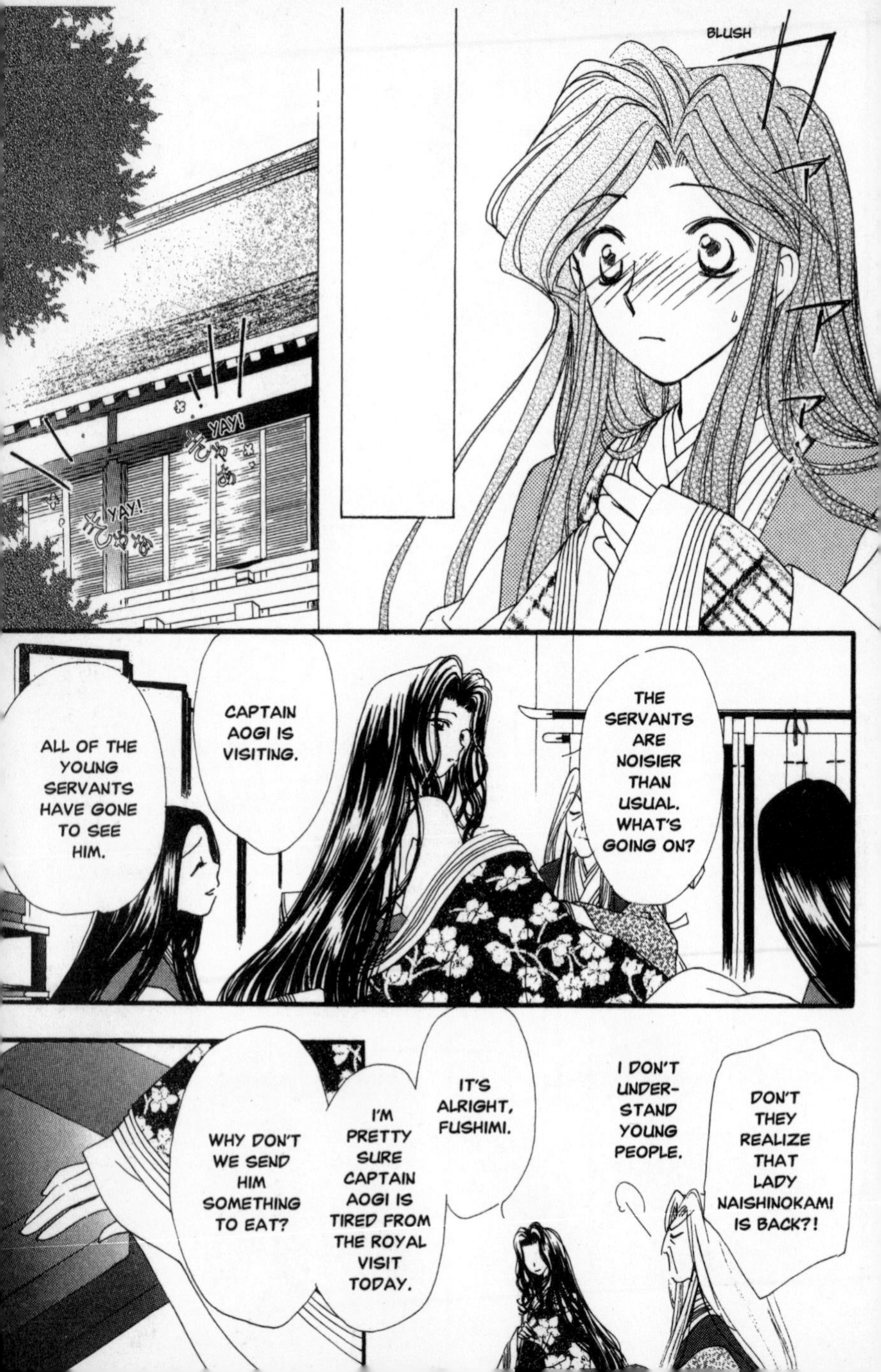
BLUSH
YAY!
YAY!
THE SERVANTS ARE NOISIER THAN USUAL. WHAT'S GOING ON?
CAPTAIN AOGI IS VISITING.
ALL OF THE YOUNG SERVANTS HAVE GONE TO SEE HIM.
DON'T THEY REALIZE THAT LADY NAISHINOKAMI IS BACK?!
I DON'T UNDER-STAND YOUNG PEOPLE.
IT'S ALRIGHT, FUSHIMI.
I'M PRETTY SURE CAPTAIN AOGI IS TIRED FROM THE ROYAL VISIT TODAY.
WHY DON'T WE SEND HIM SOMETHING TO EAT?

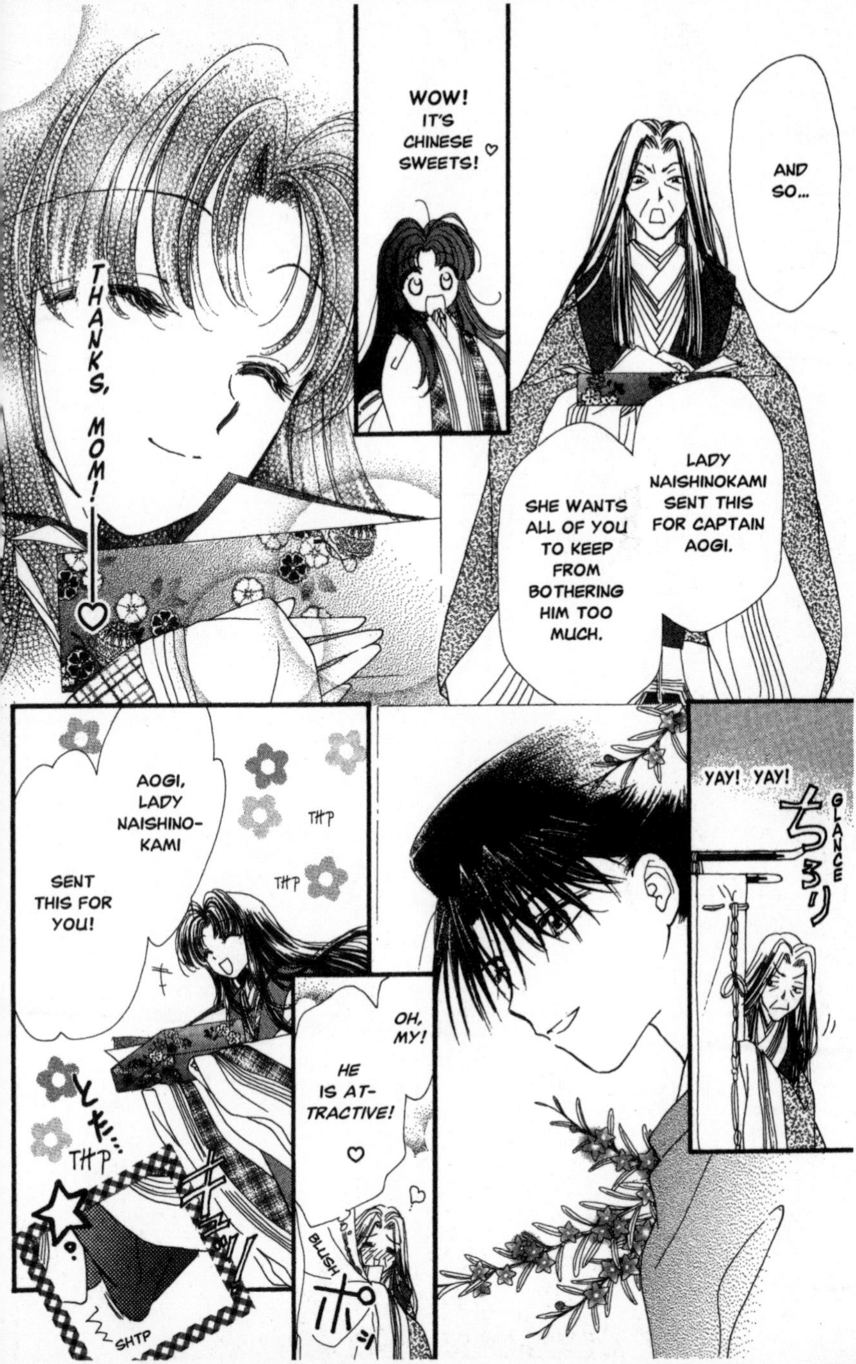

AND SO...
LADY NAISHINOKAMI SENT THIS FOR CAPTAIN AOGI.
SHE WANTS ALL OF YOU TO KEEP FROM BOTHERING HIM TOO MUCH.
WOW! IT'S CHINESE SWEETS! ♡
THANKS, MOM! ♡
YAY! YAY!
ちろり GLANCE
AOGI, LADY NAISHINO-KAMI
SENT THIS FOR YOU!
THP
THP
THP
OH, MY!
HE IS AT-TRACTIVE! ♡
BLUSH
SHTP

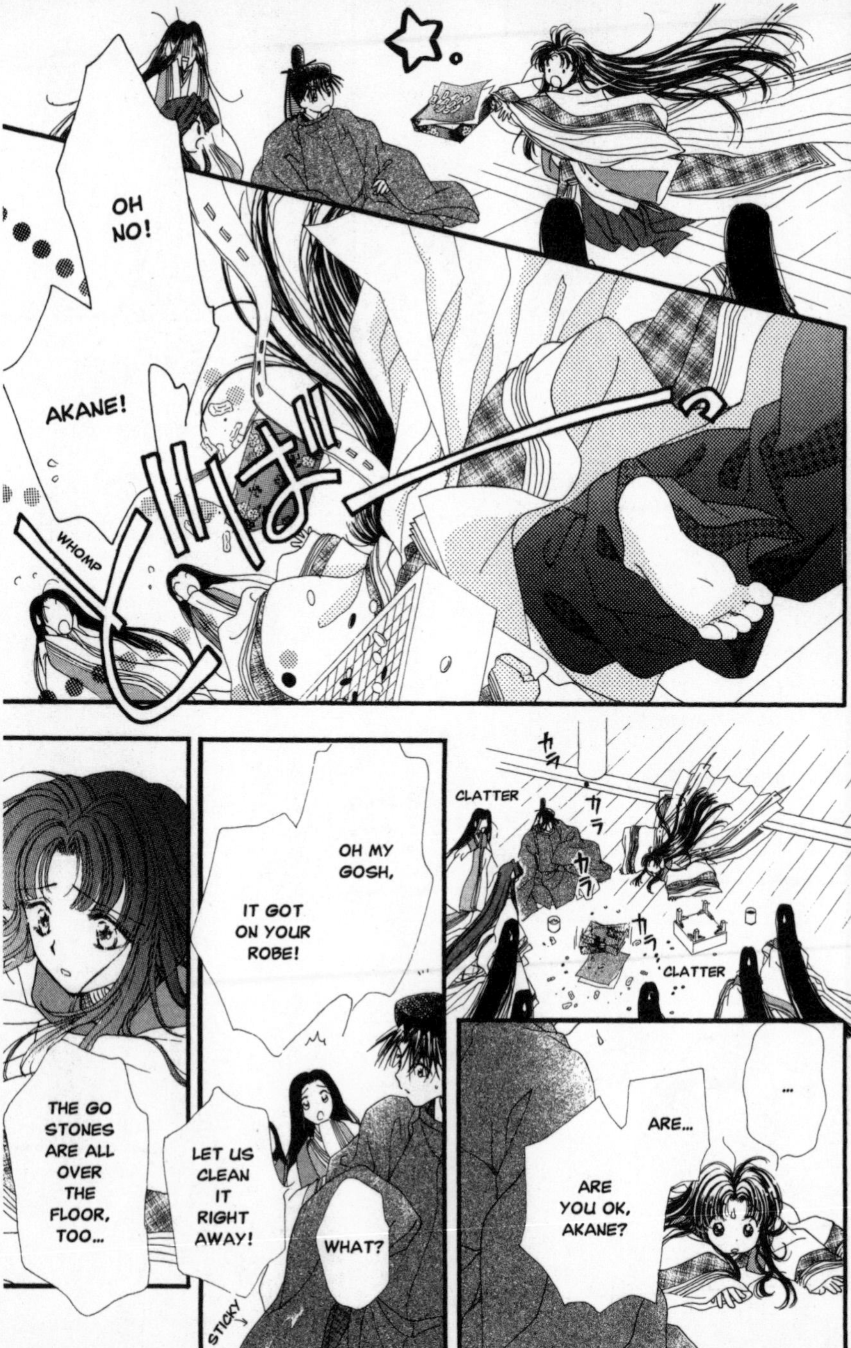

OH NO!
AKANE!
WHOMP
CLATTER
カラ
カラ
カラ
カラ
CLATTER
...
ARE...
ARE YOU OK, AKANE?
OH MY GOSH,
IT GOT ON YOUR ROBE!
LET US CLEAN IT RIGHT AWAY!
WHAT?
STICKY
THE GO STONES ARE ALL OVER THE FLOOR, TOO...

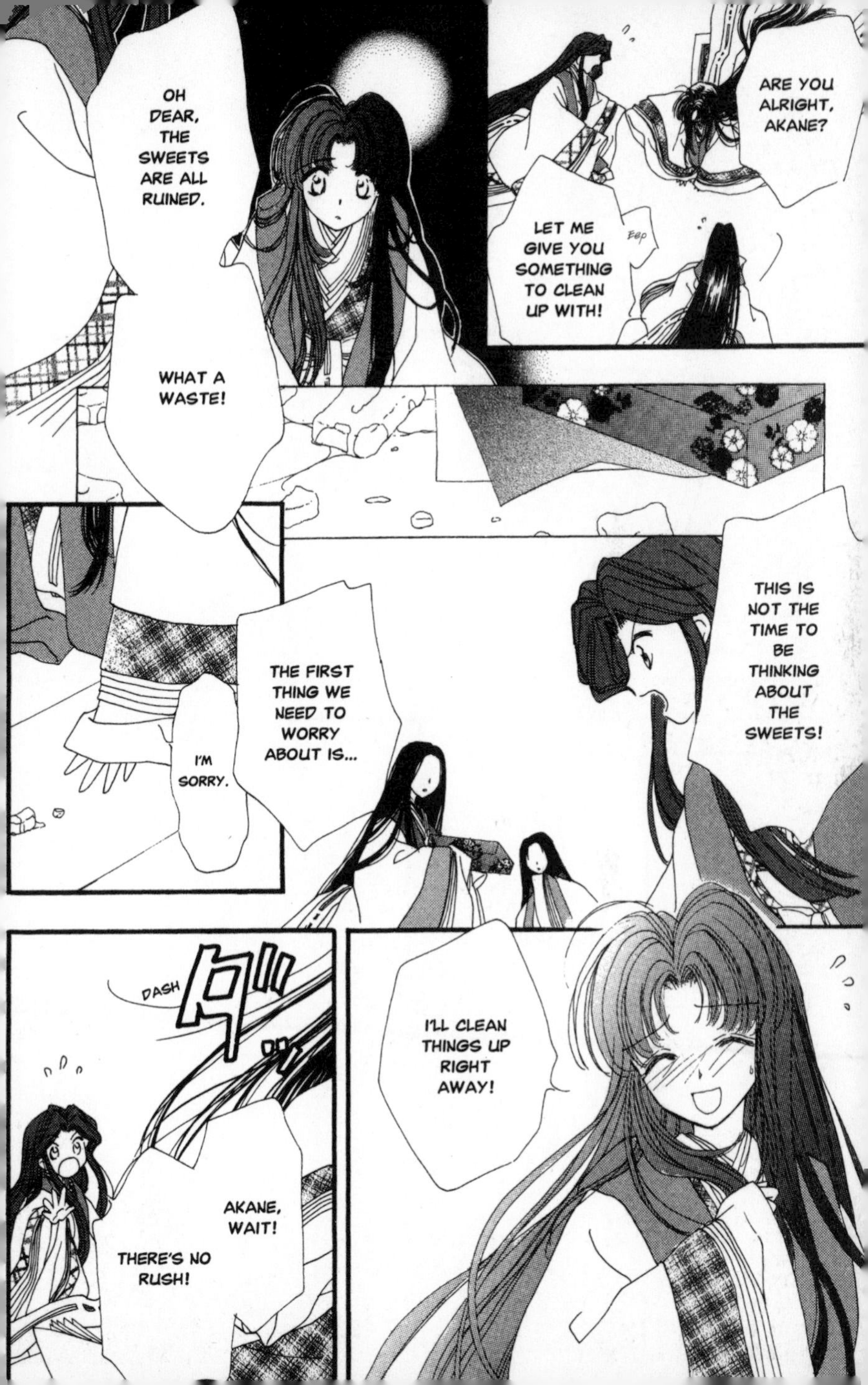
ARE YOU ALRIGHT, AKANE?
LET ME GIVE YOU SOMETHING TO CLEAN UP WITH!
Eep
OH DEAR, THE SWEETS ARE ALL RUINED.
WHAT A WASTE!
THIS IS NOT THE TIME TO BE THINKING ABOUT THE SWEETS!
THE FIRST THING WE NEED TO WORRY ABOUT IS...
I'M SORRY.
I'LL CLEAN THINGS UP RIGHT AWAY!
DASH
AKANE, WAIT!
THERE'S NO RUSH!

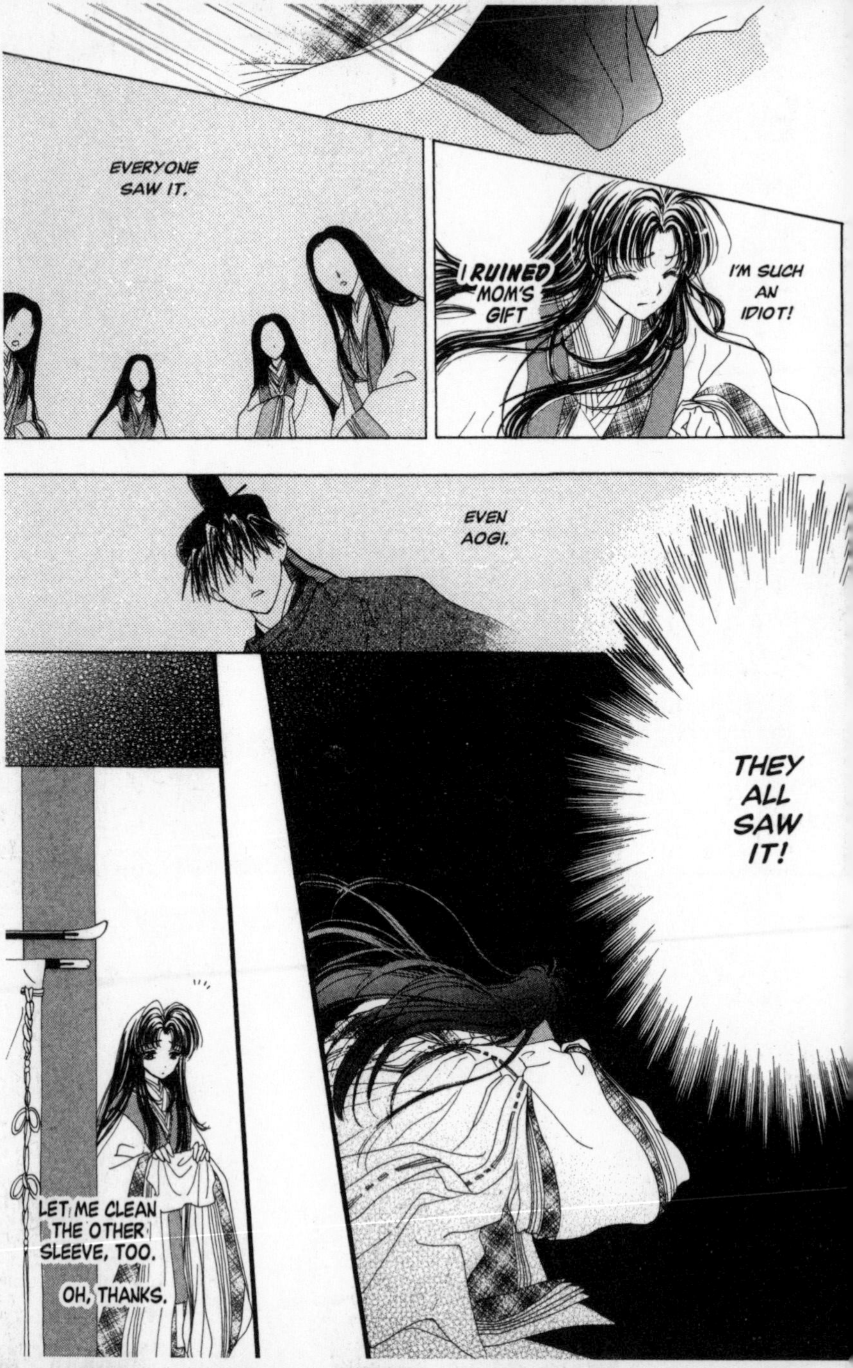
I'M SUCH AN IDIOT!
I RUINED MOM'S GIFT
EVERYONE SAW IT.
EVEN AOGI.
THEY ALL SAW IT!
LET ME CLEAN THE OTHER SLEEVE, TOO.
OH, THANKS.

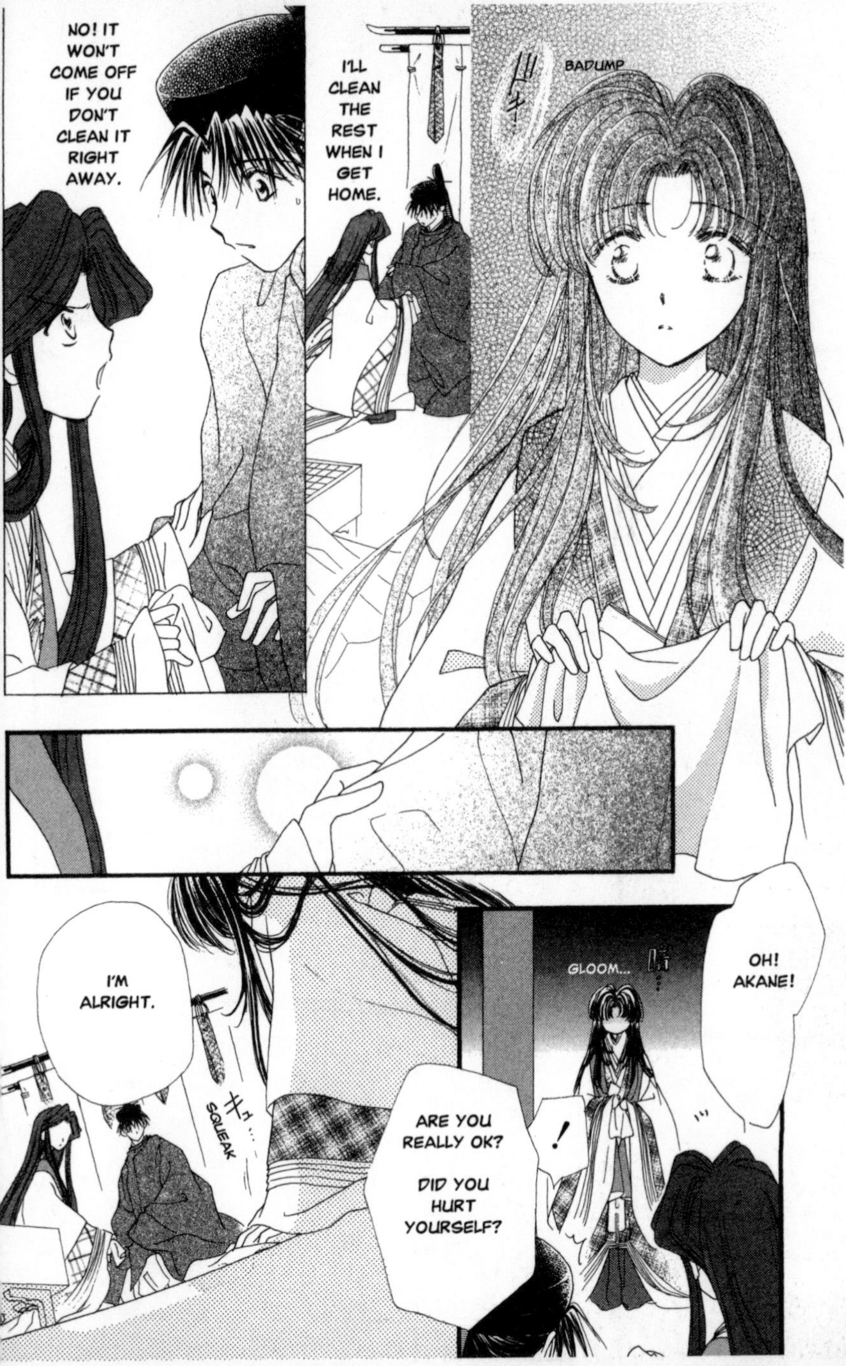
BADUMP
I'LL CLEAN THE REST WHEN I GET HOME.
NO! IT WON'T COME OFF IF YOU DON'T CLEAN IT RIGHT AWAY.
OH! AKANE!
GLOOM...
!
ARE YOU REALLY OK?
DID YOU HURT YOURSELF?
I'M ALRIGHT.
SQUEAK

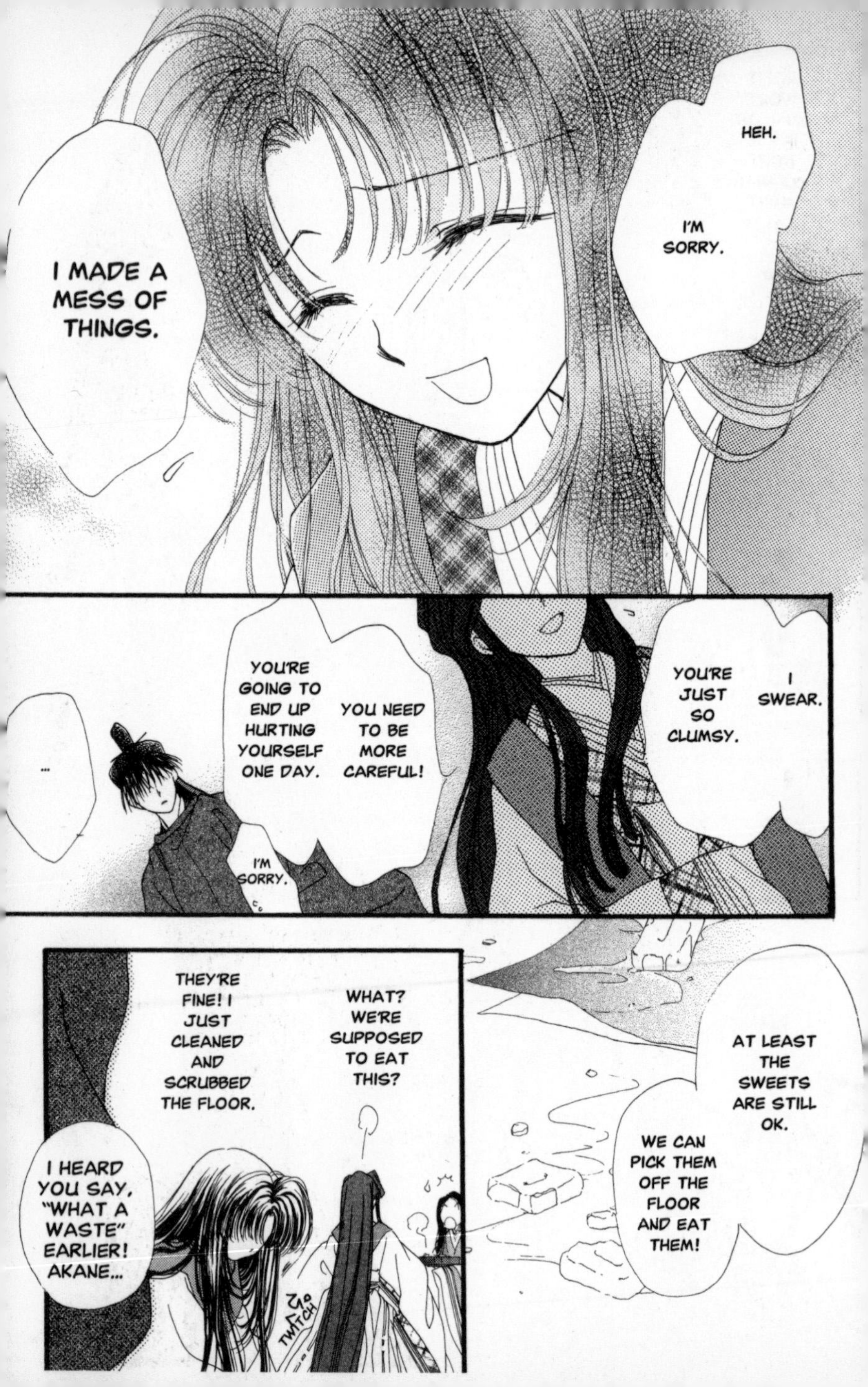
HEH.
I'M SORRY.
I MADE A MESS OF THINGS.
I SWEAR.
YOU'RE JUST SO CLUMSY.
YOU NEED TO BE MORE CAREFUL!
YOU'RE GOING TO END UP HURTING YOURSELF ONE DAY.
I'M SORRY.
...
AT LEAST THE SWEETS ARE STILL OK.
WE CAN PICK THEM OFF THE FLOOR AND EAT THEM!
WHAT? WE'RE SUPPOSED TO EAT THIS?
THEY'RE FINE! I JUST CLEANED AND SCRUBBED THE FLOOR.
I HEARD YOU SAY, "WHAT A WASTE" EARLIER! AKANE...
TWITCH

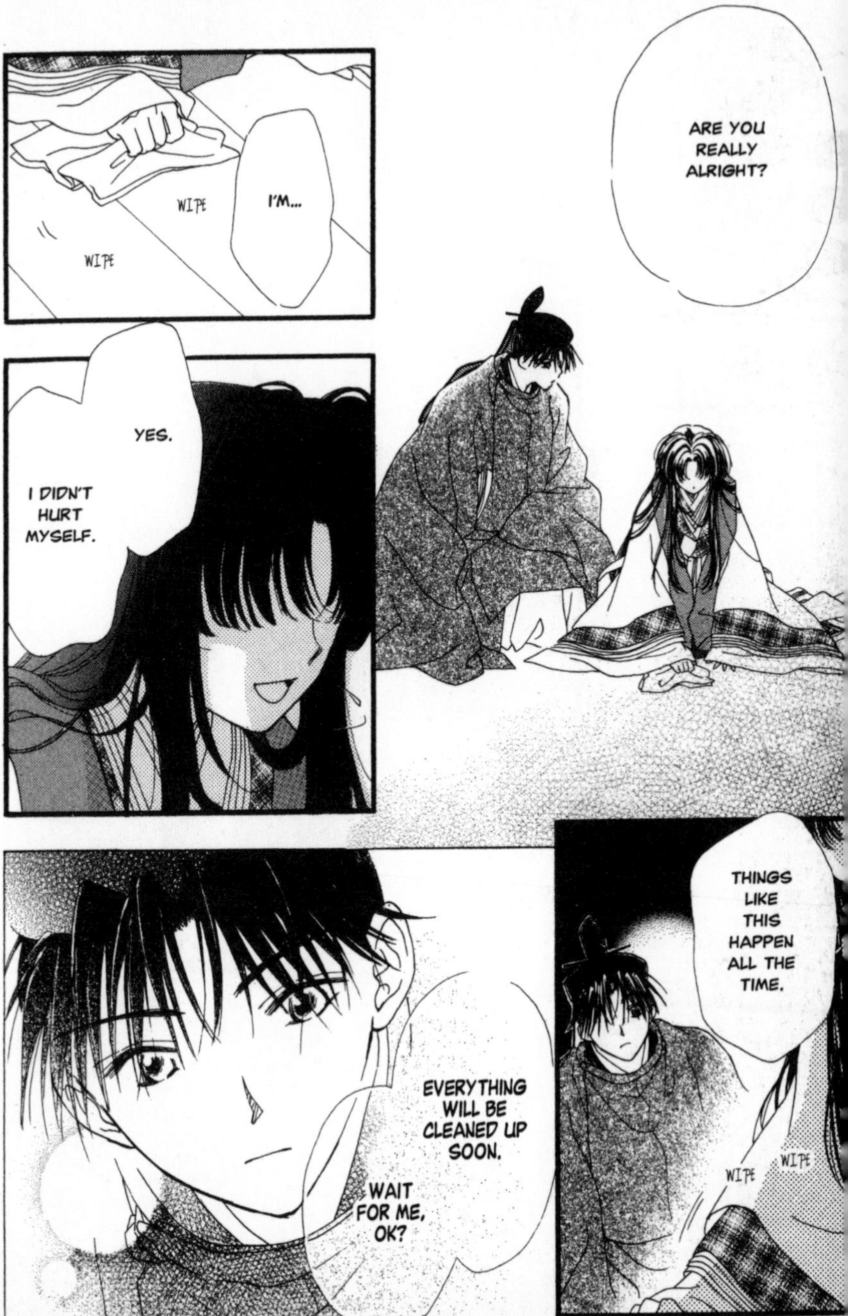
ARE YOU REALLY ALRIGHT?
I'M...
WIPE
WIPE
YES.
I DIDN'T HURT MYSELF.
THINGS LIKE THIS HAPPEN ALL THE TIME.
WIPE
WIPE
EVERYTHING WILL BE CLEANED UP SOON.
WAIT FOR ME, OK?

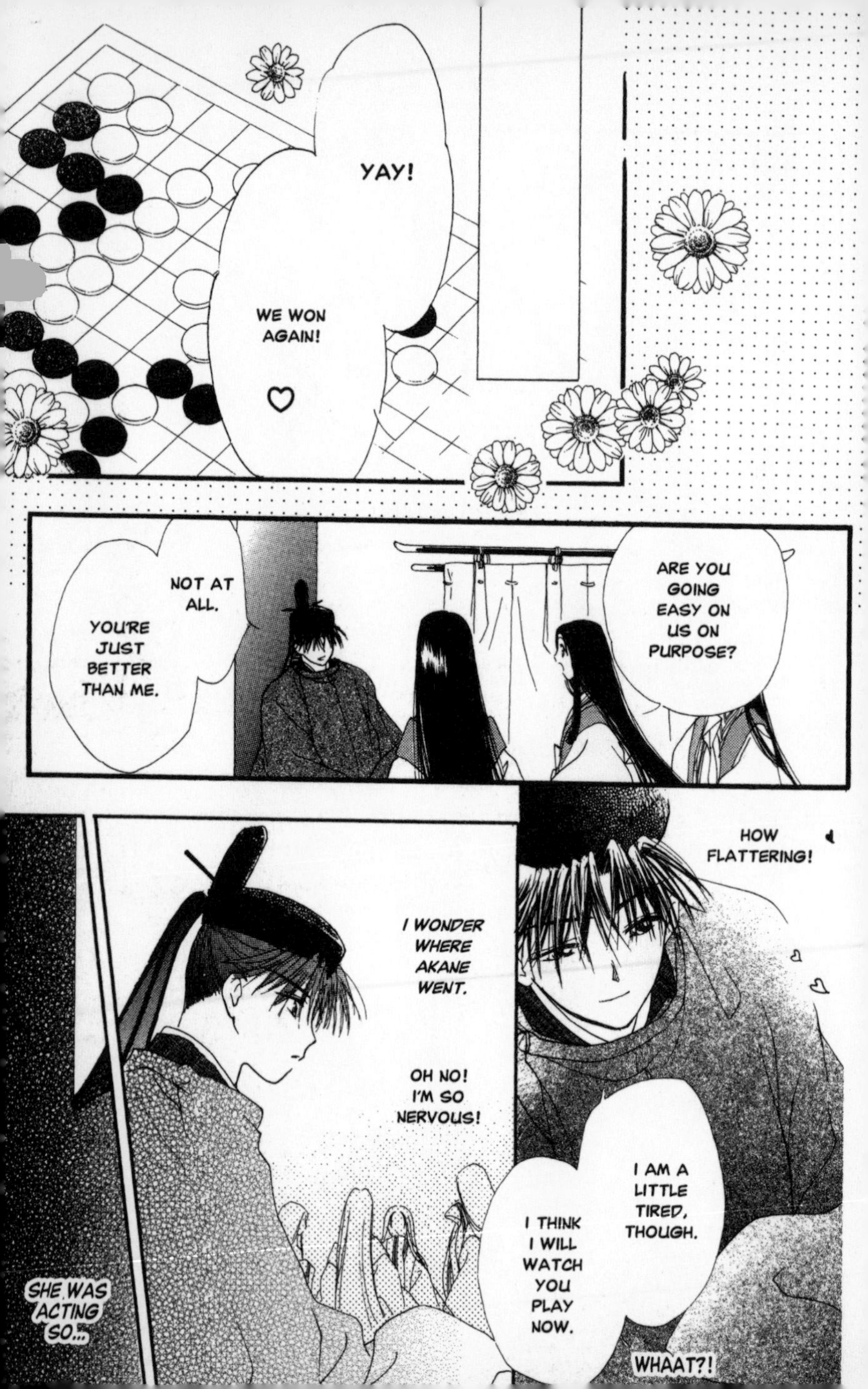
YAY!
WE WON AGAIN!
♡
ARE YOU GOING EASY ON US ON PURPOSE?
NOT AT ALL.
YOU'RE JUST BETTER THAN ME.
HOW FLATTERING!
I AM A LITTLE TIRED, THOUGH.
I THINK I WILL WATCH YOU PLAY NOW.
WHAAT?!
I WONDER WHERE AKANE WENT.
OH NO! I'M SO NERVOUS!
SHE WAS ACTING SO...

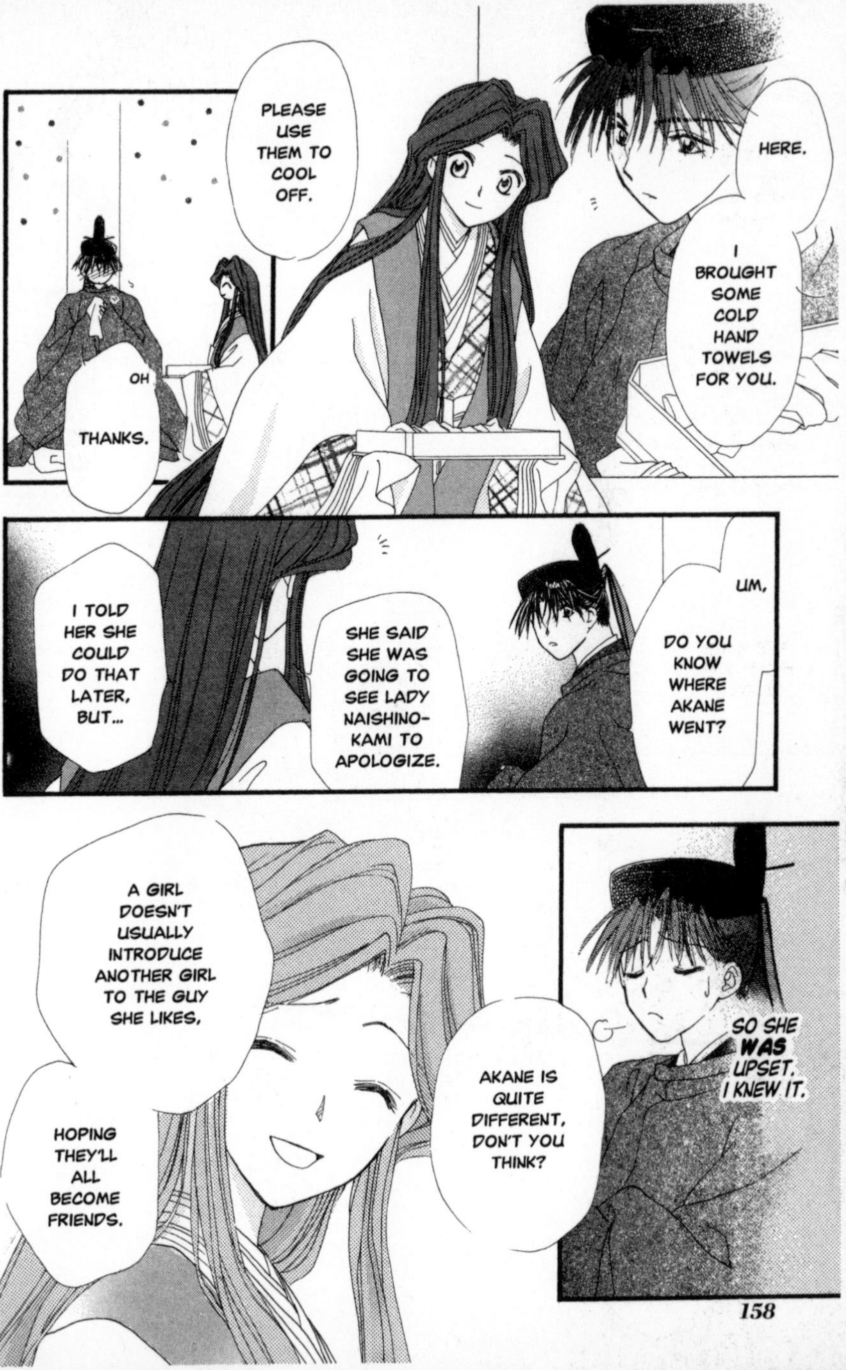
HERE.
I BROUGHT SOME COLD HAND TOWELS FOR YOU.
PLEASE USE THEM TO COOL OFF.
OH
THANKS.
UM,
DO YOU KNOW WHERE AKANE WENT?
SHE SAID SHE WAS GOING TO SEE LADY NAISHINO-KAMI TO APOLOGIZE.
I TOLD HER SHE COULD DO THAT LATER, BUT...
SO SHE WAS UPSET. I KNEW IT.
A GIRL DOESN'T USUALLY INTRODUCE ANOTHER GIRL TO THE GUY SHE LIKES,
HOPING THEY'LL ALL BECOME FRIENDS.
AKANE IS QUITE DIFFERENT, DON'T YOU THINK?

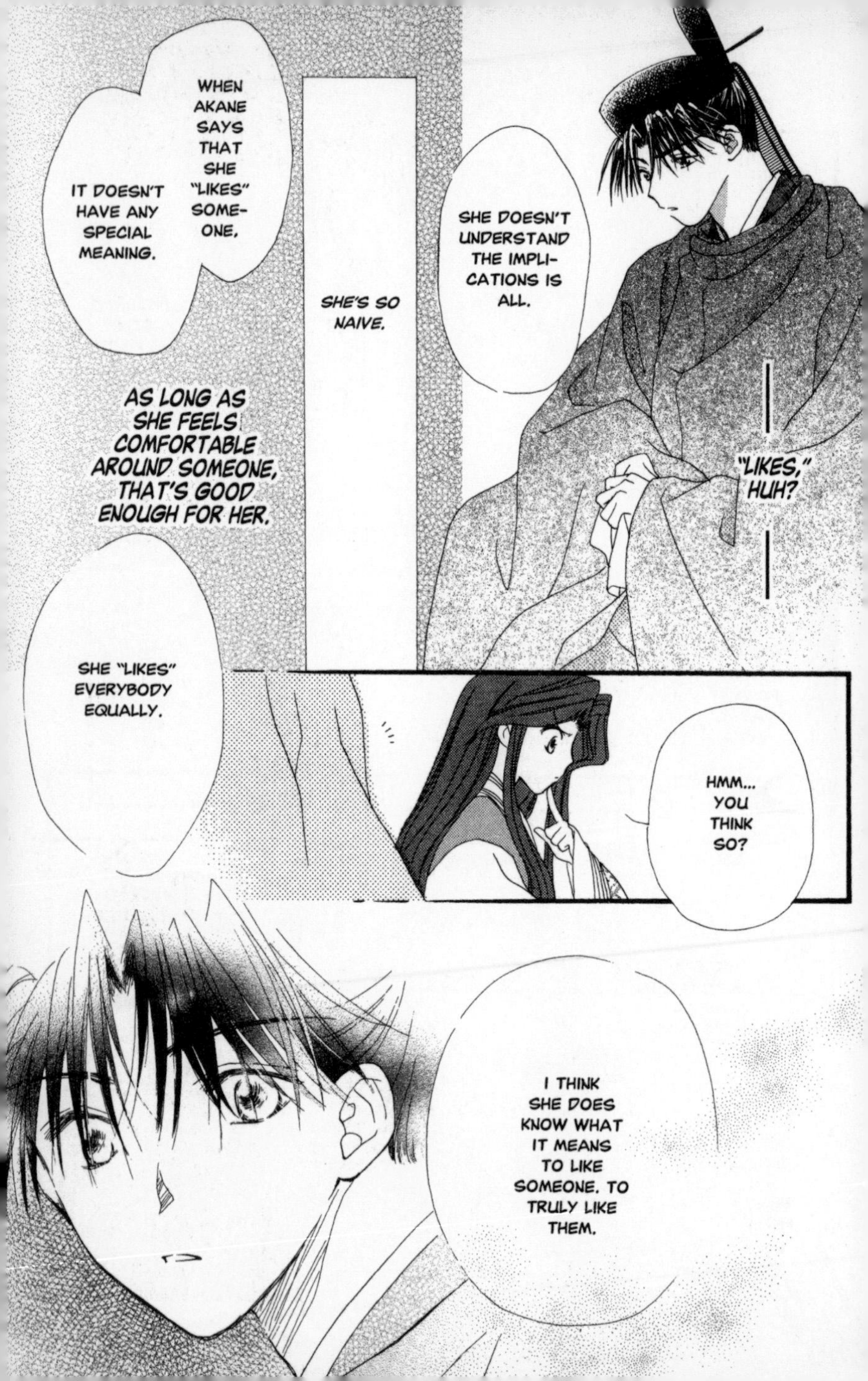
"LIKES," HUH?
SHE DOESN'T UNDERSTAND THE IMPLICATIONS IS ALL.
SHE'S SO NAIVE.
WHEN AKANE SAYS THAT SHE "LIKES" SOME-ONE,
IT DOESN'T HAVE ANY SPECIAL MEANING.
AS LONG AS SHE FEELS COMFORTABLE AROUND SOMEONE, THAT'S GOOD ENOUGH FOR HER.
SHE "LIKES" EVERYBODY EQUALLY.
HMM... YOU THINK SO?
I THINK SHE DOES KNOW WHAT IT MEANS TO LIKE SOMEONE. TO TRULY LIKE THEM.

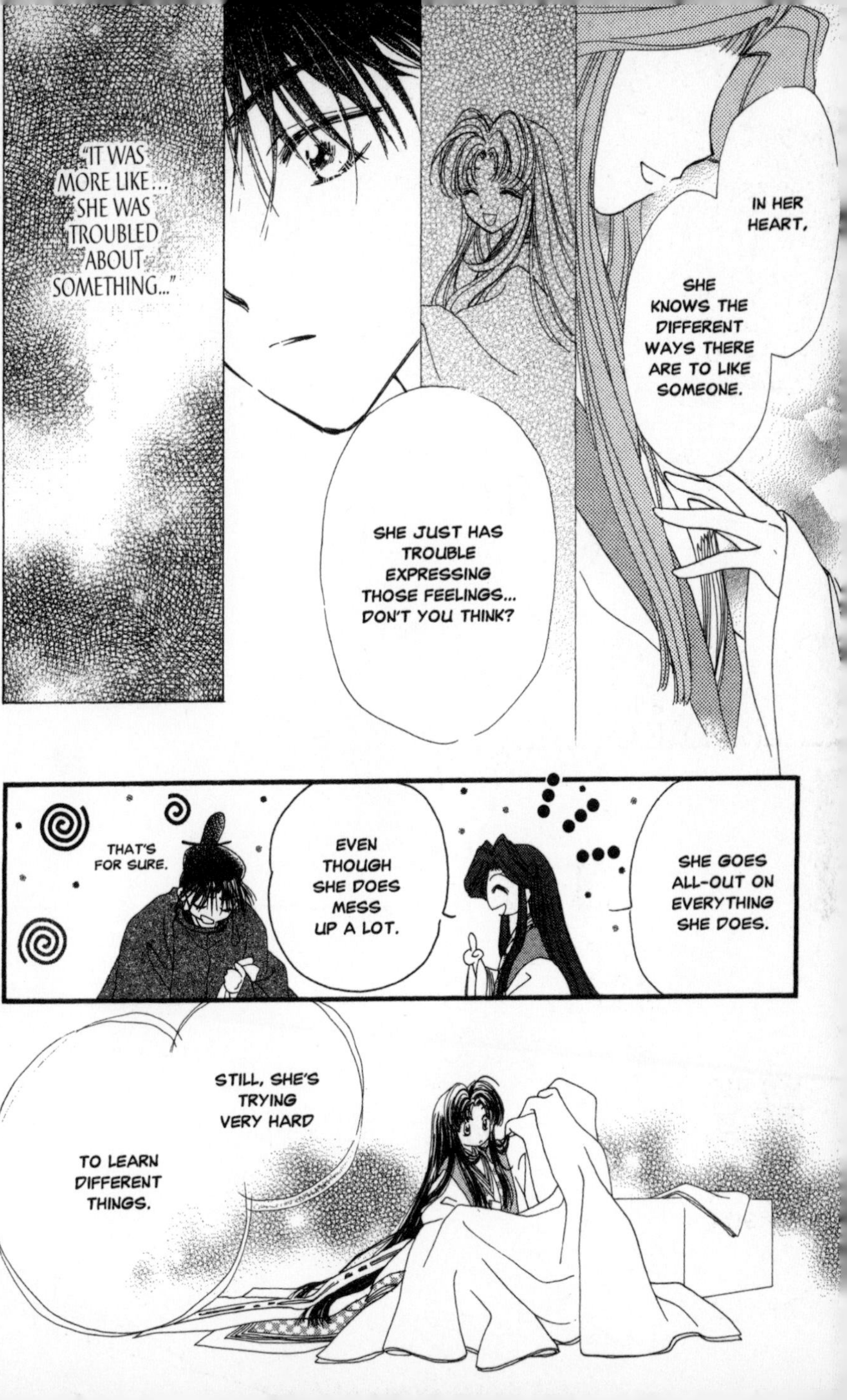
IN HER HEART,
SHE KNOWS THE DIFFERENT WAYS THERE ARE TO LIKE SOMEONE.
SHE JUST HAS TROUBLE EXPRESSING THOSE FEELINGS... DON'T YOU THINK?
"IT WAS MORE LIKE... SHE WAS TROUBLED ABOUT SOMETHING..."
SHE GOES ALL-OUT ON EVERYTHING SHE DOES.
EVEN THOUGH SHE DOES MESS UP A LOT.
THAT'S FOR SURE.
STILL, SHE'S TRYING VERY HARD
TO LEARN DIFFERENT THINGS.

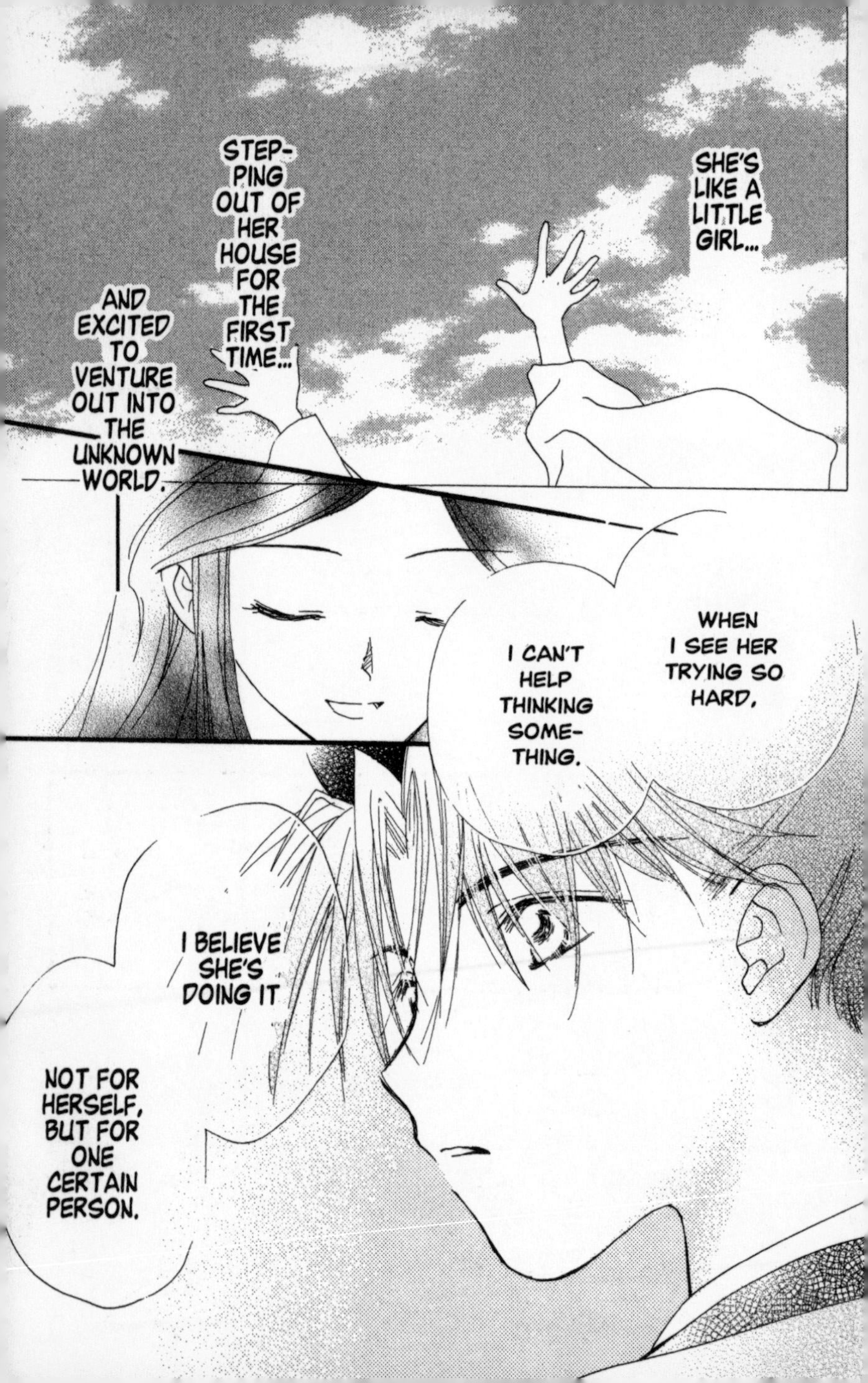
SHE'S LIKE A LITTLE GIRL...
STEP-PING OUT OF HER HOUSE FOR THE FIRST TIME...
AND EXCITED TO VENTURE OUT INTO THE UNKNOWN WORLD.
WHEN I SEE HER TRYING SO HARD,
I CAN'T HELP THINKING SOME-THING.
I BELIEVE SHE'S DOING IT
NOT FOR HERSELF, BUT FOR ONE CERTAIN PERSON.

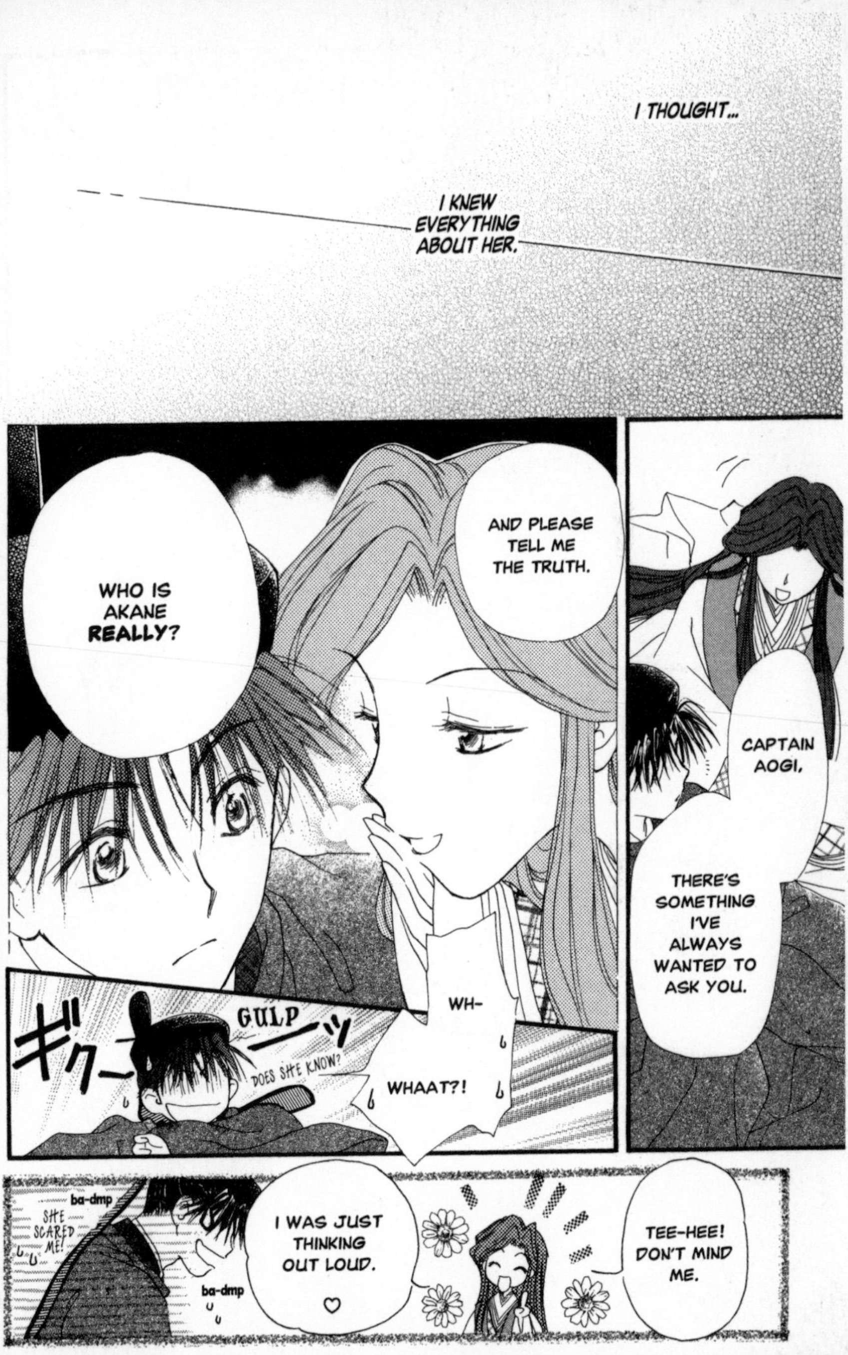
I THOUGHT...
I KNEW EVERYTHING ABOUT HER.
CAPTAIN AOGI,
THERE'S SOMETHING I'VE ALWAYS WANTED TO ASK YOU.
AND PLEASE TELL ME THE TRUTH.
WHO IS AKANE REALLY?
WH-
WHAAT?!
GULP
DOES SHE KNOW?
TEE-HEE! DON'T MIND ME.
I WAS JUST THINKING OUT LOUD.
ba-dmp
SHE SCARED ME!
ba-dmp

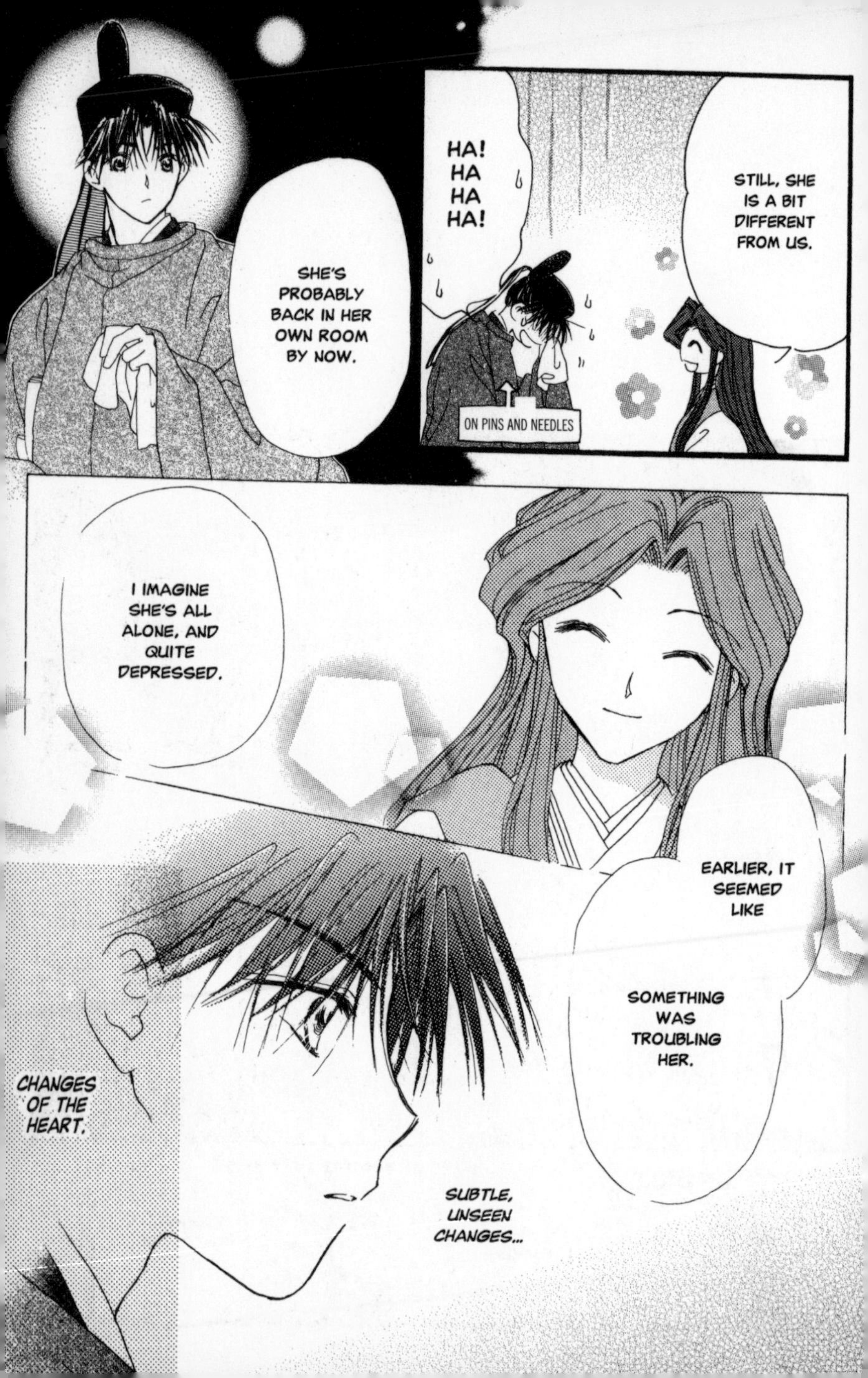
STILL, SHE IS A BIT DIFFERENT FROM US.
HA! HA HA HA!
ON PINS AND NEEDLES
SHE'S PROBABLY BACK IN HER OWN ROOM BY NOW.
I IMAGINE SHE'S ALL ALONE, AND QUITE DEPRESSED.
EARLIER, IT SEEMED LIKE
SOMETHING WAS TROUBLING HER.
SUBTLE, UNSEEN CHANGES...
CHANGES OF THE HEART.

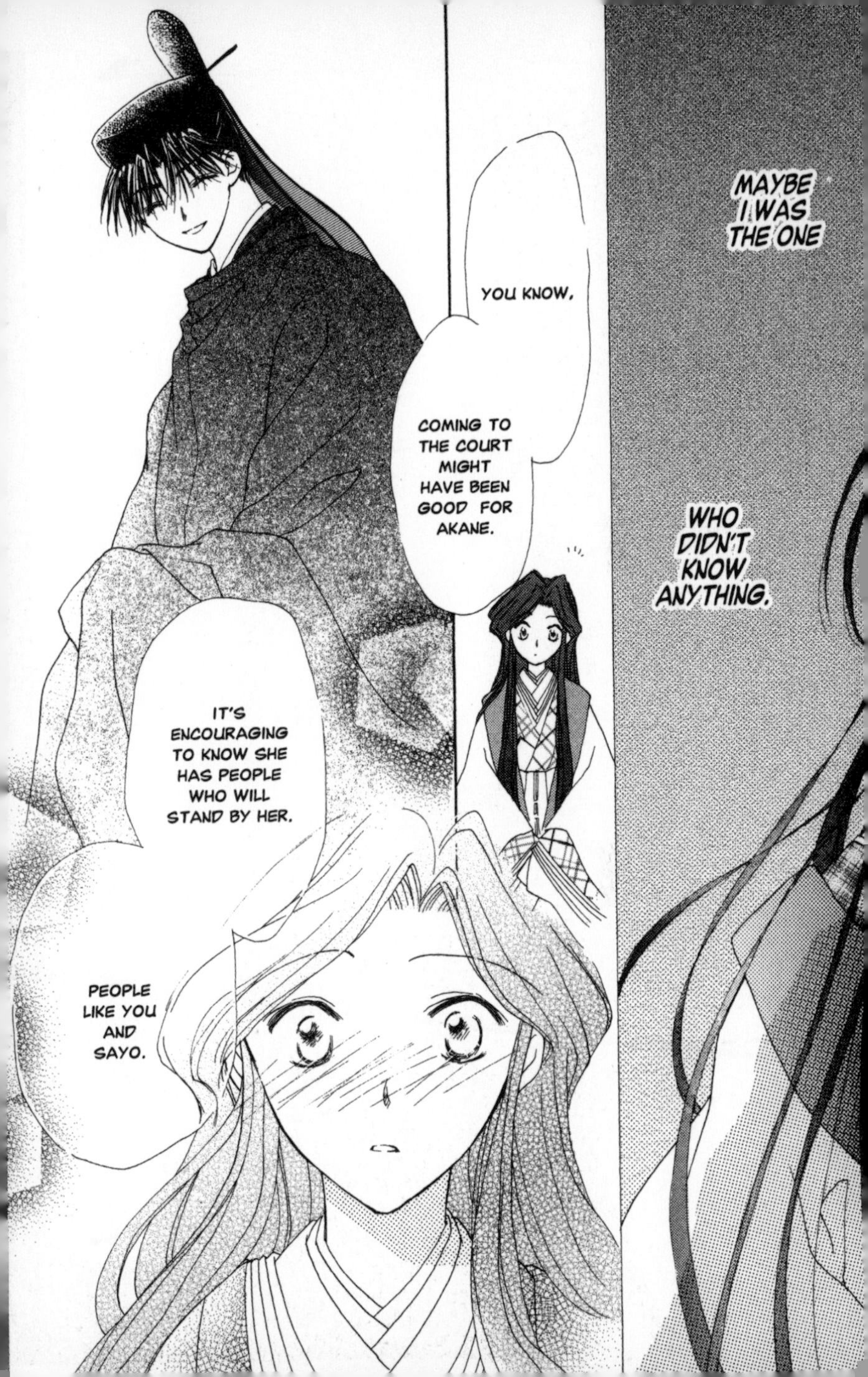
MAYBE I WAS THE ONE
WHO DIDN'T KNOW ANYTHING.
YOU KNOW,
COMING TO THE COURT MIGHT HAVE BEEN GOOD FOR AKANE.
IT'S ENCOURAGING TO KNOW SHE HAS PEOPLE WHO WILL STAND BY HER.
PEOPLE LIKE YOU AND SAYO.

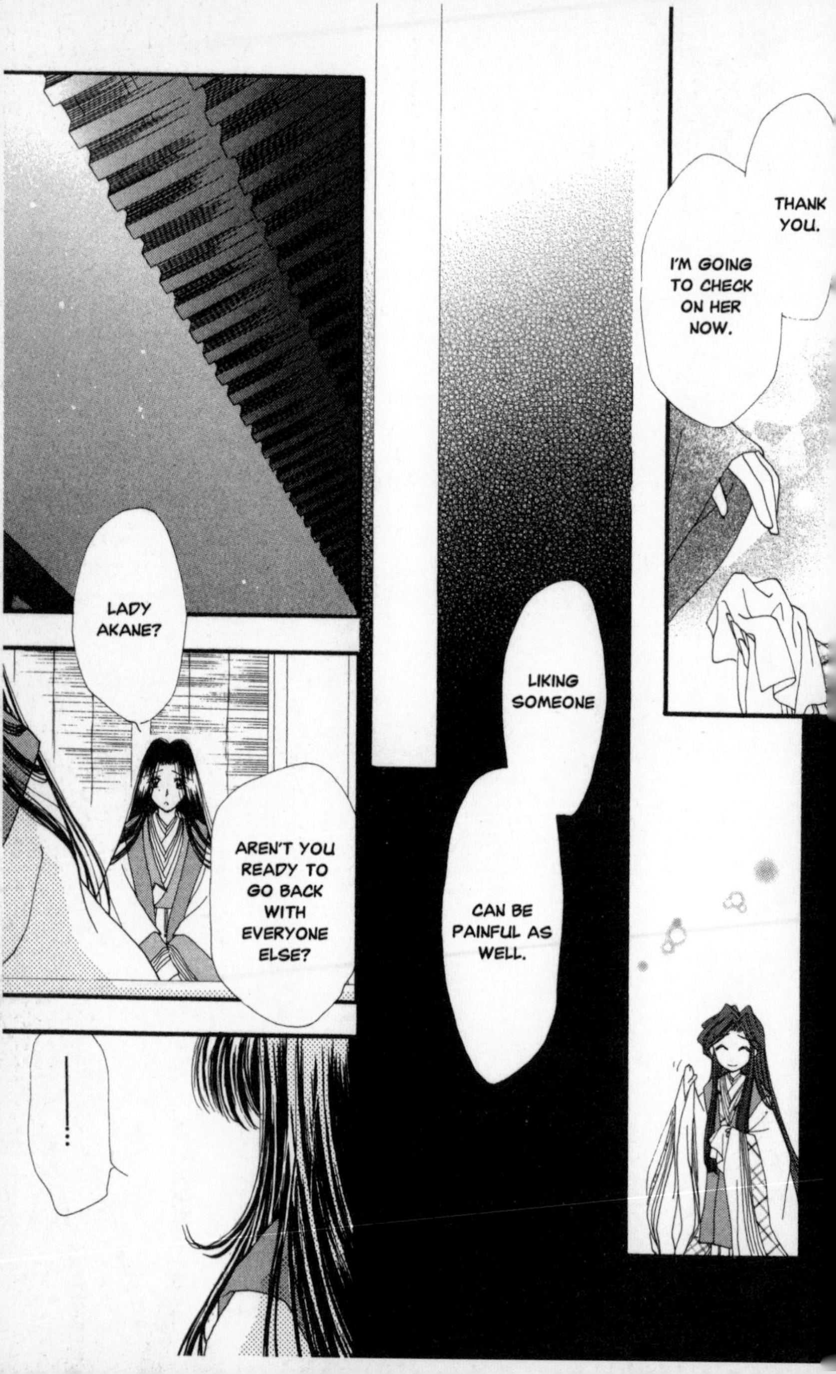
THANK YOU.
I'M GOING TO CHECK ON HER NOW.
LIKING SOMEONE
CAN BE PAINFUL AS WELL.
LADY AKANE?
AREN'T YOU READY TO GO BACK WITH EVERYONE ELSE?
......!

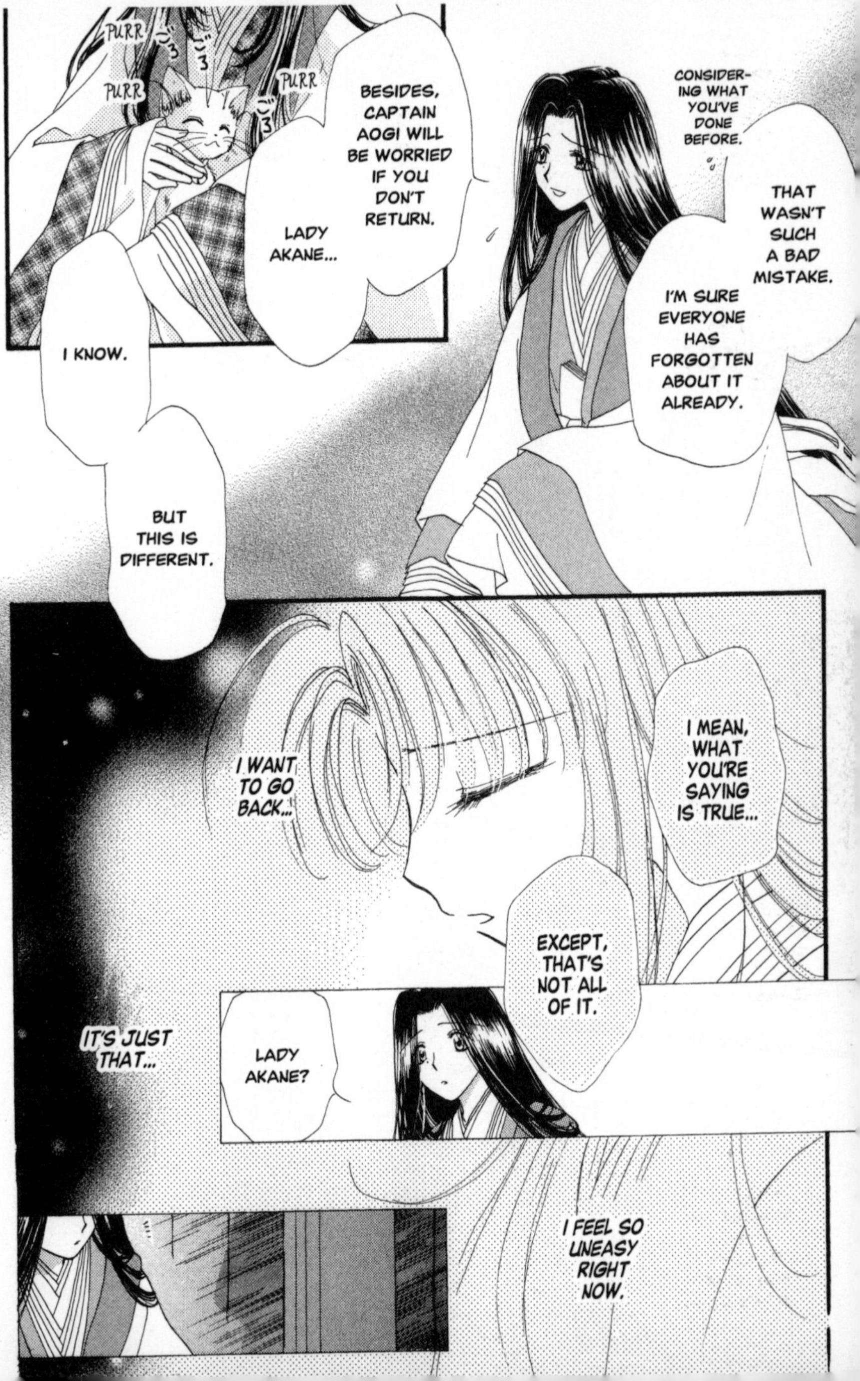
CONSIDERING WHAT YOU'VE DONE BEFORE.
THAT WASN'T SUCH A BAD MISTAKE.
I'M SURE EVERYONE HAS FORGOTTEN ABOUT IT ALREADY.
PURR
PURR
PURR
BESIDES, CAPTAIN AOGI WILL BE WORRIED IF YOU DON'T RETURN.
LADY AKANE...
I KNOW.
BUT THIS IS DIFFERENT.
I MEAN, WHAT YOU'RE SAYING IS TRUE...
I WANT TO GO BACK...
EXCEPT, THAT'S NOT ALL OF IT.
LADY AKANE?
IT'S JUST THAT...
I FEEL SO UNEASY RIGHT NOW.

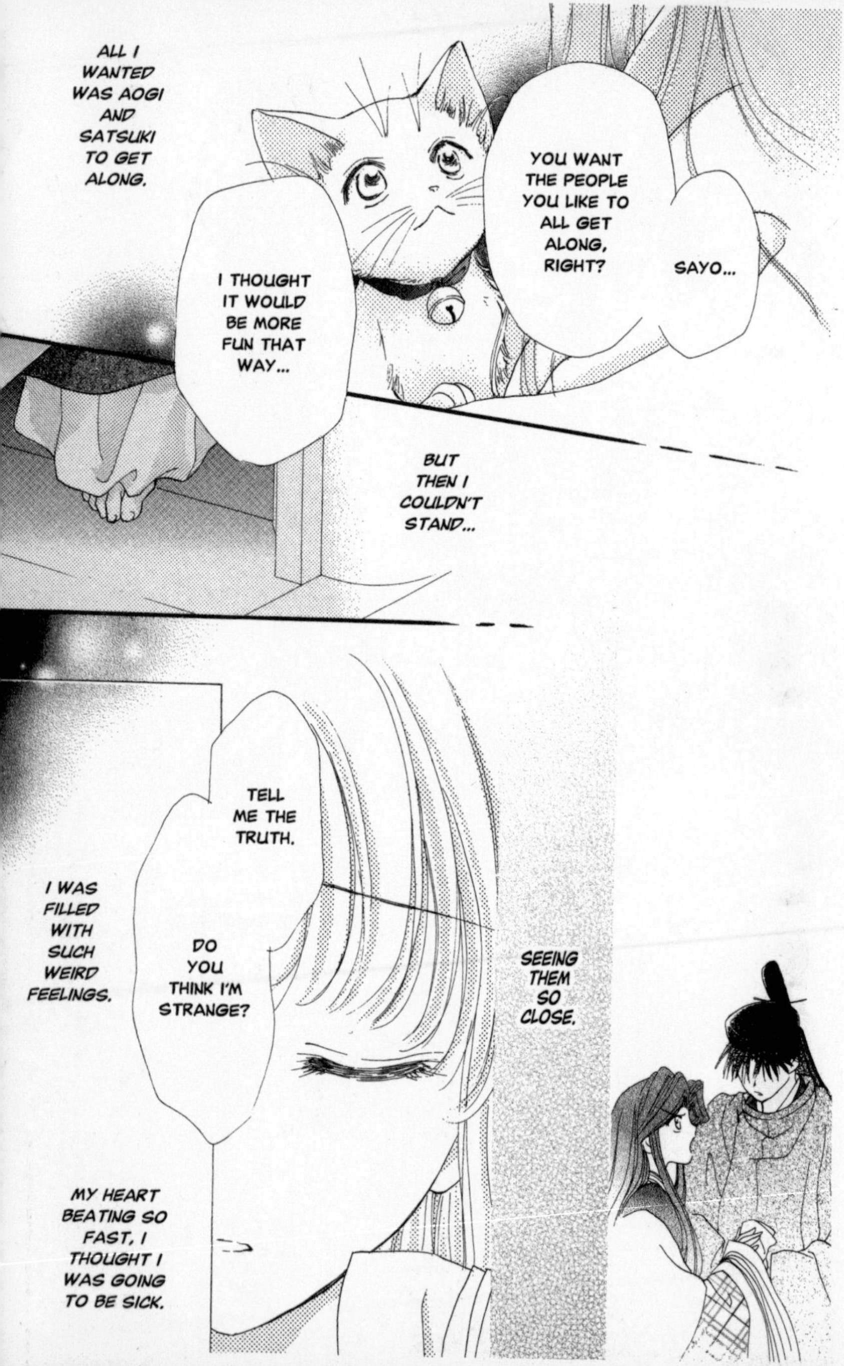
SAYO...
YOU WANT THE PEOPLE YOU LIKE TO ALL GET ALONG, RIGHT?
ALL I WANTED WAS AOGI AND SATSUKI TO GET ALONG.
I THOUGHT IT WOULD BE MORE FUN THAT WAY...
BUT THEN I COULDN'T STAND...
SEEING THEM SO CLOSE.
TELL ME THE TRUTH.
DO YOU THINK I'M STRANGE?
I WAS FILLED WITH SUCH WEIRD FEELINGS.
MY HEART BEATING SO FAST, I THOUGHT I WAS GOING TO BE SICK.

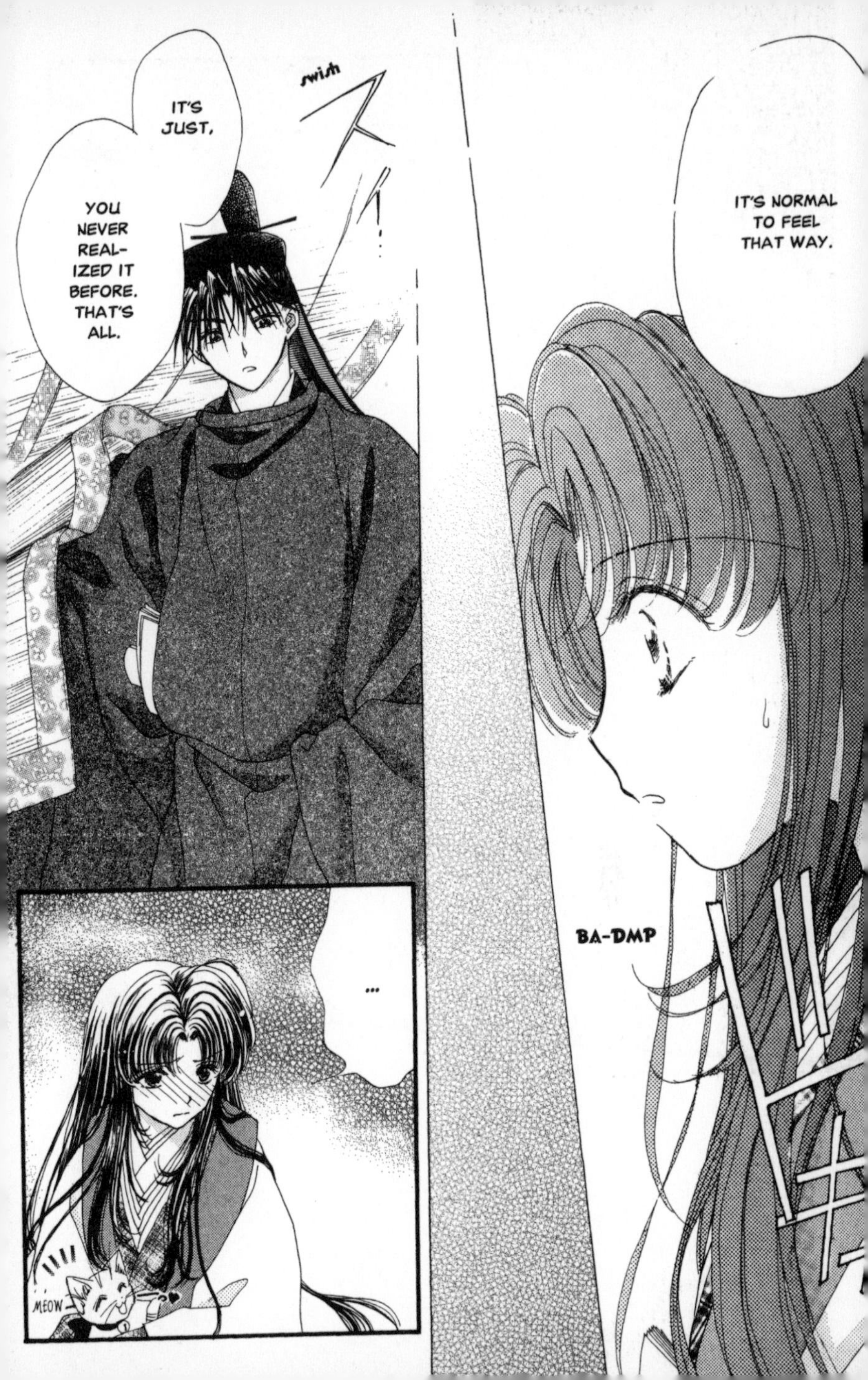
IT'S NORMAL TO FEEL THAT WAY.
BA-DMP
swish
IT'S JUST,
YOU NEVER REAL-IZED IT BEFORE. THAT'S ALL.
...
MEOW

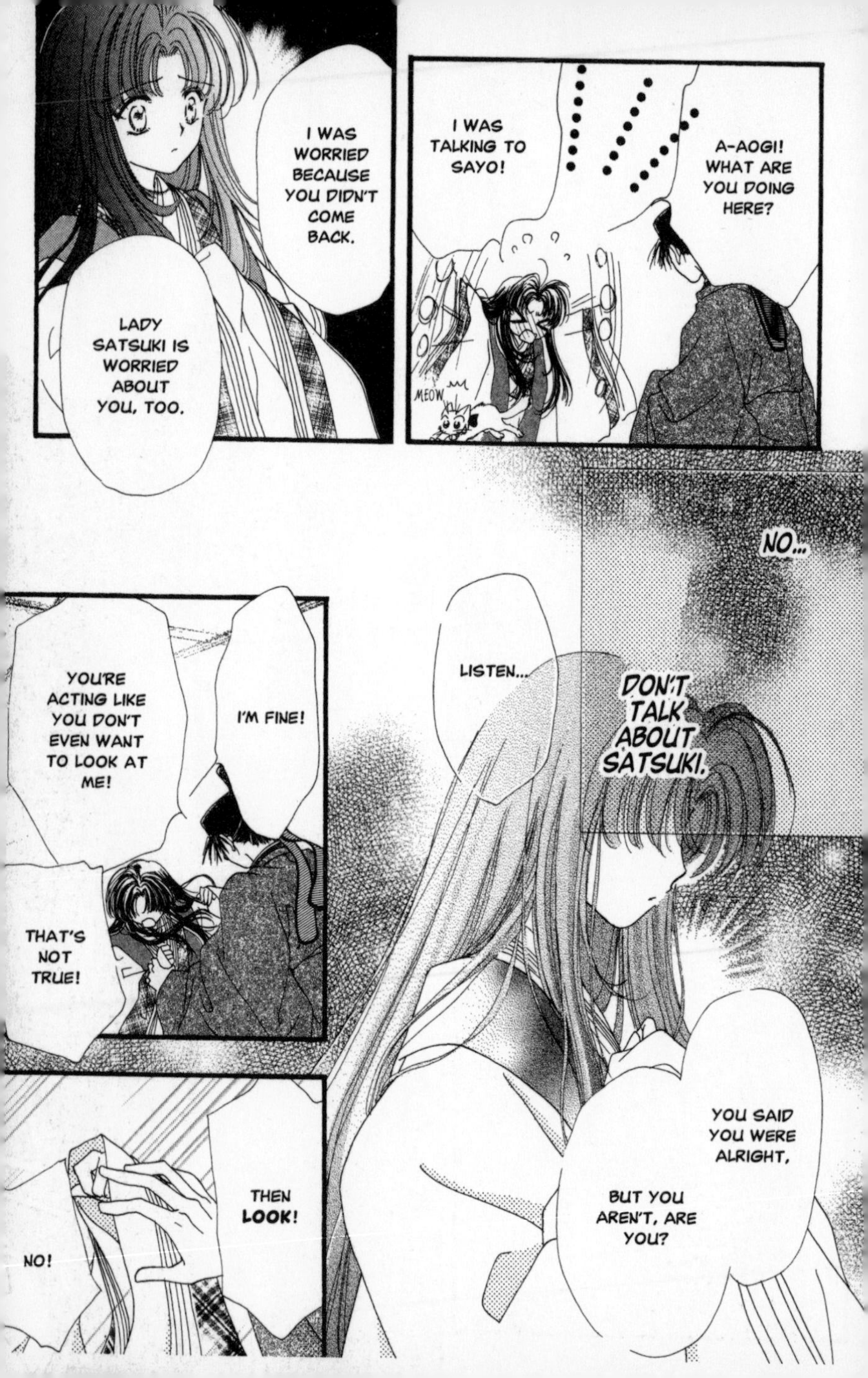
A-AOGI! WHAT ARE YOU DOING HERE?
I WAS TALKING TO SAYO!
MEOW
I WAS WORRIED BECAUSE YOU DIDN'T COME BACK.
LADY SATSUKI IS WORRIED ABOUT YOU, TOO.
NO...
DON'T TALK ABOUT SATSUKI.
LISTEN...
I'M FINE!
YOU'RE ACTING LIKE YOU DON'T EVEN WANT TO LOOK AT ME!
THAT'S NOT TRUE!
YOU SAID YOU WERE ALRIGHT,
BUT YOU AREN'T, ARE YOU?
THEN LOOK!
NO!

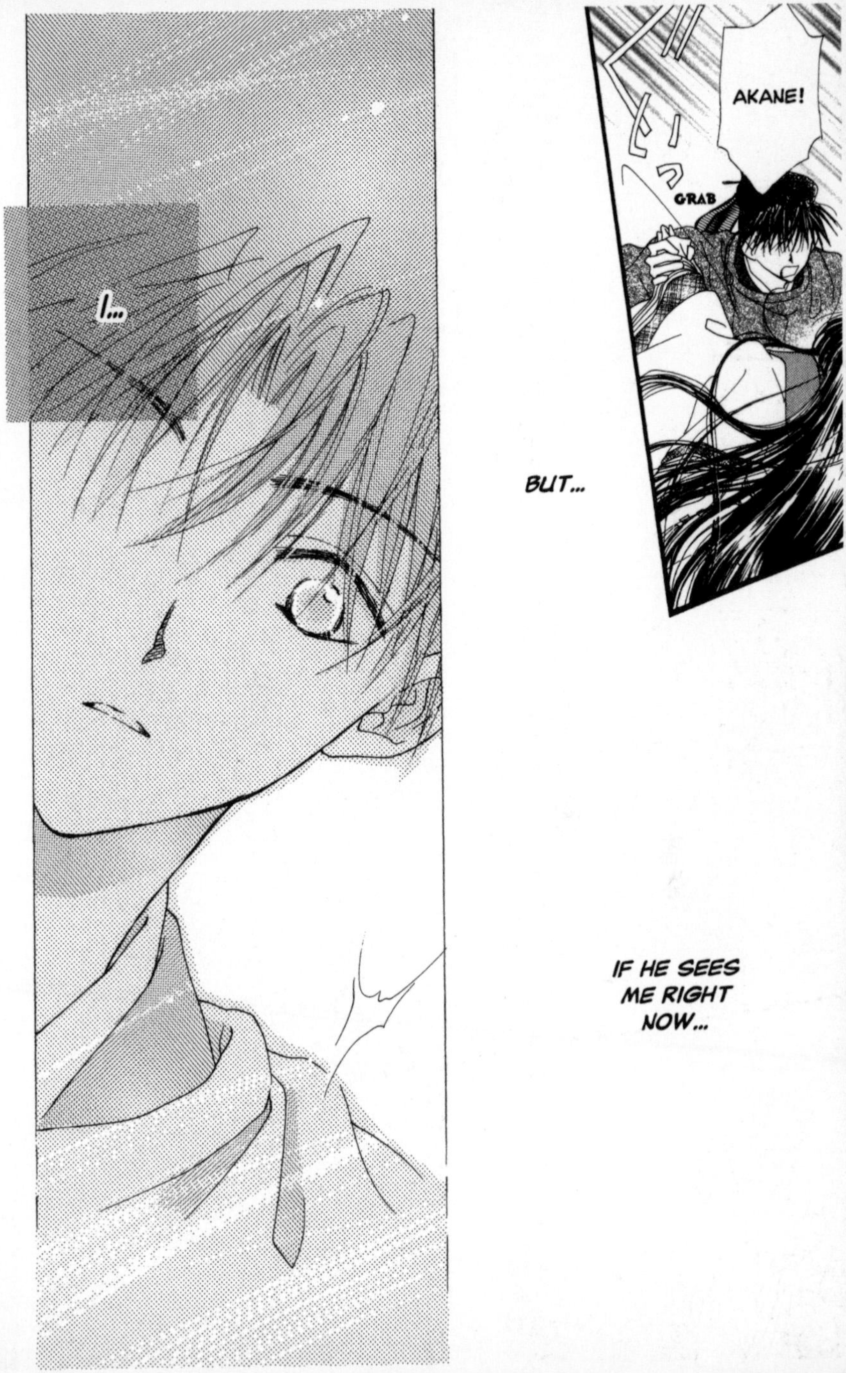
AKANE!
GRAB
BUT...
IF HE SEES ME RIGHT NOW...
I...

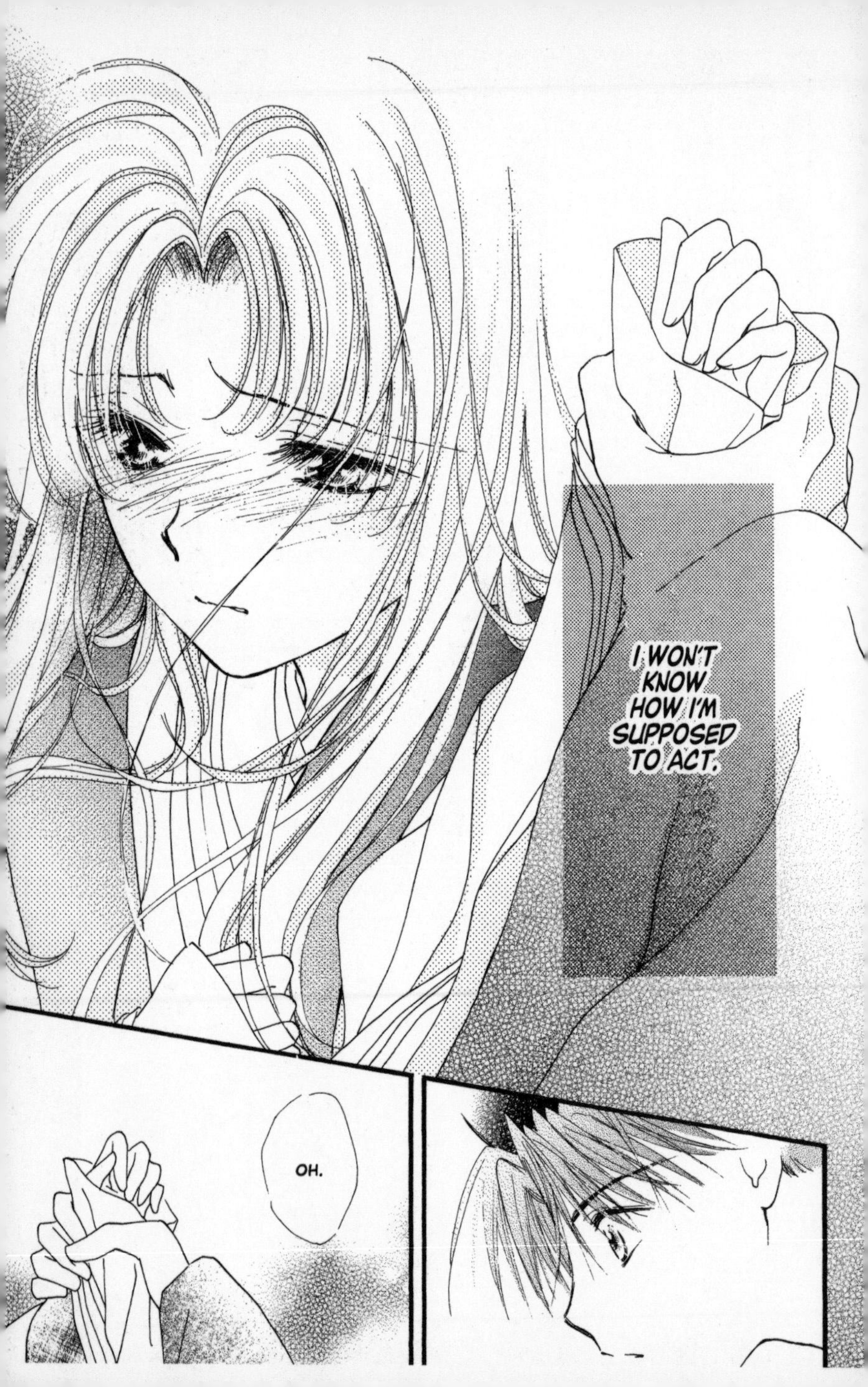
I WON'T KNOW HOW I'M SUPPOSED TO ACT.
OH.

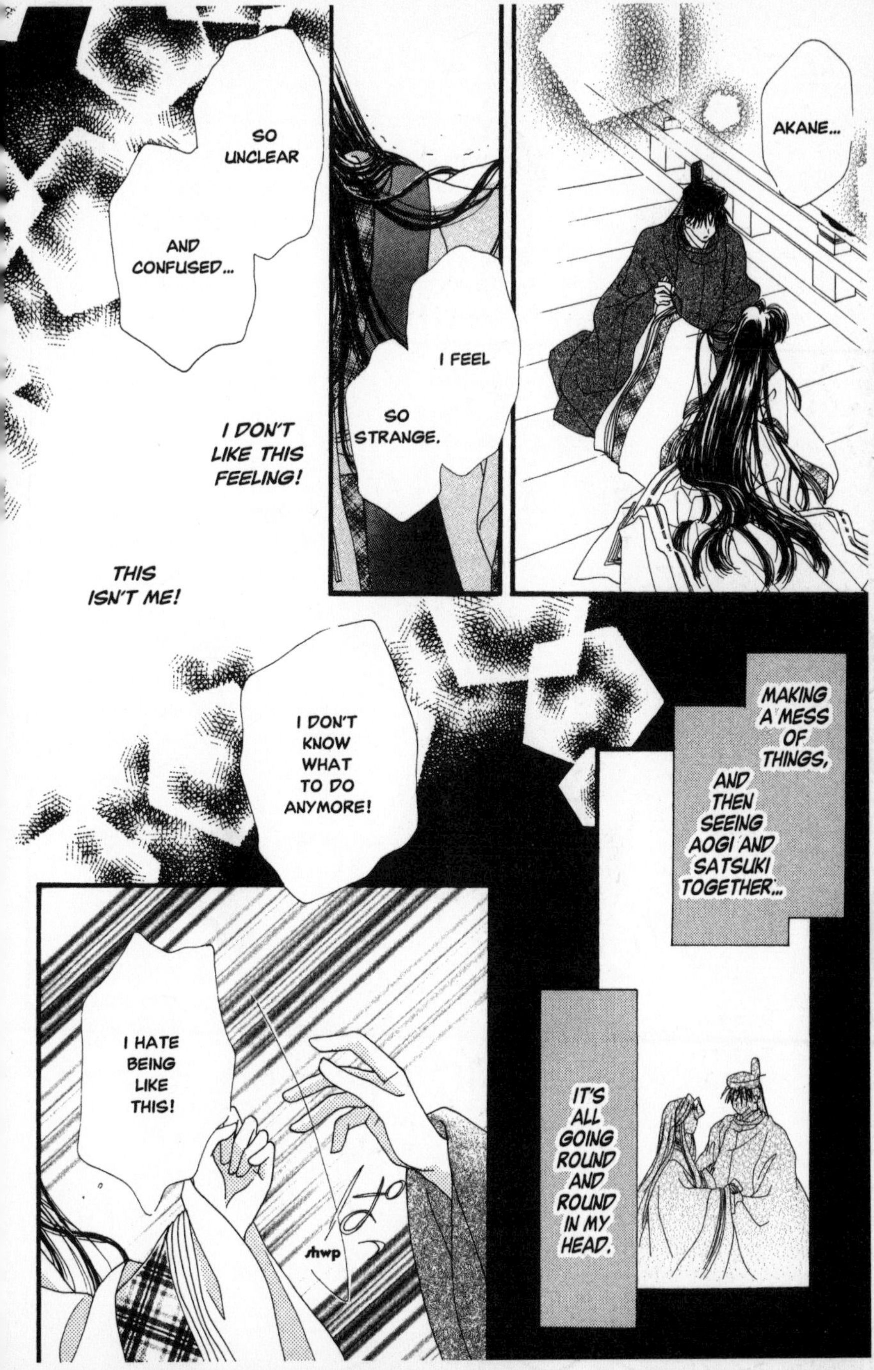
AKANE...
I FEEL SO STRANGE.
SO UNCLEAR AND CONFUSED...
I DON'T LIKE THIS FEELING!
THIS ISN'T ME!
MAKING A MESS OF THINGS,
AND THEN SEEING AOGI AND SATSUKI TOGETHER...
I DON'T KNOW WHAT TO DO ANYMORE!
IT'S ALL GOING ROUND AND ROUND IN MY HEAD.
I HATE BEING LIKE THIS!
shwp

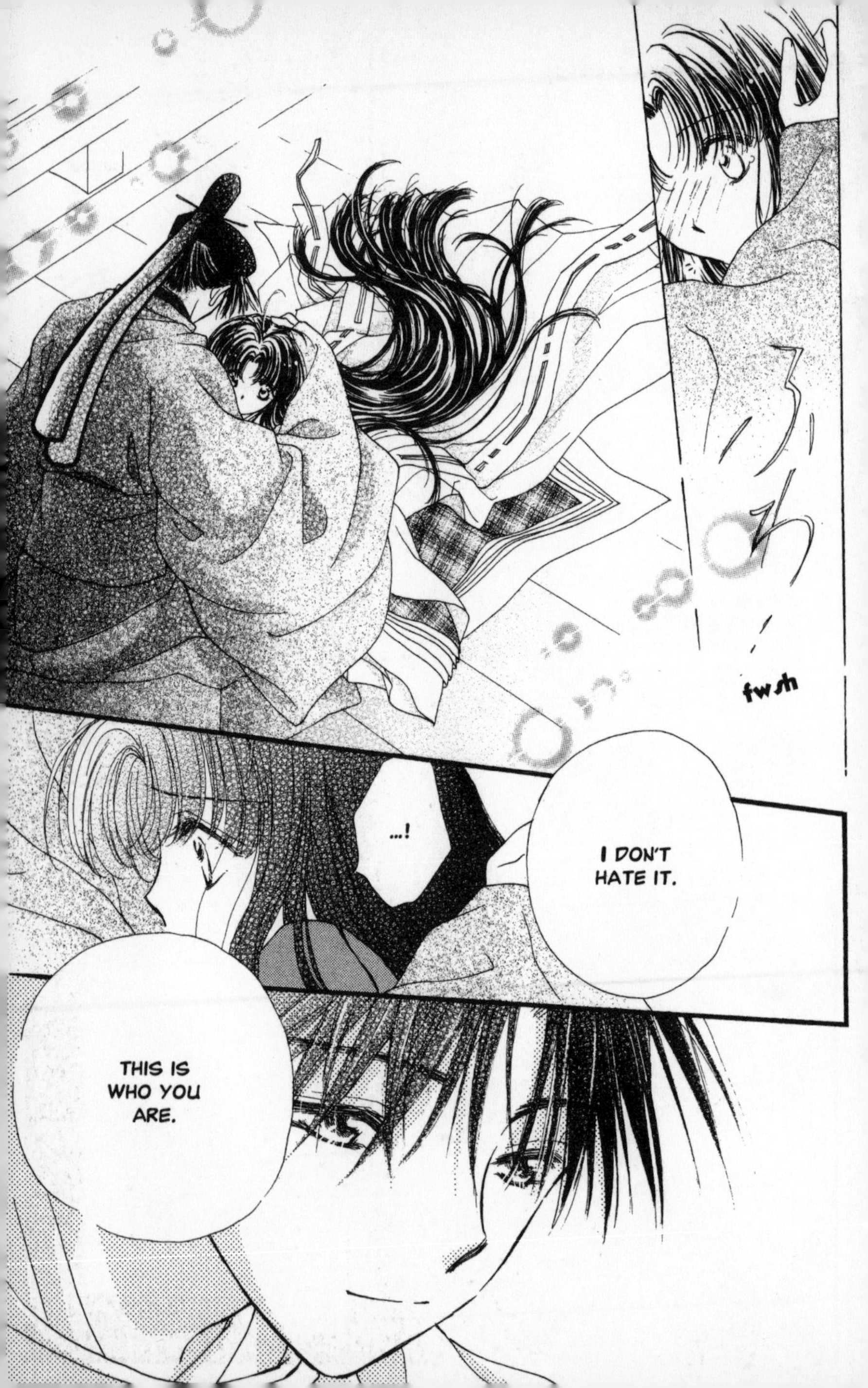
fwsh
I DON'T HATE IT.
...!
THIS IS WHO YOU ARE.

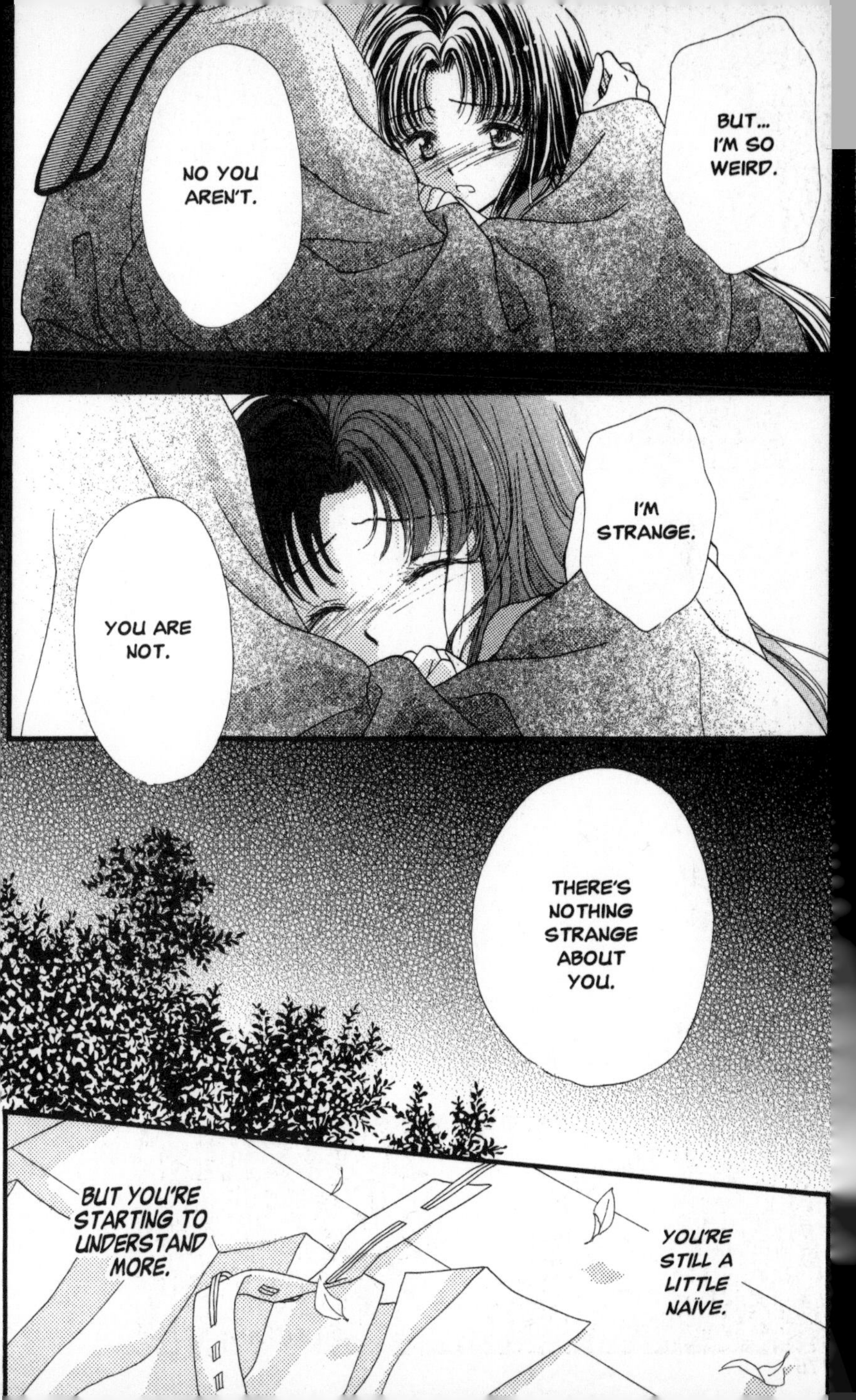
BUT... I'M SO WEIRD.
NO YOU AREN'T.
I'M STRANGE.
YOU ARE NOT.
THERE'S NOTHING STRANGE ABOUT YOU.
YOU'RE STILL A LITTLE NAÏVE.
BUT YOU'RE STARTING TO UNDERSTAND MORE.

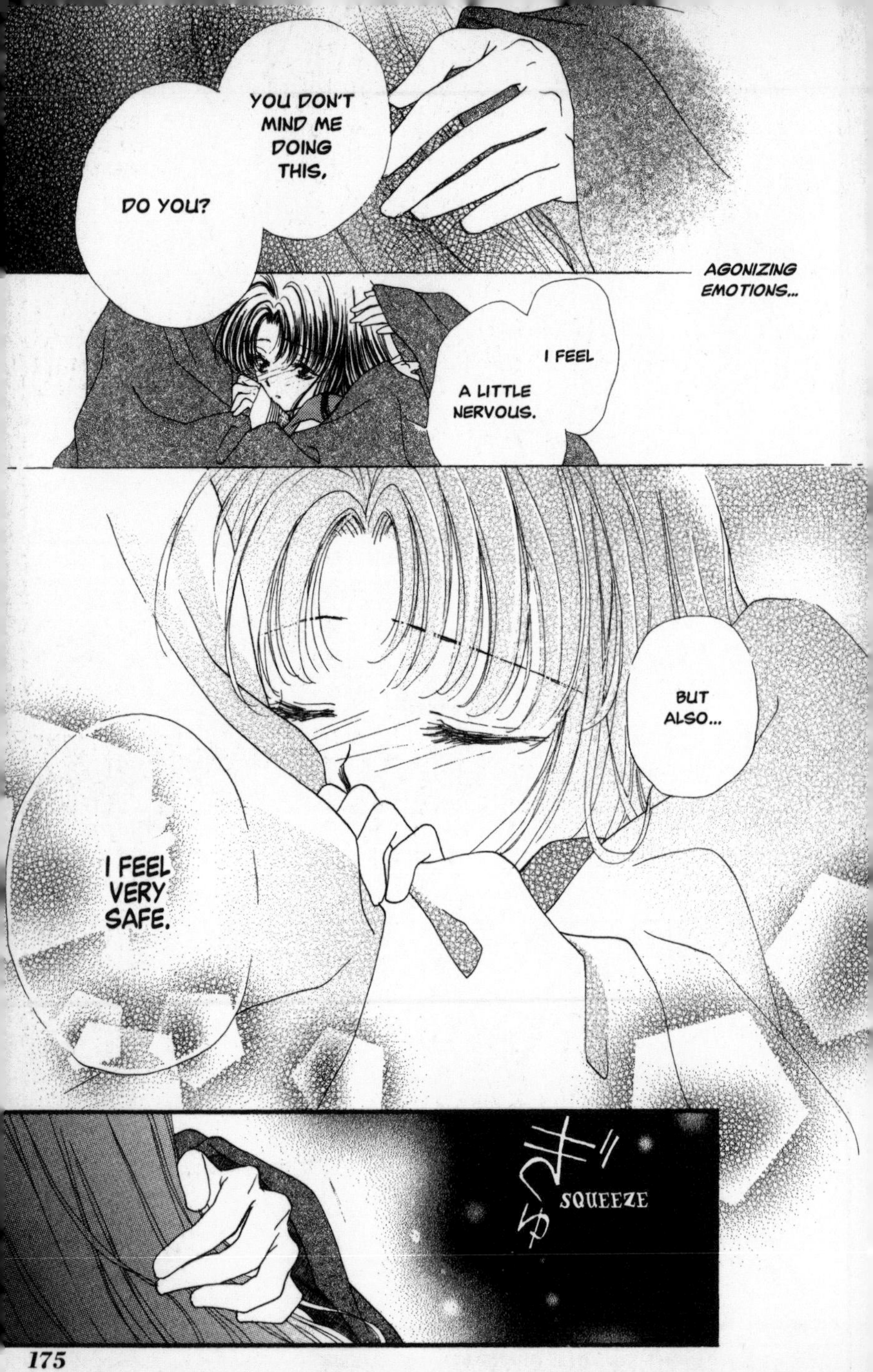
AGONIZING EMOTIONS...
YOU DON'T MIND ME DOING THIS,
DO YOU?
I FEEL
A LITTLE NERVOUS.
BUT ALSO...
I FEEL VERY SAFE.
ぎゅ
SQUEEZE

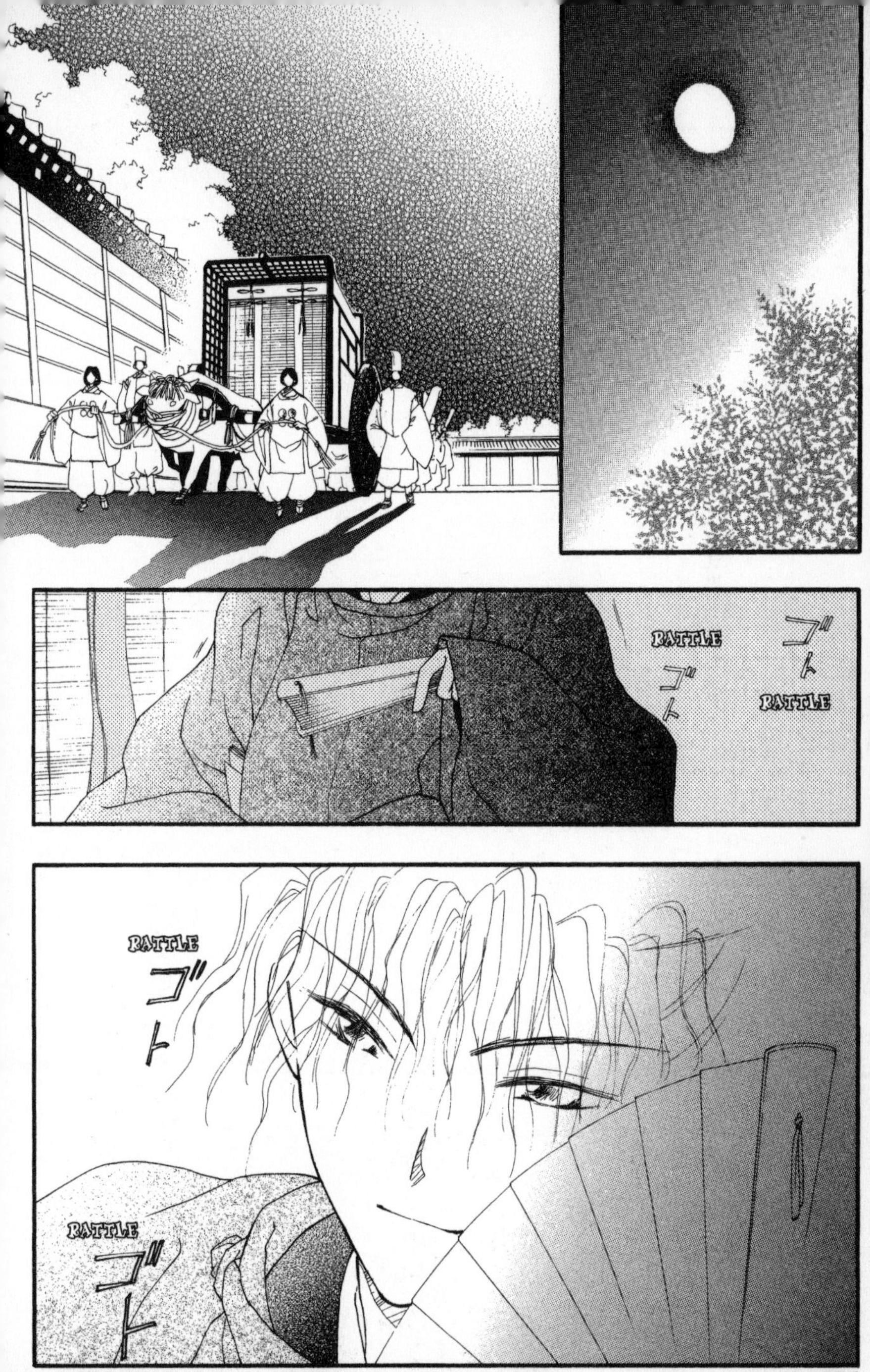
ゴト
RATTLE
RATTLE
ゴト
RATTLE
ゴト
RATTLE
ゴト